DYING EARTH AND LIVING COSMOS

The Living Gifts of Anthroposophy

The Need for New Forms of Consciousness

DYING EARTH AND LIVING COSMOS

The Living Gifts of Anthroposophy

The Need for New Forms of Consciousness

Twenty-one lectures given in Berlin between 22 January and 6 August 1918

TRANSLATED BY MATTHEW BARTON

INTRODUCTION BY MATTHEW BARTON

RUDOLF STEINER

RUDOLF STEINER PRESS

CW 181

The publishers gratefully acknowledge the generous funding of this publication by the estate of Dr Eva Frommer MD (1927–2004) and the Anthroposophical Society in Great Britain

Rudolf Steiner Press
Hillside House, The Square
Forest Row, RH18 5ES

www.rudolfsteinerpress.com

Published by Rudolf Steiner Press 2015

Originally published in German under the title *Erdensterben und Weltenleben. Anthroposophische Lebensgaben. Bewußtseins-Notwendigkeiten für Gegenwart und Zukunft* (volume 181 in the *Rudolf Steiner Gesamtausgabe* or Collected Works) by Rudolf Steiner Verlag, Dornach. Based on shorthand transcripts and notes, not reviewed by the speaker. This authorized translation is based on the latest available (third) edition of 1991 edited by R. Friedenthal and S. Lötscher

Published by permission of the Rudolf Steiner Nachlassverwaltung, Dornach

A catalogue record for this book is available from the British Library

ISBN 978 1 85584 419 3

Cover by Mary Giddens
Typeset by DP Photosetting, Neath, West Glamorgan
Printed and bound by Gutenberg Press Ltd., Malta

CONTENTS

LECTURE 5

BERLIN, 12 MARCH 1918

The Human Being's Connection with the World of Spirit

When reflecting on human life try to observe what might have happened but did not during daily life. Seeds in nature and human life that do not develop. The effect of the unconscious. The example cited in psychoanalysis of the lady who ran in front of a carriage. The hands as organ of thinking. Differences between man and animal. Gravity in the human head. A critical evaluation of our own actions shines out through the lotus flowers into time and goes on acting beyond death. Instreaming thoughts of destiny held back by arms and hands at diaphragm level. Radiations that rise from the earth and pass through feet and legs are directed through the lotus flowers.

LECTURE 6

BERLIN, 19 MARCH 1918

Sense of community and feelings of gratitude as a bridge of connection with the dead

Making contact with the dead. The dead prefigure Jupiter conditions. The significance of the hierarchies for dialogue with the dead. Developing a sense of community and commonality with the realities of existence. Human community as organism. The nature of memory. The process of memory development. Cultivating a sense of gratitude for every impression, even unpleasant ones, creates 'spiritual air' in which the dead can speak to the living. The possibility of receiving illumination.

LECTURE 7

BERLIN, 26 MARCH 1918

Trust in life and soul rejuvenation as a bridge of connection with the dead

Moods of soul that can form a bridge to the dead: 1) Gratitude for all experiences life brings, including painful ones; 2) Developing a sense of community with all life; 3) Trust in life; 4) Rejuvenating the soul throughout life. The importance of such feelings in education and teaching. The human being as duality of head and the rest of the organism; the head as older, the organism as younger entity. The heart develops more slowly than the head. Renewal of the head by the rest of the organism. Cultivating the artistic element and the life of imagination in education and teaching. The individualism of human souls between birth and death due to the physical and ether body. Soul distinctions between death and rebirth due to each soul's affinity with a very specific star constellation.

pages 89–101

The Living Gifts of Anthroposophy

Lecture 8

BERLIN, 30 MARCH 1918

Folk souls and the Mystery of Golgotha

The earth as ensouled being. Different forces at work in diverse regions of the globe. Human dependency on these forces. The folk souls. How the folk spirit works through material processes. Italy: action of the folk spirit through the air. France: action of the folk spirit through the watery element. Britain: action of the folk spirit through subterranean forces. Russia: action of the folk spirit through light radiating back from the ground. Central Europe: action of the folk spirit through warmth upon the head. The contrast between East and West. Overcoming our dependency on the folk spirit by understanding the Mystery of Golgotha.

pages 105–117

Lecture 9

BERLIN, 1 APRIL 1918

The relativity of knowledge and spiritual cosmology

The one-sided nature of modern science. The need to shed light on things from various different angles. The spiritual wall erected between heaven and earth by the Copernican view of the universe and Kantian philosophy (theory of cognition). The earth as seen by the human being between death and rebirth: eastern regions of the globe blue-purple, western regions flaming red; centre: greenish. Jerusalem as a luminous crystal form. The spirit is incalculable; we must pass from outward to more pictorial perception. The head contrasted with the rest of the organism. Darwinism and Kantianism are connected with etheric animality expressed in the human head. During Jupiter evolution the human being will have become angelic.

pages 118–131

Lecture 10

BERLIN, 2 APRIL 1918

Life between death and rebirth

The need for new ways of thinking. The loss of old spiritual ideas during Roman times, for instance due to destruction of the ancient Celtic mystery centre in Alesia. Certain views, e.g. about the nature of sensory-based thinking, must change radically. Critique of 'unprejudiced science' which in fact is subject to the dominant authority of the Council of Constantinople in 869 (abolition of the threefold view of the human being); Wundt, Frohschammer, Dr Johannes Mueller. Threefold development in life between death and new birth: 1) Forming of the 'soul being' (Imagination of spirit-corporeal configuration); 2) Development of the 'life soul' (Inspiration); 3) Forming of the 'soul self' (intuitive aspect of the soul). Pre-existence as idea for the future, earthly life as a continuation of spiritual existence.

Lecture 11

BERLIN, 9 APRIL 1918

The eternal and the transient

The need to give people access to certain esoteric truths. The mystery of the contrast between the living person and the corpse. The dissolution of the corpse in the universe is an outward picture of I consciousness. After death, three forces bear the various material particles of the human being into the universe: the power to stand upright, and the capacities of speech and thinking. In pictorial terms, these are: one linear force and two spiralling ones. Human flesh tint (the colour of incarnation) as an expression of the world of memory after death. Suppressing such esoteric truths is a way of wielding power in political life. The English-speaking peoples' efforts to gain global dominance. The contrast between East and West in relation to language. Esoteric knowledge must serve the whole of humanity, not just a part of it.

Lecture 12

BERLIN, 16 APRIL 1918

Thoughts on life and death

Reference to the public lecture the evening before: 'The Human and the Animal World'. The significance of conception and death in the life of animals. Our human I experience comprises both. In animals, a momentary I consciousness flares up at the moment of death. Conception and death in the human head. Thought is born from the will; in our will impulses, the thought dies into will. The one-sided nature of Schopenhauer's ideas. The brutality of the modern scientific outlook: Hertwig, Mauthner. Strong, courageous thinking is needed. The activity of ahrimanic powers: sundering of the sun from Christ. Julian the Apostate. The law of conservation of matter and energy a mistaken doctrine. Julius Robert Mayer. Ueberweg's History of Philosophy. Joule. Helmholtz. Darwin. Lamarck. *Naval Timber and Arboriculture* by Patrick Matthew. Hammerling's skull.

Lecture 13

BERLIN, 14 MAY 1918

Spiritual science, practical life and human destinies

The importance of spiritual science for our time. So far it exists in only a fragmentary way. Spiritual science concerns itself with the nature of the human being, his supersensible individuality, birth and death; the evolution of the Earth and cosmos. It offers more comprehensive satisfaction of the human quest for knowledge. The importance for human soul life of perception, thinking, feeling and will. Head, trunk and extremities in the human being. As science regards evolution, this occurs only in the trunk/thorax. The human head develops towards greater simplicity, for instance the human eye where physical development is held back in order to give space for the spirit and soul. Sensory perception and thinking represent a 'hunger process' in the head. The action of the I from our past incarnation in sensory perception, and of the life between death and rebirth in thinking. Spiritual science is a remedy to heal the philistinism of our era. Leninism: a coupling of the crassest contrasts. Our era informs feeling with philistinism, will with ineptitude. Tests to assess 'giftedness' and suchlike result from ahrimanic influences. Max Dessoir's 'Beyond the Soul' given a favourable review in the 'Kant Studies' journal.

Lecture 16

BERLIN, 3 JULY 1918

The Dornach building

The engineer Reuleaux distinguishes two groups of human beings, those with a 'natural' and those with a 'manganistic' world-view. The significance of technology, and mechanical as opposed to human labour. The luciferic element in human will as a correlate of the ahrimanic element in outward culture. Reuleaux's ideas about the need to intensify artistic powers in order to balance the destructiveness of material reality. New impulses flowing into art from spiritual science, coming to expression in the Goetheanum building. Its sculptural and architectural forms. The 'cake tin'. The intersecting cupolas. The columns, glass windows and their motifs, the cupola paintings, the sculptural group. Mention of a book by George Korf.

Lecture 17

BERLIN, 9 JULY 1918

East and West

Until the eighth and seventh centuries BC, people could still look back to their past incarnations. This living vision will return in the fifth post-Atlantean era. In the West, Anglo-American initiate circles seek to suppress any awareness of reincarnation. Souls being materialized by sport. Western humanity of the future is at risk of becoming 'ghostly'. In the East, acceptance of the truths of reincarnation is suppressed by inner dullness. Soul tragedy relating to the emergence of the Spirit Self. In central Europe we need to reconnect with forgotten cultural currents: Schlegel, Fichte, Schelling, Goethe. Grotesque aspects of today's Goethe Society. Layard's report on what the Cadi of Mosul said.

Lecture 18

BERLIN, 16 JULY 1918

History and reincarnation

Until the eighth and seventh centuries BC, people could look back to their former earthly incarnations and see how these had unfolded on the physical plane; in future we will look back to the soul experiences of former lives. In the intervening period, human self-knowledge was suppressed both by Freemasonry and by the Church. Bernhard of Clairvaux as an example of the soul configuration of his day. Bernhard as representative of the power of faith. The draining of money towards the Orient after the collapse of the Roman Empire. Worship of one's angel instead of a sacred experience of the divine. The tendency of the Crusades to replace Rome with Jerusalem and found an anti-Roman Christianity. The Doge Dandolo. Collecting sacred relics as the basis of capital accumulation. Johann Valentin Andreae and the *Chymical Wedding*.

Lecture 19

BERLIN, 23 JULY 1918

Human nature and human development

External historical accounts deny that human souls change in nature as the ages pass. An obstacle to perceiving the true nature of the human I: the human being always imagines himself to be sundered into two parts: his body and an abstract I. Our idea of the body is ahrimanic, that of the I luciferic. In reality we should see ourselves as threefold in nature: as we are now, and our past and future incarnation. Mythical representations of these three figures. Christ and the true nature of the human I. The 'descent of heaven'. Gnosis. Catholic rites. The Church divides souls from Christ. Petrus Waldus. Passages quoted from a book by Hertling, 'The Principle of Catholicism and Science', and from Dr B. Muenz, 'The German Chancellor as Prophet'. The book 'Life Questions' by Father Heitler.

Lecture 20

BERLIN, 30 JULY 1918

Contemporary problems I

Three eras in the fourth post-Atlantean epoch: 747–27 BC: loss of the human being's connection with the cosmos; sense of human totality in the Greek period. 27 BC to AD 693: the Church hinders understanding of the Mystery of Golgotha and humankind is directed towards the external world. 693–1413: the human being's connection with the supersensible realm becomes obscured. Bernhard of Clairvaux. 'Revelation' and 'faith'. Modern socialism's rejection of the supersensible a consequence of the laming of supersensible powers by Catholicism. The split

EDITOR'S PREFACE

The three lecture cycles that comprise this volume were given towards the end of the First World War. Parallel to the first two cycles, Rudolf Steiner was also giving a public lecture series, now published in GA 267. At the same time he was giving lectures in many other cities including Nuremberg, Munich, Stuttgart, Leipzig, Vienna, Prague and Hamburg. Following this tour Rudolf Steiner returned to Switzerland.

This volume concludes the great Berlin lecture cycles which together form a kind of compendium of anthroposophy of the time. Subsequently Rudolf Steiner's work focused increasingly on Dornach and Stuttgart. The Goetheanum building, which was nearing completion, the social threefolding movement, and the development of anthroposophical education associated with the Waldorf School in Stuttgart henceforth took up most of Steiner's time and efforts.

INTRODUCTION

In describing the innovative architectural impulse embodied in the First Goetheanum, Steiner made some key remarks (see lecture 16) which in a sense reverberate throughout this volume in diverse ways. One was about walls—usually confining and space-delimiting structures—whose forms in this new building expressed, as he said, an openness to and connection with the surrounding cosmos. Another was about the carved motifs on the architraves of the building's wooden pillars. These were not, Steiner said, fixed 'symbols' but living and therefore continually metamorphosing forms.

Extending and deepening our connection with the world and the cosmos is a primary theme in this wide-ranging series of lectures: going beyond our usual narrow limits, perceptions and definitions to engage in 'community with the realities of existence', with worlds we so often remain unaware of; that of the dead, say, who remain with us but find it difficult to live in our self-absorbed and sense-bound thoughts. By cultivating openness and gratitude we can create space for them to greatly enrich our lives, at the same time 'making an enormous difference to their souls'.

All areas of life would be enriched, in fact, if we could develop greater trust in its depths and mysteries, cultivating what Steiner calls a 'never-fading hope' in the knowledge that nothing is worthless, however difficult and stuck it may seem to us; that all experience is a gift if we learn to unlock its meaning.

The distinction between fixed symbols and living motifs likewise takes us straight to the heart of the 'project' of anthroposophy: never coming to rest in inert forms of thought—in education, say, where Steiner was already sounding alarm bells about the 'external measuring' of pupils in inflexible 'psychological' tests, and linear models of cognitive learning—but rather to dwell in the artistic realm of ever-fluid interplay, in subtle perceptions of each child's unique being and development. All this means 'grasping reality'—he keeps reiterating this—rather than imposing 'what one wishes' upon our perceptions, in a rigidifying and deadening gesture. It means looking further than abstract schemas of all kinds—social and political 'programmes' for instance—to engage instead with life itself. As William Blake wrote,

> He who binds to himself a joy
> Does the winged life destroy
> But he who kisses the joy as it flies
> Lives in eternity's sunrise.

It is a hard task, of course, for we ourselves must then also be as alive as we can be, must reject every comfortably fixed position in favour of an open-mindedness which makes space in us that life itself can fill.

Robert Frost wrote, 'Something there is that doesn't love a wall'. Steiner would concur. He keeps asking us, in all kinds of ways, to break through the walls, or mind-forged manacles, we ourselves have constructed, which induce a kind of somnolence in us, curtailing our vision on all sides. In another image he uses here, that of the magnetic needle point to North, he states something simultaneously obvious yet revelatory: that all earthly phenomena similarly point beyond themselves to the invisible forces that configure and create them. In realizing that, in some sense, thoughts are not fabricated by us but given to us if we make the right effort of will to receive them, and likewise that there are orders of being far beyond our own, Steiner invites us to participate much more deeply and fully in the cosmos as conscious participants and co-creators: to become, in fact, fully human.

Matthew Barton, April 2015

DYING EARTH AND LIVING COSMOS

LECTURE 1

BERLIN, 22 JANUARY 1918

MY dear friends, I scarcely need tell you what a pleasure it is for me to be with you again at this difficult and testing time. It has been a long while since we had the opportunity to discuss spiritual-scientific themes; and in these grave times it will be especially apparent that, far removed from mere theory, a science of the spirit must instead be a real and firm foundation that unites human souls. Not only here on the physical plane: it should unite us too with souls at present living in worlds of spirit. This is a special concern for us at this time since numberless souls have left the physical plane under circumstances we have so often spoken of. So many souls in the world are still exposed to trials perhaps graver than any so far seen in history. Quite apart from the general thoughts alive in us as we embark again on these lectures here and elsewhere, I would like to try to specifically formulate words in which our feelings can turn both to those in the thick of combat and to those, too, who have already crossed death's threshold as a result of these events.

Spirits, guardians of earthly souls
who live and weave within these earthly souls
safeguarding and protecting them with love
flowing from universal wisdom:
O hear our plea,
perceive our love
that wishes to unite with your

radiant, helping powers;
that desires to send
our spirit-surrendered love.

And towards those who have already crossed the threshold of death, we send these thoughts:

Spirits, guardians of sphere-borne souls
who work and weave upon these sphere-borne souls
safeguarding and protecting them with love
flowing from universal wisdom:
O hear our plea,
perceive our love
that wishes to unite with your
radiant, helping powers;
that desires to shine forth
our spirit-intuiting love.

For many years now, through the knowledge of spirit to which we aspire, we have sought to approach closer to the being who resolved to pass through the Mystery of Golgotha for earth's healing and for the freedom and progress of humanity. May this being be with you now, in your difficult undertakings.[1]

It may be that these grave and testing times will increasingly reveal to human souls how important it is to deepen their spiritual focus. If so, this difficult era will not have been in vain for humanity's present and future life. And yet one gets a sense—and I am not saying this as any kind of criticism of anyone, but rather as an appeal to the right and proper feelings—that people have not yet sufficiently learned the lessons of current events. One gets a sense of the need to speak ever more clearly and directly, out of the spirit of our times, to human hearts and souls. You see, voices other than human voices can also speak to us, can resonate mysteriously from present realities that are grievous on the one hand but also profoundly significant.

Everything I can say today, in stumbling and inadequate words, is vivid before me especially because, in my recent trip to Switzerland, I witnessed many things that showed me how our spiritual movement relates to the needs of our time. If you have read the lecture cycle I gave in Vienna before the war[2]—about human experiences between death and rebirth and everything this involves in relation to human life in general—if you have read this carefully you will know that at the time I pointed to the deeper causes and foundations of events which later came to such dire expression. Reading between the lines of present experiences, of what is now happening, we can find living proof of the truth of what was said then, before the war. At the time I characterized the general ailment of our age in radical terms. Here and there one sees that some lessons have been learned from these tumultuous events. But there are unmistakeable signs, too, especially apparent if one correlates separate and seemingly unimportant things, that human thinking on the physical plane has become very inflexible over the past few hundred years, and that human beings are very slow to take the decisions and adopt the measures they need to. To start with today, I would like to speak about some of the things I experienced in Switzerland. It seems to me necessary for those who are interested in our movement to have a fuller picture of the whole context of its work. But I will only give a few, aphoristic details.

It struck me as especially pleasing while I was in Switzerland that there were some young academics at Zurich University who wished me to give a series of lectures relating anthroposophy to various academic disciplines. In response, I gave four lectures in Zurich,[3] relating anthroposophic spiritual science to, respectively, psychology, history, science and sociology, the latter dealing with major social and legislative issues of modern society. I think I am right in saying that there was a certain interest—though naturally it fell far short of what one might wish for—in this relating of anthroposophy to academic disciplines. I showed in these lectures how such disciplines need to be complemented—or one could say made complete—by what can only come from anthroposophically oriented spiritual science, and that they remain only partial disciplines, only half or even just a quarter of what they could be, if they are not complemented in this way. Wherever I was able to give lectures in Switzerland I made sure that I illustrated what was lacking today in this regard, and what we need to do to incorporate developments that can lead society in the right direction. One gets the sense that an initial, strangely powerful resistance to our efforts in Switzerland has not grown less recently but rather intensified, though alongside this resistance a livelier interest has developed too. Since karma led to the building of the Goetheanum in that country, it may be that our work there might have great importance, especially if it is undertaken in the way I sought to shape it: by testifying at the same time to sources of spiritual-scientific enquiry that are concealed within German cultural life especially, but regrettably untapped and disregarded. This sense can fill us with a certain melancholy. There is something tragic about it, but on the other hand also something very satisfying. You see, if we realize this significant and dire fact, that German culture is today condemned as some kind of heresy by four-fifths of the world, we can feel melancholy on the one hand but also very hopeful that an anthroposophically oriented science of the spirit might offer a public voice to German spiritual and cultural life, might be able to give it the voice it has to find if injury is not to be done to the evolution of our earth. If we really speak to people about the spirit, if we speak of the true sources of spiritual life, we will invariably find a way to speak to all human beings irrespective of national differences.

It could also make us melancholy to see that while our efforts in spiritual science have gained some ground it is clear still that a country like Switzerland finds it increasingly difficult to hold its own against fierce encroachments. It is not easy to preserve any kind of independent judgement against pressure from four-fifths of the world. And it is hard in such a country—which may be neutral but in which four-fifths of the world still play a major part—to say everything that needs to be said. Circumstances in the world have been greatly exacerbated.

But in Switzerland we have the advantage that mere words, mere teachings are underpinned by the forms and creative elaboration of our Dornach building, which visibly reveals the aims of our spiritual science and thus can show that this spiritual science, wherever it is permitted to engage in practical life without brutal dismissal, is capable of meeting and mastering the great challenges modern life poses for people today.

In speaking of the relationship between anthroposophically oriented spiritual science and other disciplines and intentions at large in the world today, we need to introduce very new and unaccustomed ideas to people. In their unconscious depths, people have a dim and obscure knowledge that something new must come from somewhere. But their thinking is incredibly inflexible and incredibly slow to absorb new things. A fundamental trait of our modern, fast-moving times is that people think so terribly slowly, as we can see in all kinds of small ways. In Zurich, as I said, it was possible to connect aspects of anthroposophic spiritual science with academic disciplines.[4] I spoke in public in Basel before I gave the lectures in Zurich. A little while before I was due to leave Switzerland, I also received a request from Basel, from entirely academic circles, to speak about the relationship between anthroposophic spiritual science and other disciplines. But it was of course too late by then, and could not be done. I mention this for two reasons: firstly because it would have been very important to speak about our science of the spirit in a hall dedicated solely to academic pursuits, and organized by students in Basel; and secondly because it shows how slow people were to take the initiative, arriving, really, as the doors were closing. It is characteristic that people resolve on something belatedly which greater mobility of thinking, a greater capacity to assimilate things, could otherwise lead them to undertake sooner. We ought to discuss such things amongst ourselves, so that we know what we are dealing with. If we consider only one of these themes I have been speaking about recently, we can see that significant developments are needed.

In Zurich I spoke among other things of the relationship we can discern between anthroposophic spiritual science and the history of humanity. Today history is taught to children, and then as a subject at university. But what kind of history is this? It has no intimation, even, of the powers at work in humanity's history; and this is simply because the whole of modern intellectual life appeals to and activates human reason, sets in motion ordinary, supposedly fully conscious ideas and concepts, and then uses these to grasp everything.

Well, it's true; we can grasp the sense-perceptible natural world in this way, and the kind of thinking that has chalked up such great achievements in the field of mainstream science. But the moment people tried to apply this same thinking to history, they were endeavouring to make history into science. In the nineteenth century efforts were made to observe the course of history in the same way as sense-perceptible phenomena. But this can't be done—simply because historical realities have a quite different relationship with life from phenomena studied in science. What are we observing when we study history? What impulses are at work there?

We cannot discern the impulses at work in history by using the kind of rational enquiry that can be applied perfectly well in mainstream science. The impulses at work in history act in human evolution in the same way as dreams in our dream life. These impulses do not infiltrate the ordinary awareness with which we encounter and master daily life or phenomena studied in science. We can say that historical development is humanity's great dream. The fleeting pictures that play into dreams, though, become clearly delineated in the faculty of Imagination which spiritual science develops. For this reason there is no history that is not at the same time a science of the spirit; and history in the way it is taught nowadays is not history at all.

Herman Grimm[5] noted that the historian Gibbon,[6] when describing the first Christian eras, only gave an account of the decline and fall of the Roman Empire and not the gradual rise of Christianity, its growth and flourishing. Grimm of course was unaware why a good historian can describe decline extremely well but is nonplussed by growth and development. It is because history, as understood today, can only grasp what goes under and not what grows and thrives, which enters human evolution in the same way that dreams enter our individual lives. For this reason history can only be described by someone who can form Imaginations. Without these, historians—say Ranke[7] or Lamprecht[8]—describe only history's corpse and not the reality at work in historical development; and this is because the impulses at work in history are only dreamed by our consciousness. When ordinary consciousness tries to grasp historical currents it can only do so from a vantage point in the subconscious.

The modern era also offers interesting illustrations of this. If you trace modern developments you will find that in recent decades people's interest in larger philosophical questions has faded almost entirely or, much the same thing, has been stultified by academic theory, has become a kind of small-minded doctrinal disputation. It is not for nothing that a schoolmaster currently heads the world's greatest republic and feels entitled to speak on behalf of the rest of the world.[9]

If we ask where, in recent decades, one could discern a sense of broader philosophical scope in issues relating to humanity, an almost religious dimension if you like, albeit of a brutal kind, whereas everything else was more or less in thrall to the dead hand of academic dispute, then it has to be said that this was in socialism. There were real ideas here, though ones which never focused on a life of spirit but only on brutish, material realities. Unfortunately no other world of ideas surfaced to counter this one. If we perceive these socialist ideas that rose to the surface of life we find that they are, in a sense, historical ideas, are humanity's dreams. But what kind of dreams? You have to develop a sense for this dream nature of the events in humanity's history. In my lectures in Switzerland[10] I tried to demonstrate this by saying the following. Try appointing people who are very clever, but have no understanding at all of what I call dream impulses, to leading positions of responsibility in society; and then it will soon become apparent how quickly it is possible to systematically destroy a state or society. All you have to do is establish a parliament to hold sway over this state or society, and fill it with nothing but scholars and professors. And this will be a sure means of destroying society. You don't have to appoint professors to these leading positions, since socialist leaders will do it equally well—and the socialist movement has enough professors of its own. One just has to have a sense for such things, and then ask how this whole edifice of socialist theory arose. If attempts were made to introduce these socialist theories in reality—and sad evidence of this may soon be apparent in the East—they could have nothing but a destructive effect. So how did it come about that these socialist ideas took root in human heads, and what is the real nature of these theories?

To answer this we have to have an intimate knowledge of the history of the past four hundred years, and especially of the eighteenth and nineteenth centuries. We have to know that this history is quite different from the way it is portrayed in history books, and that it is really a picture of conflict between social classes. All Karl Marx[11] did, in essence, was to establish a theory of what humanity had been dreaming over the past four, or two, hundred years—what actually existed but has now been dreamed to its end and must make room instead for a new era. The socialism he propounded in his theories at the moment when the reality they related to was past shows that human reason draws on what has already gone under, already become corpse, when it employs modes of enquiry that, for instance, are perfectly valid in science. Such enquiry and knowledge show us that the world now stands, in fact, at a point of transition and that people must learn to think differently when they consider humanity's historical developments—which include the present, and future too, that likewise become historical since we approach them through historical development. People will have to recognize that historical development can only be understood through a science of the spirit. We cannot even form a proper picture of very recent events if we don't employ spiritual science. Let me give you an example which I have often cited recently.[12]

An important event which occurred between the lines of history, as it were, in Europe in the Middle Ages—we can say these things amongst ourselves, though outsiders would ridicule such an idea—was European humanity's loss of knowledge about the western parts of the world. Connections had always existed, especially between Ireland, England and the region we now know as America. Ireland and England cultivated these connections, and only at the time America was said to have been discovered was a papal decree issued forbidding any such contacts with America. Naturally it was not called 'America' back then. This connection with America really only failed at the time the Spaniards 'discovered' it. But external historical accounts are so unclear that nowadays people have the sense that in Europe no one knew about America before 1492. Almost everyone believes this. And other similar facts can be discovered through spiritual-scientific sources. Today we stand at a moment of transition when history must be considered from the spiritual-scientific standpoint. But now people might ask, since spiritual science as we see it can only emerge in our present era, how things were in former times.

If we look back to earlier times we find something different, which does, though, relate to what we call 'Imagination' in spiritual science. We find myths and legends; and from the power of these myths and legends, these great pictures, impulses—even political ones—were drawn, and were in fact a good deal more real, more in tune with reality than modern abstract teachings about history or socio-economics. You see, what makes human society cohere and determines communal life does not have to be formulated or grasped in abstract concepts. It used to be expressed in mythological form. Today we cannot simply start creating myths again but have to develop Imaginations, and use these to grasp history and, from this understanding in turn, form political impulses that will be utterly different from the phantasms so many people dream up today, or that arise, as I would say, from their abstract and schoolteacherly impulses.

It is not easy nowadays to tell people that historical developments are something that really unfold in the human subconscious rather than in ordinary, alert thinking. And yet this life of history, hidden from human beings, has a great impact on actual events and on human impulses altogether. One can say—and this became apparent in my lectures in Zurich—that people everywhere wish to embrace knowledge that seeks the spirit, but they do so with inadequate means. In Zurich one encounters the discipline of academic psychology, so-called psychoanalysis; and following my lectures some strange exchanges occurred on the subject of the relationship between anthroposophically oriented spiritual science and psychoanalysis. Psychoanalysts approach this world of spiritual science with their eyes blindfolded, in spiritual terms, and are unable to get anywhere with it. Yet this same world is knocking at the door which people nowadays need to open.

Professor Jung[13] in Zurich has recently written another pamphlet about psychoanalysis—one of many he has written—and touches there on various issues. But he does so in a way that shows he has inadequate means to embark on all this. One fact I will mention will show you straight away what I mean. Jung cites an example[14] that many other psychoanalysts refer to also.

The following happens to a woman who is invited to supper one evening at somebody's house. After supper her hostess is due to depart for a spa town for a health cure. The guests eat supper together, and then the lady of the house departs, as do the others. The woman in question accompanies one group of guests. As sometimes happens after a party, they are walking along in the middle of the road, instead of on the pavement, when a cab comes driving round the corner. All the guests step back on the pavement to get out of its way, but not the lady we're speaking of. She ran along in the middle of the road in front of the horses while the coachman shouted to her to step away. She kept on running nevertheless until she reached a bridge over a river, where she decided to throw herself over the edge to escape her predicament. She did so, and was saved by the other guests who had run along behind. And since the most obvious thing at this point was to carry her back to the house of her now departed hostess, that is what they did. Here she found her hostess's husband, and was able to spend a few hours there with him in his house.

Consider now what someone with inadequate means can make of such an incident. If we approach it as psychoanalysts, we come upon those secret provinces of the soul that tell us the psyche of the person had a particular experience connected with horses at the age of seven. Accordingly, as the woman left the party and saw the horse-drawn cab, this earlier experience was invoked from her subconscious; and she was so disconcerted by this that, instead of jumping aside, she carried on running in front of the cab. For the psychoanalyst, therefore, the whole incident results from the connection between a current experience and 'unresolved riddles of the soul' from former upbringing and so on. But this is to study things with inadequate means. The psychoanalyst is unaware that the subconscious powers at work here are more substantial in nature than he assumes—a good deal cleverer and more subtle than the conscious mind. This subconscious is also often much more courageous. You see, the psychoanalyst does not know that there was a demon sitting in the woman's soul, and that she left the house with the unconscious idea of being alone with the man once his wife had departed. The whole incident was most cleverly arranged by the subconscious; for, you see, one does everything far more certainly and surely if one's conscious mind plays no part in it. The woman ran in front of the horses in order to be saved at the right moment. But the psychoanalyst is unaware of this because he does not assume the existence of a world of soul and spirit to which the human soul is related. Yet Jung does have an intimation of this.[15] From the numerous phenomena he encounters, he senses that the human soul is related to numerous other souls. But he has to be a materialist, after all, since otherwise he wouldn't be an intelligent modern man. So what does he do? He says the following. The human soul—and we see this from all the things that happen to the human soul—is in relationship with spiritual realities outside it. Yet these do not exist! So how can we understand this? Well, the soul possesses a body that is descended from other bodies, and these in turn from earlier ones. This is genetic inheritance, and Jung constructs his thesis around the idea that the soul therefore inherits and re-experiences relationships people once had, say, to heathen gods. These experiences are still in us, he thinks, resulting from physical inheritance, and they become 'isolated soul provinces' that the human soul can only free itself from if they are first invoked. He has insight, in fact, into the human soul's need to have a relationship with such things, and understands that they will wreck a person's nervous system if not called up into the conscious mind. He therefore expresses something that is absolutely right in terms of a modern outlook:[16] that the human soul cannot be devoid of all relationship to a divine reality without being inwardly deadened. This is just as true, in his view, as the fact that no such divine reality exists! For him, the question of the human soul's relationship to God does not have the slightest connection with the question of God's existence.

This is what he writes. And now let us consider what is at work here. Jung states that the human soul must develop a relationship to God, but that it is equally certain it would be idiotic to assume God exists. Therefore, for the sake of its own health, the soul is condemned to deceive itself by positing a God. This is what Jung writes in his book, really: 'Deceive yourself that there is a God, otherwise you will fall ill!'

These things can show us that great riddles are knocking insistently at our door, while the modern age tries to push back against them. If people were courageous enough, similar things would surface everywhere. But they are not! I am not saying these things to lock horns with Professor Jung but because I believe that he thinks in a more courageous way than anyone else. He says what he must, given the condition of the modern world. Others do not say such things for they are less courageous.

All such things must be considered if we really wish to grasp what it means, as we discover through spiritual science, that humanity's history, and consequently also the political impulses at work in society, have nothing to do with ordinary consciousness, and that these impulses can only be understood and handled if we develop a capacity for imaginative awareness. As regards what I have often recently called an antisocial view of history within political life, and its chief representative, we might say that Wilsonism needs to be replaced by imaginative perception of reality. But Wilsonism is very widespread, and many are Wilsonians without even knowing it. Names themselves are of no importance. Genuinely important are the realities alive in society. I can actually speak in a more forthright way about Wilson since I gave my verdict on him before the war already, in a lecture cycle in Helsingfors (Helsinki),[17] and did not need to wait to find out, during the war, what spirit sits enthroned in America. Many adulatory voices heaped praises on Wilson, but these have gone quiet recently. People have discovered a thing or two—such as the fact that this gentleman on the throne of America, when composing his illustrious Republican charter, merely copied it from one written in 1864 by Don Pedro,[18] the ruler of Brazil, only altering the phrases that spoke of South American interests and inserting 'the interests of the United States' instead.

Adulatory voices were clamouring in Europe too when Wilson's two books *The New Freedom* and *Mere Literature and Other Essays* appeared.[19] This was only a few years back—five or six years. People have now learned a thing or two about Wilsonism. But there is a very great deal more to be learned about deeply, deeply incisive modern events. Things that can only flourish in the soil of spiritual-scientific knowledge must be taken very seriously. People often accuse anthroposophically oriented spiritual science of being theoretical, and object that other schools of thought get directly involved in practical life without bothering people about cosmic evolution and suchlike. Such schools of thought, they say, speak of love, universal human love, of what and how one should love. Well, millennia have passed while people spoke about love in this way, and we can see where it has got us. If, instead, you allow the human soul to engage for a much shorter time with a science of the spirit, really engage with it though, you will see that this spiritual science blossoms as love in human hearts. You see, you cannot preach love. Love can only grow when it is properly cultivated—and then it grows. And it is an offspring of the spirit. It is also an offspring of true knowledge and perception, one that does not focus on matter alone but on spirit.

Today, in this introductory lecture, I simply wanted to point to some feelings that may accompany us during this period and could be important. And I have outlined what ground I wish to cover in forthcoming lectures. I will be discussing what can awaken strength, courage and hope in the human soul. I want to speak about all that the science of the spirit can give humanity that is different from what many previous centuries have given it; and I wish to speak of spiritual science as something alive that is not theoretical but can give birth in us to a second, spiritual human being, one that sustains the first and gives it stability in the world. As you know, during the medieval period many people conceived the urgent desire to create gold. Why did they wish to do this? Really they desired something that cannot be realized in ordinary earthly conditions; and this was because they recognized that unless spiritualized, permeated by spiritual impulses, these ordinary earthly conditions can never bring true contentment. Ultimately this is also the message of the Gospels. But people usually overlook the most important things; they criticize the view of the Gospels that the divine realm descended to earth. But is it not here among us? It is! Just not in any outwardly apparent signs. It has to be inwardly grasped. It must not be denied as our era denies it. And this descent of the spirit to earth is also something we will speak about over the forthcoming period.

So today I only wanted to sound an underlying note. In our time it is necessary—for there are now millions of souls who have crossed the threshold of death—to build the bridge to the realm where the dead live. They live amongst us, and we can find them. And how we can do so is something we will be speaking of too, in a renewed way.

Lecture 2

BERLIN, 29 JANUARY 1918

We have often considered the saying 'Know thyself', whose light shines through every era.[20] It stood above the temple of Apollo in ancient Greece and embodies a great, an infinite prompting to develop human and therefore universal wisdom. It is a saying, however, which was significantly renewed and deepened by the impulse given by the Mystery of Golgotha. We will be speaking of all these things this winter perhaps, if time allows, seeking to find our way to the goals they embody.

Today I would like to begin with observations on the human being of a seemingly outward nature, a form of human self-knowledge that appears external but in fact has a powerful initial impetus if we first take possession of it and then draw on it to penetrate our inner nature. I want to begin—though only seemingly—from a consideration of the outward human form.

When mainstream scientists observe this outward human form they do so in a way that is fairly unsatisfying from a higher spiritual standpoint. Science as practised today offers little stimulus for a recognition of really human qualities. You can see from various comments in my book *Riddles of the Soul*[21] what ordinary science has to say on this subject. The book offers important foundations for developing far-reaching insight into human nature, but currently these foundations appear of no concern to science. And anatomy, physiology and other such disciplines offer very little to someone who seriously questions and seeks to fathom human nature by starting with an understanding of our outward physical form. An artistic mode of enquiry actually offers far more in this respect. In many ways, modern science takes us no further. Someone who decides to seek more substantial reality through an artistic, a Goethean mode of enquiry, may perhaps find his way to greater truth today than he will by following the paths of mainstream science. As little as this is apparent today, in future a world-view arising from spiritual science, and originating in a certain human thirst for knowledge, will unite a scientific and an artistic sense of the world in a higher, harmonious synthesis. This will contain much more clairvoyance than exists in the clairvoyance many today dream of—but only dream of.

If we study the human form we can initially perceive something important in it if we turn our gaze—something more or less all of you have done—to the skeleton, this basic framework of the human form. No doubt you have all seen a human skeleton and noted the differentiation that exists between the head and the rest of the form. You will have noticed too that the head is in a sense a self-contained whole which rests as if on a column upon what constitutes the system of limbs, the rest of the human organism. It is easy, in a skeleton, to distinguish the head from the rest of the human form. In the most superficial differentiation of this kind we discover that the head is really more or less spherical: not a perfect sphere, but an approximate one. Now as a spiritual-scientific researcher one has to caution people against basing their search for knowledge on superficial, outward analogies. But this view of the approximately spherical nature of the human head is not superficial. The human being really is a kind of duality initially, and the spherical shape of his head is not in the least random. We have to give full attention to what we see before us in the human head, and first hints of this have been offered as part of our enquiries in spiritual science in the book I called *The Spiritual Guidance of Man and Humanity*.[22] There I indicated that the human head is an image of the whole universe, which appears outwardly to us as a hollow sphere of space.

In talking of these things we have to note something that modern people are far removed from applying to the most important areas of enquiry, but which they do always use in a certain domain, at the same time ignoring its huge implications. It will not occur to anyone who uses a compass, a magnetic needle, one of whose ends points to magnetic north and the other to magnetic south, to seek the causes of the movements of this magnetic needle only in the needle itself. The physicist will feel obliged instead to regard the magnetic needle and the magnetic force issuing from the earth's magnetic north pole as a connected whole—a force that directs one end of the compass needle towards the north pole and the other towards the south. Here therefore we look into the whole universe to find the causes of movements in the smallest domain. But we do not do the same where we should, where it would be very important to do so. Today when we see that a second living creature is forming inside a first and where, therefore, something is likewise occurring in the smallest space—say an egg forming in a chicken—we do not usually apply what we learn from the magnetic needle and recognize that what is happening does not lie in the chicken itself but in the whole cosmos. But in the same way that the greater universe participates in the magnetic needle, so the whole cosmos participates in the developing egg in the chicken's body, alongside all other processes involved in this. The spherical form of the cosmos is involved. The genetic processes of inheritance, leading back to previous generations, only accompany what happens when the egg cell develops in the mother organism. This is heretical to a modern scientific outlook, and yet it is true. The powers of the cosmos participate in diverse ways. And as true as it is to say—and empirical embryology demonstrates it—that the germinal form of the human head develops first in the womb, so it is true too that these developments are caused by primal powers working in from the whole universe, and that this human head is an image of the whole cosmos. By contrast what hangs down from the head, the rest of the skeleton, can show us if we observe it very carefully that its form and configuration have more connection with the line of genetic inheritance, with father, mother, grandfather and grandmother, than with what exists out in the cosmos. Initially therefore the human being is a kind of dual being, also in relation to his origins and development. His form emerges from the cosmos on the one hand, and this comes to expression in the spherical form of his head, and from the whole line of genetic descent, on the other, is expressed in the rest of his organism, attached to the head. The human being's whole outward shape reveals him to be a hybrid, if you like, a being of dual nature.

Besides the fact that this is instructive, such a mode of observation has a quite different significance too. We become immobile in our thoughts and at odds with outward life, start living in a buttress of thoughts, if we observe the human being in accordance with ordinary mainstream science—if, say, we look into a microscope and watch the developing embryo, observing only what is contained in it as if one were to study the magnetic needle very closely to find out what makes it move in a north-south orientation. And then, if we apply such thoughts in turn to the social realm, to sociology, they are simply inadequate or lead to the kind of schoolmasterly abstractions we might also call 'Wilsonism'. It does matter very much what kind of thinking we develop, what thought forms arise in us as we embrace certain ideas. Knowledge itself has less importance compared with this. The important thing is what gives rise in us to a certain mode of knowledge and the usefulness it cultivates. If we have an open mind for ways in which the human being is connected and related to the whole universe, this will awaken in us thoughts that lead us into an ethical world-view, a view of human rights which today ought to be accorded the highest value but has become something very strange. You can see therefore that curiosity, a mere desire for knowledge, is not the only impulse for seeking the kinds of knowledge I have referred to here.

Before us stands the human being, therefore, as a hybrid. This has still deeper significance. Today I only want to strike some fundamental notes to elicit in you an inner sense of the importance of what we will be considering here.

Let us stay for a moment with the fact that our head, in the further course of life—this head which we meet as an image of the whole world—is basically the mediator of our perception. I won't say the 'tool' since this would not be entirely correct. But the head is not alone in mediating our perception—let's stay with perception and knowledge, with sensory perception. The head does mediate this, but along with the rest of our organism. And since the rest of us, even as regards its origins, is entirely different from the head, so inasmuch as we are perceiving beings we consist of the head system and the heart system, as I have tended to call it,[23] since there, in the heart system, everything else congregates and is concentrated. We really are two different beings at once: a head person who stands in a perceiving relationship with the world, and a heart person. The difference is this: that however much we sometimes find fault with the world, we only use our head to perceive and know things. What is this due to? If we were to draw parallels between head perception and heart perception, this would not tell us very much. Someone capable of grasping with his heart what his head perceives would cultivate a warmer kind of knowledge than another. Human beings would be differentiated in this respect, but it would hardly be a major distinction. But if we approach things with spiritual-scientific experience, something quite different becomes apparent. After all, we acquire perceptions; gradually they approach us and develop in us, and then the following occurs. The way we relate to the world through our head, the way we perceive things, happens quickly in some respects whereas the way we perceive the world through the rest of our organism occurs slowly. In addition to all the differentiation I described last winter[24] in relation to the evolution of the world and the human being, it is also true that our head perception rushes while the rest of our organism does not. This is hugely significant. If we are educated in an abstract, schoolmasterly way, our head is educated primarily. Nowadays people are raised and educated only in respect of the head. At the very latest, if the head participates for a long time in the development of perception and knowledge—but in most people this does not last so long—its development concludes in a person's twenties. At this point the head has completed its perceiving appropriation of the world. The rest of our organism, on the other hand, requires the whole of life, until we die. And we can say therefore that the head lives roughly three times faster than the rest of our organism. The rest of the organism takes its time, takes three times as long, lives at a quite different tempo. Someone who has the gift of observing and grasping such things realizes that whenever he grasps something through his head, he still has to wait for it to unite with his whole being. For full and living assimilation of something that has been absorbed by the head in around one day, we have to wait three to four days. The conscientious spiritual researcher will never communicate what he has absorbed merely through his head, but only what he has understood with his whole being. This is extraordinarily important, far-reaching in scope and of deep significance.

In schools as they exist today we can really only offer our children a kind of head knowledge, rather than one the rest of the organism can assimilate. The knowledge conveyed there is prepared in such a way that it has to be quickly absorbed by the head so that one can recall it again later. After their last exam, though, people scarcely remember anything of what they learned in this way, and are pleased if they can't. The kind of knowledge, by contrast, that can be entirely assimilated by the rest of the organism would be one which later, in recalling it, would invoke in us qualities such as love, joy and warmth of heart. How we structure lessons so that, for the rest of his life, a person can look back on his education with warmth of heart, joy and a certain feeling of bliss, is connected with the deepest mysteries of humanity.

An awful lot needs doing in this field. You see, people versed in educational matters will know that everything we present to children nowadays has been prepared in advance in a way that prevents the rest of our organism from assimilating it; and such knowledge will not engender joyfulness later. This is also why people grow old at a relatively young age nowadays. You see, it is a secret of human development that when the head, say, is 28, the rest of the organism, with its slower mode of development, is only a third or a quarter as old. The rest of our organism runs at a tempo that is three or four times slower. We will be studying other relationships too. Now if educators took account of these mysteries, people would be able to absorb and assimilate something so fruitful and health-giving that it would last them until they died. If a person has absorbed such things by the age of 25, and then needs three times longer to process and assimilate them, then the rest of his organism would have done so by the time he reached 75. On the other hand, the knowledge we acquire through our head does not have any comprehensive importance for our whole being. Only the deep inward experience and knowledge our whole being acquires can have this importance. But there is a general disinclination for such knowledge today. People commonly seek head wisdom only. Actually you can do some simple calculations based on what I have said to find that ideas a person has absorbed through his head by the age of 15 will still need to be assimilated, and that he will not really be mature enough to engage his whole being in a particular kind of work, say public administration or as a member of parliament, until the age of 45. If it has been possible, by the age of 15, to endow someone with conceptual powers that can be gradually assimilated by his whole being, he will be mature enough by the age of 45 to be elected to a city council or a national parliament. In ancient times people still had living knowledge of this from the mysteries. Today, by contrast, efforts are largely geared to lowering the age for everything, to speeding things up, since nowadays a person is as ready for things at 20 as he would only have been at 80 in the past. Yet these things cannot be determined by wishful thinking, only by true insight.

These things can certainly be applied to life and have fundamental significance. Our whole public life is geared to what human beings are by virtue of their heads. In interacting socially with each other, people only interact with their heads. Just imagine this: all social interaction is just head interaction, and highly unsuited for shaping social life. For where does the head originate? As we saw, the human head is not of this earth but originates in and is created from the cosmos. One cannot deal with earthly matters with the head. In our head we do not belong to a particular nation or region of the globe. We should only use it to decide things common to the whole earth. But, even to be able to do that, we have to grow into what belongs to the earth throughout our life, what makes us a citizen of the earth rather than a citizen of the heavens. Any judgements we make about public matters have to be drawn from deeper insights into the human being. And then in turn—and today I am only sketching outlines that we will elaborate further on future occasions—we need to consider the profound meaning of what Goethe expressed as the idea of metamorphosis, which has far wider application than even Goethe himself was able to see in his own day.

Our head is formed from the cosmos. If we consider this from the perspective of spiritual science we see that in the whole period between death and a new birth, working in the cosmos, we are preparing to form our head. We work on our organism between death and rebirth primarily by working on our future head. In a sense this head is the grave of the soul in comparison with the nature of the soul before birth or, let us say, before conception. The activities we undertake in a life of spirit between death and a new birth come to rest in the head. And then the stream of inheritance adds and attaches the rest of the organism to what is, in a sense, formed out of the world of spirit. But what is the nature of this inherited addition? It too is connected with the head. I have said this before:[25] the rest of the human organism apart from the head is the germ and foundation of the head of our subsequent incarnation. The whole of the rest of the organism is something that can pass through a metamorphosis to become the head of the following incarnation. When we cross the threshold of death, the powers we develop throughout our life pull free from the whole of the rest of the organism, but remain in the configurations which the rest of the organism possessed during life. In the period between death and a new birth we bear this with us, forming it into our future head. And so our head is always a legacy from the last incarnation. And in the rest of our organism we have therefore something that will determine how our head is formed and configured in a coming incarnation. In this way too we have a dual nature.

When we gain this perspective on things, we see that the human being is truly embedded in the cosmos, and therefore does not originate solely in the dimensions of space and time we are aware of in our outward, physical perception but is part of a whole huge context of existence. It is a fascinating thing not only to observe a bone in the spinal column and note, as Goethe did,[26] how it relates to the skull bones and to see that the latter are only transformed vertebrae, but also to discover that everything in the head has its counterpart too in the rest of the organism. We have to observe in a very open-minded way, however, to discern not only how the nose and everything in the head is a metamorphosis of this kind, but also to see that the whole of the rest of the organism is at an earlier stage of metamorphosis compared with what we find in the head.

There are extremely important educational consequences of such an outlook, as I said. If people begin to grasp these spiritual-scientific insights, they will come to embrace some really very significant requirements for the practice of teaching.

One thing is important above all: we grow old through our life. But really we ought to say only that our physical body grows old. You see, as strange as it may seem—and I have mentioned this before[27]—our ether body, the next, spiritual aspect of our being, grows ever younger. The older we become, the younger becomes our etheric body. We get wrinkles and go bald, in physical terms, but in terms of our etheric body we become—or we can become—ever chubbier-cheeked and flourishing. But just as outer nature ensures that the physical body grows older, so we ourselves must ensure that our etheric body receives youthful powers. And this can only be done if we introduce through the head the kind of thoughts that are spiritual sustenance for us and are fit to be assimilated throughout our lives.

Think for a moment of how one might teach very young children about the human being as an image of the whole universe, an image of the divine world order—but do this in a way that the child can directly and immediately grasp rather than simply reading out words from the Bible the child does not understand. Drawn from the integrity of a science of the spirit, all this can offer a more full-blooded head knowledge than is common today, and will then become a source of rejuvenation throughout a person's life. Our modern education is no source of rejuvenation but the opposite. And if today we are fortunate enough not to have become the most withered sour-pots, this is only because the current way of addressing the head alone—which has been developing for the past four hundred years or so and has now reached its culmination—has not yet succeeded in wrecking all the inherited culture that survives from olden times. But if we continue as we are doing, we are heading for a form of education that really will produce dried up sour-pots. I said this recently[28]—the war interrupted these developments—that in the years before the war a growing stream of people were flooding the sanatoria, and much effort and expense was required to try to rid people of their nervous complaints.

This is all connected with the fact that the head is not given what the whole person needs. I have spoken about how little of the right attention or care is given to such things. I often recall visiting a sanatorium a few years ago to see someone there. We arrived at lunchtime and a whole crowd of patients was walking by. Some of them were certainly quite troubled in appearance, with their nervous condition inscribed upon their faces, and hands or feet twitching. But the most restless twitcher, the most nervous person in the sanatorium was the chief consultant there. And it has to be said that a chief consultant will not find the right approach to curing his patients if he is the one most in need of a cure. Otherwise he was an extremely kind man, but at the same time an example of someone who, in his youth, had not, at least, been able to absorb what could have rejuvenated him throughout a lifetime. Such things cannot be altered by isolated reforms, but can only be improved if the whole social organism is improved. We have to look at the whole social organism. The great universal laws of existence ensure that human beings cannot find healing, be made whole, in egotistical isolation, but only by seeking it in community with others.

If we not only picture the sensory reality commonly regarded as the only one, but look beyond this to supersensible realms as the source of powers to reform the world in the near future, we can envisage how, in education and diverse other fields, a science of the spirit can be introduced into life, can be authentically developed in tangible ways.

There is actually no need to urge visionary clairvoyance to do this. We need only understand the human being as an image of world spirituality, and then a spiritual outlook will inform what we do. It is impossible to comprehend the whole human being without understanding and considering the spirit intrinsic to him. And as I have often said,[29] it is vital to lay aside a very prevalent habit—a lethargy about knowledge and enquiry. All our spiritual-scientific observations show us that we must take one step after another, must be willing to engage in details and specifics, to build up a whole picture from these details; we must start from what is close at hand and from there raise it towards the supersensible. What lies close to hand in the sensory realm shows us the supersensible almost tangibly at work. You see, if we can study the human head in the right way we can see what is formed from the whole cosmos, and can study in the rest of the human organism what will develop back into the cosmos and in turn reappear from it in a following incarnation. If we properly study sensory reality we can certainly arrive at a true view of the supersensible. But to do so we must be willing to leave our comfort zone sufficiently to allow the true nature of the human being to emerge, at least to the extent of according him the respect one happily accords a clock or another very ordinary object. Anyone with the least mechanical knowledge will admit that he cannot understand a clock unless he considers the interrelationship of its clockwork. And yet all and sundry hold forth on human nature without the same premise, believing they can speak about the loftiest human qualities, often citing the idea that 'truth must be simple'. Spiritual science is accused of being far too complex. People might think it desirable to acquire in five minutes or less what is needed for insight into the loftiest human nature. But the human being is actually very complex, and his grandeur in the universe consists of his complexity. The inclination to lethargy must be overcome in our pursuit of knowledge if we really wish to penetrate human nature. There is no contemporary understanding of what is needed unless people are willing to try, at least intuitively, to grasp the whole complexity of human nature. If we cultivate nothing but head knowledge, and do not wish to assimilate with our whole being what the head learns, nor even in the first place give the head something that the whole human being *can* assimilate, we place the human being into a social order in a way that refuses to make earthly life into an image, a reflection, of supersensible, spiritual life. Then we suffer from a strange split in our nature—not a duality of the kind I mentioned, but a harmful split we need to overcome.

During the course of evolution, human life has undergone changes. To observe this we need to go back four hundred years, or not even that long. Those familiar with the realities of cultural history rather than history as it is usually recorded know how hugely different was the life and thinking of the eighteenth century compared to that of the nineteenth. Human thinking as a whole, as it developed gradually towards the twentieth century, formulated increasingly abstract concepts, head concepts. If we study the full-blooded nature of human concepts in the thirteenth and fourteenth centuries and consider the natural science of those times, we find a very striking difference compared to the abstract, arid principles governing modern science. Some very interesting things are contained in a well-known book said to have been written by Basilius Valentinus.[30] Recently a Swedish scholar[31] wrote a book about matter, citing various comments by Valentinus, and coming to the conclusion that no one in their right mind can understand such things. It is self-evident that he cannot understand Valentinus' book since it will be entirely incomprehensible if you bring to bear on it concepts drawn from modern physics and chemistry. This is connected with realities related to those which led to the good old German proverb, 'The early morning has God and gold in its mouth' changing over time to, merely, 'The early morning has gold in its mouth.' A good old European proverb has thus been Americanized.*

In those olden times, descriptions and views of nature were imbued with what originates in the whole human being. Nowadays we have head knowledge. On the one hand this is very abstract and arid and does not imbue a person throughout his life, and on the other hand it is very spiritual. Our dual nature is such that we engender the most spiritual qualities today, for our abstract concepts are the most spiritual thing imaginable, and yet they are incapable of comprehending the spirit. It is extremely easy to see what split is caused in us by these spiritual concepts we have developed. Strangely, we have become materialists as a result of these spiritual concepts. But if concepts were true they could never give rise to materialism. The very presence of our abstract concepts is already a first refutation of materialism. We live in this split. Over the past four hundred years we have spiritualized ourselves to a huge degree, and in this spiritual quality, which we only possess in the abstract, we need to find the living spirit again. We have developed to the point of having only objectivized concepts, but now we must return to Imagination, Inspiration and Intuition again. We laid aside what was handed down to us from earlier, primordial, inherited wisdom as Imaginations, Inspirations and Intuitions; but now, having shed a full-bodied, full-blooded form of knowledge, we must develop these faculties again.

This is something that can fill us with a sense of seriousness towards spiritual science. These two first lectures have been more introductory in nature, and it has been my aim to show that the most external view of human nature can fuel our impulse to study the spiritual foundations of the world. As humanity pursues these impulses and ideas it will discover something so sorely lacking at present: an inner truthfulness. One cannot seek the spirit in a fruitful way without inner authenticity and truthfulness; and we will never go wrong if we let our life experience and

---

* Translator's note: Benjamin Franklin is said to have coined the expression, 'Early to bed and early to rise, makes a man healthy, wealthy and wise.'

insights teach us that a proper harmony between head knowledge and heart knowledge is only possible if we place ourselves into life in an authentic way. You see, this is precisely why people today do not wish to lead their head knowledge into heart knowledge: because heart knowledge not only requires longer but also reacts, pushes back against head knowledge if it is untrue. The rest of our being then becomes apparent as a kind of conscience, and contemporary humanity, with its predilection for the head, is afraid of this.

And now to end with—since whenever we are gathered here we always also need to gauge the position of our spiritual-scientific striving in relation to the whole world—a few remarks on directly practical matters.

Spiritual science can only thrive if we stand behind it seriously and truthfully, since it needs to respond to humanity's deepest needs in the modern world. It must allow the pangs of conscience that tend to arise whenever the heart says no to the head—which it always does when we do not seek the spirit or only strive for knowledge egotistically, out of desire, ambition and so forth. For this reason it is important to avoid the least compromise in our pursuit of spiritual science. The science of the spirit has to be pursued positively, out of its own intrinsic quality; and compromises involving partial truths, or fractions of truths, are untenable. It is too serious a matter to dabble with in this way. The remarks below, following on from our introductory thoughts, are not intended personally though they do have a personal dimension. We can only understand a great deal of the opposition to spiritual science if we consider where it originates and how it develops. Here and there we witness someone who attacks spiritual science in the fiercest way. There are instances of a different kind to those I am thinking of now, but in many cases opposition to spiritual science emerges from circumstances such as those illustrated by the following specific example.

On one occasion I was due to give a lecture in Frankfurt when I received a phone call from a gentleman who wished to speak with me. I had nothing against it, and made an appointment with him. He arrived and said, 'I've been travelling around after you for ages, and am very keen to talk to you.' I had nothing against this, though nothing much for it either. The man carried on talking about all kinds of things. But the science of the spirit has to be taken seriously, and this means rejecting the empty appearance of scholarly interest. You can't keep making compromises. I remained polite to the man; I let him say what he wanted but at the same time allowed him to see that I would not be taking any further notice of him. I was convinced he was talking hot air, although seeking connection and confirmation. I'm quoting this example just as an illustration of the kind of thing that happens. I let the man go on talking until he ran out of steam. Much that he said was very flattering indeed, but the only thing that mattered was whether his 'spiritual-scientific' endeavours had any truth. Not long afterwards news reached me from Switzerland that this same man was condemning the 'demonic' and 'devilish' nature of Steiner's spiritual science. There's an afterword to this story, but I will leave that aside for now. Here, you see, is one of the ways in which opposition arises—very frequently from people who wanted to become part of our endeavours and yet who, for certain reasons, had to be ignored. There's a lot that has to be ignored in keeping spiritual science intact.

In this connection I would like to mention something else. Our dear friend Dr Rittelmeyer[32] recently wrote an article in the journal *Die Christliche Welt* about the relationship between religious questions and our science of the spirit, at the same time seeking to dispel various prejudices about the latter in an extremely laudable way. We should be thankful to him for this. I hope you will all read the article. Subsequently Dr Johannes Mueller,[33] whom many of you know, saw fit to attack Dr Rittelmeyer's article in three successive issues of the same journal. I have no wish to engage in any way with what Dr Mueller wrote there. Actually I have spent years without number trying *not* to speak about Dr Johannes Mueller, since my aim is to keep spiritual science free of dilettantism, and not muddy its waters with compromise. I think one best achieves this if one does not directly speak of things whose own intrinsic value, if they have any, will become apparent by themselves. I have never before mentioned Dr Johannes Mueller. Now in our era people have little sense for what is actually true or untrue in this domain. If you study Johannes Mueller's articles you will find that they contain a great deal of what one has to call objective untruths, whether due to unthinking superficiality or other causes. They're full of such things. In my book, *Riddles of the Soul*,[34] I described an instance of this untruth in books by Dessoir.[35] I'm looking forward to seeing what response I get to my critique of the work of this man, a professor at Berlin University.[36] Presumably there must be one! The second essay in *Riddles of the Soul* describes Professor Dessoir's manner of writing, and if reviewers of Dessoir fail to consider what I have said there, they will share responsibility for his failings. Yet people often just resort to the excuse nowadays that they 'didn't know', and were not obliged to read what others had written.

Well, I will let those who are familiar with Johannes Mueller's lectures and utterances form their own views about little squibs sent in my direction, about my supposed 'crass self-advertisement'[37] and so on, and about my lectures appealing to people's sensationalism.[38] Not very long ago an elderly gentleman whom I greatly esteem, because he is very conscientious in the way he expresses himself, told me he was surprised so many people attended my lectures since I took no pains to simplify things. It is very easy to demonstrate that Johannes Mueller's accusations are untrue.[39] In cities where spiritual science has not yet taken root, not very many people attend my lectures usually; and where many attend, this is because the lecture is given in a locality where a lot of preparatory work has been done. I don't wish to spend any more time on Johannes Mueller, but I will just comment on his last paragraph which claims that I speak of the 'drama of God' who is to be redeemed by humankind, and suchlike. He gets a column and a half of text out of quoting my book *Christianity as Mystical Fact*,[40] but does so out of context, in any order he sees fit. And by doing so, by conveniently leaving things out, what he says becomes utter nonsense. In fact, in my book on Christianity the very opposite is said about the 'drama of God and his enchantment'. Johannes Mueller talks his way out of this by saying he has been unable to grasp what I wrote. I well believe him! Without having understood anything at all, Johannes Mueller sets to work to tear the book apart. As I have often said, the book places absolute and primary importance on the Mystery of Golgotha, as distinct from all other mysteries. But Mueller has no sense at all of this. I would never ask him to understand the book since I don't believe he is able to do so; but nevertheless he criticizes it. And the remarkable thing is this: that it was published in 1902, and by 1906 had therefore been available for four years. In the first edition, as was known, I had explained my relationship to science on the one hand and to philosophy on the other, and the book was in the public domain. But if Johannes Mueller remained unaware of it, that is a matter for him. The book was in the public domain in 1906, and related to my whole world-view in the same way as, for example, *The Philosophy of Freedom*.[41] And therefore anyone who formed an opinion about me in 1906 would have been obliged to consider this world-view and not start from half or partial truths. In 1906 *Christianity as Mystical Fact* had been around for four years. Yet in 1906 Johannes Mueller sent me the book he had written entitled *The Sermon on the Mount*[42] with the dedication 'To Dr R. Steiner, with appreciation of *The Philosophy of Freedom*. Mainberg, 17.8.06.' This mention was one I felt it necessary to ignore, since, in the ways I have described, it was impossible to compromise. And I consider myself entitled to fall silent rather than to try to explain my views of someone's propositions. But silence can annoy people more than anything. As I said, one has to seek opposition to spiritual science in actual circumstances and relationships. And whoever reads Dr Johannes Mueller's essays about our friend Dr Rittelmeyer may do well not just to take this opposition at face value, but discern the background to it. We have to look closely to see truer reasons that lie beneath the surface. To fail to respond to an 'appreciation of *The Philosophy of Freedom*' can antagonize the person who is hoping to be flattered in return.

I wanted to give you this little glimpse into the psychology of Johannes Mueller, so that you have a little more background and therefore see his articles in a clearer light.

LECTURE 3

BERLIN, 5 FEBRUARY 1918

IN considering the totality of phenomena in the world, and to stand in the world in the most ideally practical way, it is important, as we have often discussed from many different angles,[43] to consider the deeper human importance—one greater than external observation accords it—of the alternation between waking and sleeping. Ordinary enquiry finds only that our awareness apparently fluctuates between states of sleeping and waking. We know this is only a seeming truth. From many different perspectives we have often discussed how the state of what we call sleep does not only last from the moment we fall asleep to when we awaken again, but that it also continues in a particular aspect of our being while we are awake. It has to be said that we are never fully awake in our whole being. Sleep therefore extends into our waking state. In one part of our nature we are continually asleep; and now we can ask what part of our nature is really fully, continually wakeful while we are, as it is called, awake.

We are always awake in relation to our sensory perceptions—all that we perceive of the sensory world through our senses while awake. The characteristic quality of ordinary sensory perception is that on awakening we swiftly enter into close connection with the external sensory world; our senses are quickly activated, and this pulls us out of the dull state we ordinarily know as that of sleep. Thus we are truly awake in our sensory perceptions. We are less wakefully alert in our thinking—and careful self-observation can show this (you can find more details about it in my book *Riddles of the Soul*[44]); and yet this state can also still be called a waking one. We should distinguish between our sensory perceptions and our actual thinking. When we reflect or contemplate without reference to sensory perception, and thus without turning to the outer world, we are awake both in the ordinary and in a higher sense, although this kind of waking in our life of thought is tinged with a dreamy quality—more in some people and less in others. While a dreamy quality can mingle with the thinking of many people, by and large we can say that we are awake when we think.

But we are not awake in feeling. Of course, feelings surge up in us from an indeterminate, undifferentiated life of soul, and by picturing our feelings, so that wakeful activity in the form of thinking mingles with this feeling, we believe we are awake in our feelings too. In reality our soul sensibility in feeling is exactly the same as in ordinary dreaming. There is a deep affinity between the state of dreaming and the condition in which we feel things. If we were always able to illumine our dreams with thinking—whereas in fact we are oblivious of most of our dream experiences—in the same way as we do this with our feeling life, we would be aware of our dreaming to precisely the same degree as we are of our feelings. You see, feelings are actually present in the soul in just the same way as dreams. Feelings, emotions, and even in a sense passions and desires, live in our soul like dreams. No one is capable of commenting in full waking alertness on what is really occurring in him when he feels. As I have said, this surges up out of an indeterminate, undifferentiated life of soul, and is then illumined by the light of thinking. But it is a life of dreaming. This affinity between emotions, feelings and dreams is something observers have recognized without recourse to esoteric enquiry. For instance, the excellent art philosopher Friedrich Theodor Vischer[45] has often emphasized the deep affinity between feeling and dreaming in the human psyche.

Will activity lies still deeper in our life of soul. How conscious are we of what happens within us when, say, we decide to pick up a book, and when our arm reaches out and does so? We are no more aware of what occurs in the interaction of muscles and nerves in our organism and what also occurs in our soul when an impulse of will passes into movement and action than of what happens in us in deep, dreamless sleep. Once again, our life of thinking casts light on the nature of our will life in a way that makes it seem we know what is happening; but in fact the real nature of this will life remains immersed in the deepest sleep while we are awake.

We are therefore really awake in the true sense in relation to our sensory perception and our life of thinking. We are asleep in relation to our feeling life, even when we're awake; and profoundly asleep in relation to our life of will. Thus the state of sleep extends into our waking life. So let us picture how we walk through the world. What we experience wakefully in our awareness is really only our perception of the sensory world and our world of thoughts; and embedded in this experience is a world in which our feelings and will impulses float, a world surrounding us as the air does, but which ordinary awareness does not enter at all. Whoever sees human experience in this way is really not very far removed from acknowledging the existence of what we may call a supersensible world around him.

All I have described, however, has more significant outcomes. Underlying it are important realities affecting all of life. In acquainting ourselves with the life of the human soul between death and rebirth—and you can do so more theoretically by reading the lectures I gave in Vienna in the spring of 1914[46]—we discover that we are living with the so-called dead in this world we traverse when asleep. The dead are always there. They move and live in a supersensible world. We are not separated from them by our reality, but only by our state of awareness. We are only separated from the dead in the same way that we are separated in sleep from the things around us. Asleep in a room, we do not see chairs or other objects despite the fact that they are there. In our so-called waking state, asleep in our feeling and will, we are amongst the so-called dead though we do not recognize it, in the same way that we fail to perceive physical objects around us in our bedroom when we are asleep. We therefore do not live apart from the world in which the powers of the dead hold sway, but are with them in a shared and common world. Only our state of awareness, of consciousness, separates us from them.

This knowledge that we live in community with the dead will be one of the most important insights spiritual science can implant in general human awareness in future. Those who believe that all that happens around them occurs only by virtue of the powers active in sensory existence know nothing about reality. They do not know that the powers of the dead continually play in to this existence of ours and are continually present here. And if you remember what I said in lecture one about the false view of history that prevails today in the age of materialism, and that the real impulses at work in history unfold as if in dream or sleep, you will be able to understand that the powers of the dead can live, too, in the historical realities we dream or sleep through. In future our view of history will include and take account of the powers of those who have crossed the threshold of death, whose souls live in a world that exists between death and rebirth. An awareness of the whole of humanity, including the so-called dead, will be able to give human culture an entirely new aspect.

The mode of enquiry employed by a spiritual researcher who can put what has been said here to practical use reveals many specific details of the shared life of the so-called living and the so-called dead. If one were able to shine the light of thinking down into one's feelings and impulses of will, it would be possible to have ongoing, vivid awareness of the life of the dead. We cannot do this in ordinary awareness, and this is because things are strangely separated in our conscious life. We can say that for comprehending higher cosmic realities a third thing is actually far more important than an awareness of our states of waking and sleep. What is this third element?

This third thing, lying between those two states, is for modern humankind a mere fleeting moment easily overlooked: the moment of falling asleep, and the moment of awakening. Nowadays people do not pay much attention to this, and yet these intermediate states are extremely important in our overall consciousness. We can discover how important by illumining ordinary, unconscious experiences with clairvoyant awareness. For many years now we have been preparing the ground for this, and can now therefore confidently illumine such things by insight into supersensible realities.

While not as straightforward an approach as what has just been described, it is certainly possible for clairvoyant awareness to acquaint itself not only in general terms with supersensible realities in the world we dwell within between death and rebirth but, specifically, if you will forgive this rough and ready way of putting it, to enter into contact or correspondence with an individual disembodied soul. You are aware of this of course. I will only add that this form of enquiry is more difficult—is difficult for a general, scientific comprehension of supersensible conditions—only because there are many more obstacles to be overcome in the process. Although so few people nowadays succeed in eliciting generalized scientific findings about the supersensible world, we cannot say that this is particularly difficult since it is not so very far removed from people's ordinary soul capacities. It is more difficult to make contact with these souls individually simply because a real, specific, individual connection between a human soul living here in a body and a disembodied soul requires the person seeking such contact to be able to really live to a sufficient degree in a purely spiritual realm, undisturbed by the fact that this tangible life in pure spirit very easily awakens a person's lower urges. I have often stated why this is so:[47] the higher capacities of supersensible beings have an affinity with lower human urges rather than with the higher promptings of embodied human beings; and in the same way, the lower urges of supersensible beings have an affinity with higher, spiritual human qualities. This is an important secret of communication with the supersensible world, one that can very easily thwart a person's efforts. But once this obstacle has been overcome, we can have supersensible communication without being diverted or led astray from a world of spiritual experiences. Yet this communication takes a very different form from anything we are used to considering as such here in the sensory world.

I'll describe this very specifically. In the sensory world *you* speak to another person and the other replies. You are aware that you are creating the words you speak with your voice, and that these words originate in your thoughts. You feel that you are the creator of your words. While you are speaking, you hear yourself; and then hear the other when he replies. And you know that as the other speaks you are listening, you have fallen silent. We become very accustomed to this form of interpersonal communication, to awareness of it. Communication with disembodied souls is different. However strange it sounds, it is the very opposite. When you yourself communicate your thoughts to a disembodied soul, it is not you who speaks but the other. It is just as if you were speaking with another person and he, not you, expressed what you were thinking and wished to communicate. And what a so-called dead soul replies to you, does not come towards you from without, either, but rises from within you: you experience it as your inner life. Clairvoyant consciousness first has to accustom itself to this: to being a questioner within the other, and to receiving his reply within oneself.

This complete inversion of one's being is necessary, but is far from easy, for it contradicts everything we are ordinarily accustomed to, habits formed over our lifetime. It even contradicts our inherent nature. It is intrinsic in our nature to think that, when we ask something, we ourselves speak, and the other listens. And yet the reverse of this is true in our communication with supersensible beings. This inversion undergone by clairvoyant consciousness will show you that people's lack of perception of the dead is very largely due to the entirely unaccustomed and seemingly impossible way the latter communicate with the living.

If we return now to those transitional, fleeting moments between waking and sleeping, we find that invariably one such state is suitable for asking and the other for replying. As we fall asleep, this is an especially opportune moment for asking questions of the dead or, in other words, for hearing from the dead the questions we ask them. In falling asleep we are in a condition well fitted for hearing from the dead what it is we wish to ask them. Since we fall asleep immediately afterwards, this means we ask literally hundreds of questions of the dead, speak hundreds of things to them as we fall asleep, but know nothing about this since we have fallen asleep afterwards. This fleeting moment of falling asleep is of huge importance for our communication with the dead.

The moment of awakening, on the other hand, is especially opportune for hearing the replies of the dead within us. If we did not pass immediately into sense perception when we woke up, but tarried in the moment of awakening, we would be well fitted at that moment to receive messages from the dead. But these messages would appear to rise up from within us.

You see, there are two reasons why ordinary awareness fails to hearken to communications with the dead. One is that the moments of transition are followed by awakening on the one hand and falling asleep on the other, both states extinguishing what we experience in these transitional moments. The other is that the form of communication involved is one we find unaccustomed or impossible. As we fall asleep, the hundreds of questions we could and do ask the dead are submerged in sleep itself, because we are so unaccustomed to hear, rather than speak, what we are asking. And what the dead say to us as we awaken is something that does not seem to come from the dead themselves since it rises within us, and so we regard it as our own.

These general phenomena are sometimes however transformed in the following way. What we experience as our questioning of the dead, which comes towards us from them, seems to continue through sleep. As we continue to sleep, we look back unconsciously to the moment we fell asleep, so that dreams arise in consequence. Such dreams can in fact be embodiments of the questions we ask the dead. And it is true that we approach much closer to the dead in these dreams than we realize, and speak to them, although what we experience in such a dream was spoken already immediately before we fell asleep. The dream draws it forth from the soul's undifferentiated depths. But we easily misinterpret it; when we recall these dreams we do not usually understand what they signify. Dreams are really always a communal life with the dead proceeding from our feeling life. We incline towards the dead, and a dream often presents us with the questions we asked them. It embodies our subjective experience, but as if this came to us from outside. The dead soul speaks to us, but really we ourselves are speaking, and it only appears as if the dead person were speaking to us. What we encounter in such dreams, as a rule, are not messages from the dead but an expression of our need to be in communication with them, and the fact that we succeeded in meeting them for a moment as we fell asleep.

The moment of awakening *does* bring us messages from the dead. This moment is extinguished by the life of the senses that follows immediately. But it can also happen as we wake up, if we practise very careful self-observation, that we discern something we know does not come from our ordinary I. And messages from the dead often come to us like that.

You will only properly understand these ideas if you pay due regard to time relationships in the supersensible world. The moment of falling asleep is well suited for asking questions of the dead, and the moment of awakening for receiving their replies. These two moments are therefore distinct from each other. As Richard Wagner so aptly expressed, with remarkable intuition, 'there time becomes space'.[48] In the supersensible world, time really does become space, in the same way that one point of space is here and another there. In other words, time has not passed, but a point in space is just at a lesser or greater distance. Supersensibly, time becomes space, and the dead soul gives a reply only by standing further away from us. Again, we are very unaccustomed to such a thought. In the supersensible world, the past is not past; it exists, is still present. And the present moment means only that we stand at a different point in relation to what occurred previously. The past is as little past in the world of spirit as the house has vanished that you left earlier this evening to come to this lecture. It remains in its place, and likewise the past remains in the supersensible world. It goes on being there. And whether you are standing close to the dead soul or further away from him depends on you, on how far you have travelled with him. It may be a very great distance, or very close.

You see, as well as being asleep or awake, we also of course fall asleep and wake up, and because of this we are in continual contact and correspondence with the dead. They are always amongst us, and so we are by no means only influenced by the physical human beings around us but also by those who have crossed death's threshold and are connected with us.

Today I want to emphasize realities which, from a certain perspective, can lead us ever deeper into the supersensible world.

Now having understood that there is continual contact with the dead, we can distinguish between different souls who have crossed over into death. Passing continually through the realm of the dead ourselves, either by posing questions as we fall asleep or receiving answers from them when we wake up, our connection with the souls of the dead will be different depending on whether they died young or in old age. The realities at work here are only apparent to clairvoyant awareness: knowledge of this is one thing and its reality another. Each and every one of us is connected with the dead, as clairvoyant consciousness can teach us. But when younger people die—children or adolescents—their connection with those who are still alive is different in kind from that between the living and people who have died in the evening twilight of their years. There is a marked difference here. When we lose children, when people die in early youth, they do not really fully leave us but stay close to us instead. Clairvoyant awareness can discern this in the fact that the messages we receive on awakening are vivid and lively if they relate to children or young people who have passed away. The connection between those still alive and those who have died is one we can describe by saying that we have not actually lost the child or adolescent: they stay here with us. And they do so above all because after death they show a lively urge to work into our awakening moments, to send us messages as we wake up. It is remarkable but true that a person who has died in childhood or youth has a great deal to do with everything related to awakening. It is particularly interesting for clairvoyant consciousness to discern that those who develop a certain piety in outward life, who feel a certain inclination to pious devotion, owe this to souls who have died young. Souls who died in childhood or youth send messages that elicit this, and their influence on such piety is really very great indeed.

It is different when people die in old age. Then clairvoyant consciousness shows us that *they* do not lose *us*. They remain close to our souls. Please note the subtle difference here. We do not lose the souls of those who die young; they remain amongst us. And those who die in old age do not lose us—we can say that they take something of our souls with them. I am speaking metaphorically. Souls who have died at an older age tend to draw us towards them, whereas those who die young draw closer to us. This is why, at the moment we fall asleep, we have much to say to souls who died when they were old; and we can forge a strong connection to the world of spirit by dwelling upon these older dead as we fall asleep. There is really quite a lot we can do in relation to these matters.

We have an ongoing connection with the dead, a kind of asking and answering, an interaction and interplay with them. Our capacity to ask and thus to approach more closely to the dead is especially enhanced if we avoid ordinary abstract thoughts, thus ones drawn from materialistic life.

If they belong to us in some way, the dead suffer, too, from the way we are distracted by purely material life. If, by contrast, we hold fast to what connects us in feeling and will with the dead, and cultivate it, this is good preparation for posing the right questions to them and for entering into contact with them at the moment we fall asleep. The relationship we have with them primarily exists by virtue of the connection we had with them while they were alive. Our connection with them in life is the basis for our further connection with them after death. Naturally it matters whether my connection in life involved speaking to the other with indifference or sympathy—whether I speak with him as someone I am fond of or with an indifferent air. There is a great difference between just chatting to someone randomly at tea-time or showing real interest in what I may learn from him. During life we can cultivate more intimate connections with others that engage our feelings and will impulses, then further cultivate these after death in a feeling way, through interest in the other soul and real curiosity about any replies the soul may give. Or we may feel a prompting to remain important to the other soul, and nurture our reminiscences of him—reminiscences that do not issue from our thinking but from soul relationships. All this will fit us to approach the soul in question at the moment we fall asleep.

We can best fit ourselves to receive messages at the moment we wake up, on the other hand, if we have been able and willing to engage perceptively with the person in question during his life. Just reflect how easily we pass others by, especially nowadays, without really getting to know them. What do people really know about each other today? To take a very strange but striking example of this, there are marriages that last for years on end without the husband and wife ever really getting to know each other. Yes, this happens. But it is fully possible—and this does not depend on some special talent but just on love, really—to enter lovingly into the being of the other and thereby to carry in oneself a real picture, a world of thoughts, about the other person. And this is very good preparation for receiving replies from the dead soul at the moment of awakening. This is also really why one may be more likely to receive replies on awakening from a soul who died young, since we often more easily get to know young people than those who, growing older, have become more inward.

We can therefore do something to cultivate the right relationship between the living and the dead. Our whole life, really, is permeated by this relationship. As souls we are embedded in the sphere where the dead also dwell. The degree of piety we develop—as I said before—is very much connected with how souls who died young act upon us. And if these souls did not impinge on life, there would probably be no piety at all in us. It is therefore best for us to relate to the souls of those who have died young by keeping our remembrance of them more general. Funerals and memorial services for children or young people should always have a more general and ritual form. Some kind of ritual service should be held for the death of young people. The Catholic Church, which sets great store by youth and childhood and really would prefer to have only children amongst its flock, to have children's souls in its care, tends to avoid holding individual addresses at children's funerals. This is actually very good. Our grief and mourning for children is of a different kind than for older people. I would call the mourning for dead children a 'grief of sympathy', for the grief in this case is often a mirroring in our own soul of the being of the child who remains, really, in our close proximity. We go on living the child's life with him, and his being joins in with the grief—a grief of sympathy therefore, of shared feeling. Our mourning for older people is not of this kind; and if it is, it becomes egotistical. It is best sustained by the thought that really the person who has died at an older age takes us with him. He does not lose us as long as we try to fit ourselves to accompany him. For this reason we can celebrate a more individualized kind of memorial service for the soul, can carry him more in our thoughts and remain united with the thoughts about him we have cultivated, and try not to be an awkward companion for him. He takes us with him, but he possesses us in an uncomfortable way if we have thoughts that he simply cannot assimilate. We remain with him but we can become a burden for him if he has to drag us along with him because we fail to cultivate thoughts he can relate to, that he can spiritually discern.

Consider how tangible our relationships with the dead become if we can really illumine them through spiritual science, if we are really able to view the whole connection between the living and the dead. In future humanity will find it important to consider this. However trivial it may sound—since we could say that every era is a 'period of transition'—our time is indeed a transitional era. It must pass into a more spiritual era. It has to become acquainted with what comes to us from the realm of the dead, and realize that we are surrounded by the dead as much as we are by the air we breathe. A time will come when people develop the real sense that they ought not to be a brick wall for someone who has died, but that they are a brick wall for him if they bear thoughts within them that the dead cannot assimilate. Imagine how rich life would become if we realized this—it will make our community with the dead a real togetherness.

I have often[49] said that the science of the spirit has no intention of establishing a new religion nor of introducing something sectarian into the world. This would be to completely misunderstand it. On the contrary, I have often emphasized that it can deepen human religiosity by creating real foundations for it. There is a religious aspect to rites and services for the dead, to memorial services; and a basis is created for this aspect of religious life if we illumine life through spiritual science. When the right thing is done, life is raised from abstract considerations into realities. For instance, it is not a matter of indifference whether a funeral service is held for a younger or an older person. Such things—the right or wrong way to hold a funeral or memorial service depending on whether the person who has died was younger or older—are far more important for human community than, say, a decision taken by the local council or by parliament, however odd this may seem. You see, the impulses at work in life will emerge from human individuals themselves when people have the right relationship to the world of the dead. Today people try to organize everything through abstract social structures. They are happy if they don't have to think too much about what they are supposed to do. Things look very different however if we develop a living awareness not just of a pantheistic union with a spiritual world but of tangible community with a differentiated world of spirit. It is possible to envisage religious life becoming pervaded with specific thoughts and insights if this religiosity can be deepened through spiritual science. As I have often said,[50] the spirit was 'abolished' for western mankind in the year 869 by the Eighth Ecumenical Council in Constantinople. A Catholic dogma was established that the human being should no longer be seen as consisting of body, soul and spirit but only of body and soul, the latter being assigned certain added 'spiritual qualities'. This abolition of the spirit is hugely significant. In Constantinople in 869, the dogma was asserted that the human being could no longer be regarded as endowed with 'anima' *and* 'spiritus' but should be seen only as possessing 'unam animam rationalem et intellectualem'. The 'soul with spiritual qualities' is a dogma that has spread dim twilight over western culture since the ninth century; and it is time for this to be overcome. The spirit must be acknowledged again. It was heretical in medieval times to acknowledge the doctrine of trichotomy—of body, soul and spirit—but now it must be accorded its proper place again, its true validity for understanding human nature. It may be difficult to persuade people of this today, especially as they naturally repudiate authority, and insist that the human being has only a body and a soul. This is true not just of those who confess a particular faith but also students of philosophy and other disciplines. The philosophers, as you can read, only distinguish a body and a soul and leave out any mention of the spirit. This is what their 'unprejudiced' world-view amounts to—and yet it originates in nothing other than a Church decree in the year 869. World-famous philosophers, such as the much-trumpeted Wilhelm Wundt,[51] assign only a body and soul to the human being. Wundt thinks this is his own, unprejudiced, scientific view, unaware of his obedience to the Ecumenical Council decision of 869. It is important to consider the facts if we wish to understand what occurs in the real world. If we consider realities such as those described today, we can come to realize how we are connected with the realm that history dreams and sleepwalks through. History, and the human life it records, can only be seen in the proper light if we can also develop a proper awareness of the connection between the so-called living and the so-called dead. When we meet again we will speak further of these things.

Lecture 4

BERLIN, 5 MARCH 1918

In a recent lecture here[52] I spoke about the relationship that can exist, or in fact always does, between embodied human souls and disembodied souls—the so-called dead. Today I wish to continue with these reflections by adding some further thoughts.

Through various insights we have gained from spiritual science we know that the human spirit undergoes its own development in the course of earth's evolution. It is also apparent that we can only really know ourselves by asking the fruitful question as to how, in a particular incarnation—in the incarnation we live in at present—we relate to the spiritual worlds, the realms of spirit. What level or stage of humanity's general evolution has been achieved, one may ask, when we ourselves live in a particular incarnation?

By detailed reflection on humanity's overall evolution it becomes evident that in former times, in former epochs of human evolution, humankind possessed a certain clairvoyant capacity, which we have called atavistic. This was a time when the human soul was in a sense closer to worlds of spirit. But in its closer connection with spiritual worlds, humanity was more distant from its own freedom, its own free will than it has now become at a time when in general people are more sundered from spiritual worlds. If we can really appraise human nature in the modern world, we find that the same relationship to the whole world of spirit actually still exists unconsciously in people's intrinsic spiritual being. But they are not generally able to be consciously aware of this connection and relationship in the same way as they once were.

Certain individuals can, but in general humankind does not recognize this connection as it did in former times. If we try to discover why people today fail to become consciously aware of the relationship between their soul and the world of spirit—a relationship that naturally still exists as strongly as ever, albeit in a different form—we find this is because we have now passed beyond the midpoint of earthly evolution and find ourselves in a descending evolutionary stream of earth existence. Our physical organism—although, of course, this is not apparent to external anatomy and physiology—has become more physical than it used to be once; and between birth, or conception, and death, we no longer have an organization capable of bringing our connection with the spiritual world to our full awareness. In unconscious regions of the soul, however materialistic we are, we actually experience far more than we are consciously aware.

But this goes still further. And here I come to a very important point in modern humanity's evolution. Modern people are in general unable to really think through all that they would otherwise have the capacity to inwardly experience; they cannot fully sense, feel and experience it. Today people have a disposition that would enable them to have far more intense thoughts and feelings than is possible within what I might call the coarse materiality of their organism. What this means is that, at the current stage of humanity's evolution, we are unable to fully develop the potential we possess in earthly life. This is irrespective of whether we die at a young age or when we're old. Due to the coarse nature of our organism we cannot fully unfold capacities we would unfold if our body were more finely, delicately organized. This is true whether we die young or in old age. Whether we cross the threshold of death when young or old, a residue of unprocessed thoughts, feelings and emotions remains in our earthly organization. These thoughts, feelings and emotions are not worked through fully by the time we die, whenever that is. They remain undigested, unassimilated in a sense. This is true for all of us. And after we have died, we retain, really, an urge to think, feel and experience in the earthly realm, in earthly ways.

Let us think for a moment of the implications of this. Only after death do we become free to develop certain thoughts and feelings. We would achieve much more on earth if we could fully unfold these thoughts and feelings during our physical existence. But we can't. It is true to say that each and every one of us could achieve a great deal more if we could realize our inherent potential. This was not the case in former times, when the human organism was finer and subtler in nature, and when people were able to look consciously, to some degree, into the world of spirit and act out of the spirit. In those times, as a rule, people were able to achieve all that their potential allowed. However proud people are today of their potential capacities, nowadays things are as I have described.

Given this, we can understand that the unintegrated thoughts and feelings the dead carry with them across the threshold should not be lost to earthly life. We can only ensure they are not, however, if, as often stated, we really cultivate our connections with the dead in ways that are guided by spiritual science—if we really sustain these relationships and seek to make our connection with the dead with whom we are karmically connected into a conscious, fully conscious one. Then the unrealized thoughts of the dead are conducted through our soul into the world. These stronger, more vigorous thoughts a dead soul can have through being released from the body can act within our own soul. We cannot fully realize and unfold our own thoughts, but these thoughts can work in us.

Thus what materialism has brought us should at the same time highlight for us the importance, the absolute necessity today and in the near future, of seeking a real, tangible relationship to the spirits of the dead. The question is only how we can entertain in our souls in the right way the thoughts and feelings seeking entry from the realm where the dead dwell. We have previously spoken of this too. Not long ago[53] I spoke of important moments we should try to observe carefully: those of falling asleep and of waking up. Today I would like to give a fuller characterization of things related to this.

The dead cannot directly enter this world in which we live with our ordinary waking consciousness, which we perceive externally and in which we act through our will based on drives and promptings. They have been drawn away from this world by crossing the threshold at death. And yet we can still share a world in common with these dead if, spurred on by spiritual science, we attempt—something that is certainly difficult in our materialistic age—to take both the inner world of our thinking in hand and also our life, the way we live, rather than letting them run on unguided as we are accustomed. We can develop certain abilities that grant us common ground with the spirits who have crossed the threshold of death. In ordinary modern life, of course, there are a great many obstacles to finding this common ground. The first is something I may not have touched upon very much yet, although it does follow naturally from our other observations. It is this: that in general we are usually too spendthrift of our thoughts today. We are too dissipated and dispersed in our thoughts. What do I mean by this?

A German proverb holds that our thoughts are 'duty-free'—or, in other words, that we can allow anything at all to pass through them; and that there is no harm in doing so. But it is easy to see that what we say is a reflection of what we think, and that most people's speech nowadays—the way they flit from one idea to another—betrays a random thought life that allows one thing to follow another without much rhyme or reason. This is a waste of the power with which we are endowed for the purpose of thinking! Our thoughts are diffuse and dissipated. We permit ourselves quite arbitrary thoughts. We desire whatever occurs randomly to us, or forget it again as another thought takes its place. In other words, we are disinclined to control our thoughts. Someone starts speaking, and we listen to him for a minute or two, as he passes from one idea or theme to the next. This can be a quite unpleasant experience: we want to discuss with him what he first started saying, but to do so we will have to remind him what it was! This happens all the time: one has to remind people of the subject one was discussing initially and bring them back round to it, if there is to be any serious discussion at all. This profligacy of thinking, wastefulness of the power of thinking, prevents thoughts surfacing from the depths of our soul that are not ours but which we share in common with the realm of spirit, with the general sway of spirit. This arbitrary flitting from one thought to the next does not create the conditions in our waking life enabling us to wait for thoughts to surface from the depths of our soul life. We fail to attend to what I will call intuitions. But this is something that really should be cultivated, especially in the modern era for reasons I have outlined. We should create in ourselves a mood that entails waiting observantly for thoughts to rise from the deep subterranean places of the soul—thoughts that, it is clear, are given to us, not made by us.

It should not be thought that we can swiftly develop such a mood in ourselves. It has to be nurtured. But if nurtured—if we really try to be awake and not just fall asleep again after shutting out arbitrary thoughts, try simply to be alert and to wait for what rises in us—this mood will slowly develop. Then a capacity forms in us to receive thoughts in our soul that arise from its depths, and therefore originate in a world that is broader than our ego nature. If we really develop this capacity we will start to perceive more in the world than we see with our eyes, hear with our ears, receive through our external senses, and then combine by our powers of reason. We will begin to discern an objective reality of weaving, living thought. Nowadays very few people indeed have this primary and immanent experience. To discern this universal reality of living thought, in which our soul really dwells, is not yet an esoteric experience of particular significance, but is something everyone can have by developing the mood I have described. An experience arises that goes beyond sense perception and the rational organizing and combining of such perceptions in daily life. We feel ourselves now to be standing by the shore, then to be immersing ourselves in the ocean and weaving there in its waves. Standing at the boundary of sensory existence, I can enter the weaving ocean of thought. It is really like plunging into a living ocean. At least one can have a dim sense of a life that is stronger and more intense than mere dream life, although, in the same way as dream relates to sensory perception, this life is different and distinct from outer, sensory reality.

If you like you can speak of such experiences as dreams. But they are not! The world we immerse ourselves in here, this world of surging thoughts that are not our own but are, instead, a thought world we have plunged into, is the realm from which our physical, sensory world emerges and arises, or crystallizes if you like. Our physical, sensory world is like lumps of ice floating in water. Just as ice consists of the substance of water though in a different state, so our physical, sensory world emerges from the surging waves of this ocean of thought. That is its real origin. Scientists speak only of what they call 'ether', of spiralling atoms, since they are unaware of the nature of this primary substantiality. Shakespeare was closer to the mark when he had Prospero say, in *The Tempest*, 'We are such stuff as dreams are made on.'[54] In relation to these things people easily deceive themselves; they conjure a world of atoms, of 'building blocks' behind physical reality. But if one wishes to speak of any such 'reality behind the physical world', it is the objective world of living thought. We can only discern this, though, if we cease allowing our thoughts to wander randomly, and instead develop a mood that arises if we can wait for what is known, in popular parlance, as intuition.

Those who have been preoccupied with spiritual science will not find it so difficult to develop this mood. You see, the kind of thinking necessary for studying anthroposophically oriented spiritual science is well suited for creating such a mood. If you study it seriously, a need will arise in you to develop this delicate, weaving life of thoughts. At the same time it creates the common sphere between ourselves on the one hand and the so-called dead on the other. It is the common ground where we can encounter the dead. They cannot enter the world we perceive through our senses and organize by our powers of reason; but they do enter the world I have just described.

The second condition for removing hindrances is something I described last year:[55] the observation of subtle, delicate connections. You may remember that to illustrate this I cited an example that can be found in studies of human psychology. Schubert also highlights this.[56] It can be found in older literature on the subject, but similar examples can frequently be found in life itself. A person accustomed to going for a daily walk suddenly gets the sense, on arriving at a particular point on the path, that he must stop and stand to one side. At the same time the thought occurs to him that walking like this every day might not be the best use of his time. At that very moment, a stone that has been dislodged from a rock face above falls on the path, and would certainly have struck him if the thought had not caused him to move to one side.

This is a pretty striking instance of the kind of experiences many people have had. Although usually far more subtle in nature, they impinge on our life on a daily basis, but we usually disregard them. In life we only consider what actually happens and not what might have happened but didn't because something occurred to prevent it. We disregard the fact that something happened to keep us at home for a quarter of an hour longer so that we took our walk a little later than we intended. Strange things would frequently become apparent if we considered how things would have been different if we had not been delayed and, say, taken our walk a quarter of an hour later than planned.

Try to observe this systematically in your daily life. What would have been different if, just as you were going out, someone had not arrived and detained you for a few minutes—perhaps someone you were angry with? Such things continually impinge on life. We always seek a causal connection between things that actually happen, neglecting to observe life with a subtle discernment that might perceive, in the interrupting of intended causal sequences, the way life is endowed with an atmosphere of differing possibilities.

If we take this into account then really we always have a sense that if we do something or other at midday, having been delayed for ten minutes during the morning, then this action at midday may not only be affected or influenced by preceding events but could also have been subject to the countless things that did not happen, which we were kept from doing. By conceiving a connection between potentiality, rather than only external, sensory reality, and our life, we come to sense that the search for connections between what happens and what happened previously is a very narrow way of regarding things. When we really pose ourselves such a question, this stimulates something in our mind that would otherwise remain dormant. We start observing between the lines of life, if you like, acquainting ourselves with life's multiple meanings and ambiguities. Then in a sense we come to see ourselves embedded in surroundings that shape us, and slowly but surely help us progress. Usually we take far too little account of this. We normally only consider the inner powers driving us forward. Let us take a simple, ordinary example which can illustrate how we often connect outward events in only a very fragmentary way with our inner life.

Try to examine the way you are used to picturing how you get up in the morning. In attempting this you will mostly get a very clear idea of it—the idea of what prompts you to get up out of bed, although this too may remain a very nebulous thought for you. Now try to reflect for a couple of days on the kind of thought that gets you out of bed each day. Try to become completely aware of the specific thought that actually makes you get out of bed on each occasion. In other words, yesterday you got up because you heard coffee being made in an adjoining room; this drew your attention and gave you the impetus to get out of bed. Today it was something different. What I mean is that you should become aware specifically of what in the external world prompted you to get up. We commonly forget to seek ourselves in the outer world around us, and therefore we find so little of ourselves in this outer world. But if you pay more attention to such things it will be easy to develop a mood which people today are so shy of having, a mood evoked by a continuous undertone of thought we do not really possess in ordinary daily life. Let us say a person enters a room or arrives at a particular place but gives little thought to this. How does the place itself alter when he enters it? Some people have a sense of this sometimes, but it is a fairly rare way of regarding outer factors and conditions. I do not know how many people have any sense of this. In a room with a group of people in it, one of the people there is often twice as strong as another; one is strong, the other weak. And this is something that depends on imponderable factors. You can easily discover that someone in a group flits in and out again as if he were an angel, while another person is so strongly present that he not only stands there on two visible legs but on many other invisible ones too. The other people in the group are not usually very aware of this, and the person himself not at all. A person does not usually perceive the undertone he induces in his surroundings by his presence. We normally remain in ourselves, do not enquire as to the change we ourselves introduce by being there. But we can teach ourselves to perceive a hint, an echo of our own place in and effect on our surroundings. Just imagine the subtle intimacy that external life would acquire if something like this became a customary practice: if people did not merely fill places with their presence but also developed a sense of the effect they have by being there, by their influence in it; of the change they bring about by the very fact of their presence.

That is only one example, of which there are many more in all areas of life. To put it differently, it is possible to condense the medium of life in a healthy way—not by tripping over one's own heels all the time, but in a healthy, natural way—so that we come to feel what effect we ourselves exert on life; and this is the beginning of a sense of karma, of destiny. You see, if we developed a complete sense of what is caused by our own actions or by our presence in one place or another, always having a picture, if you like, of what our actions or presence elicit from our surroundings, then we would have a clear feeling of our karma, which is woven from all these shared experiences.

But for now I only wish to indicate how life is enriched by such intimate awareness, by reading and observing between the lines of life, by learning to observe life with attentiveness to the fact that we are more fully present when we live more consciously, with 'conscience'. Through such an awareness, once again, we develop the sphere which we share with the dead. In such awareness, developing an inner mood that is conscious of the two 'pillars' I have described—conscientious attentiveness to life on the one hand and thriftiness of thinking rather than profligacy on the other—we will succeed in a way necessary for both the present and future in coming closer to the dead. If we then form thoughts in which we draw on the life we shared with a dead person, doing so not only in thoughts but in our feelings, with heartfelt interest in the other, weaving further at the fabric of shared life situations, thinking of shared experiences we had in which feelings were involved—thus not just an indifferent kind of co-existence but moments in which we were interested in what the other thought, experienced and did, in which he, too, was interested in what we elicited from him—then we can use such moments to continue what we might call our conversations with the dead. And then, allowing such thoughts to rest and passing over into a kind of meditative state, as it were offering up these thoughts we have had at the altar of inner, spiritual life, a moment arrives when we receive a reply, in a sense, from the dead, and when they can communicate with us again. We need only create the bridge between what we elaborate in relation to the dead person and what enables him to cross over again in turn towards us. For this approach towards us it will be particularly useful if we are able to develop a picture in our deepest soul of the being of the dead person. This is something really very alien to people today. As I have said on previous occasions,[57] people pass each other by like ships in the night. They may live together in the closest proximity and then their ways part without them really knowing one another. Knowing another person does not have to be based on intellectual analysis. If we feel analysed by the person we live with we will experience this, if we are sensitive, as a kind of punishment or beating. It is not about analysis. One gains the greatest insight into others through heartfelt accord.

This nurturing of our relationship with the so-called dead is particularly necessary today, as it seems to me, because we live in a materialistic age. This is an evolutionary reality, not just a chance occurrence. Because of this we are not able, before we cross the threshold of death, to fully develop and elaborate all our potential thoughts, feelings and emotions. Since an unprocessed residue remains once we have passed through the gate of death, it is necessary for the living to cultivate their relationship with the dead, enriching ordinary human life by this means. If only modern people could hear this—could understand that life will be impoverished if the dead are forgotten! And the only ones who can properly remember the dead are those who have in some way been karmically connected with them.

We can cultivate direct communication with the dead just as we do with the living. In the past I have also said[58] that these things are usually felt to be so difficult because they are unconscious; yet not everything real is conscious, nor is everything unconscious unreal. If we cultivate this kind of relationship with the dead, then it exists, and the thoughts which remained undeveloped in their lifetime can enter life. What I am saying here is probably too much for modern people to take on board, but I say it because of a conviction, based on spiritual realities, that our social existence, our ethical and religious life, would be infinitely enriched if the living took advice from the dead. Nowadays people think there is no need for someone to attain a certain age before offering others advice. It is thought best if people become city councillors and MPs at the youngest possible age, that they are mature enough to do this however young they may be. In former times, when greater knowledge of human nature prevailed, a person had to wait until a certain age to reach such positions. And now I'm even suggesting that we wait until a person dies and then ask his advice! Yet our era does need to hearken to the advice coming from the dead. It will be truly salutary if we try to hearken to them—and ultimately the only healing thing.

Spiritual science does ask real energy of people, and they need to understand this. It asks people to try to act clearly and consistently. Today, amidst catastrophic events, the search for clarity is of the very greatest importance. The things we have been discussing today are connected, far more than people realize, with the great challenges of our day. Many years before this current catastrophe of the world war broke over us, in lecture cycles on the European folk souls, I tried to highlight some of the realities at work today in humanity in general. If you read the cycle on *The Mission of the Individual Folk Souls in Relation to Teutonic Mythology*[59] which I gave in Oslo, you can gain some insight into current events. It is not yet over; these things are still ongoing, and the cycle can offer some insight into events over the next few years.

People's earthly relationships and circumstances can only really be understood by perceiving the spiritual impulses at work in them. The time is fast approaching when people will need to ask themselves how eastern ways of thinking and feeling relate to those in Europe, and how these in turn relate to western thinking, to that of America. All possible permutations of this question should be pondered. We can start already by asking how people in the Orient regard Europe. In the East people look at Europe and have a sense that its culture and civilization are leading nowhere, leading to an abyss. An oriental person has the feeling that, in adopting what Europe can offer him, he ought not to lose the spirituality he has retained from ancient times. Easterners do not despise European machines, for instance, but—to quote the words of a renowned oriental[60]—in accepting the tools and machines that Europeans have created, they want to keep these in their proper place in the toolshed, and not in their temples, nor in their dwellings as Europeans do.[61] In the East it seems to people[62] that Europeans have lost the ability to perceive the spirit in nature, the beauty in nature. Only in the East is it apparent that Europeans have sought to limit their thinking and actions to external mechanisms, and to outward sensory reality; and in consequence oriental people feel called upon to reawaken ancient spirituality and save this for humanity. An oriental who speaks of tangible spiritual realities—such as Rabindranath Tagore in recent comments—believes that Europeans have integrated into their culture impulses only rendered possible by harnessing the devil to their cultural wagon, and that they are employing Satan's power to further their progress. Rabindranath Tagore believes that eastern people must uncouple Satan again, and bring spirituality to Europe once more.[63]

Here we find a phenomenon which, sadly, is too often overlooked today. Much has been excluded from our cultural evolution which should have been introduced into it if it were to have really living spiritual substance—of the kind found in the works of Goethe, to name only one. You might object that eastern people can find Goethe's works still alive in European culture today. But what do they actually see if they enquire more carefully? You may say that the Germans have founded a 'Goethe Society'. But let us imagine that an oriental person wished to make closer acquaintance with this society, and discover what it really stands for (since the great question of East and West is very topical at present, and ultimately depends on spiritual impulses). This oriental person could say the following. Goethe was such a decisive figure and so influential that in the 1890s it became possible, in a remarkable way, for his works to bear fruit for German culture when Countess Sophie of Sachsen-Weimar[64] took over his literary estate, caring for and cultivating it in an unparalleled way. This is true. But if we look at the Goethe Society and its public presence today, we discover that a few years back the post of president of this society became vacant. Of all possible candidates in the whole sphere of culture, a former finance minister was chosen to be this society's president![65] This is an external but nevertheless striking fact, and such things are more important than people realize. It would be very important for people in the East, for whom spirituality is a vivid, keen and real concern, to know that an anthroposophically oriented spiritual science exists here. But they cannot know this—it cannot reach them as yet, cannot penetrate everything else that is there and obstructs it, not only in this particular instance of course. It is merely symptomatic of a more general malaise that the current president of the Goethe Society is a former finance minister. I could list endless other examples of course.

Here we find what I would see as a third necessity: thorough, reality-connected thinking—a thinking that makes no compromises and does not countenance lack of clarity. On my last trip someone handed me a review of a book, a brief excerpt of which I will read here, starting with a quote from the book:

> 'Anyone who has ever graced the seats of a Grammar School will have an unforgettable memory of the hours he spent "enjoying" Plato's dialogues[66] between Socrates[67] and his friends—unforgettable for the excruciating boredom they are bound to invoke. You may well remember that these dialogues struck you as amazingly stupid, though of course you did not dare say so since Socrates was the Greek philosopher *par excellence*.' With such sweeping generalizations, the book *Socrates—the Idiot* (by Alexander Moszkowski,[68] published by Dr Eysler & Co., Berlin) makes short shrift of the good Athenian, depriving him at a stroke of his dignity as a philosopher.

The first likely reaction of many people on hearing that the author, Moszkowski, has sought to show that Socrates was an idiot is to consider this very strange perhaps. And yet this relies on hazy thinking and compromise, rather than clear and precise thinking and a willingness to penetrate reality. I want to compare this with something else. Today books are published about the life of Jesus from a psychiatric angle.[69] Such books investigate everything Jesus did from the perspective of modern psychiatry and compare it with all kinds of pathological forms of behaviour. Such authors try to draw on the Gospels to demonstrate that Jesus was sick, that he must have been an epileptic, and that in fact the Gospels can only be understood from a Pauline point of view, and so on. You can read detailed reviews of these books.

It is extremely easy to ignore things like this, and pass them by with a smile. But realities lie somewhat deeper. If you subscribe fully to modern psychiatry, you will inevitably come to the same conclusions about the life of Jesus as the authors of these books. You cannot be authentic as a modern psychiatrist if you think in any other way. Nor, in the true sense of the word, can you be a modern psychiatrist if you think about Socrates in any other way than Alexander Moszkowski does. You have to regard Socrates as an idiot. Moszkowski is only distinguished from other adherents of these theories, who nevertheless think Socrates was not an idiot, by his authenticity compared to them. They are untruthful while he speaks the truth as he must see it. He refuses all compromise. It is impossible to authentically subscribe to Alexander Moszkowski's world-view and not to regard Socrates as an idiot. If you want the best of both worlds—to subscribe to a modern, scientific world-view and nevertheless to value Socrates and not disparage him as an idiot—you become inauthentic. Likewise you are untruthful as a modern psychiatrist if you accord a religious value to the life of Jesus. But modern people are shy of pursuing things to such a clear conclusion, for if they did they would have to ask themselves some challenging questions. If they did not wish to regard Socrates as an idiot they would have to try to find out more about him, and this would require them to reject a world-view such as that of Moszkowski. Likewise they would have to reject modern psychiatry if they came to see Jesus as the bearer of the greatest ideas ever known upon earth.

We need a thinking oriented to reality, clear thinking that does not make the usual lazy compromises—which we can only avoid by being rigorously truthful. It is easy to feel indignant at someone like Moszkowski calling Socrates an idiot. But he has to do so based on his world-view. To think consistently in this way is something people shy away from. They do not want to reject a modern view of the world, for this would make their lives still more uncomfortable. If they came to the conclusion that Socrates is not an idiot after all, might they not have to acknowledge that Moszkowski is one? He is not such a renowned figure, but there are very renowned figures who might then take a tumble—anything could happen!

You see, to penetrate the world of spirit, we need reality-oriented thinking. We have to see reality clearly. Thoughts are realities, and untrue thoughts are evil, inhibiting, destructive realities. It is no good pulling the wool over one's own eyes as to one's own untruthfulness, by allowing Moszkowski's world-view and that of Socrates to co-exist. It is untruthful to allow both an equal place in your soul alongside each other, as modern people do. We only become truthful if we are clear that we must either, like Moszkowski, take up a purely scientific and mechanistic view of the world and regard Socrates as an idiot, or else realize that he was not, and then inevitably reject mechanistic views. They cannot co-exist. Truthfulness is an ideal which modern people need to embrace. Thoughts are realities, and true thoughts are wholesome ones. Untrue thoughts, however much concealed by the mantle of circumspection in relation to one's own nature, create inner realities in us that obstruct and hinder the evolution of humanity and the world.

Lecture 5

BERLIN, 12 MARCH 1918

In connection, especially, with human souls who have crossed the threshold of death, we have been trying to study how the world we live in between birth and death is related to the one we dwell in between death and a new birth. Our aim here will be to try to explore these relationships from the most diverse angles.

As humanity increasingly comes to approach the world of spirit with enquiring insight—as it must do if it is to meet its pressing tasks in forthcoming times—it will discover that a proper, exhaustive understanding of the world and humankind goes far, far beyond what can be discovered through the physical, sense-based sciences, and the powers of reason on which they rely. If we draw only on what we perceive through our senses and on the powers of reason bound up with these senses, we can discover only a very limited part of the real world—by which I mean the world of active reality in which we ourselves are also integrated as active participants. In the course of these lectures I have suggested how we can refine our powers of observation, expanding their scope to include various aspects of life that are not usually considered because we tend only to focus on what actually happens during our waking life from morning to evening, and not what could or might otherwise have happened—what, in a sense, we were prevented from doing. In order to offer you at least some tentative ideas about such things, which have to be felt initially more than thought, I asked you to envisage, say,[70] being prevented from leaving the house at a previously intended time because someone comes to the door. You might have planned to go out at 11 in the morning, but can only do so half an hour later. Now try to picture what difference it may—only may, though—have made to your whole day to leave half an hour later. During this half an hour it is possible that something could have happened to you that did not then happen. Try to consider all the possible similar events and incidents that can impinge on us in daily life—and you can form an idea of all that might have occurred but did not. Then—especially attending to a feeling sense of it—try to compare this idea of what might have happened with what did actually happen during your day, how one thing led to another by cause and effect.

To form a really clear picture of such things it is a good idea to compare them with similar phenomena in the natural world. In nature there are processes at work that must be seen in a similar light. I have often pointed out[71] how many seeds are lost and do not grow. Ask yourself how many herring eggs actually grow into herrings in the course of a year, and how many are lost. Then broaden this idea across the whole of life. Try to picture how many seeds with the potential for life do not actually develop, are left out of the rest of nature's sprouting, flourishing life and never unfold. Do not for a moment think this is not intrinsic to reality. It is as much a part of it as all that does develop fully, but instead of unfolding it comes only to a certain point and then takes a different course, in the same way that, in our own daily lives, we are prevented from doing something. These events that did not happen in life are comparable to natural processes that never developed but which instead evolve in a different direction.

There is something else, surely very similar to these two examples, that poses a riddle for us, and greatly affects human life. A normal human lifespan is between 70 and 90 years, but a very large number of people die earlier than this as we know. Life does not, therefore, come to its full fruition. In the same way that in nature seeds are held back at an early stage and do not unfold and ripen, so human life often does not reach its full maturity. Our daily actions, as we have seen, often do not unfold and mature completely either, for reasons we have seen. All this can show us that, between the lines of life as it were, a great deal exists that we fail to consider and that, instead of entering realms where it becomes tangible, sensory reality, it remains in spiritual realms.

If we dwell on this thought in really fruitful ways rather than seeing it only as a fantasy, it can lead us towards a picture, if not yet fullproof, of something very important. In ordinary life we reflect upon our actions, our deeds and will impulses. We think what we ought to do and carry out what we have thought of. But life is not only like that—planning actions and carrying them out. There is another element to life whereby things happen and often appear to us as a collection of random events, seemingly without rhyme or reason, chance connections and incidents which we can sum up as 'destiny' or 'fate'. For people who think in materialistic ways, fate is composed of occurrences that just happen to them on a daily basis. Of course, many people have an inkling, nevertheless, of some kind of hidden plan at work in this fate. But they do not usually make any headway in really understanding what is at work here. Although these things are of great importance, little attention is generally paid to them. Currently analytic psychology, as it is known, psychoanalysis, is delving into various things that are knocking on humanity's door, The proponents of this analytic psychology, however, approach these realities with inadequate means. In our circles I have often described a paradoxical instance[72] much used by psychoanalysts because, as psychoanalysis was just starting, it led to an insight into all the elements of the psyche at work in life, concealed from most people's view. Although some of you have heard this before, I would like to describe this paradoxical example to you again here.

A woman is invited to a dinner party one evening, which is being held as a farewell to the lady of the house, who is ill, and is about to depart for a cure at a spa resort. The evening goes very smoothly, the lady leaves for her spa cure and, more or less at the same time she leaves, the other guests also depart. A group of these guests walks down the street together, when all of a sudden a horse-drawn cab comes round the corner. Please note: not a car but a horse-drawn cab. The cab hurtles down the street. One of the ladies in the company separates from the rest of the group and while the others step aside to avoid the cab, she alone has the odd idea of running along in front of the horses. She runs down the street in front of them, and feels she has to do something to save herself from the horses behind her. Arriving at a bridge over a river she conceives the idea of saving herself by jumping into the water. But the other guests have of course run after her in the meantime, and manage to head her off in time. Then she is taken back to the house they had all left, and is received there. All well and good: the lady of the house has left; the woman is given accommodation there and is now able to continue a relationship with the man of the house which had begun some time previously.

Exploring hidden regions of the psyche, the psychoanalyst discovers that, as a child, this woman had certain experiences with horses, and that these have resurfaced from the unconscious, and so forth. But if we know something about the human soul we will not concur with all these theories. Granted, hidden regions of the soul do exist, but they are only the precursors of what really counts here and not the full reality. The thing of importance here is that the woman in question has an unconscious awareness which, in certain circumstances, is far slyer and more refined than her surface consciousness. In her conscious mind, as you will agree, the woman in question has behaved in a fairly clumsy way, but in her subconscious was something far slyer and more scheming. This *something* in her subconscious thought as follows. The lady of the house has left. I must find some way or other of meeting her husband; I must use the next opportunity that presents itself. The subconscious can be rather prophetic and has an intimation of what will happen if one runs in front of horses. It can organize things in the slyest way. The conscious mind is not so crafty. The subconscious has this craftiness, enhanced by a certain prophetic gift. I mention this example here because it illustrates something generally true: we all bear within us something that is far more comprehensive and also far more intense in various ways than our ordinary consciousness. If we were consciously aware of all that we know in our subconscious, we would be terribly clever and crafty, and would be able to conceive of and think out all kinds of things.

We can now ask whether what lives in our subconscious is entirely inactive. If we know how to observe the world spiritually we find this is not so. On the contrary, it is continually active, is at work all the time. What occurred in the case of this lady, and in similar instances only comes to the fore abnormally under the influence of quite particular events, desires and inclinations, is always present in us in a certain realm, accompanying us throughout our waking life. The way the subconscious manifested in this woman on one occasion—and it could of course have been a man—is due only to the fact that our subconscious knowledge of life occasionally bursts its bounds. This can also be true of ordinary awareness—that sometimes we do something particular that does not form part of our customary way of doing things, that seems exceptional. The same is true of the subconscious. But here, in this case, something unusual emerged that is always active in people. *How* is it active?

What we call fate or destiny is really a very complex thing. Our destiny seems to approach us in the form of events that happen to us. Let us take a striking instance of destiny, something many people will be familiar with. Let us assume a person meets another who then becomes his friend, or wife, or husband. To the surface mind it seems that this happened to us, and that we ourselves did nothing to bring it about. The other simply entered our life. But this is not the case. The truth is quite different.

From the moment of our birth, and still more from the moment we start to say I of ourselves, we arrange our path in life with the power residing in the subconscious in such a way that it crosses another's path at a certain moment. People are unaware of the remarkable things they would find if they could trace someone's path in life, say that of someone who gets engaged. If we traced this person's life path through childhood and youth, from place to place, until he gets engaged we would find a great deal of purpose and meaning in its sequence. We would discover that he did not simply arrive at a place where this happened to him randomly but that he moved purposefully towards circumstances where he met the other. The whole of life is filled with such a searching, and the whole of destiny is a search of this kind. However, we have to realize that this search does not take place in the same way as actions we decide on and then carry out in a linear fashion. Subconscious actions occur with strong, personal impetus. There is a purpose at work in our subconscious. It isn't actually correct to speak of the unconscious, but we should refer to the surface or upper consciousness and the subconscious, since it is unconscious only for our ordinary awareness. In the case of the lady who arranged things so craftily in order to return to the house of the man she was drawn to, the subconscious was far more conscious of what it was doing than the lady herself in her surface consciousness. The same is true of what guides us through life, so that our destiny is a weft that leads us, and is in fact very, very conscious. The fact that people often resist their destiny does not contradict this. If they could survey all the factors involved they would stop resisting it. The surface or upper consciousness is not as sly and crafty as the subconscious and therefore often judges the latter's reality wrongly. It thinks something unpleasant has occurred to it whereas in fact the person has actually himself sought what he superficially thinks unpleasant, doing so out of profound deliberation. Insight into deeper contexts would lead him to see that a greater intelligence seeks the things that become our destiny or fate. On what is all this based?

In speaking of these things for which ordinary language has no proper words, we have to resort to metaphors. Our ordinary mind, focused in the head, and highly valued by many, is like a sieve. This simile has some truth. Our head-based consciousness is a sieve. If you pour water into a sieve, it runs through and does not fill it. The things which our subconscious deliberates upon, and which then come to expression in the fabric of our destiny, pass through our head consciousness as though through a sieve; and this is why our surface awareness knows nothing of them. Our head consciousness lets them pass through as if through a sieve while our subconscious retains them. We know nothing about them only because they pass through the sieve of our surface awareness in this way. Nevertheless, we retain them.

When science develops to the point where it studies these things properly, people will enquire into these processes in animals as compared to the human being. In the case of an animal the whole creature is a sieve, and these things pass right through it. In the human being, on the other hand, they pass through the head but are retained in the whole of the rest of the organism. Under ordinary circumstances, though, since the whole person does not think, but only his head, we do not think these things, we are unaware of their existence in us. Only where hysterical conditions arise—a pathological, abnormal state—that involves the rest of the human organism beginning to think too do we discover exceptional instances where awareness arises of processes of destiny, in which, if you like, we weave our destiny—as happened in the case I have described of the lady who took destiny into her hands. So we do retain these things within us, and here we find something very remarkable. Why do they pass right through the animal whereas they are retained in us human beings?

It is because the animal has no hands. In other words, the creature's limbs are always connected with the earth, whether these limbs are legs or wings—though the picture alters somewhat in the latter case. The fact that we have transformed animal limbs into our arms and hands means they are integrated in our organism in a way that enables us to retain our thoughts within us in our destiny. But we cannot think with our hands; we can only retain or hold back our destiny with them, and therefore we are unaware of it. The hands are organs of thinking in the same way that the etheric aspect of the head is. In thinking, the etheric part of the head does something very similar to what we do with our hands. Using our hands, we bring to cessation the flow of action pervading our destiny. Our nature is such that only the coarser reasoning activities of hands and arms come to expression. Everyone knows that we possess a special 'fingertip' sensitivity, but this represents only the very coarsest aspect of what I am describing, which is something extremely subtle—a very weak, scarcely glimmering thinking which we develop there, and which we can express in artistic activity. Our hands are actually integrated into our overall organism as organs of thinking for our destiny. At our current stage of evolution people have not yet learned to think with their hands. If they did, if they learned the secrets of the hands, this would at the same time lead them to insight into the fundamental laws of destiny.

This sounds very strange but is true. Spiritual science can show us that destiny is thought in our hands, that the latter develop a subconscious thinking. Science is as yet unaware of this. Inevitably, scientists regard the human being as just a more perfect animal—which is also true. But the major distinction between the human being and the animal lies in factors scientists are unaware of or do not consider. Think for a moment what the animal's head is. It rests directly above the earth. The earth carries it, whereas the human head rests upon us in a way we ourselves sustain or carry. The pull of gravity passes first through the human organism, through the diaphragm, before it meets the earth. We relate to ourselves as the animal does to the earth. The pull of gravity on the animal's head passes directly into the earth without first passing through its organism and diaphragm. Our human orientation to the whole cosmos is the essential factor, and connected with this orientation is the fact that our arms and hands are differently organized from the corresponding limbs of animals. This is one thing science will study in future, asking how we relate dynamically to the cosmos, what forces are at work here to make us two-legged instead of four. We are organized like this through the influences of the cosmos! And we meet this organizing power of the cosmos by virtue of the fact that the line of gravity from our head passes into and through us ourselves, so that we become our own earth. By configuring and organizing our hands and arms in a distinctive way, our hands can meet and engage with destiny, can grasp it, just as the organization of the human head also relates to our upright posture. Our more perfect brain is something we possess because the line of gravity of our head does not pass directly through the earth but instead first through ourselves. There are powers at work everywhere in the cosmos, and when something is differently orientated, mass is differently distributed. This is acknowledged in respect of inorganic substance but as yet people fail to discern the same thing at work in the human being. And in consequence people fail to see how our material body works towards and meets the spirit, just as spirit everywhere permeates matter.

That is one aspect. Here we can say that we discern the human being resting upon his own diaphragm, and, whereas our understanding otherwise only extends to conscious actions, in thinking down to the diaphragm with the subconscious we can gain understanding of destiny. Thus we have seen, firstly, that if we go beyond a one-sided view of the head and consider the whole of the rest of our organism, we can deliberate upon and evaluate our destiny, albeit subconsciously: we can determine and know our destiny.

But, secondly, something else is true too. We engage in actions. In life these cause us either a certain satisfaction or dissatisfaction. If you consider a kind action you have performed for someone, this will give you a sense of satisfaction, whereas something you did to defend yourself in some way is connected with a sense of dissatisfaction, and so on. We are continually doing diverse things. But besides the things we do that cause us conscious satisfaction or dissatisfaction there are other kinds of action. We can examine this best if, through spiritual science, we study actions that have little impact on life. Chopping wood is an action which may have little intrinsic moral significance. It makes us feel tired. People think all kind of things about tiredness. As we saw in the last public lecture I gave,[73] people think that tiredness is the cause of sleep, that the first leads to the second. We all know that tiredness can arise as an accompaniment to actions such as chopping wood. But in fact this tiredness turns out to be very significant if we study it through spiritual science. It is not at all what we usually consider it to be, but something quite different. (Actions of a more intellectual or moral character are similar in this respect, but more refined, and there it is harder to discern what I am speaking of than in more elementary actions such as wood-chopping.) You can easily see that the tiredness arising during such actions is a dual process. First we need to apply our flourishing life forces to the task in hand, powers connected with our growth, and then we expend or exhaust these powers, giving rise to a degradation process we experience as tiredness. In fact this tiredness is a numbing or stupefaction whose deeper importance we in fact experience as something quite different from a consequence of—in this case—chopping wood. For ordinary life, tiredness is only a numbing of something. What is it we are really experiencing here?

Of course, only real spiritual-scientific research can cast light on this. When we are tired after chopping wood, we discover that one of the so-called lotus flowers,[74] part of the human being's spiritual organism—you can learn more about this in my book *Knowledge of the Higher Worlds*—starts to shine out strongly. A success has occurred of which we are unaware. This spiritual success remains unconscious, and what we consciously experience is the numbing that occurs in order for us not to perceive this success. A real spiritual emanation occurs here. And we can understand this still better if, to grasp the spiritual nature of such emanation, we consider, say, an action involving a moral judgement. Let us imagine that we have not merely chopped wood but instead accomplished an action arising from a moral judgement—something usually only viewed within the narrow confines of ordinary life. It does however have a different dimension too. Everything we do, even a single action, has significance within the whole course of humanity's evolution. But in our ordinary consciousness we have as little grasp of the worth of every action for evolution as our head grasps how destiny works and acts. In this case, however, the evaluation of an action does not pass through our being as though through a sieve, but as a beam or ray; it radiates outwards through the lotus flowers. Subconsciously we continually evaluate every single one of our actions. Even if you were an angelic type of person and did good to all others, in your subconscious you would evaluate how you behave and act and its value for the whole of humanity's evolution. You do this very objectively, and the outcome may sometimes be very different from what your surface awareness might think. Even if you are a thief you will judge your own actions even as you perform them, doing so quite objectively according to their effect on the overall process of human evolution. This inevitably radiates out through the lotus flowers. Just as our judgements about destiny pass through our head as though through a sieve, to be held up and retained by our arms and hands, so, with the aid of our astral lotus flower organism, we conduct the judgements we make about out own actions, also about our thoughts as actions. Through our lotus flower organism these are radiated outwards like light, and emerge from us. This shining emanation goes a long, long way. It passes over into the realm of time rather than remaining in the spatial dimension. This is why it is so difficult to picture the lotus flowers—they are in continual movement and continually cross over into time. Here space really does become time. We all cast a light before us, one which passes into time, becoming a continual beam that endures way beyond death. Someone is judging within us, in our subconscious, throughout our life. Just as someone thinks our destiny in us, so someone judges our every action, and this judgement we shine out as a beam from ourselves.

Naturally this is put metaphorically, but nevertheless it corresponds to a reality. Life is like a beam cast far ahead by a floodlight. You must picture this happening in time, though, rather than space. For instance, assuming you are 40 at present, let us say that you do something or other, and then your life continues: you grow to be 50, 60, then you die and continue to exist in the life after death. As you pass through this further existence you gradually live your way into what you shone out into this existence from your lotus flowers while alive on earth. You meet again everything that you shone forwards into the future. To put it metaphorically again, this is like pointing a floodlight forwards so that its beam shines far into the distance, and then moving along it. You meet again everything that you shone forwards into the future. And what you meet here in the life between death and rebirth are the judgements you made about your actions. In this regard the human being is not a sieve; or actually you can say that he is, for he allows through everything that he himself subconsciously engenders.

Thus there is something in us that acts as a continual critic—not using this word in a pedantic sense—of our own actions, and shines these judgements forwards into our own future. Here again one can, if one so wishes, see the scientific aspect of this. The fact that we have an upright stance and posture, so that our tool of consciousness rests upon us as upon our own earth, means that at the place where the lotus flowers are situated we retain or hold back what proceeds from our sojourn on the earth, our travels across it in the broadest sense. It is retained there, turned at right angles and sent forwards into life.

In a complex but certainly comprehensible way, as we see, what is usually encompassed in the generalized term the 'unconscious' enters and works upon our life. Our subconscious connects with our whole destiny by virtue of the fact that our diaphragm closes us off in a downward direction.

There is no such emanation through the lotus flowers in the animal. Why? This is again connected with the animal's universal orientation. We have a vertical spine, at right angles to that of the animal. Because of this we can develop something impossible for the animal because its spine lies horizontally rather than vertically. The animal cannot therefore have a 'critic' beside it nor send judgements about its animal life ahead of it into the future. Science will become much more productive when it succeeds in going beyond its trivial comparisons between the structure and form of animal limbs and those of the human being, or between the animal head and the human head. While the human being has a more perfect brain, the human head is really not so very different from the animal head, and for this reason materialist theories have easily assigned human beings their place in the animal world. What really distinguishes the human being from animals, however, is his spatial orientation. A thorough study of this would produce quite different scientific insights. Here spiritual science will show the way, as it does in other areas by pointing to specific life processes that only then can be properly understood.

In the human being therefore we can find aspects that, on the one hand, appear cleverer than he is—sometimes more subtle and astute even—in relation to the way destiny is judged, and on the other hand aspects that reveal a more objective critic of his actions that he himself is consciously. In a complex sense therefore we can say that there is another human being within us, and this comes to expression in life. Usually people do not observe their actions. The inner critic remains in the subconscious, and only becomes conscious between death and rebirth as we gradually advance along the beam we ourselves have emanated as I described. However, a judicious, detailed observation of life can show us how this critic behaves differently inside different individuals.

Let us compare two different types of people commonly encountered in life. One is often described as a 'busybody'. You can find them everywhere. They never have any spare time, are always on the move and like to have a finger in every pie and their nose, often, in other people's business. Such behaviour is held to be a habit formed during life, based on subconscious motivations and so forth. What people do not realize is that the inner critic in such a busybody, in this particular incarnation, has assumed a particular stance. Such a critic also has its distinctive individuality, which people discover after death. It is good to speak of such things with a certain humour. A sense of humour in spiritual science overcomes a mood that is otherwise really very counter-productive. The inner critic in a busybody like this is a kind of actor or performer who wishes to be seen by all and sundry—not just by other people as he may imagine, but by all kinds of spiritual beings. He takes pleasure in the fact that all the beings thronging in the world of spirit can always see him as he rushes about. This type, the busybody is, in the world of spirit, someone who keeps rushing about and wishes to be seen, and it is this motivation, translated into an unconscious prompting, that gives the person the character of a busybody.

What about the opposite type? This is the kind of person who conscientiously does what life requires and demands of him, the duties it imposes. He is not always very visible but often acts behind the scenes, doing whatever is needed. Here too the critic assumes a distinctive stance. Spiritual science can shed light on these things. Here the critic adopts such a position due to an unconscious belief that everything we do, even if not seen—as the busybody wishes—by the teeming spirits, is not in vain, and that no power in the world is in vain but has its own significance. It is a lovely thought: everything you do has significance, some meaning in the overall scheme of things, even if this only emerges in millennia to come. This awareness is rooted in the opposite type from the busybody: a certain trustful resting in the world, a certainty originating in the faith or belief I have described.

Life is illumined by perspectives above and beyond outward circumstances in the sense-perceptible world, when we see that there are relationships between our life and the world of spirit.

My comments today seek primarily to highlight two elements in human nature. One is connected with our physical organism between birth and death, where our physical organization points to a subconscious realm. Here it becomes apparent that our arms and hands are organs of thinking, albeit in the remarkable sense of giving special ground or soil to what passes through the head as through a sieve. In this respect we are a special kind of vessel; our head is a sieve for destiny. But thoughts that destiny creates coagulate as the arms and hands stop and retain them. The second element is what radiates from the lotus flowers and enters our life between death and a new birth. The relationship between these two streams or currents in us is of great significance. You see, if you consider the whole human being in terms of the diaphragm level, there too you find a dual nature. Something enters us, comes into stasis or stalls due to the power of arms and hands, but nevertheless passes down to the diaphragm level. It stalls, comes into stasis because we are vertical beings rather than horizontal ones like the animals. This sounds very strange, but the world is full of riddles and mysteries. The animal's legs relate to the latter differently from the way our arms relate to us, and this has something to do with the earth. One sees the rays or beams coming through the earth and entering us but then, guided or directed by the lotus flowers, shining out into the future. The two streams show us to be a dual being. In ordinary life they are entirely separate from each other, and life depends on this. If they were to join together, life would be different from how it is. In a confluence of the two, humankind could not develop I consciousness, which depends on these two streams being kept distinct and separate. And yet they are only partially sundered, and in a particular, different sense they do merge. What radiates from us to shine forward into the life between death and rebirth can, if we succeed in doing this, unite and combine with that other influx of forces usually stopped and held by the arms, *before* these pass through the sieve of the head. The streams can unite with each other outside of us. The two streams which normally pass through our body but do not join and merge can unite if we stop them. This in turn makes it possible for us to encounter those who have passed through the gateway of death.

This picture of the two streams will serve as an introduction to explorations in the next lecture of the connections with the dead we can develop here on earth, which we will then illumine from a different point of view.

Lecture 6

BERLIN, 19 MARCH 1918

A week ago we explored more intimate questions of the life of the human psyche: questions that can aptly prepare the ground for consideration of how the so-called living—that is, the human souls living in physical bodies—relate to disembodied souls, to those at present living in the period between death and rebirth. When exploring this theme we need to familiarize ourselves with certain basic ideas to lead us into the right kind of soul engagement—the way in which we can and should think of ourselves within such relationships. The reality of such a relationship, you see, has no bearing on whether or not a person living here on earth is aware of his connection with this or that being in the world of spirit. What I say now will be self-evident for anyone who reflects upon such things; but in the realm of spiritual science it is sometimes necessary to remind ourselves clearly of self-evident matters.

We always have a relationship to the world of spirit, and always also a certain connection with the dead with whom we are karmically connected in some way. It is therefore quite different to speak of the reality of this connection or of a greater or lesser awareness of its possibility. But it is important for everyone—even for those compelled to discount this—to learn what such an awareness tells us. It tells us, in fact, of realities in which we enduringly exist. As far as our relationship with the so-called dead is concerned, we have to realize one thing in particular: that this relationship is harder to be aware of, in a sense, than our relationship with other beings of the world of spirit. It is somewhat easier to develop awareness of the beings of the higher hierarchies through imaginative perception and even to receive certain revelations from these higher hierarchies, than to become aware of a quite specific relationship we have with the dead—in other words, to become aware of it in a true and authentic way. This is due to the following.

In our life between death and rebirth we pass through conditions of existence that are very different indeed from those in the physical world, and, as I explained in the lecture cycle *The Inner Nature of Man and the Life Between Death and a New Birth*,[75] require correspondingly different thoughts and ideas. Why, you may ask, are the ideas we employ to describe these realities so different from what we are otherwise familiar with? As we will study this winter, this is because, between death and a new birth, we prefigure in a certain way the conditions that will only arise during the next planetary embodiment of the earth, that of Jupiter. After death we live in a finer spiritual state, which is reminiscent of future Jupiter conditions. Here, during our life, our earthly incarnation, we have retained something of the earth's former embodiments—those of Moon, Sun and Saturn; and therefore in the life between death and a new birth we balance this by absorbing something of the future. By contrast, all the beings of the higher hierarchies, in so far as we can understand them with our human vision, relate to the present form of the whole world of spirit, are connected with the way it manifests at present. In future these beings will manifest future conditions. It sounds very paradoxical, I know, but it is so. It sounds paradoxical because one can then ask how these beings of the higher hierarchies can act upon the dead since the latter already bear futurity within them. Naturally the beings of the higher hierarchies also bear the future in them and have the capacity to form the future. But they do not do this without creating something, in the realm where the dead reside, that is directly characteristic of the present. We therefore have to prepare ourselves for awareness of our dialogue with the dead by perceiving what the hierarchies accomplish. And only when we succeed in invoking in the soul a more or less conscious sense of the beings of the higher hierarchies will it gradually become possible for the soul to become aware of communication with the dead, based on a new capacity for perception and feeling. This does not necessarily mean that we should perceive the higher hierarchies clairvoyantly, but, in so far as spiritual science allows us to do this—and it does—we should understand what it is that flows into existence from these higher hierarchies. Understanding is important in relation to all these things. Only when we make efforts to understand them through spiritual science can the conditions arise in which we become aware, to some degree at least, of a connection between the so-called living and the so-called dead. To grasp this we need to consider the following.

The world of spirit in which we exist between death and rebirth has its own very distinctive nature, involving conditions of existence that we usually scarcely notice in our ordinary life on earth and which, when voiced as part of a person's outlook, sound fairly paradoxical and peculiar. For a conscious sense of such things, it is of the greatest importance to acquire a feeling which I will call a real sense of community with the realities of existence. To gradually develop this feeling of community and companionship with the realities of existence is something required by humanity's ongoing evolution from the present, this catastrophic present, onwards. The foundations of this sense of community, albeit not yet in a developed form, are already present in the subconscious. But rather than speaking in very general terms, as the pantheists do, of some kind of universal spirit, of a feeling of community, we must gain detailed clarity about the meaning of such a phrase and how this feeling can form and unfold in the soul. You see, this feeling of community arises through life itself. And here we must consider the following.

You have no doubt heard of criminals, in whom instinctual nature works very strongly in the subconscious, who are driven to return to the scene of their crime. They seek out the place where they committed their crime, driven by an undefined sense. A phenomenon like this is only a specific instance of something that works more generally in people. When we have done something, anything at all, even an act of no apparent significance, something remains in us—which we can only express in a kind of picture—of the thing we took hold of when we performed our action. The object we took hold of remains in us as a certain energy, remains connected with our I. We inevitably enter into certain connections with all the entities we encounter and the things we take hold of. I do not of course only mean the grasping hold of a physical object. We connect with everything which our actions engage with; and everywhere we leave behind signs of our activity. And in our subconscious there remains a sense of our connection with the things we have engaged with through our actions. In criminals this comes to abnormal expression because their subconscious shines up very powerfully and instinctively into their ordinary awareness. Yet in the subconscious all of us have the sense that we must return to what we encountered and engaged with in our actions.

This is also what our karma is founded on, and where it originates. We have a general feeling of community with the world which initially impinges on our existence in only a nebulous way. And this sense of community with things is due really to the fact that we leave signs of our presence everywhere. We can intuit this sense of community in ourselves, creep up on it as it were. But to do so we have to consider certain subtleties of life. You have to really feel your way into a picture or idea. Say you are walking along a road and, in doing so and having done so, you keep picturing yourself doing this. By invoking this always as you walk along, you draw forth from your soul a general sense of community with the world. In someone who becomes more tangibly aware of this sense of community, it develops to the point where he can say that a connection exists, albeit invisible, between himself and all things, and its nature is similar to the connection between all the limbs of an organism. Just as each finger, every ear lobe, everything in our organism belongs to us, and all is connected with everything else, so there is a connection between all things and everything that happens, in so far as it impinges on our world.

People alive on earth today do not yet have a fully developed sense of this collective or social quality, this organic permeation of things. They are not yet aware of it but it exists in the unconscious. During Jupiter evolution this sense will be the foundation of life; and as we gradually evolve from the fifth post-Atlantean era towards the sixth, we are working to develop this feeling. Developing it is necessary as we move from our present era to a future one, and this must create a distinctive ethical or moral foundation for humanity, one much more alive and vibrant than morality is today. I mean this in the following way.

Nowadays people are not greatly bothered by the thought that they are enriching themselves at others' expense. It is not just that they don't feel many qualms of conscience about this, but that it does not even occur to them to think about it. If they did, they would discover that we live at the expense of others to a far greater extent than is realized. Awareness will gradually develop that living at the expense of others, also in society, is the same thing as if a particular organ developed inappropriately and lived at the expense of another bodily organ. People will come to see that an individual's happiness is in reality not possible without the happiness of all. They do not yet have any inkling of this, but it must gradually become the principle at work in true human morality. Today each person seeks his own happiness initially and does not reflect that one's own happiness only has a sound basis in the happiness of all.

Thus a connection exists between the sense of community with the world which I described and a feeling that the whole of social existence is an organism. People can develop an enhanced sense of this, a greatly intensified awareness of it. We can develop an intimate sense of our community with all things around us. If we enhance and intensify this feeling, we gradually create a capacity to perceive what I described in the last lecture[76] as the beam of light we shed forward into the future, beyond death into our development between death and a new birth, when we perceive it and form our karma from it. I wish only to indicate this today. When we develop this sense of community and companionship with the world, we also acquire the capacity to fully accept and accommodate the situations, thoughts and actions of another person as if they were our own. This involves a certain difficulty for our psyche: to imagine another's reality so that we can experience what he thinks and feels as our own. But if we are going to think back in fruitful ways to what we shared and had in common with the dead with whom we formed karmic connections while they were still alive, we will only succeed in making real contact with them in their disembodied state if we are able to remember the shared experiences we had with them, even of minor significance, with the quality of thinking we possess when aware of this sense of community. So imagine that you think about something that occurred between yourself and a person who has since died; say you were sitting at table with him or went for a walk, or some other minor event. The soul will only be able to fully enter into this situation in a way that makes it reality if it truly possesses this sense of community. Otherwise it will not have sufficient strength to do so. Let us be clear about this: a dead soul can only impinge on our awareness from a place—I'm speaking metaphorically, but you will understand me—upon which we shine this feeling of community. You can picture this in spatial terms if you like, but you must remember of course that this is only a picture. Nevertheless it is the picture of a reality.

Let me return to what I was saying before. You picture a specific situation with a person now dead, say sitting at a table or going for a walk with him; and then you focus your whole soul on this thought. If, in this thought, you develop a soul community with the dead person in a way that accords with the sense of community I have described, his gaze from the world of spirit can discern this thought in the same way that your thought, your orientation of thought, finds the reality upon which it is focused. Allow this thought of the dead person to be present in your loving soul, with the degree of intensity I have described, and the focus of your vision of soul will meet that of the dead person. By this means he can speak to you. He can only speak to you from the place upon which the focus of your sense of community with him falls. Thus are things connected. We learn to feel our karma by acquiring a picture of how we leave marks or signs of our thinking everywhere. If we learn to identify with things in this way, we develop the sense that can bring us into ever more conscious communion with the dead. This is the basis for the dead to speak to us.

The other thing necessary is for us to hear it, to really be able to perceive it as time goes by. Here, above all, we must attend to the 'air' that must lie between us and the dead person so that what he utters can find its way across to us. One can make a comparison here with physics. If there were a vacuum between us you could not hear what I am saying. Likewise, between the living and the dead something must exist, a medium whereby the dead can approach us. This is spiritual air, and we can now describe what this spiritual air consists of in which we have a shared existence with the dead. What is it composed of?

To grasp this we must remember something I have previously

described in a different context,[77] that is, how memory arises. You see things are all connected. Orthodox psychology sees human memory like this: I receive an impression from the outside world and this creates a picture or thought in me; then this picture travels somehow through my subconscious, is forgotten and, when a particular cause arises, it emerges again from the subconscious and I remember. As far as memory is concerned almost all psychologists have the sense, more or less, that an impression causes a thought which fades after a while, is forgotten and makes its way through the subconscious, then comes to our awareness again through some cause of other. We remember, and believe we have the same thought or picture again that we originally formed. But this is utter nonsense, despite being taught in almost every school of psychology. This simply does not happen. When we form an impression in response to an outer experience that impinges on us, and later recall this experience, the original thought or picture does not surface in us again. Instead it is like this. As we think or picture something, a second, subconscious process is occurring at the same time, but we are unaware of this while we have the initial experience. This is happening below the level of our awareness, and, in processes that I will not describe now, what occurred today unconsciously occurs again tomorrow in our organism. On the first day an outer impression elicits a thought or picture, and on the next day the subconscious effect of this calls forth the new picture or thought. A thought I have today fades and disappears and no longer exists. It does not travel around in a subconscious realm but, when I remember the event or outer impression tomorrow, this is because there is something within me which calls forth this same thought. But it has been engendered in the subconscious. If you think that thoughts or pictures are absorbed by our subconscious, journey around there and eventually surface again from there, you might as well imagine that when you write something down with the aim of recalling it in three days, the person, say, whom you wish to remember, has taken refuge in what you wrote and walks out of your jottings again three days later. Just as these jottings are composed only of marks on paper likewise our memory contains only a sign or indicator; and this evokes again what we experienced, though in a weaker degree. There are various spiritual-scientific aspects of this that we can explore, and we will do so; and then what I am about to explain will become very clear. Today, though, I just wish to recall one thing.

Anyone who tries to memorize, or teach himself something that is retained—which can be very hard graft as we may remember from our youth—is fully aware that simply absorbing or perceiving something is not sufficient to ensure this. To lodge something in our mind or memory we may often have to resort to very external props and aids. If you observe someone who is trying to lodge something in his mind, you will see what exertions he has to make to gain the aid of the unconscious activity that occurs in the process. One makes efforts to somehow support this subconscious activity. There are two very distinct things involved here: firstly lodging something in the mind, and secondly recalling it at need. If you study people and their character, you will soon discover that these two things are different. Some people can quickly grasp and absorb something, but have a terribly poor memory; and vice versa there are people who are dull as ditchwater when it comes to grasping something quickly, but who have a good power of recall, in particular a well-developed capacity to think and judge. These two things are quite distinct, and spiritual science will need to highlight what actually happens here.

When we absorb and grasp something in daily life, which we do of course from first thing in the morning until we fall asleep again at night, what we absorb is more or less consciously accompanied by our sympathies and antipathies, and we are usually pleased to have grasped or understood something. But the activity that leads subsequently to memory is a far broader and more diffuse one than the activity needed to grasp impressions. In the soul a very great deal occurs subconsciously, and this subconscious activity sometimes strangely contradicts what is happening in our conscious mind. Sometimes an impression can elicit antipathies in us. Our subconscious has no sense of these antipathies at all, for it experiences our impressions in a quite different way from ordinary awareness. The response of the subconscious to all impressions is a sense that I can describe in no other way than by saying—though this is put metaphorically, and must always be so when one takes expressions from the physical world and applies them to the realm of spirit, but here the expression is very apt—that the subconscious feels a sense of gratitude towards every impression, quite irrespective of what occurs in our conscious mind. Someone can be standing in front of you and hurl the worst insults in your face and yet it is still true to say that your subconscious feels a certain sense of gratitude towards these impressions. This sense of gratitude exists because everything that touches on the deeper elements of our being enriches our life, really enriches it. Even all unpleasant impressions enrich it. This has no bearing on how we have to respond to outer impressions. Our conscious response or reaction has nothing at all to do with what occurs subconsciously, where everything leads only to a certain sense of gratitude. Our subconscious takes every impression as a gift for which it feels gratitude.

It is extremely important to reflect on this reality occurring below the level of consciousness. What is at work there, and issues in a sense of gratitude, acts in a similar way to how an outward impression impinges on us and starts to become internalized as memory; this runs alongside and distinct from thinking, and we can only become aware of these things if we acquire a clear sense of the fact that we are dreaming throughout our waking life. In a public lecture[78] I have said that we are continually sleeping and dreaming, even in waking life, as far as our feelings and will are concerned. As we let the world impinge on us, our impressions and thoughts continually occur, but beneath this we dream about everything. This dream life is far richer than we think, and is merely outshone by our conscious mind just as a weaker light is outshone by a stronger one. It is possible to experiment with this, and gain insight into it, by attending to diverse subtleties in life. For instance, try the following. Imagine you are lying down asleep, and then wake up. Usually we pay no attention to this moment since the world immediately starts making its impression on us. But you can also remain in a tranquil state as you awaken, and then you may notice that you were already perceiving something before you awoke. You can become especially aware of this if someone knocked at the door without knocking a second time. As you wake up you can realize that something has happened, and that you know this from an overall sense of the situation.

When we observe something like this we are not too far removed from acknowledgement of what spiritual science must show: that we perceive our surroundings in far broader and more wide-ranging ways than we are consciously aware of. It simply is the case, say, when you walk down the road and then see someone coming towards you round a corner that you sensed him beforehand. In countless instances you will have a sense of having seen him before you actually did. Before we ever perceive something we are already in a soul-spiritual connection with it. This is true, though usually our subsequent sensory perception conceals the fact, and we do not give proper attention to what occurs in the intimate subtleties of our soul life.

Again, similarly, this is something that occurs unconsciously, like memory or the feeling of gratitude I described towards all phenomena around us. The dead can speak to us only through the element infusing the dreams emerging in our life. They speak what they have to say to us into this intimate, unconsciously occurring mode of perception. And they can do so if we are able to share a soul-spiritual atmosphere with them. If they are to speak to us we have to introduce into our awareness something of the sense of gratitude I described, one towards everything that reveals itself to us. If we bear no such sense of gratitude within us, are unable to thank the world for giving us life and enriching it continually with new impressions, are incapable of deepening our soul experience by bearing in mind that all of life is a gift, the dead will not find a common atmosphere with us. You see, they can only speak to us through such a feeling of gratitude, for otherwise there is a wall between them and us which obstructs communication.

We will soon discover how many hindrances exist to this communication with the dead. As we have seen from other contexts,[79] this communication is always with the dead we are karmically connected with. When we have lost them but keep wishing they were still there, we cannot cultivate the thought that we are grateful for their part in our lives irrespective of the fact that they are no longer there. Then our sense of gratitude does not come into play towards the being whom we wish to approach; and then the soul does not find us, or at least is unable to speak to us. The very feelings we often have towards the dead we have been close to will prevent the dead from speaking to us. Other dead souls, who have no karmic connection with us, usually speak to us only with greater difficulty. But in relation to people close to us we cultivate too little gratitude for the part they played in our lives. We fail to see that we ought not to cling to the thought of having lost them, for this has no gratitude in it, in the broader scheme of things. If we realized how greatly the sense of loss overshadows our sense of gratitude, then we could comprehend the full scope of what I am saying. We feel the loss of a close relative. But then we should really try to find in ourselves a sense of gratitude that this person was there in our life. We must try to reflect selflessly on what he meant to us until he died, rather than on our feelings of loss and grief that he is no longer there. The better we can feel what he meant to us while he was alive, the more easily he can find ways to speak to us, and, through the shared atmosphere of gratitude, he will be able to approach us with what he has to say.

But other things are necessary too if we are to enter ever more consciously into the world where these things hold sway. Imagine that a child of yours dies. You can cultivate a feeling of togetherness with him, for instance, by picturing yourself sitting and playing with him, and being as interested in the game you are playing as the child is himself. If you can be as interested in a game as the child himself, you will have that shared feeling you have when you actually play with a child—something worth doing only if the game means as much to you as it does to the child. This creates the kind of atmosphere that is necessary for the feeling of togetherness. So, if you picture yourself playing with the child, and really engage in this in a lively way, you create a locus upon which your gaze and his can both fall. And if you are able to grasp what the dead soul is saying, then you cultivate a conscious connection with him. And this can, in turn, be sustained by various other things.

You will think this is not so, but some people find thinking extremely easy. If people find it difficult, this engenders a different feeling. Those who give little thought to thinking are precisely the ones who find it most difficult, and this is because they are lazy thinkers. When I say that most people give no thought to thinking, I mean they take it very lightly, terribly lightly; they just think without any idea that it could be a difficult undertaking. They formulate their thoughts, and have them, and live in them. But then other things, such as spiritual science, approach them. Spiritual science is something so many people steer clear of not because it is hard to understand but because we need to make a certain effort to absorb it. People are wary of such effort. As we delve further into spiritual science we gradually discover that grasping the thoughts it contains requires a real effort of will, and that an exertion of will is not just something you do when you lift weights, say, but also when you form thoughts. But people are generally disinclined to engage in such effort. They think easily and effortlessly. Precisely when we make headway in thinking we discover that our thinking becomes harder and harder, increasingly ponderous, if I can put it like that, because we increasingly have the sense that real effort is needed for a thought to form in us. There is really nothing better for helping us delve further into the world of spirit than finding it harder and harder to formulate thoughts. The best progress in spiritual science is made, really, if we no longer regard thinking as something easy, an ordinary part of life, but instead as something we really have to sweat over, like threshing—an effort and exertion similar to that needed when threshing corn!

The feeling I mean is something I can only hint at. But it really can emerge, and is a very good and favourable development. This also relates to various other things: for instance the gradual fading of something common to a great many people. Many people's thinking is so quick that they immediately grasp a whole context of ideas when someone just refers to it in passing. They know the context and can immediately reply. Discussion in literary salons would be hard pressed if thinking grew more difficult! But we can discover that as we gradually become more acquainted with the inner nature of things, it becomes harder for us to fire off a quick retort, which is something accomplished only by easy and superficial thinking. As our knowledge advances, we become ever more Socratic: we become aware that much effort is needed and that we only gain the right to voice our opinion about something by making strenuous exertions.

This feeling—that an exertion of will is needed to grasp thoughts—is related to another feeling within us that we sometimes have when we work hard at committing things to memory, and find that we cannot retain them. There is certainly a connection between these two things: the difficulty of retaining something we are trying to commit to memory, and the difficulty of trying to grasp thoughts which require a great exertion of will. But this can be practised. We can apply what I would call conscientiousness and a sense of responsibility towards thinking. For instance, if, based on a certain experience of life, someone comments that so and so is a 'good person', another may fire back agreement without thinking: 'Yes, a really good person.' Consider how often answers consist only of a comparative intensifier. In fact there is no reason whatever to use the comparative form here. We ought to have a real experience of what we utter, rather than simply going one better than what the other has said. But naturally this should not be taken too far since otherwise silence would fall in many salons.

It may be hard to believe, but it is true: this awakening feeling of responsibility towards thinking, this sense that thinking is hard work, is a foundation for the capacity to receive illumined insights. You see, illumination does not come to us in the way thoughts emerge for most people, but always attended by a sense of difficulty. We must first learn to experience thoughts as difficult undertakings, and the memorization of something as different from merely thinking. And then we can have a feeling of how thoughts surface in a faint and dreamlike way in the soul—and are hard to pin down, are fleeting and fade as quickly as they come. We can help ourselves to grasp them if we develop a sense of the reality of thoughts we live with. For instance, be clear what happens inwardly in you if you decide to go somewhere and then arrive where you intended. Usually we give no thought to such things, but it is possible to reflect on what happens in the soul when we form an intention, realize it and achieve what we decided on. Something has altered inwardly in us. We can get a vivid sense of this in a mountain climber who huffs and puffs up a steep slope and then, arriving at the summit, cries out, 'We did it!' You can feel that something has changed inwardly in his feelings. But a similar kind of feeling can develop in us, though in a subtler, more intimate realm, if we begin to reflect on our relationship with someone who has died, if we try to share interests in common with him and connect with the other's thoughts and feelings. Then we will feel ourselves to be embarking on a path. And then a moment will come when we feel we have, as it were, come to rest in these thoughts. If we can do this—first move into and in a thought and then bring it into equilibrium—we can have the sense of first moving or walking, and then coming to a stop and standing. By doing this we have done much to facilitate illumined insights that can form in us as thoughts. This illumination through thoughts can enable us to put our whole being into something, rather than the little we usually bring to bear on situations. And naturally this leads us into greater and subtler intimations.

If you invoke awareness of this otherwise unconscious feeling of gratitude I spoke about earlier, you will immediately notice that, unlike ordinary feelings of thankfulness, you seek to connect your whole being with it—through into your arms and hands at least. And here I must remind you of what I said about the aspect of human sensibility[80] in which we grasp our ordinary thoughts while subtler ones pass through the brain as if through a sieve. These latter are, really, received by our arms and hands. This can be a real experience. We do not actually have to move our arms to experience this, but can gain a sense that the arms wish to express this feeling of gratitude, and other similar feelings too such as wonder and reverence. This experience comes to expression in partial ways, a kind of impetus in arms and hands as witness to subconscious impulses, when we feel suddenly moved to fold our hands together at the beauties of nature or as we contemplate something that has occurred. Everything that occurs in our subconscious comes to subtle or partial expression in life. We don't necessarily move our arms, but we have a sense that they want to move in sympathy with outward impressions. Only the ether body moves, our etheric arms and hands. The more we become aware of this, and the more, indeed, that we become able to feel the nature of outward impressions with our arm organism—that blue, say, makes you want to move your hand in a certain way, and red in another way, and that this movement belongs to each impression—the more we can also develop a feeling for illuminations, for inner impressions that seek entry to the soul. If we give ourselves up to such things as I described in relation to a child playing, we find our self by losing ourselves in these impressions. And then illumination can enter us once we have become able to make our whole being receptive for an impression, once we have also learned to plunge into our own thoughts of the dead person and there create a sense of real togetherness with him, and then, awakening from this experience again and uniting it with the whole of our being, learn to let feelings of gratitude flow right through into our arms and hands as I described. You see, the spiritual reality in which the dead person exists between death and a new birth is such that we, as living people, can find him by meeting him in a shared locus of spirit in a thought that he too can perceive, as long as we can meet him there with a full sense of commonality and togetherness. In the medium of gratitude, we have the means to do so. The dead speak to the living out of a space that is woven from a feeling of togetherness, through an atmosphere formed from a sense of universal gratitude towards the world.

Lecture 7

BERLIN, 26 MARCH 1918

To keep the thread, I would like briefly to return to what I said here a week ago about the 'soul atmosphere' we need to consider if we are to cultivate a relationship between physically embodied human souls and disembodied souls in their passage between death and rebirth. This atmosphere is what unites the living with the dead so that a relationship can exist between them. Initially we saw that certain inner moods must exist in the living for a bridge to be created with the realms where the so-called dead exist. Inner moods always, in fact, indicate the presence of a certain element of soul; and we can say that when this soul element is present, and reveals its existence in appropriate feelings in the living, the possibility of a relationship with the dead arises.

Then we also showed how this possibility, the soul atmosphere, is created by two tendencies of feeling, one of these being a sense of universal gratitude towards all experiences in life. I also said that the human soul generally relates to its surroundings in a subconscious and a conscious way. We are all aware of the conscious aspect, which involves directing our sympathies and antipathies, along with our ordinary sensory observation, to whatever we encounter in life. The subconscious aspect, on the other hand, involves us developing a subliminal feeling that is nobler and better than those we can usually cultivate in our ordinary mind. It is a feeling we cannot describe in any other way than by saying that, in our deeper soul, we always know we should be grateful for every experience in life, even the smallest thing that happens to us. Difficult experiences in life may be painful, but if we survey existence from a broader perspective even painful experiences will allow us to be grateful—not in our conscious mind but in our deeper soul—for the continual gifts that the universe gives us. There is a real, subliminal sense of this in the human soul. Now the other aspect is that we unite our I with every being or creature with whom we have had anything to do in life, even inanimate objects as well. But whenever we do something that involves us acting upon and connecting with another being, a residue of this remains and forms the foundation for a lasting connection or affinity of our being with everything we ever connected with. I have said that this deeper feeling of affinity—of which the conscious soul is usually unaware—is the basis for a deeper feeling of commonality with the surrounding world, a sense of community with it.

We can live with increasing awareness of these two feelings and bring them to expression: a feeling of gratitude and a sense of community with the surroundings with which we have in some way been karmically connected. We can try to raise into awareness what lives in these feelings; and the more we do so, the better able we are to create a bridge to the souls currently living between death and rebirth. The thoughts of these souls can only find their way to us through the medium of the feeling of gratitude which we develop; and at the same time we can only find our way to them if our soul learns, at least to some degree, to cultivate a real sense of community and commonality. Our capacity to feel gratitude towards the universe, the fact that we have practised engendering such gratitude within us and are capable of feeling it, creates a mood which offers the dead a path to reach us. And to feel that our being lives in an organic community of which it is a part, as our fingers are part of our body, makes us mature enough to feel gratitude towards those, too, who are no longer physically embodied; and this feeling in turn allows our thoughts to reach them. Having first acquired the capacity to feel gratitude or a sense of commonality in a particular area of life, we can then use these feelings in specific instances.

But such feelings are not the only ones. There are many other such subconscious feelings and subliminal moods of soul. Everything of this nature that we develop in our souls builds connection with the world in which the dead exist between death and rebirth. A very specific feeling, which always exists subliminally in us but can gradually be drawn up into our awareness, accompanies gratitude. It is a feeling humanity has increasingly lost as it embraced materialism. Yet it remains there in our subconscious to some degree, and even the most extreme materialism cannot eradicate it. Yet life is enriched, enhanced and ennobled when we draw such things up into our awareness out of subconscious realms. The feeling I am referring to could be described as universal trust in the life flowing through and beside us—a trust in life! It is extremely difficult to cultivate this sense of trust in the context of a materialistic outlook. Similar in some ways to gratitude, and accompanying it, it is nevertheless, a different feeling. Trust in life means that an unshakeable mood exists in the soul that whatever life may bring us it always brings a gift—and that whatever this may be it will never be worthless. Certainly we suffer and meet very difficult experiences, but in a broader context it is these in particular that most enrich and strengthen us. This continuous subliminal mood is one we can try to raise up a little into awareness. 'Life,' one can say, 'you lift and sustain me, and ensure that I gradually progress.'

If a mood like this could be cultivated in the education system in some way, a very great deal would be gained. To found our teaching on this sense of things, allowing such a mood to inform our whole education system, showing in specific instances that we can trust in life precisely because it is often hard to fathom, would be of great significance. You see, if we consider life from this perspective by asking whether it deserves our trust, we discover many things that otherwise remain hidden. I don't mean the superficiality of finding everything in life absolutely marvellous. On the contrary, in certain cases this trust in life can lead us to a severe critique of idiotic or pointless things. It is when we do not trust fully in life that we often avoid criticizing things that are idiotic or misguided because we try to ignore or overlook what we can have no faith in. I am not speaking here, therefore, of blind trust in everything that we encounter, for of course we trust more in some things than others depending on their different nature. I am talking rather of trust in life in general, in the inner coherence of life. If we can draw up from subconscious depths something of the trust in life that always holds sway there, this starts to enable us to really observe the spirit at work in life, the wisdom of destiny and inner guidance. This is not a theoretical insight but one we must really feel: that the way life shapes itself and presents me with things, the way they affect me and are related to me, is something I can trust in. And then, gradually, we are preparing ourselves to really perceive the spirit living and working in the world. If we do not have such trust, by contrast, we close ourselves off from this spirit at work in all things.

This also has an effect on the relationship between the living and the dead. By developing this mood of trust, we enable a person who has died to find the way to us in his thoughts. On the currents of this trust, as it were, our thoughts can sail to him. If we cultivate a general or universal trust in life, a faith in life, we can create an inner state of soul that allows thoughts sent to us from the dead to appear in us as inspirations. Gratitude for life and trust in life as I have described it, belong together in a certain way. If we do not have this universal sense of trust, we cannot gain trust in another person that is strong enough to reach beyond death, but instead have only a memory of once trusting him. You have to realize that feelings which are to reach and affect those no longer in physical embodiment have to be somewhat modified from those we send towards people still inhabiting a physical body. We can certainly trust a person living in a physical body, and this trust will also be of some benefit for conditions existing after death. Yet such trust has to be strengthened by a more general and universal trust since, after death, the dead person lives in different conditions. Above and beyond remembering the trust we once had in a person, we also need to keep re-enlivening our trust in a being whose physical presence is no longer there to awaken our trust. To do this we have in a sense to shine out into the world something that has nothing to do with physical things. And this universal trust in life that I have described has nothing to do with the physical world.

In the same way as trust and gratitude belong together, so the sense of community, of shared commonality, is accompanied by something always present in the subconscious soul that can likewise be drawn upwards into our awareness. Again, this should be considered more than it usually is, and could be so if it played a greater part in our educational system in this materialistic age. A very great deal depends on this. To relate to the world in the right way at our current stage of evolution we need to develop a quality—or, you might say, draw it forth from the under-soul—that people naturally possessed in former times of atavistic clairvoyance. It was once there quite naturally and did not have to be cultivated. Only scanty remains of this can still be found and are gradually waning, like everything else human beings once possessed in ancient times. Nowadays it has to be consciously cultivated, through knowledge of the world of spirit rather than by vague instinct. The quality I am speaking of here is the ability to keep refreshing and renewing our feelings for everything we encounter in life. We easily grow weary from a certain age onwards, losing our living engagement with life and failing to find joy in its phenomena. Just think of the difference between how a young person in the first flush of youth experiences life and the weary way an old person meets what it brings. Consider how many disappointments a person may have had. It makes a real difference whether someone is able to keep reviving his powers of soul and renew them each and every day in his soul or whether he grows weary as life continues.

It is extremely important to consider this nowadays, and could have very important repercussions on our education system. In such respects we are approaching a significant turning point in humanity's evolution. Our history, which is just a *fable convenue*, gives us a very warped view of former epochs. People are unaware of how, in recent centuries, children's upbringing and education has increasingly become something that fails to sustain them in the right way later in life. In current circumstances, at most, our educational efforts in youth leave us with only a memory of something. We recall what we learned, perhaps, and what was said to us when young; and usually we make do with that. But in doing so we entirely fail to consider that here, in particular, a vital secret affects human life. On a previous occasion I referred to this secret from a different angle.[81]

The human being is a complex entity. But an initial view of him ascertains a duality, as I mentioned on a previous occasion here, and this comes to expression already in our physical form: the head and the rest of our body. So let us firstly see the human being in terms of the head contrasted with the rest of the organism. Just considering this distinction in the whole edifice of the human being would lead to very important scientific discoveries. In purely physiological and anatomical terms, we can see the structure of the head as governed by materialistic, 'Darwinian' views of descent.[82] As far as our head is concerned, we are part of this evolutionary stream of physical lineage—but only in respect of the head and not the rest of our organism. To understand the nature of human descent, you have to picture the rest of the organism as an attachment growing from the head, despite the relative size of the two parts. You can picture the continuing course of evolution in these terms: as we evolve into the future, various organs could acquire further distinct organs attached to them. Evolution could continue in this way; and this is how it was in the past—in ancient times we existed only as a head being. This head developed increasingly and became what it now is. And what is attached to the head only came later, despite being larger in physical size. It is younger, a more recent development. As far as our head is concerned we derive from the most ancient organisms, while the rest of us came later. This is also why our head, at our present stage of evolution, is so important—because it recalls our previous incarnation. And in this sense we are a dual entity, the head being quite differently constituted from the rest of the organism. The rest of our organism—as I have often said[83]—is a preparation for our next incarnation. In this sense we are a very divided being, and the head is quite different in nature from the rest of the organism. The head is an ossified organ. If we did not have the rest of our organism, in fact, we would be very spiritual and yet only a spiritualized animal. The head can never feel human on its own without being inspired to feel this: it points us back to ancient Saturn, Sun and Moon phases of evolution, whereas the rest of our organism points back only to ancient Moon and, in fact, only its later period. It attached itself to the head and in this respect is really like a kind of parasite upon it.

Picture this. The head was once the whole human being, having extension organs underneath it by means of which it nourished itself. It was a very odd entity. But as it evolved further and the openings below developed by closing off from what was around them, no longer serving as organs of nutrition or connecting the head with influences emanating from the surroundings, the head ossified above and the rest of the organism became necessary. This other part of the physical organism only emerged at a time when there was no further possibility for the rest of animal life to emerge. You will say that it is hard to conceive of what I have just described. I can only reply by saying that you have to make an effort to conceive it. The world is not as simple as people think, or as they like to imagine so that they do not have to think too hard about it. In this respect we can experience all the ways in which people insist on making the world as easy as possible to understand, often displaying the oddest views. There is a wealth of literature on the philosophy of Kant[84] by all sorts of huge admirers of his. But this is only because people fail to understand other philosophers, and find that trying to understand Kant himself is already enough of an effort. And since he is, after all, a great philosopher, and also considers himself to be very brilliant, a great genius, as people so often do, they never get beyond his view of things to engage with others. In fact, people only regard Kant as a great philosopher because they find it so hard to understand him. There is a connection here with the reluctance people feel to acknowledge the full complexity of the world, and to make the effort to understand it. We have previously spoken of these things from the most diverse perspectives. When my lectures on *Occult Physiology*[85] come out, you will be able to read in detail of embryological proofs of the nonsense of saying that the brain evolves from the spinal column. The reverse is true: while the brain is a metamorphosis of a former spinal column, today's spinal column only developed as a secondary attachment to the modern brain. We have to learn to see that something simpler in us arose later than what appears more complex; that what is more primitive in nature, that lies at a subordinate level, arose at a later stage.

I have digressed here to talk about the duality in human nature only so that you can understand its consequences, which include the fact that our inner life, developing of course under corporeal conditions, is also informed by this duality. Besides the physical, organic development of our head and that of the rest of our organism, we also have two different tempi, two speeds, in our soul development. Our head develops relatively fast, while the process of development for the rest of our organism—which I will here call 'heart development'—is slower in comparison, roughly three to four times slower. The determining factors in the head's development are usually more or less concluded by the time we are in our twenties. As far as our head is concerned, we are all already old by the time we are 20. And it is only because reinvigoration comes from the rest of our organism—which develops three or four times more slowly—that we go on living in a reasonable way. Our head development happens quickly; our heart development, the development of the rest of our organism, takes three to four times longer. And our experience exists in this duality. In childhood and youth, our head development can absorb a great deal, which is why we learn so fast at that period of our lives. But what is absorbed during that time has to be continually renewed and refreshed, has to be encompassed repeatedly by the slower passage of the rest of our organism in its heart development.

Now just consider this: if education is as it currently is in our age, focusing only on the development of head capacities because, in education, we only accord the head its full dues, the consequence of this is that the head is integrated into the slower development of the rest of the organism like a dead entity. Thus it holds back the latter's development, and people become prematurely old in their soul. This phenomenon of premature inner ageing is largely connected with our educational system. This is not an easy thing to remedy nor can we sum up in a few words what needs to happen to address the problem. Almost everything in education would have to be done differently—so that it becomes something that not only addresses the memory, and available to recall, but something which refreshes and renews us. So many people today, when they think back to their schooldays, to what their teachers told them, really only remember being instructed how they should do things. Very few indeed can immerse themselves repeatedly in the vivid experiences of their youth, lovingly recalling every hand movement, every remark, their teacher's tone of voice, the feelings that permeated the lessons they received; very few can find in such things an ever-renewing source that refreshes and reinvigorates them. This is connected with the different tempi which we can experience within us: the quicker development of the head which concludes in our twenties, and the slower course of heart development, of the rest of our being, which can nourish us for the rest of our lives. What we must not do is merely give the head what is due to it, but also give it something that the rest of the organism can draw refreshing powers from repeatedly throughout the rest of a person's life. To achieve this it is necessary, for instance, that all lessons, all subjects, are imbued with a certain artistic element. The artistic element is out of fashion today. People believe that cultivating the imagination—which is, certainly, something that lifts us above daily reality—will make teaching too far-flung and pie-in-the-sky. There is no inclination today therefore to pay heed to this secret of life. We need only consider specific areas where what I am referring to still exists—it does still exist here and there—and we will find that something like this can be achieved by virtue, especially, of people becoming human beings once more. A great deal is necessary for this to happen; and there is one thing I would like to emphasize in this respect.

Nowadays those who wish to become teachers are tested to see if they know their subject properly. What is discovered really by this means? Only, usually, that the person concerned once crammed into his head the information he needed to pass his exams, gathering this from a great quantity of books and thus acquiring knowledge he might need for his teaching. In fact there is no need to acquire such knowledge. What we ought to discover to test someone's capacity to teach is whether the person concerned has a heart and a mind, whether what flows in his veins will enable him gradually to develop a relationship with children in school. Knowledge is not what we should examine but the degree to which a future teacher is fully human. I am aware that there will only be one of two responses to such a suggestion: either that the person proposing such a thing is off his head and does not live in the real world, or that this is something that already happens, is something everybody desires anyway.

My reason for elaborating on this is firstly to cast a certain light on life but then also to illumine something always felt subliminally but which is so hard to lift up into the conscious soul; and yet it is something the human soul yearns for today, and will increasingly long for in the future. We need in our souls something of the energy that can continually renew our powers of soul so that we do not grow weary as life continues, but always find in us a source of hope. Then we can feel how every day brings a new beginning. We ought not to grow inwardly old—this is vital. If you look around you today you see relatively young people, both men and women, who are inwardly already so terribly old, so unwilling, really, to regard each new day as a gift given them as it was given in the freshness and vigour of their childhood or the first flush of youth. When we see this we know what is needed, what a spiritual culture needs to give. And ultimately it is true to say that the feeling I am speaking of here, this feeling of never, ever, ever fading hope in life, fits us to create the right, feeling relationship between the living and the so-called dead. Otherwise what ought to provide a foundation for our relationship with the dead remains too stuck in memory; we merely remember what we experienced with the person who is now dead. But if we are unable to relive feelings associated with what we experienced with a person who has now departed physically, we will not have such a strong sense or intimation of the need to understand that the dead soul is now present only as a being of spirit, who must act as spirit. If our hope and trust in life has grown dull, so that we cannot refresh and reinvigorate ourselves, we no longer have a full sense of the transformation that has taken place. Previously the person's presence in our life had a renewing effect, but now only his spirit can come to our aid. But we can approach this spirit if we develop the feeling of ever-renewed life forces that continually give our hope and trust in life fresh vigour.

Here I would like to make a remark that could seem strange to you. A healthy life, healthy especially in the sense described here, will never lead us to regard life as something we are weary of. A life lived in a really healthy way will lead us, when we are older, to the desire to begin this life again anew and afresh each day. It is not healthy to think, once grown old: Thank God life is nearly over! At the age of 40 or 50 one feels instead that one would like to go back and start the whole thing all over again. And it is healthy if we acquire a wisdom that comforts us by showing that, although we cannot do so in this life, in a future life we will be able to remedy and redress what was imperfect in this one. It is healthy to look back on what we have experienced without regretting any of it, without wishing anything had not happened, and to find the wisdom that teaches us that we can wait for another life for things not vouchsafed to us in this one. This is trust, real trust in life, founded on the hopefulness about life that we manage to keep alive.

Thus we cultivate the feelings that ensoul our life in the right way, and at the same time build the bridge between the living in this realm and the living in the other. These feelings are: gratitude for the life we receive, trust in the experiences we have, an intimate sense of togetherness, the capacity to keep our hopes in life alive and fresh. These are inner, ethical impulses which, intimated in the right way, also provide the very best outward social ethic because ethical conduct, like historical understanding, can, as I described in the public lecture,[86] only be grasped by fathoming it in the subconscious.

Something else I would like to raise is the difference it makes to a relationship if two people are physically embodied or if one of them is physically embodied and the other not, or if neither of the two souls are at present in corporeal embodiment. There is something particular I want to say in this regard.

If we study the human I and life of soul—the latter can also be called the astral body, and the I, as I have often said, is the youngest part of our organization, the baby if you like, whereas the astral body is somewhat older though it originated only in the ancient Moon phase of evolution—we ascertain the following: they have not yet developed sufficiently to give us the power, if we relied on these aspects only, to sustain ourselves as independent entities in relation to other people. If each of us here were together with the others only as I and astral body, without our etheric and physical bodies, we would all merge in a sort of mush. Our beings would flow through each other. Instead of being distinct and separate, we would not know how to distinguish ourselves from the others. No one would be able to know which was his hand or leg and which that of another, though of course this comparison is at odds with the fact that arms and legs would not figure here at all. But feelings too could not be discerned as belonging to one person rather than another. That we can sense our separateness is due to the fact that each person here is detached from the whole fluid mass—which is an accurate picture of a former condition—in the form of a drop. But so that all the souls do not run together again into one, we can imagine that every 'soul drop' has entered a piece of sponge that keeps each separate from the others. Something like this is actually what has happened. Only by virtue of inhabiting physical bodies and etheric bodies are we properly distinct and separate from each other. When asleep, we are only separate from one another by retaining a strong desire for our own physical body. This desire, ardently directed towards our physical body, separates us in sleep for otherwise we would flow entirely into each other when asleep. Sensitive souls might find it a very uncomfortable thought if they knew how closely they connect, in sleep, with the inner being of others in their surroundings. But this is not too extreme compared to the conditions that would exist if this ardent longing for one's own physical body did not keep us related to it while we are physically embodied.

Now we can ask this. What separates our souls from each other in the period between death and a new birth? During life our I and astral body belong to an etheric and physical body; and after death our I and astral body belong, similarly, to a quite specific realm of stars, different in every individual case. An instinct for this gives us the idea of a 'guiding star' particular to each person. In terms of physical projection, the realm of stars is spherical, and can therefore contain the most varied divisions. These areas overlap but each one belongs to a different person. To put it in terms of the psyche, each of us belongs to a different range of archangeloi and angeloi that live with the souls belonging to them. Here on earth each person apparently has his own physical body. You may be surprised that I say 'apparently', quite intentionally, for there is a mystery involved here that I do not wish to broach at present, though I have studied it fully in the same way that I can say that every person has his own star configuration but that these overlap. Imagine a certain group of archangeloi and angeloi in the life between death and rebirth. If only a single one of these is replaced by another, this creates the domain of a different soul. In the drawing, two souls have the same star configuration apart from a single star that they do not share.

No two souls have an exactly identical realm of stars. Between death and rebirth, souls are individualized by virtue of each having his own realm of stars, and this makes the distinction between each. Here in the physical world we are distinct in physical terms as we know. Each of us has his own encompassing skin, and views the world from this vantage point: everything that approaches us must do so via the physical body. And similarly, between death and rebirth, everything that enters a soul is connected with a distinct realm of stars to which the I and astral body relate. This tells us how we remain distinct from each other after death.

Today I have described how we can create a bridge between the so-called dead and the living by developing certain feelings in the soul. What I have just said now, too, can draw towards us thoughts—let us say feeling thoughts or thinking feelings—that likewise help to create this bridge. Whatever we experience, we can try increasingly to develop a mode of feeling that is motivated to ask how a particular dead person would experience the same thing, at the same time imagining that the soul in question is sharing in it alongside us. If we can do this very vividly, in a sense we are imitating the way in which the dead interact either with the living or with each other. We are relating the individual gift of different star configurations to the mutual soul connection between us. We are imitating what lives in the interplay between one soul and the other through different star configurations. Concentrating on something of direct interest to us via the presence of the dead soul, and feeling the dead person to be with us in an immediate, living connection, then we can increasingly sense the dead really approaching us more nearly. Here we must have trust that such things can happen. You see, if we do not trust, if we are impatient with life, this impatience drives such experiences away, clouds our perceptions. Nothing is worse than to cloud our vision with impatience.

THE LIVING GIFTS OF ANTHROPOSOPHY

Lecture 8

BERLIN, 30 MARCH 1918

If you have rightly understood what I said in the last few lectures about the soul determining how we relate to supersensible worlds, how we ourselves can work to nurture this relationship, you will not need to feel anxious when you hear the simple truth that we are also, in a sense, reliant and dependent on the whole cosmos, on all our surroundings. Human life swings back and forth between these two things: between freely creating a relationship with the world of spirit, and dependence on our surroundings, on the whole cosmos, due largely to the fact that we are bound up with a specific physical body between birth and death. In the coming days I want to speak about a particular aspect of this dependence on the universe, which can seem especially relevant to us nowadays.

Your study of spiritual science will have shown you, in particular, that the whole earth we inhabit as all of humanity is a kind of great, living being, and that we ourselves live within this living entity as its limbs. In various lectures[87] I have spoken about how this great living entity, the earth, manifests in diverse phenomena. The life of our earth is expressed in the most varied ways, among other things in the kinds of relationship that exist between distinct areas of the globe and the human beings living there. While it is superficially true to say that the human race is one, a unified whole, it is equally true that this human race is differentiated depending on geographical locality, and that human beings are dependent not only on the many forces studied by mainstream science and geography but also on many hidden forces in diverse places across the face of the globe. Human beings have an inner relationship with the places where they live and the parts of the world where they originated, and ordinary science usually does not delve deep enough to reveal these. These connections and relationships are ones created over longer historical periods. We can discern something of this in the changes undergone by Europeans who move to America and settle there. Of course, the period during which America has been settled by Europeans is so brief still that there are as yet only hints, though strong and clear ones, of what I mean. The European's external appearance changes—or at least there are hints and indications of this—when he settles in America. This does not happen immediately but after several generations. It can be detected in the form of arms and hands for instance, but also in the countenance. Gradually and subtly the faces of Europeans begin to resemble those of native Americans, slowly beginning to acquire the qualities and characteristics of that people.

Such things can indicate certain connections between the great organism of the earth and the diverse parts of this organism, the different peoples who live upon the earth. We know of course that we live on earth in connection with supersensible beings, with beings of higher hierarchies. What we have called the 'folk soul' is not an empty abstraction but rather a kind of archangel being. If you read the lecture cycle I gave about folk souls in Kristiania [Oslo][88] you will find that such a folk soul is an actual, real being in whom our lives are in a sense embedded. We are in general always connected with higher and lower beings of the higher hierarchies in some way. Today and in the next few days we will study this connection from a certain angle—for such things can only ever be studied from a particular perspective.

To start with it is important to remind ourselves that what is regarded in the materialistic outlook as matter or substance does not actually exist for the spiritual scientist. A really careful and detailed mode of observation finds that substance resolves into spirit. I have often used a comparison[89] to show what I mean here. Think of water: it turns to ice if it freezes, and then looks quite different. Yet ice is still water, only in a different form. The same is roughly true of what we call matter; it is spirit in a different form. It assumes a different form just as the water does when it becomes ice. In terms of spiritual science therefore, when we speak of material processes we keep spirit in view. The dynamic spirit pervades everything; and the fact that it also comes to expression in material processes shows one way in which it manifests. Spirit is active everywhere. And so, if we consider more material phenomena, we are really speaking of the way spirit acts—how, in a certain domain, it reveals itself in outward and more or less material processes.

Material processes, which are really spiritual processes, continually occur within us. We eat and thereby assimilate substances of the outer world into our own organism. Solid substances, rendered liquid, are absorbed in the human organism and undergo a metamorphosis. The human organism consists of all kinds of substances which it assimilates from outside. As it does so, these substances pass through a process. Our bodily warmth is generated by the warmth we absorb and by processes which the substances we assimilate undergo within our organism. We breathe and in doing so we take in oxygen. Yet we not only take in oxygen but also at the same time enter into the rhythms of the outer world since our processes of respiration are connected with what occurs in the outer atmosphere. Our own rhythm is embedded in the rhythm of the whole universe. On one occasion I even described this relationship in numerical terms.[90] We are related to our surroundings in a certain way through the rhythmic processes at work in our own organism. Outer processes in nature play into us, play on in us, and this also means, in fact, that the effects of the folk spirit, for instance, are mediated to each individual. We not only breathe oxygen, but something spiritual lives in it; the folk spirit can live in our breathing of oxygen. In eating we assimilate substances, and here too the process is at the same time also spiritual, and one in which the folk spirit can live. The folk spirit lives with us in a way that is not merely abstract; its life informs all that we do each day, the processes in our organism. Material processes are at the same time the expression of spiritual modes of action. The folk spirit thus enters us in a mediated way through our breathing and our nutrition.

The various different folk spirits we described from another point of view in the lecture cycle on folk souls and Nordic mythology act on human beings in divergent ways, and this distinguishes the different characteristics of nations and races on earth. These characteristics depend on the folk spirits. But if we study the mediated ways in which different folk spirits act, we find such things as the following.

We breathe in and out, and this means we are continually connected with the air around us. And where, in a specific instance, the folk spirit chooses to act through the medium of breathing, thus creating the distinctive characteristics and configuration of a particular people, we find that it acts on this people via the air or atmosphere. This is especially striking in races that have ever inhabited the Italian peninsula, where air mediates the effects of the folk spirit on human beings. We can say that the air of Italy is the means or medium which the folk spirit employs to act within people who live in Italy, giving them the characteristics that have made them Italian and, further back in the past, the Roman people. In other words, apparently material effects can be traced back to underlying spiritual causes if we study these things through spiritual science.

What about other folk spirits? What medium do they choose in other cases to bring a particular nation's distinctive characteristics to expression? The folk spirit of peoples who have inhabited France, or still do today, acts via the fluid element—through everything they not only imbibe as fluid but also all the fluids that work within them. So this folk spirit weaves and reverberates in the French through the way in which fluids shape and influence the organism, and this gives rise to the distinctive characteristics of this people, both today and in the past.

But this relationship between a people and their surroundings is somewhat more complex. There is more to it than this. Remember that I said human beings have a dual nature,[91] with a head distinct from the rest of the organism. The actions of the folk spirit on the Italians and the French as I described them relate only to the rest of the organism other than the head, while another kind of effect proceeds from the head. The full character of a people arises only from a combination of the effect emanating from the head and that proceeding from the rest of the organism. We can say that the effect issuing from the head is neutralized by the other action which comes from the rest of the organism. What the inhabitants of Italy breathe in with the air, which has a determining effect on their organism, except for the head, via breathing, combines with the way in which the head's nervous system is configured, the way in which it is spiritually differentiated in so far as the head's neural activity is concerned. In France it is different. There, what lives as rhythm in the organism is a distinctive rhythm for the whole organism, and distinctive again for the head—the head has its own rhythm. Whereas in Italy the head's neural activity combines with the actions of the air on the human being, in France the rhythm, the rhythmic movement in the head, the resonance of the rhythm in the head is caused by the actions of fluid in the organism. Thus the character of a people develops through the specific interaction of something individually human in the head with the actions of the folk spirit coming from locality and surroundings.

Spiritual-scientific observations enable us to study how these things are differentiated across the globe. We cannot actually understand the distinctions and differences between nations if we do not look at them in this way.

What about the British character? Just as the folk spirit of Italy is mediated by the air and that of France by everything fluid, so the British folk spirit is mediated by everything of an earthly quality, chiefly salt and its compounds in the organism. The chief element here is solidity. In contrast to the fluidity at work in the character of the French people, the British character is informed by the consolidating element of salt absorbed through breathing and nutrition, and this gives rise to the distinctive quality of the British. But here again an effect proceeds from the head and somewhat neutralizes what enters from outer surroundings. As well as rhythm in the head and the rest of the organism, both these also possess digestion and metabolism. The British character arises from the way the head accomplishes its metabolism, an exchange of substances, in interplay with the salt element in the rest of the organism. This character emerges from the earthly element in combination with the head's metabolism; and we can say that as it works through the salt element, the folk soul here encounters or comes up against the distinctive nature of the head's metabolism.

In this way, taking account of these differently mediated metamorphoses, you can study all the different characters of a race or nation.

Looking further westwards, we find a sub-earthly element working in the American people. While the British character is connected with the earth element, salt, a sub-earthly quality is active in the American character, something that resonates below the earth's surface, and this is what primarily influences the organism there. The folk spirit in America acts especially by rising through subterranean magnetic and electrical currents, meeting a stream descending from the head which in turn neutralizes this influence, and has the quality of human will. That is the distinctive character of the American people. While the British character is largely connected with the earthly element absorbed into the organism and entering into interplay with the head's metabolism, the character of the American people arises from the distinctive nature of the will combining with what rises from a subterranean sphere. This is also connected with something I said in the public lecture.[92] We can only develop freely and independently where we connect with an element on or above the earth. If we are influenced by sub-earthly actions of the folk soul, we do not develop free characteristics but are in a sense possessed by this folk soul. In my public lecture I described this by showing that although an American and a European may seem to say the same thing—I'm thinking of Woodrow Wilson[93] and Herman Grimm[94]—we find that in the latter case everything has been hard-earned by human effort whereas the words of the former betray a kind of possession.

There is something important to note here, especially important in our day and age. If two or three people apparently say the same thing,[95] people consider only the abstract content of their words. Yet while the content of two people's words can be identical, while they seem to be saying exactly the same as each other, one of them may be expressing things he has struggled hard to formulate while the other has simply acquired them effortlessly through a kind of possession. The content is often not the thing of primary importance but the degree to which this content is the fruit of inner labour or has simply been received through a sort of possession. This is important. Nowadays people only have a sense of things in the abstract. In the case of Herman Grimm you can see that he only uttered things he had pondered many times inwardly. You can takes phrases written by Wilson and put Grimm's name to them, and vice versa, but that is not what matters. What Herman Grimm writes has been hard earned whereas Woodrow Wilson's phrases have a quality of possession, something entering from subterranean entities. These things can be perceived. There is no need to get emotionally worked up about them but we can just bring objective discernment to bear on them.

We will come back to Germany in a moment; but first let us move on further eastwards. The nature of eastern people will only gradually emerge from chaos to reveal its intrinsic quality; and here we encounter something striking. In Italy the folk spirit works through air, in France through water, in England through earth and in America through a sub-earthly element. In Russians and Slavs the folk spirit works through light. The folk spirit with whom we are concerned in these eastern regions works through light's reverberation. As we advance towards the future, from embryonic forms something will gradually emerge in the East and show a folk spirit active in eastern Europe that is quite different in quality from the western folk spirit. I said that this folk spirit works through light; and yet the curious thing is that it does not do so directly, through light's intrinsic vibrations, but through light that first descends to earth and is reflected by it. The folk spirit uses this light, reflected back from the ground, to act upon the Russian people. But this works upon the head rather than the rest of the organism; it works upon modes of thought, on the way in which ideas, feelings and so on are developed. Here, therefore, the way in which the folk spirit acts is polar opposite to what happens in the West, where it works through the organism and encounters something descending from the head. In the East the folk spirit works in the medium of light streaming back from the ground, and this acts primarily upon the head, with a counteraction coming from the rest of the organism, especially from the heart. Coming from the heart organism is a response directed towards the head, altering the effect issuing from there. Today this is still in chaos, enveloped in embryonic sheaths. The respiratory rhythm impacts on the head and neutralizes what comes from the folk spirit, mediated by light. This phenomenon in the Near East exists still more strongly as we move further eastwards. It is in general a remarkable and distinctive characteristic of Asia that the folk spirit still acts through the light absorbed and reflected back to work upon the head. Or the folk spirit also acts through what is no longer light, is no longer even visible: the harmony of the spheres that resonates through everything and which, for the spiritual humanity of the Far East is much the same as the actions of a folk spirit. The folk spirit here works directly through the harmony of the spheres, this too being reflected back by the earth and acting upon the head. And the rhythm of breathing works against this. And here lies the secret of oriental spirit seekers, that they have always sought to connect with the spirit by developing their breathing in a special way. If you have studied yoga you will know about specific breathing requirements. This is due to the fact that the individual, as member of all humanity, does not need to find spirituality individually through the folk spirit. He seeks it instead in a way really founded on his national characteristics. So the further eastwards we travel, the more we find this to be so. Refinements of these effects of folk characteristics, or also deviations from them, both more or less common, can show us some of the possible aberrations here—disharmonies for instance, arising when the effect coming from the head harmonizes with that from the rest of the organism and so on. But conditions today mean that it is probably not a good idea to go into detail about possible states of disharmony that arise in different peoples. It might sow dissension instead of love between nations. People might respond emotionally to such ideas instead of reasonably, and misunderstand them. At some point in the future, when times change, we may be able to talk about the people of the East and other problems.

Now let us return to the people of Central Europe. I am referring to geographical locations rather than to socio-political states. Nor am I speaking in terms of race but of spiritual-geographical conditions. Let us therefore speak of a Central Europe which does not include France and Italy.

The distinctive nature of the folk spirit working in Central Europe is that it acts directly through heat or warmth, rather than through air, water or salt as in other regions I described. In central Europe the folk spirit has chosen this medium of warmth. But this is not fixed or clear-cut; it can be individualized. There are people in Central Europe in whom the folk spirit acts in different ways—sometimes coming from the rest of the organism, sometimes affecting the head. This depends also on whether the external air directly brings warmth or whether it is conveyed through food or breathing. It is all a medium for the folk spirit. And this action is likewise counteracted by warmth in turn; and so in Central Europe the outer effects of warmth are the medium for the folk spirit, and encounter self-generated warmth or heat working from within the organism. We can therefore say that the warmth working in the organism through the folk spirit encounters the head's self-generated warmth. Where the warmth of the folk spirit works through the head, it meets the warmth of the rest of the organism streaming towards it. Warmth encounters and affects warmth, and specifically is dependent on a greater or lesser vitality of the senses, especially of the capacity of sensory perception. Someone with a lively and attentive mind, who loves to observe everything around him, develops more self-generated warmth. By contrast, someone whose attention is fleeting and superficial, whose gaze merely flits over the surface of things, has much less self-generated warmth. Full engagement with one's surroundings, having an open heart or gaze for one's environment, is what counteracts the warmth working through the folk spirit as warmth meeting warmth. That is the distinctive way in which the folk spirit works in Central Europe, determining much in the quality of national characteristics, because warmth and warmth are so intimately related. The other modes of interaction do not have such mutual affinity. The will is not so closely related to electrical phenomena, nor does the element of salt have such a close affinity with digestive or metabolic processes in the head; the same is true of the other interactions I described. But the [Central] European character is determined by warmth, and this comes to expression too in its capacity to more or less merge with everything. These are not value judgements but characterizations, and so each person is free to understand them as he likes, whether as a virtue or its opposite. Warmth meeting warmth: this gives a flexible, plastic quality, a capacity to enter into everything—also into the characteristics of other peoples. If we trace the course of history we can certainly see how the different Teutonic tribes were absorbed by foreign peoples, how they accepted and assumed the foreign element. All this can support what I have been saying.

What I have said today also gives a striking sense of the gulf and contrast between the Asian Orient and the American Occident. The folk soul in the East employs light and even what lies higher than light in the etheric realm—albeit reflected back from the earth—to approach humankind. In the West, it employs the sub-earthly element. This can lead us deep into the organic and soul life of the whole earth organism and its co-existence with humanity. There is absolutely no intention here to affront any part of the earth's population or flatter any other. And yet it is true to say that in the Orient we have a spirit-oriented flowing and streaming whereas towards the West we meet something weightier below, binding the human being to the earth. I will leave it up to you to decide whether this somehow corresponds to the character of the American people. So that is how life is: in the East a rising surge, in the West an ebbing activity that works more deeply into the earth.

Not all at once but during the course of a lifetime and through successive generations, a person adapts to earthly conditions in each region and develops an affinity with them. If a European moves to the Orient, has children there and grandchildren, the geographical conditions start to act and hold sway. Just as a shoulder can never turn into a nose, but an arm will always emerge from it, so good yogis will never emerge in America. Yoga can be transplanted; but of course you can grow all kinds of plants in a greenhouse. I am not speaking of such things but of the natural development that arises in different conditions and localities. Mainstream biology does not offer any explanation of different conditions on earth, and for this we need to consider the different ways in which the folk souls act, as we discussed today, seeing how what is hidden comes to manifest expression.

So the human being is embedded in modes of activity and influence connected with the earth. If you consider this carefully it will be fully and depressingly apparent to you how greatly people are dependent on powers connected with the portion of earth on which their karma has placed them in a particular incarnation. Naturally this is part of a person's karma, but there is nevertheless perhaps something oppressive about this fact, and the sense of oppression can become still greater if we do not have insight into all the related circumstances. Looking back to older eras of earth's evolution, we find an increase in this dependency and ever greater differentiation of humankind across the globe. Yet evolution potentially enables our inner life—albeit not our external configuration—to overcome this dependency.

What, let us ask for a moment, could conceivably moderate this dependency on a particular region of the earth, so that people might emancipate themselves from its imperative and develop more freedom? We have considered all the impulses that apparently render humankind dependent on different earthly powers in a particular region. Now something would have needed to occur to oppose the dependency I spoke of, to counteract and alleviate such conditions. It is clear that something of an entirely different nature from this dependency would, by living upon earth, have a redressing and neutralizing effect on conditions there. What could this be?

The Mystery of Golgotha occurred at the beginning of our era. We have emphasized many distinctive effects of this in the past; but we need only consider a very apparent, generally acknowledged aspect of this Mystery to see that even in terms of something so externally self-evident it introduced a unique and distinctive quality into earthly life. Christ Jesus lived amongst a people with pronounced cultural characteristics, a people whose actions also arose from a pronounced cultural awareness and character. But everything surrounding Christ Jesus—the Mystery of Golgotha, the death at Golgotha—entirely contradicts these cultural forms and assumptions. You see, the people in whose midst this Mystery of Golgotha occurred took no cognizance of it. They did not affiliate themselves with it at all in any individual, personal sense but killed him, cried out, 'Crucify him! Crucify him!' Here occurred something which cannot be for *one* cultural group or nation alone, which has sense only in terms of contradicting all that follows from limited national characteristics, and which the people in this instance rejected and sought to annihilate. This is the secret of the Mystery of Golgotha. It does not have a delimited cultural character, does not emerge from national attributes. Instead it contradicts everything we described earlier as human dependency on folk characteristics. It is an event occurring upon earth that has nothing to do with such characteristics, a being that contradicts them. Only the annihilating element, death, is connected with such characteristics. The event in question has nothing to do with the nature of the Jewish people nor with the Roman people likewise influential in the same region. The Jews cry out: 'Crucify him!' The Roman figure in these events can 'find no fault in him'—which means he is unable to make anything of what is going on there. The whole event is lifted out of all that can happen by virtue of national characteristics. If you study it carefully, therefore, you will find that the Mystery of Golgotha cannot be compared with anything else. There have always been martyrs of course, in other times and places, but nowhere else have martyrs been killed in this way and for these reasons. The more you study the Mystery of Golgotha the more you will find that it occurred precisely because it has no connection with a specific national or cultural milieu, but because it is connected with all of humanity. Firstly, therefore, we have the principle at work in human evolution that acts in a differentiating way upon humanity, but then, emerging from this differentiation, something that does not belong to it but is distinctive in its independence from national characteristics.

Increasingly it will become apparent, certainly, that the core of the Mystery of Golgotha requires individual understanding. As people increasingly encompass its meaning, they will come to see that whereas earthly conditions, human conditions are of this or that nature the Mystery of Golgotha stands alone and must be understood as something entirely unique and distinctive, whichever field of enquiry we pursue. Today we traced how folk souls affect human life. We can explain everything in terms of these folk souls, from the very beginning of humanity's evolution on earth through to today—except the Mystery of Golgotha and everything connected with it. In all possible fields of enquiry we can ascertain every aspect of human evolution on the one hand, and, distinct from it, the Mystery of Golgotha and its effects. As I have often said in the past,[96] learned theologians today have to admit that no historical evidence exists for the Mystery of Golgotha. It cannot be assigned a place in history. Things are not usually assigned a historical significance where no evidence of their occurrence can be found, and this applies in a singular fashion to the Mystery of Golgotha and all that is connected with it. Nor *ought* there to be material, historical proofs of this event. The Mystery of Golgotha is not meant to be accepted by any person who requires material proofs alone, for it only exerts the right effect on someone who, by inner effort, summons the will to accept the historical validity of something for which there is no material evidence. External proofs of the event of the Mystery of Golgotha will gradually be swept away and vanish as evolution continues; scholarly critique will sweep them away. But a spiritual grasp of human evolution will regard this Mystery of Golgotha, nevertheless, as the nodal point of all earthly occurrences. It has to be grasped spiritually, and accorded its place in the spiritual history of humanity. That is its secret. As time continues, human beings will increasingly seek not for historical evidence but for an understanding that this event, occurring as a physical event on the physical earth, must be grasped by supersensible means, and that only then can we come to fully understand its connection with the historical, earthly evolution of humanity. Next time we will speak further of this.

Lecture 9

BERLIN, 1 APRIL 1918

THE day before yesterday when I tried to describe how human beings are influenced and affected by the geographical location where they live and develop, my primary aim was to paint a vivid picture of the whole earth as an organism, an ensouled and spirit-imbued organism. Like an organism in which each part has its special role—the arms having a different function from the legs, and the heart a different function from the brain—so every part of the soul- and spirit-filled organism of the earth likewise has its distinctive task. We can see the special task of human limbs in their shape; the arms are formed differently from the legs, and the heart differently from the brain. This is not so apparent in physical terms in the case of the earth organism. It will not be clear to a materialistically minded geographer that the diverse continents or regions of the earth have different modes of action, different functions. Only when we can consider the earth's soul and spirit, as it were, can we come to see this. To do so we need to gain a really tangible sense of the earth as an ensouled, spirit-imbued organism, and of the physical human being living upon it as a part of this organism.

This gives rise in turn to various questions, and anyone who thinks that we only have one life, are born and die once, will not make headway with such questions. Physical human beings can only be incorporated into one particular region of the earth at any one time, and if we lived only once we would be fated to adapt specifically to the one region where we lived, and never have any prospect of becoming whole. We would remain confined to one aspect of the earth organism. Insight into the ensouled, spirit-filled nature of the earth, however, in turn shows something very important—that our real, deeper being, which we refer to in saying 'I', cannot be directly but only indirectly connected to this differentiation of humankind in different regions of the globe, and that the soul-spiritual core of our being in a sense only *inhabits* what is differentiated in specific ways in diverse regions. We can therefore gradually acquire insight into the fact that the outward appearance of human beings, as we first perceive it, is not identical with their soul-spiritual core, and that this outward form is really only a dwelling place formed in accordance with distinctive regional conditions. Those already familiar with spiritual science will not find this in the least surprising, and I mention it only to show that a really thorough consideration of regional conditions across the globe could lead people quite rationally towards what spiritual science teaches. It is a most misleading prejudice to say that spiritual science can only be comprehensible to someone who can grasp spiritual realities. This very erroneous idea—that because one cannot perceive clairvoyantly one is right to see spiritual science as something of no concern to humanity, as an unproven hypothesis—allows people to stay in comfortable ignorance. In fact, really thorough and detailed thinking can comprehend spiritual science. Such thinking must be willing to study actual phenomena in the light of what spiritual science states. Someone who takes knowledge available to him about the character and qualities of diverse peoples across the globe and studies this in relation to what spiritual science says about it will soon find that the comments I made last time prove their worth in relation to the phenomena. Realities we encounter must be studied in terms of these insights. We have to be willing to test spiritual-scientific knowledge against actual experience in an open-minded and unprejudiced way, and then rational understanding of any field can lead to a recognition of spiritual science.

This is something of great importance today. And in fact, far more than one thinks, there are esoteric traditions that possess such knowledge, and yet at the same time they often hold fast to a view that was justified until recent times and is still perpetuated—that deeper insights should not be made public. I have often explained the reasons[97] why people who have such knowledge do not wish to share it, but why, also, these reasons no longer hold good today. But there is a difficulty here: firstly one is up against the refusal of most of humanity to countenance spiritual science, and then also meets opposition from those who think it wrong to reveal truths discovered by spiritual science in the same way that other truths are revealed. Those who still think that the veil should not be lifted on certain truths can modify their outlook if they acknowledge important things I stated—albeit in a somewhat theoretical form, but clearly enough as it seems to me—in the foreword and introduction to my book *The Riddle of Man*.[98]

One thing that needs to be understood is that the concept of true or false that most people have nowadays should be overcome. As I have repeatedly stressed, also in my preface to *The Riddle of Man*, the dualism of right or wrong needs to be enlarged by seeing every view as one aspect of truth, like a photograph from one particular angle. If you photograph a tree first from one side and then from another, the second picture shows the same tree as the first, despite looking different. Today, in our modern and abstract age, when people think in such theoretical terms despite regarding themselves as pragmatists, a *single* view of something is thought to be the only true one. People think that they can express the truth in a single idea, and actually this is a form of arrogance. It is arrogant to think, for example, that the Copernican world-view is the only right way to see things and that before Copernicus[99]—no one says this but they do think it—people were like children, or even perhaps cattle, since they did not possess this view of the world. This world-view is right, and other views were wrong, they think. Yet this is something that has to be overcome. Even the Copernican world-view is only one view—a particular way of thinking about the world, of picturing it. There are people who, the moment they notice that spiritual science is putting one view of things, will oppose it with another. In fact, no one who knows there are diverse views of anything will deny this. Nowadays, however, many wish to further their enquiries in a way that can be summed up metaphorically as turning off the light in a room and feeling one's way around it to avoid any single, partisan perspective. This they think will give a true picture of the room as opposed to multiple perspectives. In a sense this is the ideal of modern science: switching the light off and just feeling around in the dark. To counter this, spiritual science has to turn the light on again, and acknowledge all the different possible angles on everything.

We base our efforts on circulating around things and seeing them from many different angles. That has been our aim for years; and in response some may say that the different angles are contradictory. But it is important for us to acknowledge the contradictions since this is what gives us an all-round view of things, which is precisely what we want. It is not a comfortable position of course, for people like best to fit their whole view of the world into a small pamphlet if possible, with as few pages as possible, or make one view the central hub of all their ideas. That of course leads to a narrow perspective, whereas our publications are continually expanding[100] to illumine things from different sides, and to compile a great many views from which a whole picture of reality can emerge. But at the same time, you will understand that we affront people when the truths we discover through a science of the spirit increasingly transgress against their dearly held prejudices. And especially too when we ignore the demands of certain occultists to keep important matters veiled in secrecy. We find ourselves speaking of things that shock, annoy or irritate people, partly at least also because many think something has to be one thing or another, either right or wrong. Instead they ought to see that as humanity evolves there can never be a single status quo, an absolute truth in relation to any field or discipline. We can never say, either, that something is utterly wrong. There is no such thing. It is not to provide some final answer that certain views are emerging now, nor should this mean that we look back on previous generations as childlike. Such views are coming to the fore now for a quite different reason.

Let us recall here something we all know. In the fifteenth century humanity entered the fifth cultural epoch of post-Atlantean development, which we call that of the consciousness soul. In other words, the fifteenth century saw the beginning of what has emerged particularly in this fifth cultural epoch. Until then, humanity's cultural development had been marked chiefly by the rational or mind soul. But for the consciousness soul to emerge, certain thoughts and modes of thinking assumed a very specific form. The Copernican world-view did not arise because it is completely correct—I have often emphasized that it had to arise, and I will continue to emphasize that in certain respects it is appropriate for our times. It did not emerge because it was the only true way of seeing things but because it serves the development of the consciousness soul; we best develop the consciousness soul if we gradually allow the Copernican world-view to become intrinsic to our outlook so that we calculate constellations and planetary movements in the way that happens today.

The positive thing about the Copernican world-view is not that it has finally told us the 'truth' to replace the 'falsehood' of former millennia, but that it erects a spiritual wall between heaven and earth, between the physical and spiritual world. This sounds terribly paradoxical and will of course cause offence to people who have the kinds of prejudice I spoke of earlier. Yet it is true: people began to think of the cosmos in terms of the views of Copernicus because in placing them into this cosmos, the earth's surroundings, it enabled them to erect a spiritual wall through which they could not penetrate. They were shut off from the spirit and were thus able to remain earthbound in their study of the cosmos, thereby developing the consciousness soul. The Copernican world-view was given us so that, in erecting a spiritual wall around the earth, we can confine ourselves in as egotistic a way as possible to earthly things. As the Copernican world-view develops ever more fully, it becomes ever more certain that external investigation of phenomena will sunder us from the world of spirit, and ever more necessary, also, that we rediscover our connection with the spirit through inner vision, by enlivening our inner perception. Strange things go hand in hand. In discussing them, what I say inevitably becomes hard to follow; but since there is no other means of understanding them than through anthroposophy, it is anthroposophists who will have to make strenuous efforts to understand them.

The philosophical discipline based on Kant[101] is today called epistemology. In fact, this epistemology, or theory of knowledge, is a nail in the coffin of human knowledge. One chief idea that commonly springs to most people's minds when they think of the Kantian theory of knowledge is that the 'thing' outside us is really only an ether vibration, something that has nothing to do with colour or tone but that exists as the motion of the smallest particles in space. Outside us the air vibrates tonelessly. These resonances of the air enter our ears—Schopenhauer[102] says somewhat dismissively of the theory of knowledge that they crash on our ears—and then become in us what we call tone. Outside us everything is mute, and only air vibrations exist. Then there are also ether waves outside us that approach our eyes: these waves enter our eyes and an image is created on the retina. But we know nothing about this image unless science studies it. And then these processes—which can only be material in nature—are communicated to the optic nerve and pass on into the visual cortex, where a mysterious thing happens. Here the soul succeeds in making what was first dark and mute outside us, luminous and colourful, warm and cold and so forth, creating things within itself and thus 'dreaming' the whole world.

It is very strange, this path whereby the theory of knowledge seeks to show how the outer world of matter reaches the human mind. But what does this epistemology involve? It is strange that if we stay outside in our surroundings and credit things with possessing tones and colours—which the theory of knowledge regards as the naive realism of the uneducated—we do at least still have a world of tones and colours. But now, in the theory of knowledge, we lead this world towards the eye, say, and now we have an image on the retina, followed by its reproduction in processes affecting the optic nerve. In our brain nothing of the outer world exists, but our inner life magically conjures the whole world out of vibrations. It reminds one of Baron Muenchhausen, who pulls himself up by his own hair! First of all we get rid of everything that constitutes the world and then we have nothing but brain vibrations; and then the soul creates a whole outer world for itself again that we have previously got rid of. Like Muenchausen we take hold of our own hair and raise ourselves upwards. Yet this is the philosophical world-view of our day, and anyone who objects to it is out of step with modern knowledge!

It is odd: in trying to trace how the whole, manifold world enters us we are left ultimately only with processes in the cerebrum which in fact are of the simplest kind, less complex than processes in the optic nerve. If we study how the world exists within us we arrive at something extremely simple; we seek the mind or spirit but arrive only at a spirit that dreams the world into being. Here we have to make a leap of imagination, since no one has yet succeeded in isolating or distilling the mind. In our quest for the human mind we first arrive at brain vibrations and then we are [compelled to recreate all that is no longer there]. This is the path pursued by science in order to trace how the outer world reaches our mind.

On earth we find a multiplicity of conditions and living influences, a great cornucopia that can amaze us. If we study how different people are in different regions—quite irrespective of whether we feel more drawn to some and less to others, which is irrelevant here—and consider the great scope of human differentiation, it is really as manifold as the phenomena of the sensory world itself. In olden times, when people are thought to have been childlike or even animal-like, they tried to understand this great multiplicity by ascending from sensory things to a spiritual realm—something they no longer do. As one ascends ever further from the wealth of phenomena on the earth it seems very much like passing from the external sensory world and passing through the eye and brain to reach the human mind. We arrive at the picture Copernicanism derives from the great, spiritual cosmos. Just as physiological epistemology has resorted to a method in which brain vibrations form a barrier that prevents the outer world reaching the human soul, so in the same way Copernicanism erects a great obstacle to a world of spirit.

If one wishes to test the worth of a world-view, one has to know the point of view that has given rise to it. The perspective of Copernicanism does not replace falsehood with truth but seeks to erect planks and barriers so that humankind can develop the consciousness soul inside this earthly shelter. That is the thing that really counts here. One needs to appraise things with a keen and sober eye. We must first be able to shake the foundations upon which others like to stand so comfortably today with their world-views. Without shaking these foundations we will fail to see that Copernicanism erects barriers to spiritual vision, and will therefore fail to find any relationship with spiritual science. You see, this science of the spirit has certain requirements.

It is worth moving away from an earthly standpoint for a moment and imagining what a merely Copernican world-view means to the cosmos itself: nothing but a mental calculation! Spiritual science, by contrast, needs more than mental calculations; it needs something that opens itself to spiritual perception. Why do we have a field of geology that subscribes to the idea that the earth evolved solely from a purely mineral world? Because the Copernican world-view inevitably led to this—to modern, materialistic geology. It contains nothing that could show us how, looking in from the cosmos, as it were, in a spiritual perspective, the earth can be seen as an ensouled, spirit-imbued being. The universe, conceived on Copernican lines, can only give rise to a dead earth! A living, ensouled and spirit-filled earth has to be conceived from the perspective of a different cosmos altogether—really from a quite different cosmos. Looking back towards earth from the cosmos, we can of course only ever describe certain traits or features of the life of this earth being.

Is this perspective an entirely imaginary one? Is it fantasy to think of the earth from the perspective of the cosmos? No, it is very real. It occurred to Herman Grimm, though having written about it he immediately excused himself with the caveat that this idea was not an article of faith but 'merely fantasy'. In an essay in 1858,[103] he wrote that the human soul liberated from the body might freely encircle the earth and could then look down upon earth to see everything that happens there in a quite different way. He would see things from a quite different perspective, says Herman Grimm, for instance looking into human hearts as 'into a glass beehive'. The thoughts arising in human hearts would emerge as if from a glass beehive! A beautiful image. And then, said Grimm, one could imagine that after floating around the earth for some time and looking down on it from without, the soul would reincarnate upon earth—would have a father and mother, a country and all that exists on earth, and would have to forget all that it had experienced from the cosmic perspective. And if the soul became a historian in the modern sense—Herman Grimm is talking subjectively—he would inevitably have to forget all he had known before, since one cannot write history with that different perspective.

This picture comes very close to the truth. It is true that the human soul floats around the earth, in a sense, between death and a new birth, and looks down upon earth—but in a way determined by karmic connections, as I have often described. The soul certainly has the feeling, then, that this earth is an ensouled and spirit-filled organism, and the prejudice disappears that it is only a geological structure without soul. In after-death vision we see the earth in a highly differentiated way so that, for instance, the Orient appears different in nature from the American Occident. You cannot speak to the dead about the earth in the same way as geologists speak, for they fail to understand geological ideas. When they look down from cosmic space upon the Orient extending from Asia a long way into Russia, the earth in that region appears to them to shimmer with a blue colour, a bluish-purple. The western hemisphere on the other hand, tinged with a more American nuance, appears to them to be a fiery red. That is the polarity they see when they look down on earth from the cosmos. Naturally this does not figure in the Copernican world-view—it is a different kind of perception from a different perspective. If we look from this perspective we realize that the eastern hemisphere of the ensouled earth organism appears different from the western hemisphere: a blue shimmer in the East and, in the West, a blazing up from within and therefore a fiery red appearance. And here you have one example of how, between death and rebirth, we can orient ourselves to what we then learn to perceive. We learn to perceive the configuration of the earth, its different appearance at different places, in terms of the cosmos and of a spiritual perspective: a purplish-blue in one hemisphere and a fiery red in the other. And depending on the spiritual need that we elaborate from our karma, this will have a determining influence on the place where we wish to incarnate again. I am simplifying of course, and things are far more complex in reality; but this does give you a sense of the conditions after death from which a person develops powers that subsequently lead him to incarnate again in a specific corporeality on earth.

I have only described two colours to which destiny is oriented but there are of course others, many more. I will just mention in passing that in the more central region between West and East the earth appears a greener colour, seen from without—green in the regions where we live for instance. Here there is already a threefold quality therefore, and this can give us important insight into the ways in which what we perceive between death and rebirth can become an orientation for us in relation to our decision to be born again in a particular region of the earth.

If we give due attention to such matters we can gradually come to see that certain things never usually considered are at work in the interplay between people embodied here on earth and disembodied souls. When we go abroad and wish to understand people in another country, we have to learn their language, and if we wish to communicate with the dead we also have to gradually learn their language—which is at the same time the language of spiritual science. It is a language spoken, in fact, by all the so-called living and the so-called dead, a bridge spanning from there to here and here to there. It is especially important, when learning this language, to go beyond abstract ideas and form living pictures of the cosmos. Such an image is that of the globe floating in the cosmos, bluish-purple in one area, fiery red and yellow in another, and a green girdle between them. Pictorial ideas gradually bear us into the world of spirit, and this is the important thing. If we are to speak seriously about a world of spirit we naturally have to form these pictorial ideas and, furthermore, not think they are mere figments of the imagination but that they have a reality which can lead us further. So let us conjure this image once again: the eastern hemisphere shimmering blue and purple, and the fiery reddish-yellow western hemisphere, and then much differentiation within this. When a soul looks down between death and rebirth in our current cycle of time he can perceive amidst the purplish-blue shimmer a golden form, a golden crystalline form where Palestine lies, an enlivened place, seen from the perspective of spirit, and this is Jerusalem. In the imaginations of the Apocalypse this is also referred to as the 'heavenly Jerusalem'. These things are not invented, but can be perceived. Seen by the spirit, the Mystery of Golgotha resembles the wonders a modern astronomer may see through his telescope when he sees the sudden flaming of a star. From a spiritual perspective, seen from the cosmos, the event of Golgotha was the flaming up of a golden star in the blue earth aura of the eastern half of the globe. Here you have a vivid picture to accompany what I described at the end of the lecture the day before yesterday. It is very important that we form such vivid pictures of the cosmos so that the human soul can once again find its way feelingly into the spirit of this cosmos.

Trying to accompany the soul of a dead person with this imagination of the gold-shimmering crystalline form of the heavenly Jerusalem within the blue-purple earth aura can bring you closer to him; for this belongs to the imaginations into which we pass at death: Ex Deo nascimur—In Christo morimur!

We can either shut ourselves off from spiritual reality or try to approach closer to it. We shut ourselves off from it when we try to calculate reality numerically. While mathematics is still spirit, pure spirit even, when applied to physical reality it becomes a means to close ourselves off from the spirit. The more you measure and calculate, the more you isolate yourself from the spirit. Kant once said:[104] 'The degree of knowledge in the world is exactly equal to the amount of mathematics in it.' But from a different perspective it would be just as correct to say: 'The darkness in the world is equal to the degree to which people have measured it in their calculations.' We come closer to the life of spirit to the extent that we move on increasingly from external perceptions, especially from abstract ideas, to imaginations, to pictures. Copernicus led us all into ways of calculating the universe. The opposite mode of vision must lead us to imagine the world again, to picture it vividly, to conceive a universe with which the human soul can identify, so that the earth appears within it as a shining sphere—bluish-purple in one hemisphere, with a gold-shimmering heavenly Jerusalem, and a fiery yellowish-red in the other.

Where does the shimmering bluish-purple in the earth aura originate? In looking from without upon this aspect of the globe, its physical nature recedes. The light aura becomes more transparent and the earth's darkness vanishes. This creates the blue colour that shines through—a phenomenon that can be explained in terms of Goethe's theory of colours. But in the western hemisphere, the inner nature of the earth flames up and confirms what I described in my last lecture. In America people are strongly influenced by what comes from below the earth, what is subterranean, and this is why the sparks of a reddish-yellow fire gleam and shine from within the earth, and out into the cosmos, shimmering red and yellow. This picture gives only a faint idea of the reality, but it can show you the possibility of going beyond merely general, abstract ideas about the world we live in between death and rebirth to form very tangible pictures. All such imaginations prepare us to form a stronger connection with worlds of spirit, with the higher hierarchies, with the world in which we live between death and a new birth. Tomorrow I would like to speak a good deal more about this, but today I will just mention one thing in particular.

Our current stage of human evolution, this fifth post-Atlantean epoch which is to serve the development of the consciousness soul, contains many secrets. One of these is especially well concealed by those who think such truths should not be passed on to modern humanity. This is a difficult subject, but since there is no one else anywhere in the world who will give ear to such things, you will have to heed what I am going to say. During our present era, starting with the fifteenth century, a remarkable longing started to surface in human beings. Living initially in the subconscious, it must increasingly be called up into the conscious mind. It is a longing that originates in something very specific.

As I have often said,[105] the human being is a dual being, and also a being with diverse aspects in other ways but a dual being in the sense of a division between the head and the rest of the organism. The head, as I have said,[106] is the aspect of us to which Darwin's theory can be applied especially, since we can trace it back to animal forms. During Old Moon evolution, the human being had animal forms—not those of animals living today but a more spiritual, more etheric animal form which then hardened into the human head. And today, when animals are evolving on the earth into the forms we are familiar with, the human being no longer evolves under the same conditions that once influenced his head development, which he now simply inherits, but under conditions affecting the rest of his organism. But this does not derive from the animals. Our head originates with the animals, albeit only from etheric animals. In our head therefore we bear animality, but of an etheric kind. During the fifth post-Atlantean epoch this dawned on the human subconscious. Increasingly people sensed that there was something of the animal in them, but they were no longer able to picture this spiritually. The idea took root in their heads that man must inevitably feel 'animal-like', and this culminated in Darwin's theory of humanity's descent from the animals. However, this did not just come to expression in Darwin's theory of evolution. Animals perceive things differently from people, having a more intimate connection with the world than we do. The outstanding quality of human beings on earth is due to their capacity to detach themselves from their surroundings, which then necessitates them building a bridge back to all they have sundered themselves from. The animal experiences the outer world within itself far more than we do. If animals were philosophers, they would not speak of the limits of experience since there are none for them in the sense in which people speak of them. These limits come about only through the human being's higher organization. By virtue of the animal group soul, animals sense the whole universe within them and have no awareness of limits to their knowledge. From the fifteenth century, people increasingly felt that they bore an animal within them, but they could not picture this spiritually, supersensibly, etherically, instead regarding themselves as physically related to the animals. Subconsciously they desired the same form of knowledge that the animal possesses. But inevitably this was not possible. The animal lives with the 'thing in itself', whereas this is out of reach for the human being the moment he desires to be an animal, to possess the world as an animal does but knows this cannot be. Perceiving a 'thing in itself' that is unattainable for us arose from the human longing to feel like an animal yet the recognition, at the same time, that we cannot. This is the secret of Kantianism. It is intimately connected with modern humanity's developing awareness of animal nature and of human limits to knowledge. In olden times people knew that there are no limits to the knowledge of an animal, and therefore, for instance, they felt that understanding the language of the animals was a very fortunate gift, as one finds in many old legends.

That was one thing they knew, the people of olden times—that the animal has no limits to knowledge in the sense we are aware of as modern human beings. They knew something else as well, that the beings who belong to the hierarchy of the angeloi are free, are beings of free will; and they knew that we human beings are in the process of becoming angels. When our current stage of Earth evolution is over and is succeeded by Jupiter evolution, the human being will stand at the level of the angels. He is on the way to becoming free. Freedom is developing within him. Yet what will happen in forthcoming times as the consciousness soul gradually develops, if humanity rejects this evolution towards angelic nature? Humanity will be left only with the thought that freedom is an illusion. Human actions will be seen as subject to natural imperatives. Wherever boundaries to knowledge are erected, the development towards freedom is rejected; and this is very closely connected with all that has so far emerged in rough and ready fashion from the idea that we have evolved from animals. In fact our origins are far more complex, as I have tried to show.

Some of the things I have said today were rather difficult to take in. But this was necessary; and tomorrow it will enable us to speak from a particular angle about the connection between modern life on earth in the physical body and life between death and rebirth. Those concepts will be somewhat easier. You have been good enough to attend to me as we spoke of more difficult ideas, and tomorrow this will help us in relation to other ones.

LECTURE 10

BERLIN, 2 APRIL 1918

WITH the ideas I elaborated yesterday I was especially keen to show the need, at our current phase of evolution, for new concepts or at least ones that are not yet generally available, so that they can begin to inform our cultural horizons. Human culture requires certain ideas that are either not yet there or not accessible. It is very important that this should happen. If we study the diverse aspects of modern culture we find that, despite all pride and arrogance that sometimes figures there, it has not produced any new ideas. Many diverse views exist in ethical, artistic, philosophical or scientific disciplines but they all, nevertheless, draw on old ideas that have been around a long time, which are then simply thrown together as if in a kaleidoscope and churned out again. We need new ideas. We lack precisely the kind of new ideas that we need; and this is why, for instance, certain ancient truths are no longer understood—truths that surfaced among the ancients and have been passed down to us, ideas such as those figuring, at the latest date, in Plato[107] or Aristotle.[108] In still earlier times such ideas were even more incisive. Nowadays, though, they are either not understood or rejected, or rejected because they are not understood. Let me give you an example of one such idea.

When a person sees an object today he thinks the object is outside him and that he can see it due to the light that passively—one cannot say mysteriously—enters his eye from it, engendering what the soul senses as colour for instance. Plato has a different idea.[109] Here we encounter something which, if we take it literally, we can only understand as meaning that the human eye sends out something that mysteriously grasps hold of the object. It is as if the eyes extend feelers to grasp the object. This is what Plato writes. Modern scientific views cannot make anything of this of course. It is an idea that you can find recorded in scholarly books on the history of philosophy, but you cannot make much headway with such books because such ideas are based on something that existed in ancient times and has now faded—a certain atavistic clairvoyance or clairsentience. In our time we need to rediscover this in a different way. Since ancient times, you see, ideas have been lost that we need to reacquire.

They were lost, in particular, due to the Roman culture that poured across Europe, especially western Europe. Proper study of this Roman culture in its spread across Europe would be very illuminating. We need to realize that there is nothing left now in Italy of this ancient Roman influence, and whatever else they may be responsible for, modern Italians have no part in what I am going to say. The spread of Roman culture through Europe had a really devastating and pulverizing effect on certain fundamental ideas—ones that now need to be brought back to life. We need think only, for instance, of the destruction of the town of Alesia[110] shortly before Christ's birth. Situated in what is now the Côte d'Or region of France, this centre of ancient Celtic-Gallic culture was eradicated by the Romans. Napoleon the Third[111] erected a monument to Vercingetorix[112] at the site of this old town of Alesia, a centre of ancient Celtic, Druidic culture which Caesar[113] destroyed. It was a place of great learning; ten thousand Europeans studied there, in the way people studied in those times. All this was eradicated and replaced by Roman culture. This is merely a historical observation which can show that in Europe, too, influential ideas of a more ancient kind existed in ancient cultural centres, and were eradicated.

Today I chiefly want to focus on two ideas that need to be incorporated into scientific enquiry and life in general if a better understanding of the world is to arise. The first is to understand how we really perceive the world with our senses, which happens in the following way.

Whenever we see a coloured object before us, while it is true that this acts upon us, there is also a process of destruction at work in the human organism intervening between ourselves and the coloured object. I have often described this;[114] a kind of small death occurs, with our nervous system as the organ for ongoing breakdown processes. The blood however balances and counteracts these destructive processes caused by the outer world impinging upon our organism. In the human organism there is a mutual interaction continually at work between blood and nerve, and this interplay involves an enlivening process from the blood on the one hand and a kind of death process from the nervous system on the other. As we perceive a coloured object in the external world and this impinges on us, a process of destruction takes place in our neural system; something is destroyed both in the physical body and in the ether body. A kind of channel is bored through our organism due to a process of destruction that runs in a quite specific direction. When we see something, a channel is bored from our eye to our brain. Rather than something dissolving its way through from the brain to the eye, it is the opposite: a hole is bored and through this the astral body slips in, in order to be able to see whatever the object is. Plato still knew this. It could be seen by ancient atavistic clairvoyance, and we will have to reacquire such knowledge by really getting to know the human organism again through modern clairvoyance, discovering this channel that arises, this hole where a tunnel is bored from the eye to the brain by means of which the I unites with what impinges from without. Humanity has to learn to form different concepts from those common today in modern epistemology or physiology, instead seeing that a channel or tunnel is bored from the eye to the brain and through this the astral body and I connect and engage with the outer world. This is alien to modern ideas, and therefore people are likewise unaware of the physiological factors that follow from this. Nowadays students at university learn all the received wisdom about physiology but never anything about how things are in reality. What they learn is meaningless.

Another such concept is one you commonly find today in modern academic discourse. Human development is described there in these terms: we are born as undeveloped creatures, and then our psyche and mind slowly develop, coming to expression slowly through our organism as it grows more complex and refined. This view appears everywhere today amongst psychologists and academics in general, and also in books for the general public. People can relate to this idea, which seems highly probable. But it is all only appearance, maya. In many respects this is actually the opposite of the truth, the opposite of what really occurs. Instead—and here I need only refer you to what I described in *The Education of the Child*,[115] though expressed in a slightly different way there—we should understand that in infancy the soul and spirit are still of the nature of soul and spirit, and, as the child develops, these gradually transform into material configuration, into the body. Gradually a person becomes a full picture or reflection of soul and spirit. It is very important to have this insight. If we have it, we will no longer regard what runs around on two legs on the ground as the 'human being' but will see that this is a reflection or image of the human being, and that when we are born in supersensible terms we gradually grow together with the body and create a full image or reflection of soul and spirit. Soul and spirit vanish into the body and manifest less and less in their own right. In other words, we need the very opposite idea from the one commonly regarded as true. We need to know that we become, say, 20 years old by virtue of the spirit descending into and being subsumed by the body, the spirit transforming into the body since the body itself is an external image of the spirit. Then we will also see that gradually, as we age, a reverse transformation occurs. The body calcifies and hardens, but the spirit becomes ever more soul-spiritual in nature. We cannot hold fast to it however because it is at odds with the physical world and seeks to express itself through the physical body. The spirit becomes ever more autonomous and only comes to full manifestation after death. So you see, it is not that the spirit and soul gradually wane and grow dull as we age but the opposite: they become ever freer again. Naturally a materialistic thinker faced with this idea will very often object that Kant, for example, a very clever man, lost his faculties when old; and so it can scarcely be true to say that spirit and soul were emancipating themselves. But such objections are made only because a materialist cannot perceive or take any account of the spirit and soul that has gradually grown into the world of spirit. It will be a hard nut for many to crack to think that as we grow older we do not actually grow feeble-minded but more spiritual. It is just that the body has worn out and the soul and spirit we have developed cannot be expressed through the body any more. It is like a piano player who might go on and on developing his skills, but if the piano is worn out and broken it will be hard to discern this. You won't perceive much of his skills if the piano is out of tune and there are several strings missing. In old age Kant, though apparently feeble-minded, had actually become glorious for the world of spirit.

To discover reality we sometimes have to turn received wisdom on its head. We have to give real credence to the view that what is at work in the world in this respect is maya, a grand illusion. If we become aware of this great illusion of maya, we will start to be able to properly acknowledge that the appearance of weakness and feeble-mindedness in outer physical terms in a person 70 years of age is deceptive, and that his spirit is just elsewhere than on the physical plane. Obstacles to understanding spiritual science often consist in our inability to form appropriate ideas about what happens on the ordinary physical plane. We form erroneous ideas about what happens here, and these mistaken concepts sunder us from reality, prevent us reaching it. But if we develop concepts such as the one I just described, we will come much closer to the knowledge which spiritual scientific research discovers in relation to what happens immediately after death.

Entering into physical life at birth, we gradually and increasingly come into relationship with our physical body. You have now heard the right way to view this relationship. There is always so much to say that sometimes we fail to consider the fact that something similar also occurs between death and rebirth. Here we likewise engage in a relationship with something that resembles our increasing connection with the physical body here on earth. Our physical corporeality is not merely physical corporeality but as we know it encompasses the physical body, the etheric body or body of formative forces, and the astral body or outward soul, the soul body. Just as, in physical life here, we have to appropriate these three vessels or aspects, we likewise have to appropriate three vessels in the time between death and a following rebirth. To ensure these are not confused with anything else, I will name them here. They are: the soul human, soul life or life soul, and the soul self. In the same way that we here appropriate the physical body for life in the physical world, so after death we appropriate the soul human; and likewise the life soul corresponds to the ether body or body of formative forces, and the soul self or individual soul corresponds to the astral or soul body we acquire here. I have chosen these terms so that they are not confused with what humankind will acquire in a different way in the Jupiter, Venus and Vulcan stages of evolution, which will be similar but, since a different phase of existence is involved there, has to be distinguished carefully. The terms themselves do not matter. What we need to do is enquire a little into how these vessels are appropriated after death.

After entering upon the life that unfolds between death and rebirth, we are initially surrounded by a composite of pictures that originate in our experiences during the life that has just ended or also from still earlier experiences. But for now let us stay with the experiences of our previous life, which arise for us as pictures surrounding us. It is important to realize that these pictures are in our surroundings after death and, remarkably, that we find it somewhat difficult to realize they belong to us. What I described in *Theosophy*[116] as our experiences in the soul world, a recapitulation of our life in pictures, is only a part of this whole world of pictures. Apart from those there are others. And our life after death involves gradual recognition that these images belong to us. Our consciousness engages with these pictures in order to recognize in the right way that they belong to us.

We can only fully understand what this involves if we realize that our life here between birth and death is far richer than only our conscious life. We live in certain conditions and relationships, in community with certain other people. What happens between us and plays a conscious part in our lives is only a part of this. Things continually occur—you have to recognize that we are consciously aware only of a small part of what we experience in our life unfolding here on earth. Let us take an ordinary event. You have gathered here this evening, and every person here has therefore entered into some kind of interaction with every other. But if you try to discern how much of these interrelationships you are conscious of, it will be very little. If you are at a distance of three metres from someone, and then approach him, this approach involves a whole sum of facial expressions: how you see a person's face changes continually as you come closer to him. Our ordinary physical reason cannot possibly trace in thought everything we actually experience during physical life. What we consciously experience is only a small portion, and what remains subconscious is far more significant.

When you read a letter, for instance, you are usually aware of its content; but much more is going on in the depths of your soul. Without being aware of it, you are mildly annoyed or gladdened by the beautiful or ugly handwriting. But more than this, something of the writer actually enters into you without you being aware of this with every letter of his handwriting. This lives in you like a dream continually infusing your life. This is why we find it so difficult to really understand dreams—because they manifest a great deal of what we overlook in our ordinary awareness. Assume that one lady is sitting here and over there another. If the attention of one of them is not drawn to the fact that another lady is sitting over there, she does not observe her more closely, she can fail entirely to become aware of her gestures and whatever else she does. Yet this takes root in the subconscious, and what we paid scarcely any attention to in waking life can enter our dreams. Or imagine you are wrapped in your own thoughts when a friend passes you by without you noticing him at all perhaps. And then you dream of him, despite being unaware that you passed him in the street. A very great deal occurs in life, and so little of it enters our waking consciousness. Yet all these manifold occurrences in life that remain in our subconscious become images around us. Coming here tonight and going away again later, the image of this whole room will stay with you, although only in so far as it has all made some kind of impression on your soul. There are no demarcated boundaries where soul impressions are concerned.

Human life is therefore associated with the creation of countless pictures and images. All of them—I can think of no other expression—are rolled up in human life. And the first thing that happens after death is the unfurling of these pictures, as one could call it, the unrolling of pictures, of post-mortem imaginations. Around the human soul a world of imaginations gradually forms, and our consciousness then consists of our perception of this world of pictures.

I described this from a somewhat different perspective in my Vienna lectures on life between death and rebirth.[117] It is important to consider these things from various different angles. This unfurling of images can be compared in a way with what happens when we are young children, have just been born, when our body is as yet largely unformed. People other than mothers sometimes think an infant resembles a frog—not yet fully human. It gradually takes shape and form. And just as we gradually assume clearer form as we grow older, so that something we bear within us becomes materially manifest, so in the same way a life grows after death that we can describe as the unfurling of images of our life. In this unfurling or unrolling, the aspect of our nature we called the soul human assumes form. You have to picture that what exists of us after death is spread out, and that in the imaginations of our past life the soul human initially grows: the human being of images, the developing spirit corporeality consisting of Imaginations.

Here again we can offer enormous help to the dead if we accompany them with such ideas which are, at the same time, those of spiritual science, or such images as we elaborated yesterday of the bluish-purple earth with the golden Jerusalem. These are pictures that the dead soul longs for, for he thirsts for orienting and ordering imaginations. This gives him real support and help. We help him especially if we accompany him with thoughts of what we have experienced with him, as a point of reference for this unfurling of images. It is especially beneficial if we accompany him with thoughts of things in life that were scarcely noticed at the time. Picture, for instance, if you can recall it, how a person entered the house on his return from work, how you welcomed him, and the soul quality coming to expression in this greeting. Such things can contain an infinitely loving quality, though also other quite different qualities too of course. In doing this you will meet the dead person in thought. I have described all kinds of ways[118] in which we can mingle our own thoughts with this world of pictures within which the dead soul has to develop, within which his consciousness has to spread and unfurl. Ideas which the dead soul strove for but was unable to attain fully, and that explain something to him, become his world of pictures. And here we can help him, collaborate with him in forming his soul human aspect.

In the period following death, of course, the other aspects are also present and developing: the soul life or life soul, and also the soul self. These aspects, in particular, develop increasingly and assume increasing definition so that the dead soul immediately after death feels them to be future potential in him, something he only slowly develops. In this respect the dead person has the sense that he has to elaborate the soul human, has to work to develop it, but that the life soul is something he must just allow to develop, which emerges gradually of itself. It is of course already present just as the power of reason is innate in a child, but like this too it has to develop gradually. Immediately after death, an inspiring power arises in the dead soul in consequence, and develops to become ever stronger. If we help the dead soul as described we also help him to develop this inspiring power. You see, something must gradually come to speak to the dead soul from these pictures. They have to become more than a mere memory of the life that has passed, must convey something new to him that life was not yet able to convey to him. What they now tell him must become the seed or germ of what he shapes as his next life on earth.

Thus the life soul begins to develop, and the pictures become ever more eloquent. Initially the dead person directs his gaze—if I can put it like that—to the earth primarily. Just as we direct our thoughts upwards to the world of spirit, so the dead person always orients his soul to the earth. For instance he sees, as I described yesterday, an earth globe whose eastern hemisphere is bluish, and whose western hemisphere is reddish in colour. These pictures appear and are interwoven with him. Within the general picture of the earth he initially sees his own life, his life with us on earth. And this is also why we can help him to make sense of these pictures. He has departed from the earth but does not yet leave it with his eye of soul. And gradually the earth starts to resound for him, as Inspiration increasingly develops. The pictures he sees gradually tell him more and more.

People often ask me whether this help given to the dead can only be given soon after death or whether one can still offer it years or decades later. The need for such help never ends. No one can live so long on the earth that it becomes unnecessary to help someone who has died before him. Even if someone has been dead for 30 or 40 years, the karmic connection remains. Of course we should remember, though, that if the soul of the person still alive on earth is less developed, he will have a more vivid awareness of his connection with the dead soul to begin with—it can be felt very strongly to start with since the pictures then still arise more passively [in the dead soul] and mostly relate to what he did on earth. Then these pictures start to resound—the music of the spheres sounds forth from them. This is harder for those on earth to relate to, and we can only gain insight into it through spiritual science by knowing what will happen in future epochs of the earth. But after all it is not very common for people to feel the need to come close to the dead person over decades compared with their feelings immediately after his death. Experience shows that as living people we grow less and less attached to the dead and our living feeling for them fades, and this is at least partly why our connection with the dead becomes less strongly felt as time passes.

This can show us that the first period of life between death and rebirth is primarily given up to developing the soul human, to what hovers round us as a world of Imaginations. Later on—though this also exists from the beginning—we turn our attention to the inspiring power of the soul, to the life soul. And then the soul self also stands before the dead soul like an ideal. This too is present from the outset, since it is what gives us individual consciousness. Just as the power of reason needs to develop through childhood although it exists innately from the beginning, so between death and rebirth we develop the soul self. To a very large degree it is developed in the period during which we gradually approach a new life on earth again. When we start blooming with spiritual youth in the period between death and rebirth, our soul self has reached the culmination of its development. On earth we gradually age whereas in the world of spirit between death and rebirth we grow young again. Here we grow grey with age, and there we grow ever more youthful. Not so very long ago people knew such things. One need only remember the phrase in Goethe's *Faust*, 'grown young in the misty age',[119] which refers to being born in the northern world. In the old days people did not speak of being born but of 'becoming young', and this referred to a person's life before birth. Goethe picked up on this expression.

In the last period of the time between death and rebirth, the soul therefore chiefly develops the power of Intuition. In the first period, the imaginative aspect of the soul came alive, that is, the soul human. Then the inspired aspect of the soul, the life soul, gradually emerges to its full extent. And following this, there develops what gives the soul its full individuality, the capacity of Intuition, the ability to find one's way into other realities. What does the soul find its way into here? Of what does it chiefly receive intuitions?

At a certain point in the life between death and rebirth, the soul starts to feel an affinity with the succession of generations that eventually leads to a father and mother for the next life. The soul gradually develops this affinity with ancestors who marry, to their children and so on. Immediately after death we experience the pictures as these unfurl; we look down upon earth and these pictures together compose greater pictorial contexts in the imaginative realm. When we are approaching a new life on earth again, we become ever more intuitive. And here we have a broader, more all-encompassing picture as I described it yesterday: the earth's sphere shimmering blue across Asia, India, east Africa; and glittering red in the other hemisphere where America lies, with green and other colour tones between these two areas. And now the earth also resounds in a wealth of tones: the melodies, harmonies and choirs of the music of the spheres. Gradually this is interfused with the pictures one had previously of the generational line of descent. Gradually we come to discern the thirty-sixth then the thirty-fifth pair of ancestors, the thirty-fourth, the thirty-third, the thirty-second and so on down to one's future mother and father. We come to discern this, interwoven into our Imaginations informed by Intuition, until we arrive at our mother and father. This Intuition is really a process of being subsumed in what lives in the line of descent. Thus the second half of our life between death and rebirth is one in which we accustom ourselves to live ever more fully in what is occurring below, to live in this otherness already in a prefiguring way, in what will become both our closer and further surroundings; instead of living in ourselves now, we live in what is other than us. We embark on the life between death and new birth by living in what is other than us, and come to the end of it by primarily also being able to live in what is other. Then we are born and initially retain something of this otherness. This is why we are imitators in our first seven years: we imitate everything we perceive. Read what I presented in *The Education of the Child in the Light of Spiritual Science*. This imitation is a last echo of living in what is other than us, which continues into our physical life. This is the primary quality, understood spiritually, in the life between death and rebirth and likewise the first characteristic that emerges in the young child: imitation of what is around us. We will fail to understand the capacity for imitation in the child if we do not know that it originates in the grandiose intuitive life of soul and spirit in the latter period of our life between death and rebirth.

Here again we have an idea that will be important for future spiritual development to encompass. In ancient times, primarily by virtue of knowing the spirit through atavistic clairvoyance, direct vision instilled a belief in immortality, which people now regard as very dubious if they think materialistically. In former times they had knowledge of it. But in future the idea of immortality will be invoked from the opposite direction; people will come to see that this life here on earth is the continuation of a life of spirit. In the same way that people used to regard a continuation of life after death as self-evident, in future they will increasingly come to see all life here as a continuation of the life between death and rebirth. The churches have all put obstacles in the way of this insight into the pre-existence of the soul, which they consider heretical. As we know, the Church Father Origen[120] had a poor reputation particularly because he still recognized this truth. In the ninth century, as I have said before,[121] the Ecumenical Council of Constantinople 'abolished' the spirit by establishing the dogma that human beings consist only of body and soul, without spirit, though they accorded the soul some spiritual quality. The Council prohibited people from regarding the human being as constituted of body, soul and spirit. Naturally this prohibition still remains but something else has become associated with it: our 'unprejudiced science' has adopted this schema! It is very interesting. Modern philosophers commonly divide human nature into body and psyche, and very rarely is there any mention of a threefold body, soul and spirit. If you read the renowned philosopher and psychologist Wundt[122] you can find that such 'unprejudiced empiricism' divides human nature into body and soul alone. But it is not unprejudiced! It is the last vestige of the dogma established by the Eighth Ecumenical Council. Philosophers have forgotten this and regard their enquiries as unprejudiced. So here we have one obstacle—

the abolition of the spirit. The other barrier, erected by the Church, is its forbidding of the belief in the soul's pre-existence. Even unprejudiced people cannot countenance this belief in pre-existence. There was a famous philosopher-theologian or theological philosopher—whichever way round you like—called Frohschammer,[123] in Munich, who attacked the idea of the soul's pre-existence by saying this: If the soul really existed before birth and was not born at the same time as the body, the child's parents would engender a little animal which then acquired a soul. He thought this a very worrying idea—I cited it in notes to my *Riddles of the Soul*.[124] But that is not how it is either. If we know that the soul connects with a bloodline for over 30 generations before birth, we cannot say that the parents conceive a little animal. There is a whole spiritual process involved, running through more than 30 generations.

In future therefore we will not ask only whether this life continues beyond death but, by a proper study of physical life on earth, will come to see that our physical life, beginning at birth, is a continuation of a life of spirit! People will recognize that spiritual life continues into mortal life, and mortal life into immortal life; and by discerning the one within the other they will then have a sure basis for studying immortality. When people come to understand this life on earth in the right way, they will cease to try to understand it solely in terms of physical existence but will inevitably acquire other ideas in addition, such as those I have now described.

Oh, there are a great many ideas that need to be corrected. Ideas that hold true in life are often very hard to acquire, and modern vernacular can be a great obstacle here. We have to use popular language initially because otherwise no one will understand us; but it is very problematic to think that a child acquires his resemblance to his parents by direct inheritance. That is nonsense. In the public lecture[125] I also said that our mainstream scientists struggle a great deal by failing to apply to the organic realm what is self-evident in inorganic science. No one would dream of explaining magnetic force by saying that it resides in a piece of iron itself, a horseshoe say. Magnetism in a magnet or in a magnetic needle is explained in relation to the magnetic poles of the earth. But when an egg forms in a chicken, or a human embryo develops, people stop looking further afield for an explanation. And yet the cosmos is everywhere involved in such processes. However strange it seems, in the same way that in visual perception a channel is bored into the eye to open a passage for the I and allow it to emerge, reproduction is founded on the fact that space is created. The mother's organism is prepared in a way that creates space there, and what then develops enters from the cosmos, from the whole macrocosm. It is a complex process, but a space is created in the mother; the mother's organism is interrupted to create a cavity where the macrocosmic powers can enter. That is the important thing, and before long even mainstream embryology will come to see this, understanding that the most important part of the embryo is where there is nothing, where the matter constituting the mother is repulsed to allow the macrocosm to enter. This macrocosmic element is long prepared, the human soul intuitively accompanying ancestors of its future body for, at most, 32 to 35 generations. The soul is already connected with these powers working in from the cosmos, can already perceive them. From the zodiac realm he is assigned to he watches the macrocosmic ray fall upon earth and observes where he will be incarnated. And then he gradually approaches the earth.

These things, I believe, can also make an important impression on our sensibility. One cannot assimilate spiritual science in the same way as, say, mathematics. We have to unite our heart and mind deeply with it, and in reality this makes us into a different person, profoundly enriching human life and creating the foundation for a really cosmic consciousness. This enlivening effect of spiritual-scientific perception, refreshing in the best sense of the word, is of key importance. At the same time we should be aware that in the current age we find ourselves in a kind of transitional period in relation to these things, and this is the karma our era must take upon itself. People tend to object to assimilating what they consider very complex ideas in order to engage with an anthroposophic view of human destiny. Others, they say, make things plainer and simpler. Certainly, someone like Dr Johannes Mueller[126] makes things nice and simple. But the point is that we are living in a period of transition, and that these ideas are still unaccustomed ones in our day and age. We must accustom ourselves to them. The time will inevitably come when children, already, are taught such things, though in a suitable form. This will be possible, and in doing so people will discover that children will understand them surprisingly well. Much better than others, they will understand what is drawn from the pictures spiritual science presents. You see, they bring with them, as capacity of imitation they possess in the world of spirit, diverse qualities which we then expunge from their souls, which we fail to acknowledge, sometimes quite brutally dismissing them. Otherwise people would admit that some children say remarkably intelligent things, can often be far more insightful than adults. What a child says can sometimes be far more interesting, more closely connected to the real nature of the world than what a university professor says. The insights of spiritual science need to be assimilated with a certain sensibility, a certain ethos, and then it will not be difficult to present them to children in a fitting way. Naturally this can feel uncomfortable initially, which is why people dismiss such things, But if we really attend to the place children's questions are coming from, their *timbre*, we will see that they possess recollections of another life.

We have to give serious credence to spiritual science, seeing that it must also find its way into the life of society, to which upbringing and education likewise belong. A great deal more could be done in this respect than is usually thought possible. Nowadays prospective teachers are tested to see primarily what knowledge they have, although this is the thing least necessary to their profession. Whatever they need for their teaching can always be read up somewhere; and whatever one studies and learns for exams is always swiftly forgotten. You can see what I mean if I recount an anecdote from my own college days. I was due to be examined but the professor in question was ill at the time. I went to the assistant professor and he told me that I would have to wait a week to be examined, and expressed his sympathy for my 'condition' which he likened to that of a pregnant woman. He said: 'I know what it's like—you will have forgotten it all in a week. But I'm sorry, there's nothing to be done.' It is therefore common knowledge that all one is supposed to have learned for an exam will be forgotten soon afterwards; it is really very comical. The important thing in a teacher, instead, is to see what kind of person is being unleashed on our children. Instead of focusing on what a person has crammed into the mechanism of his memory and thinking, we should look for the human being in him. The real human being is what counts in teaching—someone who is capable of creating the imponderable relationship with young people that is so necessary. It will then be an easy matter to present to children and young people the aspects of spiritual science that can benefit them.

Today I chiefly wanted to draw your attention to realities at work in all human life to show that the old concepts are not enough, that we need new ones to enrich our view of the world. When spiritual science is disseminated more widely you will see what kind of response it meets with in many quarters. People have been longing for something like it for a long time. Most people dislike absorbing too many ideas at once, which is why they like going to slide shows or illustrated presentations, where they can simply stare rather than absorbing new ideas. Whenever something new is presented to people they usually wonder what on earth the speaker is going on about, and wish he would 'translate' what he is saying into terms they are already familiar with. This is not what we are doing in the science of the spirit, where new ideas and concepts are needed, ones that do not yet exist. Some of them existed in olden times, in different forms, but have not yet reappeared in a modern form. We have to resolve to penetrate new ideas, and this is often very difficult for people. If they really did so, they would not object so vociferously but would really attend to such ideas and assimilate them. Instead of asking what on earth an anthroposophical speaker is going on about, they would realize that such views we form also release life forces in us and enable us to enter into reality. They would see that spiritual vision, though subtle, is something much closer to them than they think. But prejudices will have to be overcome for them to get to that point.

There is, for instance, a popular little book entitled *Introduction to Philosophy*,[127] expounding concepts such as those I described, today and yesterday, as inadequate. The author enters especially strange territory when he speaks of 'supernaturalism', his word for the supersensible. He regards this idea as particularly harmful because, he says, the natural realm is one where we can all form and test our own views whereas in the supersensible realm, the supernatural, there is a danger that people cannot judge things for themselves but must take things on the authority of others. This is of course connected with another idea—that in all ages priests have exploited such power to make people dependent on their authority. But if we consider the actual circumstances we find that mainstream philosophers actually become rather childish when they start speaking of the supersensible. This is a childish or childlike view, for it seems the author here has no idea that the belief in authority still remains very prevalent today, however much people wish to distance themselves from it. How many people actually know, for instance, what the teachings of Copernicus are based on? These ideas are presented to them as if a person were given a chair to sit on out in the cosmos somewhere, and shown the motions of the sun with the planets circling around it. But all this is nonsense. If people were shown all that could really be disclosed to them, they would form a quite different idea of things, and would come to see how unsound all such hypotheses are. Consider the huge scope of what people today simply take on authority. In another area, though this is a related phenomenon, people are very pleased when a Bolshevik government discloses to the public secret files upon which the fate of countless people depend! Here is a natural fact that all can check; but in relation to the supersensible, they think people will lose their independence. This is to turn things on their head. And one task of spiritual science will be to put things the right way up again. It is inevitable that things have been turned upside down, for the consciousness soul needed to develop. But now it is time to set things the right way up again.

We will pick up on this again next time, and will see that this picture of setting things the right way up, standing them on their legs again, actually also has a deeper reality.

Lecture 11

BERLIN, 9 APRIL 1918

As I have often said in recent lectures,[128] throughout human evolution esoteric truths have always been available to certain individuals, albeit by drawing on sources other than ours. However, such individuals made very certain that these truths were not communicated to people who were not initiated into esoteric mysteries, but were carefully guarded. As we know, traditions are perpetuated even when they lose their meaning and justification as humanity in general develops. Today, certain truths are still kept a closely guarded secret by those aware of them. And yet many such things ought no longer to remain concealed but, like other scientific truths, must be made available to humanity in general.

While this can only be done in relation to certain basic ideas, where these are concerned it must happen. Matters we have been discussing for a long time now include some of these carefully guarded truths and insights. The spirit of our enquiries makes it necessary for us to continue to delve into these secrets. Those who receive them, to whom they are communicated in a simple form, need to recognize from their very nature that they must be treated with great seriousness, with a certain degree of reverence. You see, part of the reason that initiates today are reluctant to communicate such truths is a prevailing lack of reverence for the truth in modern humanity. It is of course hard to summon much reverence for the supposed truths of a modern materialistic outlook, and not much harm is done, at least apparently, by meeting such things without reverence. But certain matters do have to be handled with respect and reverence if they are to properly find their way into general human culture.

Here I would include knowledge about the human being himself. These insights may seem fairly simple to begin with, but are in fact of very great scope and import. Our recent observations, in particular, concerned ultimately with the connection between our life here in a physical body and life between death and rebirth, relate to a great deal that is of intimate significance for our understanding of human nature. Today therefore let us first focus our spiritual gaze on things we have already spoken about from other perspectives. We will do so now only from a certain angle, in a way that can allow us to pick up the thread of themes we have been addressing in these lectures.

As you know, modern science sees the human being in very close proximity to the animals, failing, as we have stressed,[129] to consider what distinguishes us from them. For instance, it highlights the great resemblance between the shape of bones in the human being and in animals, a great similarity in their shape and morphology. This is correct, but fails to discern the most important thing. As I described last winter in a public lecture,[130] if we approach human life with the necessary reverence and depth, fully pondering on the very significant difference that exists between a person alive on earth and a human corpse, we can discern a mystery, a secret, in this impression of polarity between the living person and the corpse. The first thing that can strike us is that powers of external nature, to which the body was not subject from conception or birth through to death, now lay claim to the corpse. The living person was not touched by these forces due to the living, feeling entity connected with the substances constituting the body. If we trace in thoughts what happens to the corpse, irrespective of whether it is cremated or decomposes more slowly, we can see that the processes involved are basically the same, just occur at different speeds. The substances cohering in the living person dissolve, either slower or faster, into the substances at work in the whole earth. With our ordinary senses and thinking we can trace everything that happens to the parts and substances of a corpse.

The spiritual scientist however can take these observations further, finding that substances in the corpse immediately after death gradually transform into a vast field of substances. Naturally this takes hundreds of years, but the substances of the corpse dissolve slowly into a vast complex of substances, into the totality of what constitutes our whole visible, externally perceptible world.

Now it is interesting to study the connection between our I consciousness here in physical life and this decomposing corpse, which strangely are related to each other in a certain way. When I say 'I consciousness' I naturally do not mean our real, actual I since this passes through the gate of death and continues to live between death and rebirth. But the picture of the I as it hovers before us here in physical life—since we do not have consciousness of the I as such but possess only a picture of the I in our consciousness—is bound to the body, to the corpse, and in particular to the complex of substances that gradually dissolves into the universe after death. This dissolution of the corpse into the universe is nothing other than the outward picture of our whole I consciousness, for in reality this consciousness belongs to the universe into which the corpse resolves. The self-evident perspective we have during our life, that we exist within the confines of our skin—which an esotericist regards, actually, as a very peculiar notion—is due only to the fact that the substances of our body cohere between birth and death. We always ascribe our existence to the fact that we fill this defined space with our flesh and blood. Actually this is absurd—we are not here at all. In reality we are everywhere and, during sleep, try in fact to spread out wherever the substance particles of our body will be after death. During our lifetime we have the illusory sense that we exist in a particular spatial context defined by our skin. Actually this is a *maya* which we learn; and among the many other things death is, it is also the refutation of this illusory consciousness of the physical, material world. Death bears the particles of our corpse to where our I consciousness in fact always dwells. This has far-reaching importance.

But now we can ask what it is that after death carries our I consciousness, and its outward image, the particles of our body, out into the wide world? What forces are they?

There are three forces involved, and we can try to gain an idea of them as follows.

The first manifests during our life by virtue of the fact that we crawl on all fours in our earliest infancy and subsequently stand vertically. We only gradually find an upright orientation, a vertical alignment. As we transform ourselves from the crawling infant into an upright person, we follow a particular force orientation into which we place ourselves and with which we identify. In terms of spiritual science, this direction of force is very clearly visible in us. A line runs through us from below, passing from the earth's centre out into the universe. In ancient times this line passing from the earth's centre into the universe was described as different for each person and even at every moment in time, and yet it was always seen as passing outwards into the universe from the centre of the earth. That is one of the important lines of force in the human being. It acts only for as long as this physical life of ours lasts, for the physical gravity of our body holds it in balance. The moment this physical gravity is no longer working as it did on the living body, that is, at the moment this body becomes a corpse, this line of force passing from the centre of the earth out into the universe starts to disperse and bear away the particles of our body. Naturally they are driven further by their own gravity; but if we were to observe what happens with these particles for a long enough time, we would find that they disperse in the direction in which this force carries them, even if this takes centuries.

The second force we must consider here is one that primarily comes to expression in human speech. As we speak, there is a certain impetus in our articulated language. It imparts a certain momentum to the air we exhale. The spiritual scientist sees this power as one that winds itself around the first. Basically it has a spiral form, encircling this vertical line. It is a force that modifies the purely dispersing trajectory of the other and imparts momentum to it. But as well as this second force there is also a third, originating in the following. Whereas speaking develops a certain outward momentum, thinking—which is what distinguishes us from the animals—opposes this power coming to expression in speech. Here we have the third force. If we were to draw this, it could be like this [see drawing]. By these three powers, the vertical trajectory, the power at work in speech and the one at work in thinking, the particles of the human corpse are gradually guided out into the universe. Of course gravity opposes them, and other forces, chemical ones for instance. But these three powers overcome what counteracts them.

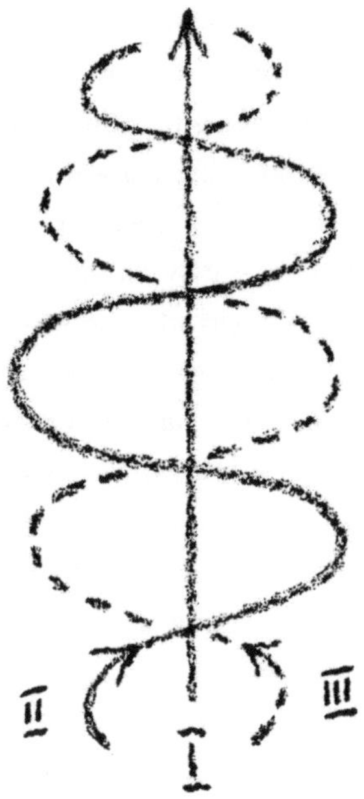

These three forces that cohere during our physical life when we stand on two legs are emancipated and disperse the form that was previously held together. What we call the ether body or body of formative forces also especially follows the direction of these three forces after death. This happens a few days after death and we have often described it as the dissolution of the ether body. The dispersal and dissolution of the physical body is less important for the dead. It reminds them of the moment of death, fixes it and so sustains their memory of their earthly I. More important than this is that these forces reveal to the dead soul the ongoing lawfulness of the dissolution of the ether body. But if nothing other than these three forces existed, the dead soul could not know that it is his own form, that it in fact originates with him. He would perceive it as something alien. It is important that he not only perceives the process of dissolution but that he is also able to recognize its connection with him, its origin in him—that he sees these are the remains of what he made cohere on earth in his human form. And this leads us to something else.

Here I have to refer to something which really is not treated with the necessary reverence nowadays, in our dry, prosaic times, even though we see it before us all the time. This is something apparent to everyone and yet its appearance is one of the most mysterious of phenomena, although its mysterious character is not felt. This is the incarnation tone of the human face, the outward skin colour. Something very individual comes to expression in the tone of each person's skin; it is slightly, subtly different in everyone, with as many tinges and nuances as there are people. If you concern yourself with this riddle of individual human skin colour, as some have tried to do, you will gain a sense of what comes to expression in this flesh colour. Something very mysterious indeed manifests here. If we study the phenomenon through spiritual science the question about the 'incarnation hue' acquires very great significance, for it depends on two opposing forces or, one could say, on two pressure forces active in us and working against each other in the human form. In a sense the ether body or body of formative forces presses outwards while the astral body presses inwards; and this happens everywhere. Whereas the astral body seeks to contract, to push inwards from without, so the ether body tries to push outwards from within, to expand. What comes to expression in our human flesh colour, the colour of incarnation, arises partly from the encounter of these two opposing pressures, from without and from within. Our skin colour mysteriously expresses what the etheric body and the astral body have to say to one another.

We see this flesh bloom in people here on the physical plane but if we could observe it from within it would appear different. Looking from within outwards, the tinge of your skin as an average European would not look flesh-pink but greenish-blue. The after-effect of this greenish-blue tone also becomes apparent after death. As our etheric body or body of formative forces expands in line with the three forces previously characterized and the dead person gazes upon this figure or pattern, he sees his flesh colour in its after-effect from the other side. After death it shimmers towards him in a greenish-blue colour.

But this hue also contains something essentially different from its outward appearance in physical life. Strictly speaking, this colour of incarnation is not only mysteriously different in every individual but it also changes in each of us during our lifetime. I'm not referring to the fact that, when suffering from one or another kind of illness, our skin sometimes looks roseate, sometimes more curdlike, for these are of course abnormal conditions. Apart from these greater fluctuations, the incarnation colour also continually subtly changes. But when seen from the other side as the dead person sees it, something else becomes apparent. This hue reveals our whole world of memory, as if embroidered on a tapestry. If we speak pictorially, therefore, we can describe this 'incarnation tapestry' as a kind of garment, a very fine one, which has been turned inside out as one turns a dress or a glove inside out. Then we see the inner lining as it were of what is usually turned outwards, which, because it is hidden from view, we can only perceive by virtue of it coming to our awareness as memory rather than the content of thought as such. It is something that gives thoughts their diverse auric colours, their living resonance. We only come to know the outward life of what we send down into our subconscious. We do not become aware of how this glitters through our skin colour, but the dead become aware of it in the after-effect of this incarnation hue. When the dead soul looks back on the dissolution of the body of formative forces, he has it before him as memory and then he knows that he is this. He realizes: I am this!

Spiritual-scientific research shows that something mainstream science gives little attention to, the great difference between man and animal, is expressed in our upright gait, our capacity for speech, for articulated speech, and the capacity for thinking, powers which we bear with us out into the universe after death; and the incarnation colour of our skin is the physical expression here of what goes on working after death as a residue of memory. After death, therefore, we impart ourselves to the universe; and what we possess here and manifest in our physical body are the outer signs of our cosmic nature and being. This is what gives us a sense of uniting with something so mysterious in the colour of incarnation: a feeling of the universal significance of what we observe in the human being. By virtue of our incarnation hue more than anything else, we are a microcosm in relation to the macrocosm. This ground tone of colour is very significant for it is, we can say, the colour of the tapestry upon which the dead person's memory appears: in greenish or greenish-blue tones for white people, purple-reddish for Japanese, and a flesh-pink colour for black people after death.

These things are intimately and significantly related to the life between death and a rebirth, and are a preparation for a new incarnation. They lead someone to choose a particular nation or race in a new life. Studying the life of spirit is not to satisfy mere intellectual curiosity. Our life here in the physical world, along with things that make mysterious impressions upon our sensibility, can only be explained and understood if we consider this life in its real relationship with spiritual reality.

As you may now realize—though the things I have been describing are presented here in fairly basic form and can be further elaborated—we can gain an intimate awareness of human nature and development in general by studying these matters in more detail. People today are wary of looking so attentively at human nature and development. They don't want to engage with it. On the other hand, as I have often said,[131] there are those who stand guard over certain concealed esoteric truths, and enjoy the power of sole possession of such truths. This has extremely important ramifications. However little inclined people are to believe this, there are some who seek to further their plans for world dominion by studying, in their centres of occultism, how world evolution develops, and how they can best exert power over humanity over the next 30, 40 or 50 years.

Nations where such figures work, studying the course of human evolution and how to influence it, and then establishing political life to further their interests accordingly, will of course have an advantage over others where this is not done. These things play a major role in global reality. We are living at a time when it would be necessary for people to be aware of such things. Today I will only speak of one related matter.

Current events are of catastrophic proportions and, in purely outward terms, to a superficial view they exceed anything previously played out in humanity's history. And yet they are only part of a larger, more encompassing context which we can only properly understand if we bring the necessary reverence and seriousness to bear upon it. In certain places a good deal is already known about humanity's evolution, but this knowledge is carefully guarded with the aim of giving power to its possessors. I do not know whether you will be sceptical about this. I say things in a way that leaves everyone free to give credence if you think what I say is credible, or withhold it. Today, in the English-speaking world, certain impulses which we may try to describe in more detail on a future occasion,[132] are striving for world dominion on a global scale. I am not speaking out of some kind of Central European chauvinism but present to you merely the results of spiritual-scientific enquiry. The figures in Anglo-American life who possess this knowledge would be the last ones to repudiate it, though they might very well deny it to make absolutely sure that it does not come to public attention. Those in the know are for instance aware of the following, which I will try to illustrate by broadening the context for a moment.

During the course of human evolution, thus from the third and fourth post-Atlantean epoch onwards into our fifth epoch as materialism emerged and took shape, former truths became devalued, really lost their currency and value. In old traditions you can discover the deepest truths in the guise of pictures. Myth, images and pictures are something that modern people only accept as poetic fancy. They accept a playwright such as Strindberg[133] for instance because he seems to clothe what he says in poetic form. And yet they do not regard poetic works as anything to be believed—nothing in them is thought to express reality. Mythic and pictorial expression has been devalued, and people no longer feel that the imagination offers deeper underlying truth. In the course of the fifth post-Atlantean epoch this process will increasingly extend to language itself amongst the English-speaking peoples. Besides devaluing images as a mode of expression, the word itself will be devalued. In the same way that materialistic outlooks oppose the image today, so in future they will join battle with the word. People will come to say that words are not a fitting means of expressing truth. In his *Critique of Language*, Fritz Mauthner[134] has already tried to make language the culprit for all the superstitions said to prevail amongst humanity. But while his tool may be sharp enough—for his critique is an apt instrument—he is working with an unsuitable material, with the German language, and is deceiving himself. English-speaking occultists however have a suitable material in the English language. In its developmental impulse of devaluing meaningful content, this language is increasingly left with the mere elaborations of words. Consider its abstract trails of words and all that is overlooked and passed over by this means. If you have studied English philosophy you will find that its language has lost any real wealth of inner content. Read John Stuart Mill[135] or Herbert Spencer[136] for instance; the language they use offers no means to enter and engage with the spirit. Here we can see how language is a very important factor in the way English-speaking occultists approach the problem of language, and this lies in the very nature of modern impulses. Drawing on occult foundations, such people dream up ways and means of exerting world dominion without resorting to language. And this represents a great contrast between Orient and Occident—the Orient with its acutely alive intensity of language, and the Occident with its dismissal of language's inner meaning. The Central European, once again, occupies a position midway between these two extremes. What is at work here, and is being shouted as loudly as possible from the rooftops to further the interests of various nations, is actually very deceitful. It seeks—again, this is not chauvinism but is drawn from the most sober, spiritual-scientific appraisal—to conceal the truth, which is that efforts to secure power are being undertaken in a realm where, through its own process of development, language is losing its dominance. The great, incisive, catastrophic events of our times are symptoms of this wide-ranging, all-encompassing battle which will inevitably find diverse expression in the near future in conflicts across the globe. This will not be like other previous wars, which concluded with peace; things will no longer be as they used to be. There will instead be perpetual conflicts, and the only way to view the incisive events of our time is in this larger context. It is no longer adequate today to think superficially about events and circumstances. We need to plumb the depths, for otherwise nothing much will result from all that we undertake. But society today finds it very difficult to get used to the insights arising in this realm from a science of the spirit. This became apparent to me very recently in a bizarre way—all the more bizarre because it emerged from an act of kindness. I was busy preparing the new edition of *The Philosophy of Freedom*,[137] which is due to come out soon. I was a young man when I first wrote this book, 32 or 33—a very long time ago. And as I worked on the new edition this brought certain things back to mind. As I have described in the journal *Das Reich*,[138] I was very gratified by a response from Eduard von Hartmann,[139] the author of *The Philosophy of the Unconscious* with whom

I was corresponding at the time.[140] I sent him my *Philosophy of Freedom*, and he wrote various remarks in his copy, and then let me see these comments. I wrote them down and still have them.[141] You see, this was a very kind deed on his part, and I was extremely grateful; and yet it was the cause of what I am about to relate.

In *The Philosophy of Freedom* I first presented the nature of spirit in the form of self-comprehending thinking; and this is because we only truly grasp the spirit if we actually experience it in self-comprehending, self-founded thinking activity. But as this became clear to me, I found it necessary to speak about some things in a different way from others who see matters differently. I therefore formulated this sentence:[142] Idea is an individualized concept, and a concept is experienced intuitively in the mind; the idea is an individualized concept and the I relates it to an outward object. This was one of the sentences that Eduard von Hartmann had underlined, noting the following: 'That is an unusual way of using words.' As you can see, it was very kind of him to engage with me, and yet at the same time highly characteristic. To compare something major with something minor, one might say the following. When Copernicus expressed the idea that the sun does not revolve around the earth but the earth around the sun, someone might equally well have noted in the margin that this was an unusual way to describe things. Naturally we need an unusual formulation to characterize something new. Yet you see that in the very quarter where one might have hoped for understanding the response is: an unusual way of using words!

As we see very clearly in this example, if people never allowed themselves to coin new formulations, there would be no progress—in the spiritual domain or any other. Even the very words that spiritual science employs meet with dismissal wherever we turn. Old views of the world are very worn out now, like an old coat, and the words in which they are formulated are no use even to these views themselves. The national clothing exchange office would not even accept such ragged word-garments if they were offered it. But people do not notice the redundancy of a world-view, founded on tired formulations, in their inner life. We need to develop a sense for this, and this is part of what people will have to find today if they are to understand the age we live in. We must understand these times!

We must take such things to heart, for otherwise partisan interests can use their secret knowledge to gain the upper hand, whereas all humanity should be served by this knowledge. Even the best knowledge, if exploited for vested interests, for the power of a few, will turn into a calamity for humanity.

Lecture 12

BERLIN, 16 APRIL 1918

In my public lecture yesterday[143] on 'The Human and Animal World' I referred among other things to an idea we can form about human soul life which is not simply hypothetical but does really correspond to reality. In speaking of the world of animals I pointed to the beginning and end of life as two moments when physical life first enters and then departs—the moments of conception and death. I said that we could see this as a ladder, with conception at the beginning of it and death at the end, and that these two experiences really pass through the whole of human soul life—that at each and every moment this soul life comprises in a whole what is experienced in animal life when the genus soul, the animal group soul, which never fully arrives on the physical plane, enters into a reciprocal relationship with the physical entity at conception. And similarly, something like a hint of I consciousness appears fleetingly in the animal at death. Someone able to observe the death of an animal, as I said yesterday, can form an idea of how something that runs throughout our human life, our I consciousness, is only present for the animal at this moment when life departs. But the important thing here is this: that these two moments, really only two fleeting moments in animal life, are combined in us in one as in a synthesis and run throughout our human life. Thus the human head, the distinctive nature of its organization as I described yesterday, can, in a quiet echo of this, develop a continual conceiving and dying; and this gives rise in fact to the justified idea of the soul's immortality. This life of the human soul therefore continually emerges from the interwoven union of conception and death.

I then added this: whenever we have a thought, this is born from the will; and whenever we will something thought dies into this will. Schopenhauer[144] represented this in a very one-sided way by regarding the will alone as real. He did not recognize that 'will' is only one aspect of the matter, in a sense only the dying thought, whereas the 'thought' is will coming to birth. If we share Schopenhauer's view of things, it is like thinking that human life only consists of the time from age 35 to death; but before 35 of course we must have been living in order to reach that age, must have been born and have developed. Schopenhauer acknowledges only the will, regarding the idea as mere appearance. Yet that is only another form of manifestation—the idea of will that seeks to be born or realized whereas thought is the dying will. In our soul life thought and will are continually interwoven; and we can see this at the same time as birth, originating in conception—which is perception—and dying.

To form this picture, and even to substantiate it anatomically and physiologically, we need nothing more than our modern science and the will, the good will, to really observe soul phenomena. We can interpret modern findings about the human brain in a different way from mainstream science. If we study the physiology and biology of the human brain with an open mind, really examine it carefully, we discover that what I just said has a sound scientific basis. There are many fantastical notions dreamed up nowadays in universities, along with psychological and physiological experiments undertaken because anatomists do not actually think but instead just sit down at their apparatus to maltreat the psyches of their students, firstly, and then attempt to study these psyches. If people refused to allow this it might be possible instead to really observe the human soul, to develop a living concept of the soul and of the ongoing process of birth and dying within it—of this metamorphosis which is only an enhancement and refinement of Goethean metamorphosis. But after a hundred years, modern science has still not managed to understand Goethean metamorphosis, let alone advance an idea of such benefit to humanity.

What I tried to outline yesterday is in fact nothing other than the idea of Goethean metamorphosis taken further and elaborated. Such things can be discovered without the need for clairvoyant perception;

they draw only on a truly scientific approach and the capacity to study the human psyche. If a number of students were introduced to such things in a way they could understand rather than having all the current idiocies foisted on them, we would move a good deal closer to spiritual science as something that can really inform modern culture. You see, such ideas, which can be scientifically ascertained today, require nothing but good will to become really fruitful for human soul life, good will to observe carefully and accurately and to have corresponding thoughts; and such ideas can create a bridge from outer science based on the sensory world to a spiritual science. The latter makes no headway not because it is incomprehensible to people who have no capacity for clairvoyant vision but because the modern scientific outlook is so fiercely opinionated that it cannot countenance something new like this emerging. In my view no harm is done if we describe things as they really are occasionally. Still more important than an idea like this spreading as an idea is its effect upon the life of the human psyche. It matters much less what kinds of thought we have than what powers we must apply to grasp a particular idea or thought. Our state of soul will inevitably be quite different if we are thinking a completely dead idea of modern 'science' or a living, spiritual-scientific one. The latter involves our whole being; it inwardly enlivens us and integrates us with the cosmos. Such thoughts as arise from modern science, by contrast, especially when it exceeds its intrinsic, narrow remit, sunder our connection with the universe.

We have to realize this, and spiritual science really must impress it on humanity. You see, precisely where things start to be of direct importance for life itself, for instance in education, in children's upbringing and everything connected with it, it is of boundless importance for the psyche to dwell in living ideas and concepts. Someone who can regard things in a living way will be able to draw on a science of the spirit to undertake the tasks and actions of key importance for our whole modern culture. The full significance of this really needs to be understood. If it were, people would recognize how much we need to review with an open mind the almost wholly distorted thinking that underlies practical measures today. People do not easily discern the symptoms of this distorted thinking.

Yesterday[145] I pointed out that amongst ourselves, too, we must strenuously avoid lax or lazy thinking of any kind. Consider what will happen if we allow lazy thinking to prevail. In all my recent lectures[146] I have been singing the praises of a book by Oscar Hertwig[147] called *The Development of Organisms*, calling it the best scientific work of recent times. My lack of reserve in heralding this book is because someone at the forefront of the scientific methods of his time had undertaken to unpick Darwinism and push it back into its proper confines. I agreed wholeheartedly with him until the last few pages. But now his next book has been published, entitled *In the Defence of Ethical, Social and Political Darwinism*; and really it is hard to find words sharp enough to object to the impotence, narrow-mindedness, triviality and nonsensical nature of this book. And this is because this research scientist has now departed from his proper, narrow field and started talking unalloyed garbage! This good fellow, for instance, states that all scientific methodology should follow the model of astronomy.[148] This is not, of course, an original idea. Dubois-Reymond[149] said it back in 1872 when speaking of the atomic structure of the world. But how on earth can we observe the realities around us if we do so based on astronomical theory which is as far removed as possible from us as human beings? In terms of logic this is as pointless as trying to understand a family living in dire poverty in the country not by observing this family itself—father, mother, son and daughter—but instead by contemplating life in a wealthy manor house and drawing on these observations to formulate laws about the poor family! Such things are simply overlooked nowadays; people lift their gaze away from reality. But we should take due regard of it. We at least should avoid either relying on authority or lazy thinking. We can be clear that a favourable judgement about someone in a particular instance does not mean that we subsequently rely on anything else he has to say. A really open mind and lack of prejudice means that we appraise Oscar Hertwig's work as outstanding in one instance but as utterly worthless in another. If we fail to practise this discernment, we overlook life's realities on the one hand, and gain no insight into the world of spirit on the other. I'd like to give a small example here. I am not sure how many of you are aware of this, at least to the degree of really gaining benefit from it in daily life.

A little while ago an article by Fritz Mauthner[150] appeared in the *Berliner Tageblatt* refuting a book which dealt, among other things, with Goethe's horoscope. This review by Mauthner was quite amazingly trivial. In a great many self-satisfied column inches, he tried to show how out of touch the author was to write about Goethe's horoscope, and to do so even in a series as popular as the one entitled *Nature and Culture*. This article struck me as taking triviality to new depths. The author of this book[151] in the *Nature and Culture* series is in fact a fairly average modern academic and it was hard to see why Mauthner was getting so worked up about it. What was he objecting to, especially since the author in question was poking fun at all the people who give serious credence to such things? So Mauthner was attacking the man merely for raising the subject. The same author who wrote this little book sent a reply to Mauthner's critique, published in the same paper,[152] saying it had never occurred to him to promote astrology. In fact, his academic approach accorded fully with Fritz Mauthner's views. The two were in agreement; and yet Mauthner still saw fit to launch his tirade about the grave social dangers of publishing such a book in that series. For its part, the *Berliner Tageblatt* noted that it agreed with Mauthner's view and did not consider he had misunderstood or misrepresented things.

This is just one, particularly striking example of the degree of spiritual debility underlying all such phenomena. If we examine whether such journalism, such inferior cultural activity, in any way invigorates life, we arrive at some characteristics of modern culture which it is necessary to be aware of if we are to understand what benefit spiritual science can have today. Above all we need to know that mendacity and lies are real powers. One can scarcely imagine anything worse than what I have described here: one person writes a book about astrology, another attacks him for it, and the first defends himself by saying he was only poking fun at the idea. If he had prefaced his book by stating that his account of Goethe's horoscope was a joke then Mauthner would have been satisfied.

These things are serious and connected with the most serious modern concerns, above all with the fact that in our age spiritual science will have a hard task in making headway, in achieving what it needs to. It requires really strong and courageous thinking; and alongside all its content we need to recognize that strong, courageous thinking is a necessary foundation, though one that has frequently been undermined. Nor is it just human beings who are active in this undermining work. For centuries the great ahrimanic powers have been at work amidst humanity. One of the many things that ahrimanic powers have worked to bring about to sow confusion amongst humanity—a state of darkness within which light must be found anew—is the obscuring of human insight that all matter is rooted in the spirit, and that all spirit seeks to manifest materially. The world has been torn asunder and things that belong together have been separated. Above all, if we study the ongoing stream of Christian history—not Christianity itself—we find ahrimanic powers working in humanity through these historical developments, working with great vigour. Among many other things, we should be aware of this: the sundering that has arisen between the sun and its power on the one hand, and Christ and the Christ power on the other. If the connection between these two things is not acknowledged again, it will be hard for the world to find a relationship with the spirit; and one of the key tasks of spiritual science is to enable people to rediscover the sun mystery in a different way, corresponding to the Christ mystery as spiritualizing impulse in humanity. In eras prior to the Mystery of Golgotha this solar mystery could not yet be the Christ mystery, though it became so directly afterwards. Julian the Apostate[153] was still aware of the sun mystery in its ancient form, but was not yet aware of it as the Christ mystery. His tragic fate was to fall prey to the delusion that he should tell humanity about the sun's spiritual power, which led to him being murdered during his Persian campaign.

But in the nineteenth century another spiritual undertaking of ahrimanic powers was to prevent humanity from knowing anything of what I have described: the sun mystery's connection with other mysteries. We have to be fully aware of these things. Here I will mention something that would be considered delusional if I were not talking to people with some preparation but to an academic association or suchlike. I am compelled to speak the truth as I see it, and we can leave aside here the question of who is actually delusional. In the nineteenth century an idea took root which nowadays dominates all of science and, as it goes on securing its dominance, will never allow healthy ideas about cultural and spiritual life to make any headway. The founding principles of chemistry and physics include the idea of the conservation of energy. Wherever you turn you will hear it said that forces only transform rather than disappear. The examples usually cited are of course all separately justifiable. If I stroke the top of a table I apply pressure, but rather than being consumed this energy transforms instead into heat. All powers or forces do transform in this way. Energy and force transform. The theory of the 'conservation of energy' is a motto that has pervaded all scientific thinking today, and is now established as an axiom showing that substances, matter and their attendant forces or energies do not arise and disappear. If we cite this theory within due confines, there is nothing to say against it. But this is not what happens. Instead it becomes a rigid scientific dogma.

In the nineteenth century, specifically, a strange ahrimanic coarsening of ideas occurred. Julius Robert Mayer[154] published a really very beautiful treatise on the conservation of energy in 1842, which most leading minds in Germany dismissed as amateurish. Julius Robert Mayer was later locked up in a mental asylum although today we know his discovery was of groundbreaking importance. Yet it is easy to show that the very people who nowadays refer to this scientific law have not actually read what he wrote. There is a volume on the history of philosophy by Ueberweg[155] which mentions Mayer in passing. If you read these few lines you can tell immediately that this historian of philosophy, who is compulsory reading for all students, has never read what Mayer wrote, for if he had he could never have written such tripe. The fine, spiritual way in which Mayer presented his work did not pass into human souls; instead it was greatly coarsened. And this is because Mayer's version of the idea was abandoned while that of the English brewer Joule[156] and the physician Helmholtz[157] entered scientific discourse instead. But no one thinks it necessary today to consider such things, which ought by rights to figure at our centres of higher learning. People also ought to study why Darwinism spread so rapidly. Believe me, if Darwin's book *On the Origin of Species by Natural Selection*[158] had simply been published like any other book it would not have spread like wildfire through popular circles. No, the ground had been prepared for Darwin's work. In 1844, a long time before Darwin therefore, a book had been cobbled together and been published, a trivial compendium of all the things later stated by Lamarck and others. This was a speculative publishing venture which Robert Chambers[159] in Edinburgh embarked upon, knowing that nineteenth-century instincts would herald such a publication. Darwin's work tumbled headlong into an atmosphere fully ripe for such ideas. He merely interpreted what he found by applying to it Lamarck's[160] theory of natural selection, with which English pragmatists had long been familiar. Previous to this, a book by Patrick Matthew entitled *On Naval Timber and Arboriculture*[161] had been published, and expressly stated the selection theory. It would be important, actually, to trace the ways in which these things found their way into nineteenth-century culture. History as it is presented is a convenient myth, a great deception in most fields. We ought instead to study what actually happened. You see, it makes a difference whether a young person knows he is dealing with a scientific fact or merely with the thoughts of Joule, an English beer brewer. It makes a difference for him to know whether something entered nineteenth-century scientific discourse as a result of efforts expended in real research or whether such ideas became prevalent due to the entrepreneurial activity of an Edinburgh bookseller, Robert Chambers. Such knowledge can lead us to a right appraisal of the truth, and truth is something humanity must take as its guideline in every matter.

This idea of absolute rather than relative permanence of substance and energy is what nowadays prevents people from discovering the place where substance does actually vanish into nothing and where new substance arises. This place could be ascertained physiologically today but the dogma of the conservation of energy prevents people from seeking or finding it. The sole place where this happens—or rather a great many of them—is the human organism. Substance does not merely pass through the human organism but, during the process that can be inwardly experienced in the synthesis of conception and death, particular substances that we have assimilated vanish from the body—forces disappear and new ones are engendered. The processes involved here have been observed for a longer time now than people realize, though no value is accorded to such observations. We need only pay careful attention to the blood circulation inside the eye. Using instruments that are sensitive enough nowadays to observe this outwardly, it would be possible to demonstrate in purely external, physical ways what I have just described. The blood can be seen to travel to a peripheral organ, to vanish into it and then to be engendered again in it, giving rise not to blood circulation as such but to creation and disappearance. These things happen, but the dogmatic ideas of modern science prevent observation of them, and this means in turn that people fail to grasp the reality of certain processes.

Modern science sees no significance at all in the merely physical death of human beings. In all other respects scientific research is greatly concerned with death since it fails to engage with the nature of life; but dying as such receives no notice. Otherwise the dead are a matter of interest, as confirmed by an example I heard only yesterday. Hamerling[162] was buried in a provisional grave in Graz in 1889. He was to be moved to another grave later, and during this transfer—I heard this yesterday from the gentleman who discovered it—the skull disappeared. There was no sign of the skull all of a sudden. The gentleman who told me this followed it up and it turned out that a plaster cast of the skull was made at the university museum. Wrapped in newspaper, the skull was kept there, and only rejoined the rest of Hamerling's body when this matter was discovered. So people are interested in the dead, but not with the fact of death itself. Actually, a study of dying, of death, can lead to the most important insights. The dust originating from human bodies, as I pointed out recently,[163] seeks to journey upwards into the cosmos. Unlike any other dust, this human dust, quite irrespective of whether the corpse is cremated or decomposes in a grave, would disperse into the whole cosmos if not encompassed by sun power, by the energy existing in the sun. The light that shimmers upon the surface of a glittering stone, or when we see plant colours, is only one of the sun's powers: the power that Julian the Apostate called the visible sun. Then we have the invisible sun, too, underlying the visible sun in the same way that the soul underlies the external physical human organism. This energy, which naturally does not descend to earth with the physical ether rays but only lives again within them, is what enlivens the dust of human bodies in a way that is distinctive and does not occur with anything else. No such enlivening happens with minerals, plants or animals. After a person has died, a continual interplay occurs between his outer corporeal remains and the powers that stream down from the sun. The two things encounter each other. But these forces that stream down from the sun to move the dust of human corpses are also those the dead person himself discovers as soul-spiritual entelechy after death. While we are incarnated in a physical body we see the physical sun, whereas after death, after passing through the gate of death, we discover the sun first of all as the cosmic entity which enlivens human dust below on the earth. This is one of the general discoveries we make after death. We learn to discern the interwoven nature of sun power and human dust; and by doing so, by becoming aware of this tissue woven from human dust and sun power, we learn firstly the secret of reincarnation altogether, from its other aspect, as preparation for our next incarnation: as what weaves our next incarnation out of the cosmos. And at the same time we also learn the other aspect of certain realities upon which the mystery of reincarnation depends, which we will speak of in the next few days.

This can show us the striking difference between the nature of ideas we form inwardly after our soul has passed through the gate of death and the experiences our soul has here. These after-death experiences have an entirely different soul configuration. Just as we alternate between sleeping and waking while alive, so the dead soul also alternates between different states of consciousness. I have already described this in these lectures but would now like to do so again briefly from a different angle.

One of the aspects of our life on earth is that we live inwardly in thoughts. Now the dead soul enters a reality composed of what are merely thoughts to us. In our physical life here we perceive the external world of minerals, plants and animals, as well as our own physical reality; but the thoughts we have are only a shadowy reality for us, whereas they are immediately vivid to the dead soul. This world into which we enter at death relates to the physical world in the same way that a solid object relates to its shadow. In our thoughts we possess only the shadows of what the dead person experiences, which is also different in kind and quality from our experience of thought. After death we learn something different about thoughts than we do here on earth, at least in our modern age. As far as our thoughts are concerned we are usually wrapped in a kind of dream. But after death we find that in thinking—that is, in living in thoughts as realities—we grow and thrive; and to the degree that we depart from thoughts and do not live in them, we grow thinner and more meagre. Creation and dissolution themselves relate in the after-death condition to living in thoughts and living outside them. If people who did not try to think grew ever thinner here on earth, the world would become a very strange place. But here we experience only the inactive shadows of thoughts, which have no real effects. The dead soul by contrast experiences thoughts as realities; they nourish or emaciate his soul-spiritual existence. And this period during which thoughts nourish or emaciate him is also the time when he develops his life of supersensible perception. He observes thoughts streaming into him and disappearing again. This is not perception as we know it ordinarily, whose nature is clearly defined, but instead an ongoing stream of thought life that continually unites and combines with our own being. However many physical things we see here on earth, we are still constituted in the same way, and nothing much has altered in our organism. For the dead soul this is different: what he perceives continually changes him. That is one condition: this perception of the influx and vanishing of a living stream of thought. The other condition arises when this ceases, leading to a tranquil sense of awareness in the dead soul of what has flowed through him: a clear memory, not like our ordinary abstract memory but one which is connected with all growth and development. These two conditions alternate, and this is also really why the dead are only receptive to thoughts that are borne towards them from a spiritual-scientific or spiritual outlook. The kinds of thoughts modern people mostly have nowadays scarcely reach them, while the mode of thinking that can reach them is one modern people have little inclination for. People today like thoughts that they can in some way derive from the external world, and are not drawn to ones they have to inwardly elaborate and which therefore already have traces of the nature of thought after death—a fluidity and mobility. That is felt to be far too difficult. People sit happily in laboratories with their microscopes and study cells, then write excellent books on the subject such as Oscar Hertwig's *The Growth of Organisms*. But the moment they actually begin to think they write nonsense, and the new book by Hertwig is an example of this. The difference is that for his second book the corpses of thought were no longer sufficient. Strictly scientific books depend only on these thought corpses, whereas living thoughts would have been required for Hertwig's second book, and he was incapable of having these. You have to be able to really love thoughts and live in them for the second type of book. And if you really wish to create a bridge with karmically connected people who have passed through the gate of death, you need an outlook which at the very least tends towards living thinking. With this outlook, the thoughts of the living really are a special gift to the life of the dead, and make a difference, an enormous difference to their existence between death and rebirth. But if there lives in human souls an undefined sense of everything on earth which the dead consider should be different from how it is, the living will have little joy from this thought. An undefined sense of this kind does exist. People are anxious about the view of the dead emerging in relation to much that they think and feel, do and believe in physical life. This is an unconscious anxiety, but it keeps the living caught up in materialism. The unconscious still acts even though subliminally. We need courageous thinking not only to ensoul our conscious life of thinking but also to fathom the profoundest depths of human nature. This is something that has to be said again and again if the full seriousness of spiritual science is to be grasped. You see, it is not enough to grasp one or another principle, to consider something or other interesting or important in itself, but instead we need to combine all the details to form a coherent organism, as it were, from all the many contributory aspects, so that together they can be configured into a whole outlook and frame of mind. This outlook is one I have tried to characterize from the most varied perspectives. It is vital that there are some people at least in our present era who, in this way, give proper and serious attention to spiritual science, knowing that it can help cultivate living, fluid thinking in our time, and that people should not attack one another even though they are really in agreement—that they should not, for example, bark their heads off just because someone mentions a horoscope, instead of giving the matter proper and serious consideration.

An era when such a state of soul prevails engenders all kinds of other related phenomena. It would be important to really focus on the nature of the age and its often so catastrophic expressions. There are some today who are starting to think seriously, but it is also apparent how difficult people find it to get beyond an inauthentic attitude to the world and humankind which holds them captive. One question I have touched on in passing today, and which we will consider more thoroughly in the coming lectures is this: How is it possible that Christianity, active for centuries, for millennia now, has nevertheless allowed our current conditions to emerge? The answer to this would require insights which humanity in general does not yet include in its scientific and religious discourses. Only spiritual science can offer them. It is after all a very serious question: What should be our attitude to Christianity today, given that this same Christianity has been at work for centuries and yet has allowed our current circumstances to arise? Most curious of all, however, are the people who propose a return to forms of Christianity that existed before contemporary developments began, and who therefore have no real feeling that returning to the same original conditions will inevitably allow the same consequences to emerge from them again. Such people will no doubt find it very hard to see that something thoroughly new, of a quite different order has to enter culture. I will speak further of this next time.

Lecture 13

BERLIN, 14 MAY 1918

THOSE who have a longer familiarity with spiritual science ought really to regard it as something that can have the most intense and energetic effects on human life. I have often said this, but it is an aspect of spiritual science so vital for our age that cannot be stated often enough. The science of the spirit is after all a kind of science, and as such it is in a process of development, remaining fragmentary as yet and only partially proven. The form it can eventually assume is something we can see only the very first beginnings of at present.

I am speaking here of the content of spiritual science, by means of which we can learn something about the nature of the human being, about our supersensible individuality in so far as this also lives and exists beyond the boundaries of physical life marked by birth, or conception, and death. The science of the spirit can also teach us something about the evolution of the earth and about the connections between this evolution and the human being. In other words, spiritual science can satisfy human thirst for knowledge in a more comprehensive way than empirical science. It can answer some of the inner questions which people have.

But spiritual science has an importance beyond its content, and we can see this when we consider what we ourselves—our soul life, mood of soul and frame of mind—can become if we occupy ourselves with the thoughts and ideas of spiritual science. It may also be the case—and this is true of course of every field of enquiry ever known to mankind!—that insights drawn from sources of spiritual life and disseminated today in all good conscience may later be superseded as the science of the spirit itself makes further, self-correcting advances: that some things will then appear in a different form. Then one or another aspect of the content of this science of the spirit might be different. But this developing content of ideas or thoughts will not alter its fundamental effect upon our inner mood and outlook, and this in turn relates very closely to certain basic traits of our current time. Today I wish to consider some of these fundamental characteristics of our age, especially as they concern the soul disposition of human beings. In doing so I will adhere to the four most important human soul capacities already very familiar to us: to human sensory perception, to thinking by means of which we assimilate and integrate these external sensory impressions, to feeling and to will. During waking life, our inner experience unfolds in perception, thinking, feeling and will.

Let us first take sensory perception. With an eye of soul honed through spiritual science we can observe a fundamental cultural characteristic of the human soul developing over the past three or four hundred years in countries we are concerned with now. This is not intended as any kind of criticism but only as a description. Even a superficial reflection will show that the capacity for sensory perception in human beings, thus the soul's immediate relationship with the surrounding world, has increasingly come to require ever more vivid, intense and absorbing stimulus to satisfy the senses. The older members of the audience might like to reflect on their youth, and compare what they experienced then with current conditions—it is still more striking the further back in time one goes. The urge for sensational stimulus has grown very markedly and become predominant, and this is because people today need strong and very rapidly changing sensory impressions in order to be excited and engaged by their surroundings. They want to be titillated and fascinated. A sensational quality has become very widely predominant and this is connected with something highly significant. The predominance of a need for sensory stimulus also modifies the strength and energy of the human I. Only spiritual science can enable us to understand why this is so, since it can tell us what external perception really is.

If you study philosophy you will find most effort of all expended on the nature of external perception or sentience, as it is also called. The most diverse theories have been formulated to explain what sentience or perception are in the context of the human corporeality and psyche. There is no need for me to expound on all this here, but I do need to explain the position of spiritual science in relation to this question.

On previous occasions—also here in Berlin in a public lecture[164]—I have suggested that science in the nineteenth century and into our own time achieved magnificent things, in particular as regards our understanding of the external world perceived by our senses. And yet it conceives of human evolution, in particular, in far too linear a way and in far too simple terms. Its hypothesis is simply that there were once lower animals, then higher ones, then higher still, and from these the human being ultimately developed as highest animal. Yet human evolution just isn't that simple. There are various ways in which we can conceive of the human being; and to us, as I have often said, his outer bodily form must appear as the image of cosmic, divine being. We can also conceive of him, in scientific terms now, as subdivided into three parts: the head or sensory part; which, since the chief senses are located in the head, we can sum up generally as the head system, though it is not a precise term; then the trunk system; and thirdly the system of extremities or limbs. Of these three parts of the human being, really only the trunk—the heart and lung system—is formed as modern science conceives it. The head system is not actually involved in an advancing developmental process but is in a sense retrograde, held back at an earlier stage. People have frequently told me that this is a difficult idea to grasp, and have asked me to explain it in easier terms. In fact, as I have pointed out on various occasions, the external scientific facts if properly understood—though this is at odds with what certain modern scientists say—prove what I say to be true. Study the human eye and compare it with the eyes of animals at a certain stage of evolution. You cannot say that the outer form of the human eye is more complex than that of an animal at a certain evolutionary stage. That is clearly not the case. There are animals that have more developed aspects of the inner eye than we do. They have structures for which there is no external physical parallel at all in us, for instance the falciform process and other organs in the inner eye which are blood vessel modifications. The prolongation of these blood vessels sustains the intimate coherence between an animal's whole feeling life and its visual perceptions. The animal feels far more intensely in its eyes than we do, and we do not have these organs. The human eye is actually simpler, and therefore our evolution has not produced an advance on the animal eye as such but has also returned it to an earlier stage. In the same way one could demonstrate that the minutest aspects of the human head are retrograde, that our head has 'evolved backwards' again compared with the rest of the forward-evolving human organism.

Someone who thought this retrograde development of the human head was a difficult idea to grasp asked me if I could offer any clarifying points of reference here. I told him that we need only consider the following. In the evolutionary sequence of animals that concludes with the human being, the human embryo is distinctive in losing the hair coat possessed by animals at a certain stage of development. We do not have fur, but the head does have a hair covering. We can see therefore that our head returns in its development to the animal stage, and this is another indicator of its retrograde nature, though of course only a superficial, external one. The inner indicators are much more eloquent of this fact. And I would ask you to consider the full scope of its significance.

The very fact that the head's development becomes retrograde, so that evolution does not progress in a linear way here but withdraws in the head, holds itself back, means that space is created for our soul-spiritual development. The researchers who believe that human feeling and cognition result only from our physical organization do not properly understand their own science. They fail to see that our soul and spirit can only unfold because the physical organism does *not* thrive and flourish but instead recedes or withdraws. It abates, comes to a standstill, makes space for the development of spirit and soul. Where we unfold spirit and soul to the greatest degree, physical development withdraws.

We can inwardly perceive this if we have undergone soul-spiritual development and, through inner self-observation, receive an answer to the question of what our ordinary thinking and perception is. What is the real nature of our ordinary waking life infused by thinking and sensory perception?

As far as the human head is concerned, sensory perception and thinking, and in fact waking life altogether, are a hunger. The distinctive nature of the inner balance of our human organization is that during waking life the head, or rather its inner organization, continually feels hunger compared with the rest of the body. Ascetics who seek enhancement of their soul and spirit have made use of this fact: they fast, let their whole body go hungry because this hunger process, extended to the whole body, is meant to induce inner illumination of a kind. In fact this is mistaken. The normal state is already for our head, in waking life, to be less nourished by inner processes than the rest of the organism; and only because of this can we be awake and alert, and think.

If our head is always hungry while we are given up to this retrograde process in the head—whereas in sleep efforts are made to overcome this stasis—what do we actually perceive? The science of the spirit can teach us to distinguish two things here, which in reality are always combined and yet are two very different things: firstly mere waking life; and then our external sensory perceptions and our ordinary memory pictures. So what is actually occurring as we hunger in our waking consciousness?

On the one hand we perceive the I from our previous incarnation. In mere waking, we perceive what we brought with us from the world of spirit and what accompanied us as we entered life through birth or conception. This fills the space created by the withdrawal of our physical organism. And when we perceive external sensory objects, these objects take the place of the I we otherwise perceive when we receive no external impressions but are merely awake. In ordinary life these two things are merged; we continually perceive external objects and are very rarely in a merely waking state. But into our outward-oriented psyche is mingled an inclination to perceive our past I, as well as to suppress it through external colours or tones. Perception of our past I alternates with suppression of it, for as soon as an external object impinges on us, it suppresses our tendency, our capacity, to perceive the I from our former incarnation. This remains unconscious; we are unaware of it. Yet our sensory perception is really a battle between the object that exists before us in the present and the I of our previous incarnation.

You may now start to realize what it means if we seek sensory stimulus by giving ourselves up to the external world. This will never strengthen but only weaken us; and this is because we are in fact weakening what our strength really consists of, which is our I from a previous incarnation. It is clear, therefore, that a tendency to seek the sensational, literally, in the form of sensory stimulus will produce a kind of weakness in human nature by weakening the I.

And what occurs when we think or picture rather than perceiving sensory reality? Either our thoughts fall quiet—though this is less common nowadays—or they relate to particular external perceptions. When our thoughts fall quiet in waking life then everything we experienced between our previous incarnation and the present one is active in us—in what can be active by virtue of space created within our organism. Thus where sensory perceptions otherwise arise, the past incarnation acts, and where ideas otherwise arise, the life we underwent between death and rebirth becomes active in us. If we develop powerful thoughts out of ourselves this means we are trying to elaborate them from what we brought with us from the period before our latest birth, out of something intrinsic to us. If on the other hand we only develop thoughts stimulated in us by our external surroundings, absorbed as pervasive soul content from without, we invariably weaken what we brought with us from the period between death and rebirth, that is, what our I consists of. The compulsive search for sensation weakens our present life. Spending lots of evenings at the pub, say, to avoid drawing as little as possible on our own resources, or the excitement of poker games or bingo or any other of the thousand little external stimuli people seek out to spice up their lives, is not a strengthening but a weakening of the I; and this is, basically, due to a feeling that they are not strong enough to occupy themselves with something drawn from their own inner life. The science of the spirit can teach us why people today seek out sensation and stimulus.

In general we can diagnose this prevalent aspect of modern culture as a kind of narrow-mindedness. Please don't take offence at this. It is simply how things are nowadays, and applies equally to modern science or other fields. This narrow-mindedness is a major symptom of our culture today and prevents people from searching in their own souls for the wealth available from their past life and from their pre-birth existence. They have no belief in such a thing, and it would be essential to acknowledge it, and to see that spiritual science could enable them to access it.

With this in mind, let us for a moment consider how spiritual-scientific ideas can affect the state and pattern of a person's soul. They certainly do not offer external stimulus or sensation, and definitely do not seek to do so. They do not captivate the senses through outer sensations, and many miss such stimulus. In relation to spiritual-scientific matters people have to reflect themselves, and are likely to fall asleep if they are unable to draw anything from their own inner resources. What spiritual science does in particular is to instigate mobility in the life of the psyche, to shake it awake. It endows us with a capacity to elaborate our own inner thoughts. It counters outward sensation, especially by enabling us to think a great deal about only very few sense impressions. There is no need to rush from one sensation to the next, but instead we can ponder greatly on all kinds of sensory impressions. Every simple phenomenon we encounter can become a riddle for us, every small detail of life gives us much food for thought. And the thoughts and ideas which many people find too complex—about Saturn, Sun and Moon phases of evolution, about the different planetary embodiments of the earth and so on—give our spirit mobility, and in a sense prevent narrow-mindedness. In this way our science of the spirit works to counter a certain cultural predisposition, fights against bigotry and narrow-mindedness in the realm of perception and thinking. This accompanies but is not the same as the content we gain from spiritual science; it forms our soul, and this is of much importance.

As regards the realm of human feelings, let us ask what trait appears in those who concern themselves with spiritual science compared to those who wish to have nothing to do with it and reject it out of hand? In the latter one finds lack of interest for the great concerns of the world. If we are to cultivate an interest in spiritual science we need to broaden our interests beyond the things closest to hand. What do most people nowadays care about some previous stage of the earth before it became our earth? What do most people nowadays care about human culture before it developed into the modern age? This requires us to broaden the scope of our interests beyond immediate and familiar circumstances. Our age tends to confine our areas of interest to a very narrow realm.

Forgive me if I state quite baldly—though I'm characterizing here, not criticizing—that our time tends towards the mean-spirited and philistine. As more and more people succumb to this philistine tendency, it will increasingly affect the public domain as well. One striking example of this can unsettle anyone with insight into current events.

In the East, in Russia, is a people whose depths of soul are as yet undeveloped, still in a childlike state, but these underlying powers of soul should evolve in future, in the next, the sixth post-Atlantean era, to special heights, acquiring a spiritual, spiritually active character. This is something one wishes to acknowledge and nurture. But this people, or a great majority of them, now labour under the scourge of Leninism. One can scarcely think of anything more grotesque than the coupling of this cultural monkey of the West—I don't mean the man himself but what he propounds—with a prophetic culture of the East. No two things could possibly be more divergent in nature and yet be coupled together. Here we have the most grotesque expression of materialism, the essence of philistinism, which Leninism is, the rejection of all broader cultural interests and the imprisoning of these cultural interests in the narrowest possible philistinism; and set against this a dynamic from the East that seeks to develop in these people something fundamentally anti-philistine. We have to see this clearly; and there is nothing that can better help us do so than spiritual science. Spiritual science also counters philistinism by appealing to broader, more generous human interests. You see, without interest in what connects us with the cosmos, surpassing the narrowest interests and pulsing into grandeur, one cannot become a spiritual scientist. In the realm of human feeling, therefore, the science of the spirit battles against the philistinism and mean-spiritedness that inevitably emerge from materialism, just as, in the domain of perception and thinking, it battles against narrow-mindedness and bigotry.

As for the realm of the will, we can observe remarkable things here too if we have developed a little perception of life. Not materialism itself but what is attendant on and associated with it develops something peculiar in the whole of human life. The will of course can only come to expression through the vehicle of corporeality if it is to act on and affect the outer world. Our modern materialistic age leads people to be clumsy. They become clumsy in a whole host of ways because, in their earliest youth, their bodily forces are enlisted in only a few, very particular actions and directions. Strange to say, there are men who cannot even sew a button on their shirt, let alone do anything more complex. If we regard spiritual science as more than mere theory or doctrine and see the warmth at work in it, absorbing this warmth into our whole being, it enters the muscles, the pulse and makes us more skilful. If we were able to introduce our children to a spiritual-scientific way of thinking, we would see the benefits in their dexterity, in their ability to do things more easily. Their fingers would become more skilful. If we can make our ideas more mobile and flexible, this also gives more mobile expression to the will. In the realm of the will, therefore, the science of the spirit battles against the clumsiness threatening humanity which, more than many imagine, is symptomatic of our age. Look around and see how many people are capable of doing anything outside the narrow remit of their profession. They have lost the knack for such things. And even in their work they are more or less just adhering to customary actions. If you take someone who has become accustomed to the more or less mechanical procedures of his job and try to get him to do something different, you will see the very one-sided nature of modern culture. This cannot be remedied by external means, however, since our national economy tends towards specialism in everything. It would be pointless to try to fight this. But what we can do is energize people inwardly so that, from the centre of their being, they acquire more skilful impulses. To do this they have to imbue themselves fully with awareness of the supersensible world, and above all of the supersensible nature of the human being. We cannot properly understand sensory perception and thinking, even scientifically, if we do not know what I described earlier: that the human organization recedes to make place in the head so that our past life and the life between death and rebirth can stream into our organism.

Scientific views about the human organism are, as I said, far too narrow. Only the human trunk can be conceived as narrowly as science regards it, but not the limb system. If we now consider our extremities, arms, hands, feet and legs—though this system also continues inwards—we can see its organization as being opposite to that of the head. Rather than retrograde development we find excess development. Here development shoots beyond what is otherwise normal, beyond what we actually need during life. This would become clear if people studied evolution very carefully. Let us take just the external limbs: the arms connected to the breasts, as secondary reproductive organs, then the legs in connection with the primary sexual organs—and thus the extremities in physical connection with an aspect which already allows a person to look beyond himself, his own life, in physical terms. At their core, the organization of our extremities does not merely serve what infuses our individual human life but what goes beyond us, thus our soul and spirit. The soul-spiritual reality underlying our extremities goes beyond what serves human life between birth and death, works beyond death. Just as there is a physical connection, in reproduction, between the adult human organization, the centre of its extremities, and what will become the child's, so spiritually, as Imagination, we also possess in our arms and legs something that bears us through the gate of death. We can perceive this very clearly through imaginative perception: we bear in the organization of our extremities, even anatomically, our soul-spiritual future after death.

A careful, diligent study of science will eventually mean that people no longer regard spiritual science as something unattainable. Instead of considering the human organism in a linear way but by observing its reality, which is non-linear, science itself will discover the need for a spiritual-scientific perspective. One thing that must be refuted in this process is the idea that all external sense impressions are of the same nature. This is a belief held not only by lay people nowadays but also by clinical researchers in their anatomical studies. They regard the heart as just another organ like the head. This isn't true. Compared to the heart the head is of a lower evolutionary order in its whole organization. But people cannot discern this, cannot observe properly. When people learn to observe correctly, science itself will give rise to a fundamental conviction of the spirit at work in the human being, and passing through births and deaths. Arriving at this insight, people will then also start to pay heed to the soul and spirit in all culture, and will realize the importance of the battle against narrow-mindedness, philistinism and clumsiness. Alongside this, above all, they will learn to take account of the spirit in practical life. Nowadays a physicist encounters no objections when speaking of positive and negative electricity, positive and negative magnetism, whereas people feel affronted if the spiritual scientist talks of two currents in the human soul, the luciferic and ahrimanic. But these two currents or streams are just as much a polarity as positive and negative magnetism or electricity in the physical realm. And if we are to understand humanity and its evolution we must try to observe how the luciferic and ahrimanic are at work in life. Let me give one example. The structure of society was one-sidedly influenced for a long time by luciferic beings. It is not that one can eradicate the luciferic aspect from life. Someone who says they will try to guard against luciferic influence will succumb to it even more. All we can do, rather, is accord this influence its proper realm in life, knowing that the luciferic is at work in one place and the ahrimanic in another. Then we can avoid exaggerating their effects and shedding a false light on them. For centuries the structure of society in Europe and in other places in the world too was dominated by strong, one-sided luciferic impulses. These strong luciferic impulses engage human drives and instincts, working from within outwards. This is not a critique, just a characterization of the times. How does this luciferic impulse work? Hitherto society, its culture and the place a person occupied within it have been shaped by people's vanity and ambition, and these are luciferic impulses. A person's vanity and ambition were invoked. I myself can recall how vanity and ambition were elicited at school not so long ago. And these impulses were often what spurred people to acquire or appropriate things that would give them an important position in society.

Now an important moment has arrived however. A careful observer can hardly avoid seeing that these luciferic impulses are on the wane. To put it baldly, they no longer have traction. But they are being replaced by something else, largely ahrimanic in nature. And an ahrimanic quality is creeping into the workings of society now. Our dear populace, free of authority as it believes, and rejecting and attacking all imposed authority, will nevertheless blindly allow ahrimanic impulses to shape society and its structures one-sidedly. As one example, something very strange has occurred in the form of psychological testing. Experimental psychology, which no doubt has a limited justification at universities, is capable of discovering some things about the workings of the human body and how it gives expression to various aspects of the psyche. But now it has devised something that avoids any need to study this psyche more deeply. A piece of equipment records data electrically. The length of time it takes for a student to register a particular impression is measured. Thus people are studied in an external, clinical way, and this is easier than searching within. I have no doubt of the value of this experimental psychology in particular areas, but now it is seeking to broaden its remit and to study 'gifted' children in this way. A number of children across the age-range are tested for attributes such as memory, attentiveness and so forth;[165] yet the way in which the methodology of experimental psychology is used is very odd. For instance, memory is tested as follows.[166] Two columns of disconnected words are written on the board, such as 'head' and 'crystal' followed by two other unconnected words and so on. And then, having rubbed the whole thing out, just the first word in each column is written again, and the child has to remember the other word in the other column. Those who can recall the disconnected companion word for each word written down are thought to have a better memory while others who either can't remember at all or take a longer time to do so have a worse memory. That's how powers of memory are tested. Or then they test intelligence. Let me read you an example of how they do so:

> For instance, if one gives words such as 'mirror ... murderer ... rescue', a whole range of diverse connections can be established between the mirror and the rescue which require no specialized knowledge but only a well-developed combinative capacity. The most obvious connection ...

and therefore one a 'less intelligent child' will make

> ... is of course that the person threatened sees in the mirror the murderer creeping up on him. But quite different motifs can be imagined: for instance a murderer creeping up on his victim might knock into a mirror and the clatter caused by this could wake up

> the threatened sleeper so that he can save himself. Or the murderer, as he takes aim, is blinded by a reflecting mirror ...

Just imagine ... this is supposed to measure intelligence!

> This can also involve motifs that elicit feelings more strongly. For instance the murderer can get such a fright at his vague image in the mirror in the half-dark that he relinquishes his intention, either because of his sudden fear or because he feels pangs of conscience when he sees his reflection; or else because he thinks that his image in the mirror is that of somebody else.

Apparently it is especially intelligent if the child thinks the murderer might see his own reflection and think it is that of someone else.

> One might also imagine that the murderer creeping up on his victim is reflected in the clear water of a lake in a wood etc.

So, the child is supposedly more or less intelligent depending on whether he thinks the most obvious thing or something less obvious, and anyone who is shown to be more intelligent by this means receives special educational funding. This is how intelligence is to be tested today, and people are enthusiastic about these methods. This is all meant to enhance the social order if not actually shape and determine it. Such proposals, currently the subject of much campaigning, will be seen by the public, no doubt, as the outcome of genuine science. By this means people attempt to find ways of according each person their 'rightful place' in society, and essays are written to support this end. One such begins as follows:

> Applied psychology has flourished during the war like no other discipline. This is not by chance. Consuming people as it did, and making many kinds of differentiated demands, the war, after all, made clear that one should not waste human resources or fail to make properly planned use of them. Hitherto only education has made practical use of the methods of exact psychology. But now three questions arise: What profession is a person best suited for (problem of choice of profession)? How can we replace the resources of intelligence that have been lost in such high numbers

> (selection of talented students)? And how can we best heal those suffering from head wounds and other nerve injuries (psychotherapeutic practice)?

And so on, and so on . . . This represents a very misguided outlook of our times, which generally escapes notice all the more since there are, of course, professions where such an approach is called for—such as aircraft pilots, whose reactions and responsiveness do need testing. But such things should not be generalized for this will introduce an ahrimanic quality of the narrowest kind into the structure and fabric of society. Everything would be excluded from human aspirations, from human endeavours, that arises from the soul and its elementary, impulsive instigation. We can see this in very crass terms. If 'talented' children were really tested in this way, and the results actually implemented as proposed, what meaning could there be in the phrase, 'Love and delight are the wings for great deeds'?[167] If people stopped to think about the biographies of great figures they would discover, of course, that someone like Helmholtz, say, would have been marked down as a very untalented chap. Just read Helmholtz's biography![168]

This is an ahrimanic trait at work here. These things emerge in a masked way. If people cannot observe things as spiritual science does they fail to notice where the harm lies. It is not enough, today, to give way to all kinds of delightful sentiment. We have to awaken and judge life clearly. If a few people, at least, could form an objective view of this nonsense of 'talented pupil testing' that would be a very good thing. You can be sure that this approach will develop and thrive, and will be regarded as objective and open-minded. It will be glorified as one of the finest outcomes of a philosophical school of thought which has, finally, shed all old, idealistic preconceptions and methods.

Connected with these things, above all, is the need for the human soul to develop fundamental qualities of breadth of interest and authenticity. Let me offer two examples here of the lack of these qualities today. Please don't be offended if I reach for examples close to hand. In Munich, recently,[169] I gave a lecture about a seer's relationship to and experiences of art. I never imagined that a newspaper reporter would be likely to understand spiritual science or write anything worthwhile about it. On the contrary, if this were to happen I would be greatly surprised. In this lecture I was speaking about the art of music and the fact that musical experience encompasses our whole being in important ways; and that, in all real musical experience, a rhythm develops and unfolds within us. Then I spoke both about the human soul and spirit and about physiological aspects, mentioning how the cerebrospinal fluid rises and falls through the subarachnoid cavity, and showing, furthermore, that the spinal column is more or less flexible and extendable, giving rise to a wonderful inner rhythm. Through musical experience, something magnificently rhythmic occurs in us. I mentioned this rhythmic flux of the cerebrospinal fluid, which I also associated with inbreath and outbreath. And since I was also speaking of symbolic ideas in this lecture, the newspaper reporter stated that I used inappropriate symbolic ideas, such as the idea of the cerebrospinal fluid! Yet we need only realize that, the brain, without the cerebrospinal fluid, would weigh down upon the underlying blood vessels and crush them. The Archimedes principle means that the brain is rendered lighter by the cerebrospinal fluid. It is something perfectly real, not just 'symbolic'. But that is the scope of people's interests nowadays, and such nonsense is written.

And then one more example, a tiny one really, of authenticity and inauthenticity. I have often mentioned that the somewhat dubious academic Max Dessoir[170] also wrote a chapter on 'anthroposophy' in his book *Beyond the Soul*. I have made efforts to point out his errors and distortions;[171] but in purely external ways, too, his approach is very comic and utterly superficial. Citing my book *The Philosophy of Freedom*,[172] he says that this was my first venture into authorship. I had to correct him and point out that I had been writing and publishing books for ten years before this. Yet Dessoir's *Beyond the Soul* was widely acclaimed and was discussed by journalists such as those who think cerebrospinal fluid is something symbolic. It drew popular attention and a second edition has now been published. In his preface,[173] Dessoir seeks to justify himself, in exactly the same distorted ways, stating that it is quite clear from the context that I have failed to understand him. He meant that *The Philosophy of Freedom* was my first 'theosophical book'. Well, apart from the fact that it is clearly ridiculous to think he can be referring to anything other than my 'first book', it is just as ridiculous to speak of *The Philosophy of Freedom* as my first 'theosophical work' given that many people have said that I put philosophy behind me when I embarked on my theosophical books. This lack of truthfulness is something we have to get to grips with. We won't make any headway without authenticity, and we cannot let such things go unchallenged. For anyone familiar with these matters, Max Dessoir's whole book—and not only the chapter on anthroposophy—is riddled with such flaws. And yet a journal, the *Kantstudien*,[174] which regards itself as very serious and places great importance on its scholarly credentials—and I'm mentioning it because it has not taken up arms against anthroposophy—discusses this book by Dessoir from various angles as a serious academic treatise. It is very sad indeed to find that a journal of philosophy deems such a blatantly superficial book as worthy of its scholarly attentions. And one has to ask where this leaves the general reading public who rely—despite their supposed rejection of authority—on a journal like this to inform their choice of reading.

Our only option, if we have the will for this, is to found our examination of human nature on the spirit once more, and this is something that only the science of the spirit endeavours to do, working towards truthfulness, a broad scope of interest, lack of philistinism, mobility of thinking and open-mindedness.

I have mentioned these things to remind us that the content of spiritual science is not the only thing of importance. The distinctive nature of spiritual-scientific ideas, thoughts and pictures affects our whole psyche, releasing it from narrow-mindedness, philistinism and general clumsiness; and this inevitably becomes increasingly apparent to those who give due regard to the impulses at work in spiritual science. We have to realize the practical value of spiritual science, and we will speak more of this in the next lecture.

LECTURE 14

BERLIN, 21 MAY 1918

IN the past, at this time of year, we have often considered matters that relate to the festival of Whitsun. But as I have frequently said, the turmoil of events facing humanity at present is so great, and diverges so greatly from the ordinary course of human history, that ordinary reflections on the festivals seem out of place. Too often and too easily these reflections may, albeit unwittingly, distract us from the catastrophic events surrounding humanity. Nevertheless, the meaning of the Whitsun festival can have a bearing on these events, and it may still be permissible to reflect upon it.

From past talks on Whitsun we know that its most essential aspect is the individualization of a common life of shared experience amongst those who participated in the great Easter event of humanity. The tongues of fire descended on the head of each single person, so that each one learned to grasp the very nature of the Mystery of Golgotha flowing through human evolution, and in a language unlike any other and therefore comprehensible to all. The tongues of flame descended upon the head of each individual. Previously, one can say, the souls of the separate disciples felt themselves enfolded in the general aura of the Mystery of Golgotha. But at Whitsun, what they only knew together in their communal life passed over into each separate soul so that each one received his own illumination. I am of course putting it in abstract terms, but this is the most important aspect of Whitsun. We have to find a sense, a feeling in our soul, of the individualization of the Easter message through the annunciation of Whitsun, if we are to understand this festival in the right way. Then, in terms of the Whitsun annunciation, we can also grasp what spiritual science seeks to achieve. You see, one of its most fundamental endeavours is to enable every human soul to find an inner spiritual core that illumines the universal goals it strives for. As humanity develops in future, individuals ought to become ever less reliant on the social structures that encompass them, each becoming, hopefully, mature enough to live in a way that allows the other an equal life alongside him. Then inner tolerance will inhabit human souls and freedom can be realized in society. There is no other way than this to realize freedom in the world. In other words, the Whitsun message must enter each single human soul.

The Whitsun message is exemplary for how each must work inwardly with others and together take up what the science of the spirit offers. Thus in a sense we can say that spiritual science itself is a perennial, continual, enduring Whitsun annunciation.

If we cultivate these insights on our own soil, the modern age can teach us the need for patience above all. There are friends among us today who, from the outset, have worked inwardly to develop our spiritual-scientific movement. Fifteen, sixteen or even seventeen years have now passed since these beginnings, yet we must always remember how little, how very little indeed so far has been achieved during this time. And from this follows the next thought: that we must arm ourselves with great patience as we reflect on how the science of the spirit, and what it can be and become through us, can actually lead to a re-enlivening of human existence.

What spiritual science can become: we must always compare this with our tiny achievements in the past decade and a half. It is true that many have assimilated what spiritual science offers humanity; and yet, as is clear from our numerous reflections, this is still only the very tip of the iceberg. Spiritual science still needs to flow into society and its structures, into the whole life of modern humanity. If we are to grasp this fully we must also relate it to another thought that rings in our ears today and at every moment from all current world events, embodying a certain conflict into which the human soul is driven, and which has now reached a certain culmination.

Our spiritual-scientific research is founded first and foremost upon a flow of supersensible, spiritual reality into the human soul. The science of the spirit allows us to perceive that spiritual life has always continually flowed into human beings as humanity evolved, and yet that everything occurring on earth can only be seen as progress in so far as people know how to awaken to outward existence what streams into them from the world of spirit. Such a thought ought really to pervade our whole life of feeling. We ought, for instance, to be able to connect it with our more academic knowledge of history and, from this perspective, see how it applies to modern culture. We should be able to ask ourselves, for instance—as a hypothesis of course, and yet such hypotheses lead to realities of thinking—what would have happened if, say, Columbus or someone like him, someone very much connected with the development of modern humanity such as Gutenberg, the inventor of modern printing, or even Luther in the eighth or ninth century, had been born at a different historical epoch. What destiny would then have awaited the individuals who bear these names? Born at a different era, they would most certainly not have become what we know them to have been from our studies of history. Of course this did not happen and is hypothetical, since world evolution has its own karma. And yet these thoughts lead to realities. Such individuals would then have become people unknown to mainstream history. And yet we cannot imagine that modern times would have arrived without, say, the invention of printing, or that the Reformation would not have occurred. This tells us, chiefly, that something is communicated to humanity from the world of spirit, so that we come to see, to a far greater degree than the contemporary world is able, that the human being is an instrument by means of which spiritual realities enter earthly life from the world of spirit.

In relation to such things, as I have said, we find ourselves amidst fierce conflict today. The contemporary world does not acknowledge that a spiritual stream of evolution flows or trickles down into earthly events. It does not acknowledge that the human being is merely an instrument, and the society it seeks to develop is one where this is not acknowledged either. It seeks to develop a social order that takes account really only of the individuals here upon earth. The most extreme caricature of this position is found today, as mentioned recently, in Leninism or Trotskyism:[175] in views of society acknowledging only the very earthly individual. I am not thinking so much of the theories involved here—that is the least of the problem—but their real consequences for life. Lenin or Trotsky are trying to organize and structure society—even in an area where it is least appropriate—as if nothing else exists than the separate, physical human being. This ideal has been developing for decades now in socialist theories, and Leninism and Trotskyism are only the last grotesque birth pangs of a view that has long been forming.

So given this, how can we find our way back to the meaning of the Whitsun event? Certainly it is true that an individual life of mind and spirit must come to illumined rebirth in each separate disciple. But this must be a life of spirit, by virtue of which the greatest conceivable degree of reality—for which we are but an instrument—is imparted to the separate parts of a whole.

At the same time, the Whitsun annunciation has another meaning too, the most important of all: the assurance that a human being does not relinquish any of his worth by becoming an instrument for the spirit that flows continually into humanity. We retain our personal value despite this. This is not just a theoretical insight but something with consequences for life, which needs also to inform the ways we conceive of the state, morality and the life of society. A thought is important in its awakening, kindling power, and an archetype of this, of course, is found in the tongues of fire descending on the head of each one of the disciples. To sleep through current events, as is so commonly the case, is to sin against them. And yet in the cycle of evolution in which we now find ourselves it is quite impossible to awaken to the real nature of events if we do not reflect upon them with a certain inner mobility, if we are unable to distinguish what is essential and true from what is inconsequential and false. Today we are inundated with a flood of newspaper journalism in which a vast amount of dross conceals perhaps just a line or two of huge, real significance, pointing to what is really happening as an archetypal phenomenon—to use a Goethean expression. The rest is just so much wasted ink. We need to awaken an inner sense in us of what is truly important and essential and what is of no consequence in all this. And this faculty can arise in us if we unconsciously acquire the great world perspectives spiritual science can offer. We have to try to integrate this sense and intimation, try to feel as we can when spiritual science comes to life in us. To do so however we need to develop inner trust in what we fathom with our feelings, in our intuitive capacity, to a far greater extent that people today are accustomed to. Anyone who expects an inkling he acquires today to shed light tomorrow on actual events will usually not make great advances with his powers of true observation. Something may be true but events can conceal it and it may perhaps only come to tangible expression in the distant future. Here it is necessary for us to place ourselves into the world in the right way, and develop true ideas about what is happening there.

Extremely important things are happening in the current stream of evolution, and these can be detected in actual events if we know how to observe them as I have indicated: by distinguishing the essential from the non-essential, and having the courage to do so.

To draw out one strand only, the British Empire is in the process of becoming insignificant, and its outward reach and power, its specifically British attributes, are transferring to a kind of general Anglo-Americanism. This is happening right now. British dominance will tend to fade into pan-Anglo-Americanism, and this is very much a part of the development we have been speaking of, and is not at all at odds with it. It is actually extremely important to focus very clearly on such a key thought, since it does matter a good deal whether we allow true or false powers to inform our thinking. As I keep reiterating, the times themselves can teach us a great deal in this respect. Many soldiers have been transformed by their war experiences, as everyone knows who is familiar with the facts. There is no scope here to discuss the nature of this transformation. But there are also a very great number who have been at the Front who still think as they did in July 1914, still resort to precisely the same concepts as they did before and have therefore learned nothing. In speaking to such people one finds that they still say exactly what they would have said in July 1914. And yet anyone who is in the least awake will give every concept a different weight and colour after these events. And this is why we will have to ask—as a very serious and, in fact, Christian question of conscience—where we can find the people today who, prior to July 1914, were fully aware of the possibility of events taking shape as they now have done. Or I could formulate the question a little differently—and you will realize this is not mere whimsy. In the lecture cycle I gave in Vienna before the war[176] you can find that I described human society as containing something comparable to a carcinoma, a cancer in the life of humanity. That was something that needed to be perceived at the time, though many still have not done so. And so I ask this: has any understanding of this idea of a carcinoma in human evolution developed yet?

You see, spiritual science must be taken seriously if it is to be applied to current events. A great part of the reason why spiritual science is so widely rejected is that people feel very uncomfortable with its seriousness. While many enjoy it theoretically, they feel very, very uncomfortable at the seriousness of its implications for life itself. All this, I hope, will lead us to understand more clearly something that I must now include in our reflections, and that it is important to consider if one wishes to understand the very foundations of spiritual science.

In trying to understand things in the world, people today always feel they need to draw their understanding from what is happening at present before their eyes. But the spirit cannot be sought only in this way. If, for example, one wishes to understand the workings of spirit in the human being, it is not enough to consider this human being in present terms only, between birth and death. Why is this? Let us say that you are 50 years old—or some other age—and have an inner life that is connected with the powers of the sentient soul. An immediate perception of the present will make you think that you possess a sentient soul which expresses itself when your inner life of feeling expresses itself. But that is simply not true. In fact your sentient soul developed between the age of 21 and 28, and what lived in your soul then, and came to an end when you were 28, ceasing to live in the soul, still has an after-effect that you draw upon today when you consider the powers of the sentient soul. You make use not of present powers of the sentient soul but of the powers you possessed back then. The past is at work in you. And it is therefore not true to say that the present accounts for everything at work in you. The past also has an after-effect. The world of spirit has to be grasped as music, a music that is real. You would never be able to remember a melody if you forgot the first note by the time the third note arrived. The first note is still working on in the third, is contained and active in it. In spiritual activity, things do not just work on by being retained in memory, in the mind, but they carry on working as a reality. The effects of past forces of spiritual life are continually present in diverse parts of the soul like the different aspects of soul and spirit, though in a different sense. Our reality as 21- and 22-year-olds continues to work in us when we are older, goes on existing. It exists in so far as it existed in the past, not as a present reality. To form new ideas—and what I have now described is, for instance, a new idea not to be found in the range of accustomed ideas today—is uncomfortable for people. They do not wish to acknowledge that when they are old and grey-haired or bald they still speak and think with the powers they possessed in their youth or childhood. And it is simply the truth to say that your experiences at school and what you do from age 18 to 28 live on in you, continue to work in you, for the rest of your life. You cannot replace this by other powers except by turning to the sources which spiritual science opens. This is the only means to make good something lacking in life. You will not be surprised to hear that many people do not make productive use of their lives, and this is connected with our education system. You see, we cannot develop something that has not been planted in us in childhood, has not been implanted through the ordinary powers by virtue of which we address our essentially human nature.

There is a great deal involved in properly understanding such ideas. As I keep trying to accentuate from many different angles, above all it involves learning to have much greater or deeper faith in life, in the spirituality of life. It is relatively easy for people today to believe, say, in their spiritual origins, to conceive of a spirit, originating in a world of spirit, connecting with genetic inheritance through the generations. But this is not sufficient. Above and beyond this we need to believe not only in the spiritual origins of some aspect of our life but of the whole of it.

Because of evolutionary tendencies in humanity that I have often described, we believe that our development has been more or less concluded by the age of 20. In our twenties we believe we are mature enough to stand for election to a municipal council or parliament, that we have all the faculties we need by that age to make the right judgements. By then, people think, they have long overcome the age of immaturity when each year brought new capacities. We expect that different stages of childhood will bring with them changes and developments in inner faculties, and this comes to radical expression at puberty in particular. But after the age of 20 we no longer think there is much further development. We think we have finished developing and do not expect to see any further incisive developments—and this is understandable if we stay with an ordinary view of things. However, we can look at it like this instead: in corporeal terms we do not grow older than 27, at which point bodily development has concluded and has nothing more to offer; anything which is to contribute to our further development must then be drawn from the spirit, and when this happens it unites with our soul. Very few will acknowledge nowadays that by the age of 45 you can gain a different order of experience through inner insight than you can have as a young whippersnapper of 21. Few credit how fertile and productive ageing can be, how much can be gained by growing older. And the very absence of such belief obstructs this inner development, does not allow it to unfold, since people do not attend to the new revelations each year would otherwise bring them. Consider how much would change in human life if this belief gained currency, so that people knew they should wait for an older age to experience things that cannot be experienced beforehand. This would cultivate expectancy and hope in life, something so lacking today. But beyond its personal significance, think what huge importance this would have for the whole of human society. Alongside all the 'levelling impulses' as I will call them, that are playing their part today, consider how human fraternity would benefit if people realized that a person of 40 can have changed and developed through experiences we cannot yet have at 20. If this were a natural sentiment, consider its effect on the way a person of 27 would relate to a 40-year-old. Today, of course, this cannot yet happen since a 70-year-old is often actually no older than a 27-year-old. Those of highest standing in society are often no older than far younger people, and do not even notice this. As yet, therefore, this hope has no reality.

But life must bring these developments. The future is asking us to start to grasp spirit as reality again. Today people generally acknowledge spirit only as a sum of abstract concepts. They arrive at a sum of abstract concepts such as can very well be developed up to the age of 27. And yet real, tangible spirituality is connected with the fact that in our life on earth between birth and death we first have a burgeoning, flourishing life in corporeal development concluding by the age of 28, and that from the age of 35 this physical life begins to decline. This tangible spirituality changes and develops in a way that we can say is opposite to that of our external development. Outwardly we grow old, get wrinkles, but our ether body, or body of formative forces, grows younger, continually younger. Today people pay no attention to this body of formative forces that grows ever younger. People go bald, get grey hair and have no idea that they have, at the same time, a body of formative forces burgeoning and flourishing all the more as they go grey and lose their hair, nor that, precisely then, this can endow them with capacities they could not possibly have had earlier on. Lack of awareness of this is due to the nature of the age we live in, but this is an aspect of the age that needs to change. Our time needs new concepts. In particular, our thoughts need to become healthier and more vigorous and cease to cling to externals, which leads to severe short-sightedness in all areas. We need to learn to use thoughts to penetrate reality in whatever field we explore. For example, we cannot understand history if we cannot complement outward knowledge with inner wisdom. For various reasons connected with the fracture or break in humanity's evolution we have ceased to understand various aspects of grandeur that were previously perceived atavistically. People today consider themselves original in various fields.

Quite a while ago now, in a lecture at Dornach, I raised this question:[177] What would an audience say about a production of Goethe's *Faust* which, after Faust has collapsed before the Earth Spirit, shows the character of Wagner as Faust in somewhat modified form, but still nevertheless identifiable as Faust?[178] Actually a director ought to try staging it like this, and I will explain why.

Think of the great figure of Faust, elevated to cloudy heights, and then of the pedantic character Wagner who is frequently portrayed on the stage as hobbling about rather awkwardly. Faust despairs of the various sciences and this is usually regarded as something very profound, although in fact there are many today of little depth who trivially entertain this idea. Many today respond to the idea that we should grasp the world of spirit by pointing to the deepest ideas in *Faust*: for instance of a self-sustaining and all-encompassing power as this figures in Faust's conversation with Gretchen.[179] People forget that Faust is speaking to a 16-year-old girl and is adapting what he says to her. The whole of humanity likes to take its lesson from these words but in doing so is reducing itself to the perspective of a 16-year-old girl. I have even known professors of philosophy who cite these Gretchen catechisms as the highest wisdom. But the telling point here, at the beginning of the play, is not that Faust is despairing of all the sciences but that he is turning away from the sign of the macrocosm, from the whole world in fact. Initially he wishes to know nothing about how the human being is connected to the whole, great, encompassing universe. Instead he turns to the Earth Spirit and thus to what will reveal to him only what human beings possess by virtue of earthly powers. What the macrocosm reveals to him he regards as a show or spectacle merely,[180] and he turns away from it. And yet the Earth Spirit dismisses him. Faust thought he would be able to grasp through the Earth Spirit something that is connected with his deepest being, but the Earth Spirit brings him to the point of collapse, and speaks these words to him: 'You resemble the spirit you grasp, not me!'[181]

So now let us ask who it is that Faust grasps or comprehends. He himself says[182] to the Earth Spirit, 'Not you? Who then?' And at this very moment Wagner enters. And the message is this: everything you have so far developed is mere feeling and yearning; and what you bear in you can be seen now before you in—Wagner! Wagner is Faust's other nature, the true, dramatic answer to his question. Faust is being asked to understand that, basically, in everything tangible he has so far developed he has not yet become anything more than his own assistant, and this moment of self-knowledge aims to help him progress a little. This reality could be depicted on stage if one showed the two figures standing side by side in close resemblance. But to do this it would require the courage to take these phrases—'You resemble the spirit you grasp, not me!'; 'Not you? Who then?'—far more seriously than has so far happened. One would have to accompany the dramatic action fully with these thoughts, which really can be found in the play itself.

Taking this further, Faust has turned away from the sign of the macrocosm and does not wish to experience the powers that connect us with it, with the whole universe. This was, fundamentally, the position of Goethe himself when he wrote Part I of his *Faust*. And in making good what he omitted in his youth, at least as he looks back on it during the Easter walk and through the Easter night, Faust advances beyond the stage of self-knowledge he encountered in the form of Wagner and arrives at the point where he can recapture what he let slip by before: the message of Easter. Read what Goethe writes here: Wagner does not wish this. The words themselves are resonant with meaning. For instance:

> How is it that a shred of hope remains
> To him who always clings to shallowness?
> With greedy hand he delves for golden coins
> Yet glad is when he digs up worms![183]

It is inevitable that 'no shred of hope remains' for such a person. This is what we discover through self-observation. Faust merely draws all the consequences, but at the same time recaptures what he omitted in his youth. He catches up with it again and recaptures it and this leads him a stage further and higher. This is what justifies repeating the question, 'Who then?' He now resembles the one who appears to him in the 'poodle', the figure of Mephistopheles. What is this really? It is the power that counters human striving and opposes us in the same way that Faust opposes the Earth Spirit when he wishes to have nothing to do with the macrocosm. These are the powers of Lucifer surfacing within us. For this reason Mephistopheles is initially depicted with luciferic features, and why, in Part 1 of *Faust*, Mephistopheles is largely a luciferic being.

But already by the end of the 1790s Goethe was growing beyond the foundations of his youth. If you read the 'Prologue in Heaven' you find that what he elaborates there is no longer bound up with the revelations of the Earth Spirit. Now he is preoccupied with the impulse that enters from the macrocosm. Goethe has grown beyond his own beginnings, and now something enters his soul that is enormously important and, if we can perceive it, allows us deep insight into his being.

Goethe was familiar with the tradition of Faust legends in Teutonic mythology, and this included Mephistopheles. But at the moment when, hard pressed by Schiller, he continues writing *Faust*, Mephistopheles becomes a figure who—although Goethe himself is not fully aware of this—inwardly bothers him, and whom he does not properly fathom. Jakob Minor,[184] a *Faust* exegesist and someone who otherwise has some interesting things to say, found an odd explanation for why Goethe got stuck when he tried to continue the drama. He says it was because he was old, close to 50, when he took up *Faust* again. I can't imagine how, if one's poetic powers dried up by the age of 50, it would ever have been possible to write *Faust*—which depends upon the power of years beyond 50 and on drawing youthful vigour from a life led as Goethe knew how to. But Mephistopheles did instinctively irritate him and prevented him getting any further; the Faust-Mephistopheles conflict would not come right. In his play Goethe had engaged with the great questions facing humanity, but now Mephistopheles was preventing him getting further. The latter had assumed a luciferic character, involving powers that emerge from feeling life. But as soon as Goethe starts writing the 'Prologue in Heaven', Mephistopheles stands there in relation to the macrocosm, and it is no longer adequate just to leave Faust battling with powers at work inside human beings. It is no longer enough to give Mephistopheles a merely luciferic character. Goethe sensed this. I really have no desire to be pedantic but I will quote a few lines simply to indicate something important. In the 'Prologue in Heaven', the Lord says:

> Of all the spirits of repudiation
> The rogue's the one who causes me least bother.[185]

In other words, there are other spirits of repudiation. Yet in *Faust* there is only one: Mephistopheles. And now let us recall that in the 'Prologue' Mephistopheles says:

> What I love best are full, fresh cheeks abloom:
> For corpses I am not at home.[186]

But at the end, as you remember, he does after all make strenuous efforts about the corpse. So what is going on? Goethe sensed that the single Mephistopheles figure he had received from the old Faust legend splits into two when you go out into the macrocosm. Goethe had a dual sense of the figure as both luciferic and ahrimanic, and could get no further because there was no science of the spirit in his day. But later, when he needed to unite macrocosmic events and human concerns in the 'Classical Walpurgis Night', and at the end, where macrocosmic universality and humanity's experience are interwoven as one, Mephistopheles had to assume an ahrimanic character. Goethe very largely succeeded in this. But really everything that Goethe himself said about his relationship to his *Faust* drama conveys the sense of being stuck, of getting no further. In passing from the medieval legend with its folk character to a play of global reach, it is necessary to split Mephistopheles into two, a luciferic and an ahrimanic being, and this was why Goethe found it so hard. Nevertheless he succeeded—naturally I am not finding fault with Goethe—in endowing his Mephistopheles with ahrimanic traits as he approached Part 2 of the play. A luciferic being loves 'full, fresh cheeks abloom', whereas an ahrimanic one is concerned with the 'corpse' since it imbues itself with all we experience in our capacities of sensory perception, and also our consciousness, between birth and death.

If we study an individual such as Goethe we find how he retains youthful powers yet continually draws on these to undergo new experiences in life. What emerges in such a remarkable way in Goethe at the end of the eighteenth century is not due to him ageing but to the crisis he went through; and this gave new birth to certain youthful powers, a kind of Whitsun miracle in him. What I have been saying here about *Faust* is elaborated further in a text about to be republished,[187] entitled 'Goethe's Faust as Picture of his Esoteric Worldview', Part One of a little book called *The Distinctive Mind of Goethe*. Part Two of this booklet will include Goethe's thoughts on *Faust*, and Part Three, some commentaries on his *Fairytale of the Green Snake and the Beautiful Lily*.[188]

In speaking of these things I wish to highlight the need to properly penetrate aspects of humanity's spiritual substance and culture, both now and in the past, and of giving proper weight to what we possess. Over the past four or five decades, you see, we have forgotten how to absorb the greatest aspects of humanity's past and give them full and serious attention. A great deal has been overlooked and neglected in the last 40 to 50 years, and now the cultural and spiritual riches that once existed need to re-emerge, though in a renewed form. Much of this was atavistic, you see, and for this reason was unable to break through certain barriers.

The time was not yet ripe for Goethe to split the figure of Mephistopheles into two, a luciferic and ahrimanic figure. Yet this duality lived in Goethe's nature. In a nutshell, we must learn to believe in the whole of human life and not just in childhood. We must learn to lead a life of expectancy. Just imagine what effect this would have if people looked forward expectantly to being 50. How many people nowadays look forward to this? How many people lead their life in a way that allows new content continually to flow into their soul? What changes would come about in society, too, if this faith in the whole of life were to take root in people? In fact, one simple thought can lead us to this faith in the whole of human life. It is this: Would there be any point in living to the age of 70, on average, if our development concluded at the age of 28? Would there be any reason for going on getting older? Here, though, to be taken seriously, we will need some help from science as a basis for spiritual-scientific insights.

I have said that the science of the spirit—and here I return to the beginning of today's lecture—has so far achieved remarkably little within our movement. Yet the prospect is not hopeless, as one can discern in many circumstances. We can best discern it—and this has often happened over recent decades—when young people studying at university approach us in an endeavour to find something that can connect their studies with spiritual science. These young people, at the outset of their lives, have a sense that every field of knowledge can be led over into the science of the spirit. This can give rise to the most fruitful seeds for the future. But the difficulties arise immediately when these young people, for instance, try to write a thesis that includes spiritual-scientific insights that are certainly relevant to it. This cannot be done, for while spiritual science has a great deal to offer, people are prevented from pursuing it or compelled to turn aside from it. I can tell you of an instance, one long enough ago to allow me to quote it—it would be inappropriate to mention more recent cases—where a student submitted a thesis here in Berlin whose only fault was to mention my book *Christianity as Mystical Fact*.[189] This was a philosophical and not a theological dissertation. The student asked me what he should do, explaining that his supervisor Paulsen[190] would not accept it as it was, that he could not quote Steiner. The only thing I could think of was to advise him to go to Muenster and submit the thesis to Gideon Spicker.[191] This did work. We have to see how things really are, enter into specific realities. The points of view one encounters in trying to embark on an academic career are sometimes very odd. A prospective lecturer—though one who got round this problem as you will hear—once told me the following. He had written a paper on the work of a poet. I won't tell you which, as this has to stay confidential. Then he wrote a paper on Schopenhauer and also of course a doctoral thesis. Now he wished to become an associate professor. He went to the university in question to see the professor about this, a person who liked him well and considered him very capable. He thought this professor would find it easy to appoint him to a lectureship. But the man told him this couldn't be done since he had written a paper about a poet, about aesthetics, but this poet lived in the nineteenth century and this was too recent, apparently. Then he had written a paper on Schopenhauer, which could not supposedly be regarded as strictly academic. 'Well, what shall I do?' the man asked. And the professor told him to find some more or less unknown figure from an earlier period and write a paper on him. This will be easy since there will scarcely be any previous literature on the subject. The prospective lecturer did this, found a literary figure in Italy from a long time back, about whom nothing had been written as yet, and wrote a paper about him which he himself thought most inadequate—an opinion shared by his supervisor. And yet this was a good enough basis for becoming an associate professor!

I do not mention this to find fault with anyone. It is not a matter of individuals since the supervisor himself found it ridiculous that he was obliged to impose these modern prejudices on his charge. And the other person, the one who wished to become an associate professor, found it all ridiculous too. These were two extremely nice people, one older and one younger. It is nothing to do with the people themselves, but with the culture of the age against which one can only make headway with strong, energetic thoughts. And strong, energetic thoughts are only possible nowadays if humanity is made fruitful by the spirit, if we found what we build on what a science of the spirit can give us. Whether we turn to Goethe or to the contemporary world, we will repeatedly hear this call: to renew our world of ideas, our world of feeling; to renew our thoughts in a way that runs strongly contrary to present developments. This in turn depends on the Whitsun miracle being fulfilled in each individual soul, so that in our catastrophic age this miracle reveals itself as a renewal of life. Then human beings, illumined by the spirit, can meet each other as individuals in a way that enables a common will, a common reflection and a confluence of powers to develop and shape the spiritual structure of humanity. From each human individual must come what is needed for the future. We should not wait for a general message to which humanity hearkens, for this will not come. But it will be possible for an influx from the world of spirit to light up in every single human soul. And then what should and must emerge will do so through the way human beings live and work together.

THE NEED FOR NEW FORMS OF CONSCIOUSNESS

Lecture 15

Berlin, 25 June 1918

Today I will summarize various things we have discussed, and expand on them, in order to create a foundation for further key thoughts that we will engage with over the next few weeks.

There are two forms of consciousness familiar to all—dream consciousness and ordinary waking consciousness. In spiritual-scientific research a third form is added, which we call clairvoyant consciousness. We regard dream consciousness really only as a kind of interruption of our continuity of ordinary awareness, and this is because we do not remember our dreams very much. In fact we do dream continually while asleep. The content of our dream life that we are aware of only makes up a part of our total dream experiences—the ones we recall when awake. Spiritual science therefore teaches that we possess three levels or also three modes of consciousness: dream consciousness, ordinary waking consciousness and clairvoyant consciousness which gains access to the supersensible world.

Now you will find it quite easy, starting from clairvoyant consciousness and working your way downwards, to gain insight into the relationship between each form of consciousness and the next. Dream consciousness gives us images. We know that our dream experiences are in images, and that they cannot easily be integrated into the causal sequence of our daily life. If you were to mingle dream life and waking life you would become a fantasist. Thus in our dream experiences we have images that are at odds with what we call daily reality.

If we now consider the relationship between ordinary waking

experiences and the content of clairvoyant consciousness, we find something very similar. You see, what clairvoyant consciousness experiences as spiritual, supersensible reality leads it to regard the experiences of our waking life as image. In an awakened, illumined state in clairvoyant consciousness we can say that we experience true reality, and that in contrast to this what we otherwise call reality is only a sum of images.

Expressing this in an abstract way, as here, has little value. It is true that many are quite content to express these things theoretically, and think that this in itself will solve great riddles of the world, but it won't. Such things only have value if we engage very practically and specifically with them, though this is only possible in particular areas.

One such area—the human being himself—has been the repeated subject of our reflections, and must be so if we are to make progress in the science of the spirit. The human being is a field of study very close to us of course and yet often so far removed. Although people are unaware of the supersensible aspects of the human being, they believe that they know about our physical nature. But this too is true only to a limited extent. Ordinary anatomy and physiology are fields of study fraught with countless illusions. Today, if only apparently, we will start from the outward form of the human being, highlighting his threefold nature as I have often described it.[192]

If we study the human being in relation to the supersensible world, but as image rather than reality, in terms of mainstream anatomy and physiology, we find that his outward physical form can be divided into three very different parts: the head system, the aspect chiefly concentrated in the head, the trunk, and the extremities or limbs. In respect of the latter, though, we have to see that this third part of us does not consist only of arms and legs but also that these limbs have an inward continuation. Let us consider these three systems first of all, which together compose the whole human being.

In fact we ignore supersensible reality in a way if we only consider these separate systems as three parts of a whole, for actually each is very distinct and separate. The diverse powers or, let us say, currents of energy that share in forming their different shapes come from very different directions. If we study the human form with powers of supersensible perception, the powers forming the head have to be seen as originating before birth or conception. To study the head we have to delve backwards into the world of spirit rather than into the stream of physical inheritance. The way in which the human head is formed—though here I am speaking of its subtler structures—originates primarily in all the powers imbuing the human soul in the world of spirit before this soul has united at birth or conception with the physical stream of inheritance. The head is chiefly formed not so much by a person's experiences in a past life, nor his outward form then, but by actions he has done, his deeds, and to some extent also his feelings. When supersensible knowledge develops to the point where we gain insight into a form such as a particular person's head, we can start to look back from this to his last incarnation. We touch here on extremely significant secrets of human development. Far more than is apparent to initiates of a less advanced kind, the form of the human head is connected with a person's karma and the way this develops from a previous incarnation.

We will bypass the trunk system for now and consider our extremities, albeit with their continuation inwards. By no means are these extremities shaped in as individually specific a way as the human head. Each of us has a distinctive head because the latter points back to former lives on earth. The organization of our extremities, on the other hand, with which the sexual organs are also directly connected, points us forward to subsequent lives on earth. As yet, everything in this system is undifferentiated. The soul correlation to this organism points us towards future lives.

It is also very important indeed to consider the trunk organization, which is an interplay of powers at work in the human spirit both before birth and conception, and after death—that is between death and a subsequent birth. In other words, what encompassed the soul during the period between our last death and birth or conception works together in us with what will encompass and surround it between our next death and subsequent birth or conception. These two aspects interweave, acting within the human trunk and becoming especially apparent in the most salient aspect of the trunk organism—the breathing process. The outbreath is primarily an image—and here again

I'm using the term 'image'—of what the soul experienced from its previous death through to its latest conception, while the inbreath is a picture of the powers around and within the soul between our next death and a following conception or birth.

These are tangible distinctions. What ordinary anatomy and physiology lump together as aspects of the human form, with head, trunk and limbs all similarly composed of nerves and blood vessels, is distinguished carefully by supersensible insight. Ordinary anatomy and physiology believes it is dealing with immediate realities whereas our science of the spirit regards the shape of the head as an image of the deeds and feelings of a past incarnation; it sees the outbreath—which is slightly different in quality in each person since the breathing process, like the head, is individual in nature—as an image of the powers that enfolded the soul from our last death through to our latest birth, and the inbreath as an image of powers that will enfold the soul between our coming death and following birth. In the process at work in our extremities we already have an image of our next life on earth. Thus in the same way that our waking life is interwoven with images when we dream, the magnificently expanded supersensible life to which clairvoyant consciousness gains access is pervaded with images too. But these pictures are the 'reality' given to us in ordinary waking life. Every subsequent set of phenomena, starting from clairvoyant consciousness, can be seen as pictures at the next or lower level. Our prosaic reality is a picture of supersensible reality, and our dream reality is a picture of the ordinary reality we encompass in daily life.

What I say here really becomes properly clear only to clairvoyant consciousness simply because the outward human form alone does not reveal all that I have now described. If we assume that someone has a lower degree of clairvoyance, of the kind that gives inklings or intimations rather than fully aware perceptions, he would still be able to arrive at an understanding of the head, trunk and limbs as I have described them. This would not be difficult even for lower clairvoyance. But there would be no certainty in these perceptions; they could not really become conviction without critically testing them by employing a clairvoyance that encompasses states of awareness that accord with aspects of the human form as I have described them. You see, our head points back to former lives not only in its outward form. Its quality of soul distinguishes it, firstly, from the other parts of our nature, but it is also remarkably inwardly differentiated too, though in a way hidden from ordinary awareness. Either this awareness is dreaming or, when engrossed in the content of daily reality, it fails to notice something underlying the head's activity, if I can put it like that. What I mean is this: in waking consciousness we undergo our daily experiences, filling ourselves with the awareness mediated for us by the head by virtue of external sensory perceptions, the pictures conveyed to us by our senses, and our thoughts and ideas about these sensory pictures. All this is so vivid and intense for our ordinary waking consciousness that we overlook a subtler awareness, which continually trickles beneath it. This is a background awareness that is not as loud or insistent as waking consciousness.

Our head actually dreams continually while we are awake. This is important: our head is engrossed in a continual dream behind our waking consciousness. You can access this dreaming by practising some exercises of fairly easy scope. You need only try to enter into that state of inner life in which your consciousness or mind is empty, alert and attentive but without sensory perceptions or thoughts. In ordinary life we are either oriented to our world of external perceptions or have memory pictures of these perceptions, or thoughts which surface and are also connected with our memories. More often than we think, though, we give ourselves up to merely attentive consciousness without noticing this. It is a dull state. But if you try to create a state in you that I will call 'mere waking attention' with nothing originating in external perceptions, memories or memory-connected thoughts, trying instead just to be awake and alert, perceptions not so fully dressed in ideas will soon surface in you. These thoughts that surface have a kind of dulled quality of feeling. One can say that they behave like pictures but without the full weight of pictures. One often encounters people in this state. They can tell you that they have a state of mind which they can perceive but cannot describe, they perceive it but not in the same way as one perceives outward impressions of the world. Such people are speaking the truth, and there are far more than you think who can tell you such things once you know them well.

What surfaces here is the weaving of this underlying consciousness I described, which is a kind of dreaming. But what is being dreamed? The dream is of one's previous incarnation, one's former life on earth. But interpreting this is difficult. And yet this is so: what resides in one's awareness, in head consciousness, is a dream of a former life on earth. In this subjective manner it is possible to access the dream of our past life even though it is difficult to interpret this. We will come back to this again later.

Our description of the human head is therefore complex, also in terms of soul quality, since two consciousnesses are interwoven there: our ordinary waking consciousness and the lower-lying dream consciousness, which is a kind of reflection of our previous incarnation.

If we now consider the other pole of the human being, that of our extremities or limbs, we find another interesting soul characteristic. This system of limbs in us is also complex in soul terms—or in other words in the soul qualities corresponding to it. I have often pointed out[193] that we are asleep in relation to our limb system whereas we are awake in relation to our head. Our will really does appear to sleep, and we have only the pictures and ideas of what our will accomplishes. When we have the picture of moving our hand, we nevertheless are unaware of the connection between this movement and our physical organism. This happens as unconsciously as the processes of sleep. Sleep continually pervades waking awareness of our limbs, this system of extremities in us, and this is because our human will is immersed in a sleeping condition.

But here is a remarkable thing: at night, during sleep, when we are outside our physical body—in other words, when the I and the astral body have departed from the physical body and etheric body so that consciousness or self-awareness do not function, or only in a dulled state—this system of extremities in us wakes up in a sense. But in our current stage of evolution we cannot fathom this with our ordinary consciousness. Because we can activate our consciousness only to a very dull degree when asleep, we cannot observe what our limb system, which sleeps by day, really accomplishes at night while self-awareness is not located within the physical body. This too is a kind of dreaming. This limb system in us dreams, one can say, during the night. Just as the head dreams by day at the same time as it possesses clear, waking consciousness, so our limb system dreams below the level of dulled sleep consciousness, or one can say parallel to it or alongside it. And what does it dream? It dreams of its next earthly incarnation. Our outward human form, you see, not only bears past and future within us but we also bear a past life on earth and a future life on earth in us in our soul life, in the form of ordinarily imperceptible dreams and in all kinds of underlying consciousness.

And now the trunk or thorax. The processes of breathing out and in are not clearly followed by our ordinary awareness, but our organic functions are more closely connected with them. These processes of outbreath and inbreath are raised to conscious awareness in oriental practices—something not appropriate for us. We should enter into clairvoyant consciousness in a different way. The spiritual seeker of the Orient tries to dull his head awareness, to suppress it, and instead to stimulate and illumine consciousness in the thorax. He really does try to make consciousness surface in the breathing process, in the breath. This is a different state of awareness. By becoming aware of how the breath breathed in spreads through the organism, and the breath breathed out streams forth and leaves the body, he raises into conscious awareness what otherwise remains very unconscious. This induces in him a state in which he has a very clear awareness of something of which the breathing process is an image: of life in the world of spirit between death and rebirth. For many people in the Orient it is no theory but a certainty—and this is partly why people of East and West fail to understand each other—that a soul-spiritual life precedes birth and follows death. This is as certain for them as you are certain that after walking for a while you can stop and look back and see the distance you have travelled. Just as you can be quite sure of the path you have travelled and the path you are going to take, so the oriental perceives what lies before birth or conception, and after death, and does so in an immediate way through the breathing process raised into consciousness rather than as a theoretical notion based on ratiocination.

This part of us, the chest, continually dreams in a sense. It does not entirely awaken when we are awake, nor does it entirely sleep when we sleep, although there is a difference between these two states. The dream consciousness of our chest is duller during the day than its dream consciousness at night when we are asleep. Then it is somewhat brighter. There is not a great difference here, but a slight difference of emphasis.

Thus we see that our threefold form is not merely one of outward appearance but also involves complex differentiation of consciousness, and this is what constitutes our inner life or life of soul. These states of consciousness interweave with each other, reflecting one another. What we call our life of thinking primarily arises through the daily waking consciousness of our head. The ongoing dream state of our chest system gives rise to what we call our feeling life; and what we call our will emerges by virtue of the dream consciousness of our limb system, which sleeps in the day and wakes at night.

One thing still remains. When we consider our external aspect, we are concerned not only with a visible, physical organism but we also bear in us a fine, etheric, supersensible organism which, to avoid misunderstandings, I referred to in my recent comments in the journal *Das Reich* as the body of formative forces.[194] Compared to our external physical organism, this supersensible organism is less differentiated, is more of a unified whole whereas only a superficial view will see our outward form as unified. The real unity of our being resides in our etheric body, and this body should be subdivided in the same way as the physical body, not in terms of distinct and separate parts but as I have now done in relation to states of consciousness. This etheric body also undergoes continually alternating states of consciousness; in daily life, from the time we wake up to when we fall asleep, it has a different awareness than it does when we sleep. We bear something very important in us with this supersensible body. It is illusory of some theoretical theosophists simply to divide the human being into physical body, etheric body, astral body and so forth, and to think that this means very much. This merely produces a kind of classification system, and such systems are never very useful. We only gain useful insights if we examine more closely what is actually happening in our etheric body. Just to say we possess an etheric body is to utter a phrase without much significance, a vague picture of some kind of thin fog, and this is illusory. In fact we have in this etheric body something of key importance although we cannot usually perceive it. During waking life, the karma of our former lives on earth continually weaves and lives in our etheric body and is perceived by us. This ether body is at work in our subconscious, and its activity is the perception or vision of our karma from past incarnations. The clairvoyant can gain knowledge of karma by learning to use his etheric body as we otherwise use our physical body. If we learn to use it we cannot avoid seeing karma as a reality. You see, from the time we wake up in the morning until we fall asleep at night, the ether body, if we grasp its reality, is constituted of a vision of our karma. During our waking life it sees our karma from past lives, and during sleep it perceives our developing karma. I am again describing this as clairvoyance sees it.

Thus we dream in our chest not only of what we underwent in the world of spirit between our previous death and latest birth; we not only look upon our past but also upon the karma it involves for us, the past karma which is perceived below the level of ordinary consciousness, as if by an eye of spirit, by the ether body through the function of the lower body. And we gaze upon all that is connected with a future incarnation, with our developing karma, not only via the consciousness of our extremities through the inbreath, but our ether body becomes the eye of spirit to perceive this future karma in a way that is unconscious for ordinary awareness. It is not easy for people today to develop an inner practice to this degree, although it is certainly necessary for every person to actually perceive what I have now described. This presents certain difficulties as I have described in more detail in my book *Knowledge of the Higher Worlds*.[195] This was a far easier undertaking in past eras of humanity. You see, history is also more differentiated than people imagine, and the transition between the third to the fourth post-Atlantean era marked an especially important moment in history, which I have also characterized in *Occult Science*[196] and other texts. This was the moment when the Graeco-Roman age began, the culture of Greece and Rome, when it became so difficult for humanity to penetrate these worlds any more, to have the perceptions I have described. Before this time it was easier, relatively speaking; and orientals have retained something of this capacity. People in the Occident no longer possess it and are therefore unable to engage in the kinds of exercise practised in the Orient. Instead they must turn to those described, for instance, in

Knowledge of the Higher Worlds. The era commencing around the seventh and eighth centuries BC was certainly one when humankind was cast further out into the physical world. Another age will come—beginning fully around the third millennium—and we must prepare for this. Something undefined will rise up into every soul from our human nature at this point, and people will be unable to interpret this without the resources of esoteric science, of spiritual science. What spiritual science must prepare and found for the future millennium is really not subjective in nature, not some kind of wishful thinking, but corresponds to a necessity of human evolution. The middle of the third millennium will bring a significant and incisive development: it will be the time when human nature has developed to the point where it will react in an unhealthy way if, by then, people have not assimilated insight into repeated lives on earth and human karma, which was lost back in the seventh and eighth centuries BC. Previously human nature responded healthily, and knowledge of these things arose naturally from it. In future this same human nature will appear pathological if people themselves do not endow it with these teachings. We can only properly understand the age we live in if we see that in this sense we are enclosed between two poles, one of which lies before the seventh and eighth centuries BC, before the Mystery of Golgotha, when human nature itself gave us knowledge of the soul's supersensible experiences. The other pole will come in the third millennium when, by its own powers as described in *Knowledge of the Higher Worlds*, the human soul must acquire supersensible knowledge by spiritual means so that the body does not succumb to illness but is infused with healthy powers.

Only by grasping this can we understand both outer and inner phenomena in our age. These things are of course only developing slowly and gradually. It is important, if we do not want to sleep through these developments, sleepwalk through them, to notice what is trying to find its way into life, which will only fully unfold by the middle of the third millennium. Gradually it seeks entry, and humanity must start to do everything consciously, consciously preparing the way for what is coming. We have to learn to observe life, and then even outward phenomena, the surface of things—initially in relationship to human life—can show us that what I have said is true. In ordinary, coarser brain development, the necessary insights described in spiritual science do not easily dawn. In a tragic way we can discern what unknown powers, which I will speak about in the next lecture, really want of humanity. At the present time there are certain pathological—and therefore tragic—natures in whom, nevertheless, certain things become apparent already that will emerge in healthy people in the future.

I have often mentioned the name of a very curious man[197] whose life swung back and forth between health and sickness: Otto Weininger,[198] who wrote the strange book *Gender and Character*. Weininger himself is an extremely curious figure. First you have his dissertation, the first chapter of his book, which some praised to the skies while others condemned it. Neither of these was an appropriate, objective response really. Then Weininger increasingly becomes preoccupied with the problems he himself raised in *Gender and Character*. He makes a trip to Italy, records his experiences there, and sees quite different things on this journey than others see there. In this Italian journal by Weininger[199] I find some very curious things. As you know, I describe many things that can only be perceived through Imaginations: from the Atlantean era, from Lemurian times, and how things appeared in times that we cannot easily grasp by contemporary modes of awareness nor through historical records. Here one has to employ certain ideas and concepts, clothe things in a way that the contemporary mind can grasp. When I read Weininger's journal much of it strikes me as a successful, artistic caricature of the truth. Weininger's life in general was rather strange and remarkable. At the age of 23 a thought takes hold of him, hypnotizes him: that he must kill himself because otherwise he will have to murder someone else; that a criminal is lurking in his soul. It is easy to explain this in esoteric terms. Grandeur and exact perception merge in him with a superficial wilfulness. He leaves his parents' home and takes a room in the Beethoven house in Vienna, stays there one night, and in the morning shoots himself.

The distinctive quality of this soul was that it never wholly connected with the body. An ordinary psychiatric diagnosis would call Weininger a 'hysteric'. Anyone who can see deeper will discern that there was an irregular connection between his soul-spirit and his physical body. Unlike others, in whom soul and spirit depart from the body during sleep and reconnect with it on awakening, Weininger's spirit-soul rises out of his body from time to time—I can point you to the passages where this is apparent—then quickly submerges in it again; and as it does so, a thought lights up, which he then records in writing, often in a very dry way. As his soul and spirit immerse themselves in the body again, he becomes imaginative in a very curious way. We can see an irregular connection of the soul and spirit with the body here, which in a very distinctive and curious way gives rise to a form of knowledge that humanity will have to have in the future. Just imagine this: in someone whom mainstream psychiatrists would call a hysteric appears knowledge that humanity will need in future, albeit in caricature form. You can therefore easily see that the precursors of the future—just as there are throwbacks to past eras—can appear amongst us in various forms regarded as abnormal by present standards: precursors of a time when people will need to know about successive lives on earth, about karma, and about how karma is dreamed in us. It is because such people appear as the precursors of future eras that their knowledge renders their organism pathological rather than healing it. By the aid of their pathology, something emerges as a caricature of humanity's future knowledge. For instance, take the following passage from Weininger's book *On Last Things*, published by his friend Rappaport:

> Perhaps it is not possible to recall anything of our condition before birth since we are sunk so deep through birth: we have lost an awareness and have demanded to be born in a quite impulsive way, without rational decision or knowledge, and therefore we know nothing about this past existence.

One thing is clear: even though the insight that has lit up here is a caricature, yet there is absolute certainty of it—that this person emerged at birth from a spiritual state where he existed previously. If anyone had written this in the tenth or twelfth century BC, or even at the time of Origen,[200] there would have been no reason to wonder at it. But when someone writes this in our day, in his own, distinctively emotive way, it is not theoretical but something of immediate reality in his awareness.

I could cite many more such examples. What do they show us?

Nothing other than the prefiguring, the announcing, of this supersensible knowledge that seeks entry into human nature. And because it is not sufficiently sought by means of anthroposophical spiritual science, it enters in cataclysmic ways, convulsing human nature, making it pathological as it did in Weininger. If I use this word I do not do so in a disparaging way. I am simply describing the facts, the reality of illness in someone who shoots himself at the age of 23 because he discovers a concealed murderer within him and wishes to kill himself to save himself from becoming a murderer.

There are hundreds, thousands more such instances. This knowledge is seeking entry! And it would be good if a great many people, as many as possible, would see that this is so. The longing for such knowledge is very widespread in the human subconscious. Outward powers I have often characterized[201] are holding this knowledge back. At the end of my essay[202] on Christian Rosenkreutz,[203] published in the journal *Das Reich*, I commented that we should pay careful attention to what has been emerging since the seventeenth century, or actually already since the fifteenth, announcing itself and becoming increasingly clamorous. The time has come to speak to our contemporaries of this, in forms of ordinary academic discourse. Back then it emerged as I described in the last issue of *Das Reich*, where I spoke of how Johann Valentin Andreae[204] wrote down *The Chymical Wedding of Christian Rosenkreutz*. Philologists have been tearing their hair out over this: Johann Valentin Andreae writes down *The Chymical Wedding*, which in fact conceals profound esoteric knowledge, and after this he behaves in what is really a very curious way. Not only does he engage in elaborate but vain attempts to define certain words relating to texts written by him at the same time as *The Chymical Wedding*, but also, despite having written down the latter text himself, he appears to have no clue to the meaning of what he wrote. The pious pastor, who subsequently wrote all kinds of other things, understands nothing about *The Chymical Wedding*, nor about other texts he wrote at the same time. He was only 17 when he wrote *The Chymical Wedding*. He has not changed, he remains the same person, but a quite different power inspired him at the time. The philologists tear their hair out and compare the handwriting of many different passages in his letters. His hand certainly wrote the text, his body sat there as he did so, but a spiritual power announced itself through his person, a power that was not incarnated on earth at the time but wished to proclaim these things to humanity.

Then came the Thirty Years War, burying much of what should have entered humanity at the time. During this period things that should have been understood were not, were buried instead. *The Chymical Wedding* was written down by the hand of Johann Valentin Andreae—it has been accurately dated to 1603; but it elicited little response since the Thirty Years War started in 1618. Such things sometimes occur before wars begin. But if we read the signs of the times we can discern that what is planted as seed in this way must also bear blossoms and fruit!

This is part and parcel of what I have been intimating: what must be read from the signs of our own, very catastrophic times, and I will speak more of this next week.

Lecture 16

BERLIN, 3 JULY 1918

NEXT week I will continue the observations we began a week ago, and draw some conclusions from them. But today I wish to speak of something apparently not connected, but in fact very much so, which relates to our building in Dornach.[205]

The very distinctive quality of this building is intended to play a part in humanity's evolution: the spiritual development we have perceived as beginning in our time and which we must assume will continue to unfold. We have attempted to shed light from the most varied angles on the characteristic nature of these present and future developments, so far only present in germinal form. Today let us consider how the aims of anthroposophically oriented spiritual science are expressed through the building in Dornach that will be dedicated to it.

One way to consider contemporary developments is to study them externally, as people are accustomed to do whose whole focus and outlook are adapted to outward reflection. But in our time there is also good reason to observe the inner aspect of all that happens. In fact we can only gain a true picture of what happens in the world by bringing spiritual insight to bear on it, on how it has long been prepared and will in future assume quite different forms from contemporary occurrences. I would like to start today with something very material in nature, which can however be spiritually observed to reveal impulses always active around us.

Though few people have formed a comprehensive view of contemporary occurrences, those who have include some engineers. Several decades ago, in 1884, the mechanical engineer Reuleaux[206] wrote an essay about characteristic aspects of modern culture, albeit from his materialistic perspective. At the time he divided modern humanity into two groups, one whose way of life and outlook he called 'natural' and the other 'manganistic'. He derived the latter word from magic, as an attempt to employ the powers of the universe to intervene in human life. Today, very briefly, I first want to consider this division of humanity into two.

In former times, in a sense, all people were 'natural', and the great majority are so still today. The minority, composed primarily of central and western Europeans, and the people of America, are 'manganistic' people. The important thing to note here is that 'natural' culture still plays an important part in modern life. It is significant that so-called manganistic culture has only really developed gradually during the past century. The most paradoxical outcome of this latter-day culture is that it has artificially introduced into the world much more human presence than the actual number of human beings on earth. Over the past few decades, this smaller portion of humanity has brought the machine, mechanical inventions, to untold development. You will not be surprised to hear that a great proportion of the work accomplished nowadays is done by machine. Yet you may be somewhat astonished to hear the scope—which can be calculated—of human work now done by machines in place of human beings. This can be calculated as I say, in terms of the millions of tons of coal that are consumed annually to power these machines. One discovers that the work accomplished in this way through coal-powered means comes to no less than that of 540 million human beings, who would need to work 12 hours every day to do what these machines do. In truth, therefore, we cannot say that there are just one and a half billion people alive on the earth. Besides these there are another 540 million more, existing by virtue of the manganistic, rather than natural, work accomplished by machines overseen by a minority of the earth's population. The population of the earth is not truly expressed by population statistics, for they should include a further 540 million people. One can say that in Europe and America—less so in eastern Europe—we are surrounded by work that continually impacts on our daily life, of far greater dimensions than we realize. This work simply replaces natural human endeavours.

The people of the West are extremely proud of this accomplishment. They highlight the fact that what machines perform produces a great deal more than is produced in the rest of the world by far greater numbers of people who do not yet employ machines to such a degree and live in a 'natural' way. Thus we can say that if the work done by machines were undertaken by people instead, 540 million people would have to work 12 hours a day. That is a lot. And, as you know, our modern global culture is very proud of this achievement, which has various consequences.

To gain insight into what underlies this, you need only consider one instance where 'natural' culture intrudes a very great deal into our modern 'manganistic' one. The match is an example of this. The younger ones among us will not remember this, but the older members will recall times when matches were still rare and a flame was kindled with steel, stone and tinder. This leads us back further still to an older way of kindling fire: to the bow-drill, which required a great deal of human effort to get a flame going by turning a wooden drill in a piece of wood. If you compare this ancient, 'natural' way of kindling a flame with the modern match, something else becomes apparent. To a large degree the whole of our manganistic culture renders invisible the laws which people were once close to. It suppresses these active laws. Consider the ancient way of making fire; the work a person had to undertake to do this was intimately connected with himself and his personal accomplishments. Nowadays physical, mechanical or chemical processes replace this and distance us more from natural phenomena and our involvement in them—in which a spiritual occurrence is also at work. Natural phenomena are removed from immediate human activity. You will frequently hear people saying that new technologies have subjugated and mastered natural forces to serve us. From a certain point of view this is fully justified, but it is very one-sided and incomplete. In everything which mechanical agency accomplishes—a term in which I also include the transformation of matter into chemical energy and its use—natural forces not only serve humanity but are pushed further away from us along with their deeper connections to what, really, are world impulses. In the machine, the human being is gradually withdrawn from a clear view of natural process itself. Technology therefore does not only serve humanity but pushes something away from us. Through technology something dead comes to overlay living nature. The living quality that once played directly from nature into human labour is pushed away from us. And if you consider that really we extract what is dead from nature to introduce it into manganistic culture, it will no longer be so surprising to you if I relate the science of the spirit to what a mechanical engineer has to say.

The engineer Reuleaux accentuates the fact that humanity's recent progress is dependent—and here he is right from his particular perspective—on enlisting natural forces to serve human culture. Above all, however, we must first turn our attention to the fact that we are dealing here with mechanisms, with machines, that replace human effort. This is not just something confined to what we see with our senses, but this process, this creation of an extra workforce of 540 million 'people' on earth has a very significant spiritual dimension. Human energy has crystallized in everything that has arisen in this way: human reason flows into it in a sense and works within it, but this reason surrounding us in machines has now become detached from human beings. The moment we detach from humankind something that is intrinsically connected with it, the powers we have described as ahrimanic in our science of the spirit take direct possession of it all. These 540 million contrived beings on earth are at the same time containers for ahrimanic powers, for the powers of Ahriman. This is something we should be aware of, and it means that the purely outward progress of our civilization is bound up with ahrimanic powers; and these are the same as exist in the nature of Mephistopheles, which closely resembles ahrimanic qualities. But nothing one-sided ever exists alone in the universe without its opposite number: never just one pole without the other pole emerging. These ahrimanic qualities arising on the earth in the material forms of industry and so on, the machine age, have their counterpart in a corresponding complement of luciferic qualities engendered in the spiritual realm. Ahrimanic nature never emerges in isolation but, to the same degree that it emerges visibly on earth as I have described, it is balanced by luciferic qualities that are interwoven with this whole, ahrimanically imbued culture. The will of human beings on earth as ahrimanic culture crystallizes is at the same time infused with a spiritual correlate, and this works into human intention, human impulses, passions and moods. A luciferic spirit being actually exists to correspond with every ahrimanic machine. As we create our machines, we slip down into a dead realm, which is therefore all the more outwardly visible and apparent as ahrimanic culture. But as a mirror image of this whole ahrimanic culture, an invisible luciferic culture arises. In other words, humanity's morality, ethics and social impulses are pervaded by luciferic moods to an extent corresponding to the increasing scope and number of machines. The one cannot arise without the other. This is how the world is composed.

We can see from this that it is never a matter of fleeing Ahriman, nor, equally, of fleeing Lucifer. All we can do is observe the emergence of this state of affairs in which polar ahrimanic and luciferic qualities balance each other and are inevitably connected with the further developments of human culture in our time. Spiritually perceived, this is what happens. And, starting in our time we must increasingly try to perceive things spiritually.

Now it is very striking that when Reuleaux, the mechanical engineer, lauded humanity's manganistic progress—which was wholly justified from his perspective (and spiritual science should never be reactionary)—he also emphasized something else. He pointed out that humankind in this developing new world of machines, especially in Europe and America, will need to cultivate stronger powers of spiritual life and culture than formerly, when culture was still more embedded in nature and when human labour related more intimately to the natural world. Naturally he did not speak of Lucifer or Ahriman but simply described things as I presented them at the beginning of today's lecture. I'm sure you will be able to discern what I have added to the observations of an engineer who lives fully in the modern, materialistic world. For instance, Reuleaux said, naively,[207] that if art is to continue to thrive, it will require stronger engagement with aesthetic impulses than was necessary in former times of more instinctive culture. But he was basing this statement on a rather curious belief, a naive belief apparent from his statement that in art the human soul lives more intensely in aesthetic laws compared to the anti-aesthetic machine—something he readily admitted. He saw the machine as invidious to art. But his naivety here is his complete lack of awareness that this will require the development of more intense and active artistic powers imbuing the human soul than used to be the case. He could see that technology is attacking everything that humanity once drew from spiritual sources, but not the inadequacy of compensating for this merely by returning to these old sources. This really is not possible. Stronger, more spiritual powers must enter our spiritual life as human culture advances on the physical plane, for otherwise humanity would inevitably succumb entirely to materialism however much it theoretically resists this.

You may perhaps see from this that, starting from awareness of the impulses at work in our modern culture, we can come to insight into the inner nature of current developments. Art needs a new impulse, a new impetus. If our anthroposophically oriented spiritual science is to offer new impetus to the old spiritual culture of humanity, then inevitably art too must receive a new impulse of this kind.

A first and naturally very imperfect beginning has been attempted here with the building at Dornach. I fully acknowledge the imperfections of what is only a first attempt. But it may be justified for us to see it as heralding further developments of this kind, further progress on this path. Those who will follow after us, who will continue working when we have long departed from our physical bodies, will hopefully do it better. The impulse for the Dornach building did have to emerge now, though. You see, we can only properly understand this building if, instead of applying absolute standards to it, we concern ourselves a little with its history. I would like to start from this since we continually encounter misunderstandings in this respect.

As you know, from 1909 onwards our work was associated with the performance of various mystery plays[208] aiming to give an artistic and dramatic portrayal of the powers at work in the world, as we see them. These performances in Munich were accompanied by lecture cycles that were always well attended;[209] and our Munich friends therefore conceived the idea of creating a building dedicated to these activities and spiritual endeavours. This was instigated not by me but by the members in Munich, and I beg you to remember this. The building was really a response to the feeling among a good number of our members that more space was needed. Given this need, it was quite self-evident for this new building to have an architectural form in harmony with our world-view. In Munich this was conceived only in terms of internal design and architecture since the building was to be surrounded by a number of houses accommodating members who wished to settle there. These dwellings would have adjoined and surrounded the new building, which, since it would not have been visible amongst the other dwellings, was intended to be as inconspicuous as possible. Only the internal architecture of the new building was therefore considered; and internal design only has significance in this case if it affords a context and framing appropriate for the activities that go on there. But this must be conceived artistically. It must not just reflect but really give artistic expression to the activities that happen in it. This is why I always compared the architectural concept of our building—perhaps a little trivially and yet also aptly—with the idea of a cake mould or cake tin, which gives the cake inside it the right form. The 'cake tin' in this case is all that surrounds and encompasses our spiritual-scientific activities, our artistic endeavours and all that is spoken, heard and felt there. All the latter is the 'cake', and the rest is the tin; and this needed to find expression in the internal design of the building. But after various endeavours to conceive and realize these plans on the site we had already acquired in Munich for the purpose, we ran into opposition not from the police or the local council but from the artistic community in Munich. We realized that people were affronted by what we wished to establish there, although they did not say what they themselves would have done instead. Whatever further modifications we might have introduced, the whole thing could have gone on fruitlessly for decades. Finally we decided to abandon the idea of a building in Munich and to use a site in Solothurn instead, which one of our members had offered us for the purpose. The building was therefore to be built on the hill at Dornach, near Basel, in Solothurn canton. Here there were no surrounding houses and the building would be visible from all sides. And people were very keen for the building to be built quickly. Without completely altering the idea I had already formulated for the internal design, all I was able to do was to try to connect the building's exterior with the internal design as already conceived. This meant that the building as a whole had certain deficiencies, which I, more than anyone, am aware of. But that is not the chief thing. What is important is that a beginning has been made as I said.

But now I would like to consider a few things briefly that aim to show the distinctive nature of this building, so that you may see how it is connected with our whole spiritual-scientific or spiritual stream.

The first thing you will notice if you look at it without prejudice is that the building's outer cladding, its walls, are conceived as quite different from ordinary buildings. The artistic idea underlying the outer wall of all buildings hitherto is to shut them off from their surroundings. Outer walls are always conceived as defining the limits of the building, and all architectural and sculptural work on these walls is associated with this overriding idea of the wall as delimitation. While we have naturally retained an aspect of this in a physical sense in our building in Dornach, in artistic terms we have broken with this customary view: here the exterior wall does not confine and delimit the space of the building but instead opens its space to the whole universe, the macrocosm. If you are inside this building, therefore, you should have the sense that the space in it is broadened into and connected with the macrocosm through the walls and their shape. Everything in it aims to represent such connections with the universe. This is the underlying principle in the shape of the walls, in the pillars too which accompany the walls at certain intervals. It is the principle too in all the carving and sculptural elements, the pillars with their pediments, architraves, capitals and so forth. In other words, the walls are conceived as transparent to the soul, as opposed to ordinary walls that shut off and delimit space for the soul. Here we should feel ourselves to be free in the infinity of the universe. Naturally physical space does still have to be delimited, but the forms of these boundaries can be artistically worked to overcome the sense of this physical confinement.

Everything else in the building is connected with this principle. The symmetries we find in other buildings had to be dissolved correspondingly. The Dornach building only has a single axis of symmetry, really, oriented precisely on an east-west axis, and everything else is arranged around this axis of symmetry. The pillars at intervals along the walls therefore do not bear identical capitals but stand in pairs, on left and right, of identical capitals and other form elements, each pair differing from the next. Thus if you go in to the building through the main entrance, you first come to two identical pillars, whose capitals, pediments and architraves are the same. And thus you pass identical pairs as you continue through the whole building. This enabled us to introduce evolution into the motifs of the capitals and pediments. The capital motif of each pillar always evolves from that of the previous one, exactly as an organically more perfect form evolves from one less developed. Here the identity of symmetry is resolved into ongoing development.

The whole building consists of two main parts—the rest of it are subsidiary or adjoining spaces—which have a basically circular plan and finish above as domes. However these two cupolas intersect in a segment, and so their base is not composed of complete but of incomplete circles. A forward part of the smaller circle over the smaller space is missing, and this is where the other circle, that of the large hall below, connects with it.

The whole is such that we have two cylinders here, one of larger and the other of smaller diameter. In the larger is the auditorium, while the other smaller cylinder is where the mystery plays and other presentations are performed. At the place where the two circles merge will stand the speaker's rostrum. There too the curtain is situated. In this way the two cupolas are joined, something that has not been done before in this way. Technically, too, it was an interesting challenge: to make two cupolas intersect and join with each other. The whole wooden edifice rests on a concrete base and platform, which really only comprises the cloakrooms. Concrete steps lead up from there into the wooden building itself, which rests on the concrete foundation.

Along the length of the wall of the larger cylinder beneath the larger cupola run seven pillars on each side, and in the smaller space six pillars on either side. Thus in this smaller space, which forms a kind of stage area, stands a circle of 12 pillars, and of 14 pillars in the larger auditorium. The sculptural motifs of these pillars develop as we pass around the circle. The motif developments surprised me myself even as I worked on them. When I made the model for them, conceiving the pillars and their capitals, one thing greatly surprised me: there is absolutely nothing symbolic about them. People who have described the building to others, saying that there are all kinds of symbols adorning it and that the anthroposophists work with symbols, are wrong. There isn't a single symbol in the whole building, in the sense they mean it. Rather, the whole building is shaped in accordance with its overall form, is conceived in a purely artistic way. In other words it does not signify—to use this word in its worst sense—something that is not actually there. Instead, this ongoing evolution of the capital motifs, and of the architrave motifs, is drawn purely from the way one form emerges and arises from another. As I developed each form out of the last in this way, it gave rise in a quite natural way to a picture of evolution, of evolution truly perceived rather than Darwinian notions of it. I did not plan this in advance but it arose quite naturally and led me to see—I myself was surprised by this—how certain human organs, for instance, are simpler than in a lower order of animals. I have often said that evolution does not make things more and more complex. The human eye, for instance is more perfect by virtue of being simpler than in animals, evolving towards greater simplicity. As I created these motifs it became apparent to me that from the fourth motif onwards a process of simplification was necessary. What is more perfect turns out to be simpler.

But this wasn't the only thing that surprised me. When I compared the first pillar with the seventh, the second with the sixth, and the third with the fifth, I discovered remarkable congruencies. In working sculpturally, of course, one has areas of relief and concavity, which I created out of immediate feeling and perception. But in looking at the capital and pediment of the seventh pillar I found that the relief areas of the seventh pillar corresponded to the declivities of the first, and vice versa. They accorded precisely with each other. I am speaking in terms of convex and concave of course. An inner symmetry arose quite naturally, and was quite different from an outward one. In the metamorphosis of the motifs and their sculptural realization, the architecture became more mobile and the sculpture came to rest. All is simultaneously wooden carving *and* architecture.

The whole building rests on a concrete understructure whose interior has motifs which are likely to surprise those who enter it. Naturally people come with preconceived ideas and judge what they see according to what they know. Many who were not sure what to make of it all have said that the Dornach building is 'futuristic'. The forms of the concrete part of the building are conceived in response to the new material, concrete and its artistic potential. But within the concrete shell we have also tried to create pillar-type supports. Quite of themselves, these assumed the appearance of elemental beings who grow, gnomelike and riven with fissures out of the earth, and at the same time have a load-bearing design. And so one sees that they give support, but they bear a heavier part, which they push back, shift back, in a different way from a lighter part. That is the wooden substructure.

The need also arose for windows, something that wouldn't have figured in Munich where we were concerned only with interior design. If you wish to understand the windows, I would ask you to try to picture the whole idea of the wooden structure first. As it stands there it is not yet really art or at least not an artwork in itself. The pillars, walls and sculptural motifs are artistic but the whole thing does not aim to have a decorative character; there was no decorative intent. Instead, it will invoke in anyone looking at it certain feelings and thoughts in every line and surface. One has to follow the lines and surfaces of the building with one's eyes, with feeling vision. What we experience inwardly as we let our gaze run over these contours really only gives rise to an artwork, in relation to the wooden sculpture, that comes into being in human sensibility. The concrete substructure and the wooden part of the building prepare this work of art in us. The work of art is something each person must create for himself, build up in himself, through his delight in these forms. In other words, this is the most spiritual part of the building. The work of art that emerges only does so, really, when the receptive soul of the listener or the speaker is inside the building. And so it was necessary to insert windows, always one window corresponding to the space between two pillars. To elaborate here too on the underlying principle of the building, we had to find an appropriate glass-engraving technique. We took coloured panes of glass and engraved corresponding motifs into them and thus we have glass windows with etched motifs. Using a larger version of the instrument that a dentist uses when he drills into a tooth, we etched into the thick glass panes to remove what we needed to, creating different thicknesses of glass. The motifs arose from these differences of thickness. Each pane is of a single colour, and the sequence of windows with different colours gives rise to a harmony. In its axis of symmetry the building, as one passes through it from the entrance, displays a sequence of coloured windows in harmonious colour evolution. But here again the work of art as such is not yet complete. It only becomes so when the sun shines through; and so we have created here in this system of glass windows something that requires living nature outside to interact with the glass engravings to create the work of art.

The motifs engraved on the coloured windows show many aspects of the content of our spiritual science, always perceived imaginatively: the dreaming human being, the intrinsic nature of the wakeful human being, diverse secrets of Creation, and so forth. These are not portrayed in symbols but in direct perception: all with an artistic intent but only complete when the sun shines through them. Here again therefore we have tried to do the same thing by other means—to overcome the confinement and enclosure of the space. With the architectural and sculptural treatment of the building we have tried to use forms in a way that overcomes space, inwardly of course, not physically, and lead the gaze out beyond it. This is already more sensory and tangible in the case of the windows, whose connection with the sunlight shining through from the cosmos, shining also through our visible world, is something intrinsic to them. These two aspects of the building therefore primarily correspond to an element of soul created from without on the one hand by the interaction of light and glass engraving to produce the work of art as such, as soul element; and on the other, the spiritual element arising through the wooden sculpture experienced as work of art in the human soul itself.

The third aspect of the building is embodied in the paintings on the inside of the cupola, whose motifs are, once again, drawn from our spiritual-scientific world-view. Here expression is given to the content of our world-view in painting, at least as this extends over a certain large, macrocosmic time frame. Here you have the physical aspect of the matter, if I can put it like that. You see, in painting—for certain inner reasons that are beyond the scope of today's lecture—what one wishes to portray can only be portrayed directly. The colour itself must express what it is intended to, likewise the forms and lines of a painting. We have therefore tried through the content depicted there to go out into the macrocosm, to overcome the boundaries of the cupola walls. The content itself carries us outwards, and these paintings depict everything, really, that belongs to the macrocosm, and thus our eyes see what is intended in a directly physical way. We have tried to accentuate the luminosity needed for painting these motifs by using pure, plant-derived colours. Naturally all this has not been as successful as it might have been if the war had not intervened. It is anyway only a beginning. The mode of painting employed here naturally has to accord with our view of things. In painting the spiritual content of the world, we are not concerned with figures and forms conceived as illumined by a light source but illumined from within and of themselves. Thus painting here must acquire a quite different character. If we paint a human aura, for instance, we have to paint in a different way from that used to depict a physical form. A physical form is painted by distributing light and shadow across it as they would be when illumined by a light source, whereas the aura is self-illumined; and so the nature of such painting becomes quite different.

In very broad outline, therefore, to the extent we can describe such things without pictures, these are our aims for the building. As I said, the whole building is oriented from west to east, with the axis of symmetry passing through the pillars in the same direction, intersecting with the small cylinder, thus the stage area, at its eastern edge. And here, as one faces east, between the sixth pillar on the right and the sixth pillar on the left, stands a sculptural group[210] carved in wood. This is an artistic representation of what I will call the most intimate aspect of our spiritual-scientific world-view, seeking to depict something that must necessarily come to inform human spirit vision in our time and in the future. Humanity must learn to see that everything of importance for the world's development and human life flows into the three streams portrayed here: in a sense the normative spiritual stream with which we are interwoven, then the luciferic stream, and the ahrimanic. Divine evolution, luciferic evolution and ahrimanic evolution are interwoven with everything: both the foundations of physical life and the manifestations of spiritual reality. Again, though, this should not be conveyed symbolically but should become living, artistic expression in this sculptural group. A sculpture in wood. This idea came to me, and I believe I grasped it as idea and yet I am not yet myself clear about the reason for this in its esoteric depths. I trust that future esoteric research will make this plain. It certainly strikes me as quite right, though, that while all ancient motifs are best represented in stone or bronze, all Christian motifs—and this is a Christian motif in the truest sense—are better executed in wood. All I can say is that I have always found it necessary to re-imagine the group in the Church of St Peter in Rome, Michelangelo's Pietà, in wood. And only then, I believe, would it represent what it should. And the same is true of the other Christian sculptures in stone. I have not yet discovered why this should be so. But at all events, our group had to be conceived and executed in wood.

The chief figure in this group is a kind of representative of humanity, a figure who should represent the human being in his divine manifestation. I will be happy if anyone who looks at this figure has the feeling that it is a representation of Christ Jesus. But even trying to create the figure of Christ Jesus would have seemed to me an inartistic endeavour. I wished to represent what actually stands there. The viewer of the piece is then free to experience whether this is Christ Jesus. I would be very pleased if this is his experience, but it was not my preconceived intention to portray this. A truly artistic thought is embodied in purely artistic form, in the figure and shape, while anything else is a novelistic or programmatic idea, a preconception of how Christ Jesus should be represented. Art, at least sculptural art, lives in form. So in this group—which stands eight and a half metres high—the chief figure is somewhat elevated, with cliffs behind it and cliffs below. Underneath, from a cavern in the rocks, an Ahriman figure emerges. The figure is half-reclining in its rocky cavern, its head directed upwards. Above, upon these somewhat undercut rocks, stands the chief figure of the group. Above the figure of Ahriman, and to the left of the viewer, a second Ahriman grows forth from the rocks, so that the figure of Ahriman is reproduced a second time. On the viewer's left likewise, and also above the Ahriman figure, is a Lucifer figure. A kind of artistic connection has been created between Lucifer and Ahriman below him. Just a little higher, above the chief figure of the group, and to the viewer's right, is another Lucifer figure. Lucifer is therefore also represented twice; and this other Lucifer has collapsed inwardly, and now falls headlong because of this. The right hand of the central figure points downwards, the left upwards. The upward-pointing left hand points to the place of rupture in Lucifer, to the exact place where he has broken in two and tumbles downwards. The right hand and the right arm of the central figure point down to the lower figure of Ahriman and make him despair. The whole is conceived—I hope people will get this sense of it—without any aggression from the central figure: there is only love in the gesture I described. Yet neither Lucifer nor Ahriman can bear this love. Christ does not battle with Ahriman but simply radiates love. But neither Lucifer nor Ahriman can allow love into their proximity. Through its proximity one of them, Ahriman, experiences despair, a sense of being inwardly consumed, while Lucifer falls headlong in consequence. The gestures of Lucifer and Ahriman convey this inner state.

These figures of course were not easy to create since I had to create spiritual beings—Lucifer and Ahriman are entirely spiritual beings and the central figure is so partly. It is the hardest thing of all to convey spiritual reality in sculpture. Yet I tried to achieve what was needed, especially for our purposes: to resolve the form, although it necessarily remained artistic form, entirely into expression and demeanour. As human beings we have only a very limited capacity to use gesture and facial expression. Lucifer and Ahriman, on the other hand, are entirely gesture and demeanour. Spirit forms do not have clearly defined outlines and confines and are never fixed. If you wish to give artistic expression to the spirit this is like trying to portray lightning. A spirit has one form one moment and another the next, and we have to take account of this. Trying to fix a spirit form as it is at one moment, in the same way that one depicts a resting human form, would give rise only to a rigid figure far removed from reality. Instead one has to invest everything in the gesture, as I have tried to do here with Lucifer and Ahriman and partly also for the central figure who naturally is a physical figure: that of Christ Jesus.

Now I would like to show you a few photographs to give some sense, as far as this is possible, of this central group. The first shows the head of Ahriman, in the form this first came to me: a person—think here of the threefold human being consisting of head, trunk and extremities—who is entirely head, and who is therefore an instrument for the most extreme cleverness, wariness and cunning. The figure of Ahriman seeks to convey this. As you can see here, the head of Ahriman is fully spirit, if I can use this paradoxical expression—but you are aware that spiritual descriptions often have a paradoxical character. The figure is true to the spirit, artistically true to nature. Ahriman had to 'sit still' so that this could be achieved.

The next one shows Lucifer, seen to the left of the group from the viewer's perspective. To understand Lucifer one has to think in a curious way to conceive his spiritual form: one has to 'think away' what is most ahrimanic in the human figure, thus get rid of the head, but at the same time greatly enlarging in your mind the ears and auricles, the outer ear, though naturally spiritualized, and forming wings; and formed into an organ, albeit one wound around the body, together with the larynx which is likewise greatly enlarged. And thus the figure's head, wings and ears together form one organ. The wings and this head organ arise when one seeks to portray Lucifer. Lucifer is a widened and broadened larynx—a larynx that becomes the whole figure and from which, through a sort of wing, a connection is made with the ear. You see, Lucifer is an entity who hears the music of the spheres, assimilating this into his wing-ear organism; and, without any interference or utterance from individuality, the cosmos, the music of the spheres, speaks through this organ which, transformed in the front into larynx, is thus another metamorphosis of the human form—a larynx-ear-wing organ. His head is therefore only rudimentary. If you go and see this group in Dornach you will find that the figure of Ahriman embodies what can be conceived as form and figure, whereas the head of Lucifer—although it is difficult to picture this being so—is something beautiful to the greatest degree. Thus Ahriman is everything reasoned, clever but ugly in the world, while Lucifer embodies beauty in the world. Youth and childhood are more luciferic, and advanced age more ahrimanic. The past is more ahrimanic and the future more luciferic in their impulses. Women are more luciferic and men more ahrimanic; but everything consists of both these streams.

The being above Lucifer arose as an elemental being growing out of the rocks. The group was more or less finished and we had taken away the scaffold when, curiously, it became apparent—as Miss Waller expressed it[211]—that the whole gave the sense of too much weight on the right, in aesthetic terms only of course, and needed a counterbalance. Rather than merely adding another lump of cliff, it was necessary to pursue the sculptural idea further. And so this being here emerged, growing out of the rocks like an elemental entity—an addition that karma asked of us, you might say. You will notice one thing in particular with this being, albeit only as intimation: that asymmetry must prevail the moment we consider spirit forms. In the physical realm this comes to only very limited expression: our left eye is slightly different from our right, and so on; the same is true of ears and nose. The moment we enter the spiritual domain, the ether body acts in a very asymmetrical way. The left side of the ether body is quite different from the right, and this comes to the fore the moment one tries to create spirit forms. You can walk around this being and it will show you different aspects from every different angle. But you will see that asymmetry is necessary here as expression of the gesture, a certain humour, with which this being looks over the cliff and gazes down upon the group below. There are good reasons why it looks down humorously like this over the edge of the cliff. It is wrong to try to rise into higher worlds equipped only with mere sentimentality. Sentimentality is misplaced in such efforts since it always has a tinge of egotism. You will often notice that in speaking of the highest and most spiritual matters I introduce a certain tone to try to dampen egotistic sentimentality. People will only be able to raise themselves to the spirit by avoiding egotistic sentimentality, entering spirit realms instead with a purity of soul that can never be entirely devoid of humour.

Now here is the head of the central figure in profile, as it necessarily arose. Here again the head needed to have a somewhat asymmetric quality, showing that the inner soul of this figure is expressed not only, say, in the movements of the right and left hands, of the right arm and so on, but that this inner life in a being such as Christ Jesus, who lives entirely in the soul, also impresses itself upon the form of the forehead and the whole of the figure. This is much more so here than can be true of human gestures otherwise. Although this doesn't correspond to reality we experimented with reversing the slide in the projector, thus giving a quite different appearance simply by means of this reversal. This gives a different impression. The artistic conception of asymmetry, though, is something you will see only in the finished head of the central figure. It is true to say that all artistic questions really do play into the elaboration of such a form. The smallest artistic question of detail invariably relates to a much broader whole. Here, for instance, we were particularly concerned with the surface treatment, which is key to a sense of life and vitality. First curving the plane and then curving the curve again, this special treatment of the surface with its double curvature draws life itself from the plane—and this is something we only notice as we work through these things. And so you will see that what we sought to achieve does not lie only in the content or represented idea but also in a certain artistic handling of the subject. Rather than a novelistic or representational depiction, we tried to convey ahrimanic and luciferic nature, and human nature too, by a kind of fingertip sensitivity to material, working right down into the surfaces in a fully artistic way. The broadening of our perception into the spiritual realm is matched in the other direction by a deepening of artistic expression.

This group is to stand in the stage area on the east side of the building, and above it arches the smaller cupola, the latter also painted as I described. Above this group we have tried to recreate the same motif again in painting. Here is the Christ, with Lucifer above and Ahriman, and we have tried to use colours to artistically express all this. You can see from the different modes of treatment that such things must be drawn entirely from artistic means.

All this was only possible thanks to a number of our friends who worked on the building with the greatest dedication. The most curious comments have been made about the building, but eventually perhaps people will come to see what dedication and commitment was shown by members of our society, artists in particular, in devoting themselves so selflessly to its creation. In relation to this sculptural group in particular, important artistic questions arose. Miss Maryon,[212] for instance, worked most wonderfully at transforming a world-view into artistic expression. Naturally the building is not yet complete, though no doubt it would have been by now if it had not been for the catastrophic global events which hindered our work.

In these brief, aphoristic outlines I wanted only to show you what we intended to accomplish with this building. I hope that this has given you at least a small glimpse of what we can now hope will eventually come to completion in Dornach. Our concern here is to place our world-view visibly and artistically into the culture of today and the future. Then people will see that this world-view is more than mere theory, is, rather, a totality of real and living powers. If we had created something merely symbolic people would be right to say that this is just theoretical. But since our world-view shows itself capable of engendering real art, it is something more—it is alive. It will engender other life too, and be vitally productive in other domains. Today there is a great longing for a life of spirit suitable for our age. But there is also a great deal of unproductive illusion in this domain. I do hope people will learn to discern what emerges from the real needs of humanity's present condition and what arises only from confusion and hallucination. Everywhere one sees, as it were, the mushrooming aberrations of what ought to arise in the life of spirit, in our cultural life. We have to learn to distinguish between half-crazed distortions and what genuinely seeks to emerge from humanity's authentic powers of spiritual development. Today you can hear much that is very misguided. It is quite natural that people hearken to such things, for this shows they are seeking the spirit. You need only open your eyes to see that people seek the spirit everywhere. A metaphysical novel by the writer Korf[213] has just been published—terrible rubbish, and really just inept propaganda for the Star of the East.[214] I do hope people can learn to tell the difference between such distortions and the real endeavours we need today that go to the very root of human existence and human striving.

LECTURE 17

BERLIN, 9 JULY 1918

As we have seen from our recent reflections, life, the whole life of the human soul, is a complex matter. The human soul is connected by many different threads to many diverse fields, powers and centres of the universe. I would first like, in only a few words, to recall something we broached two weeks ago[215] as a point of departure for realities we will today begin to consider, and which may be able to illumine the world from a particular angle.

I said that we can only acquaint ourselves with human reality by becoming fully aware of other states of consciousness besides our ordinary waking state: of dull, twilight states of consciousness within this waking condition. Furthermore I suggested that we can only fathom these states if we understand the threefold human being: the head, the trunk and the extremities or limbs. Our whole being makes use of the head, certainly, to possess the kind of waking consciousness familiar to us. But alongside this, as I said, the head possesses a dreamlike consciousness—which our waking awareness overrides—that enables us continually to gaze back into our former lives on earth. And similarly the limb system, though also connected to our whole being, continually develops a dreamlike awareness of our future life on earth. The theory our spiritual science propounds of repeated lives on earth is in fact therefore already a reality in the human soul. It is a reality of consciousness, albeit a dull, dim twilight reality. Then we also described the dreamlike consciousness we develop through exhalation, which belongs to the trunk and rhythmic system, with its sense of our life between our last death and latest birth; and that developed by inhalation, similarly assigned to the rhythmic system, which gives us a dull, dim awareness of the life we will have from our next death through to a following birth. Briefly then, these different states of consciousness interweave with each other in us, and all this can show you that our whole being is a finely woven organization and that the way people usually view the human being represents only a very small and the least subtle portion of our whole nature.

This complexity is due to the fact that the diverse aspects of our whole being are embedded in worlds initially unavailable to ordinary perception, and can therefore be called supersensible as regards ordinary awareness. What in us is thus embedded in a world of spirit, even in the case of a none too subtle life of soul in very ordinary human existence, and can be traced through various earthly lives, is not at all simple or easy to understand. And yet we can only fathom the whole meaning of human life if we consider this highly complex human nature of ours as it passes through diverse lives on earth. This finely woven fabric is actually—especially to modern perception—very concealed or masked. I will return to this idea of masking later. Really we only know the human mask, for what descends from the world of spirit and as it were sets up house here in the physical human being, and then rises again to worlds of spirit at death, does not announce itself in evident terms in human life. A great deal occurs in our palpable or easily visible life that conceals and masks processes leading us from one earthly life to another. We start to see how complex this life of ours is when we trace it over longer periods. And now, as I describe how our true life of soul passes through longer spans of time, I would beg you to entirely overlook the great difference between this description and the accounts of ordinary history. I have often said why this is so, and we will later come back to it and examine it in more detail.

As I pointed out a little while ago,[216] important developments in occidental humanity took place in the eighth to the seventh century before the Mystery of Golgotha. During this period a significant transformation occurred in the people of the West. As we know, at that time the third post-Atlantean epoch was followed by the fourth. Previously, prior to the seventh and eighth centuries BC, human souls largely possessed characteristics of the sentient soul; and now they acquired the character of the rational or mind soul. A further important point of transition occurred in the fifteenth century AD, and thus not that long ago, when the human soul acquired characteristics of the consciousness soul. The changing character of the soul we possess also alters the way in which we look back in dull, dreamlike awareness to a former incarnation. If we think of someone living, say, at the beginning of the Graeco-Roman period, thus in the fourth or third centuries BC, in the West or a region close to it, we would find that generally he would possess a rational or mind soul character. But the part of him that dreamed of former lives on earth would of course be focused on these former lives where the soul had sentient soul character. During the fourth post-Atlantean epoch, however, humankind gradually lost the ability to directly perceive recurring incarnations. Nevertheless, many did still possess this capacity, and those who did so and looked back to their former lives saw themselves as—if I can put it like this—the possessors of sentient souls. There was a relatively big difference between how people saw themselves at that time and what they perceived in a dreamlike vision of former lives. They saw a great divergence between their current and their past condition: between their rational or mind soul and the sentient soul they felt themselves to have possessed in a former incarnation.

What is the significance of this sense of having been a sentient soul in your previous life? Today scarcely anyone has this, and cannot have it: a real feeling of having been a sentient soul, of remembering this condition vividly, as people did in the first few centuries of the fourth post-Atlantean epoch. People in Egyptian and Chaldean culture in the third post-Atlantean epoch felt themselves to be sentient souls, and this means that one has scarcely any sense of being a person who thinks. No importance is accorded to having thoughts. Instead one continually has a vivid sense of being connected with one's surroundings—but these are at the same time imbued with spirit. It is really very difficult to describe this form of consciousness, this sense of being a sentient soul. It is a vivid experience that makes one continually feel one leaves part of oneself behind as shadow in all the places one passes through. If, say, you have been sitting on a chair, and then you go for a walk, you would feel you are still sitting on the chair for a long time. There was a very vivid sense of connection with outward things, and above all people continually had a very vivid, clear and tangible sense of their spatial form before them. It was due to this great awareness of their spatial form that the doctrine of reincarnation current at the time was so vivid to them. You see, as people looked back to past incarnations, growing aware in dreamlike perception of former lives on earth, they saw a vivid image of their spatial human form: they really saw themselves, their form, in diverse situations.

During the course of the fourth post-Atlantean epoch this vivid perception gradually faded. In consequence people were no longer able to draw upon sufficient strength to grasp the dreamlike recollections in them of their former lives. This was due, particularly, to the fact that as time went on people were no longer recalling the vivid and immediate perceptions of the sentient soul but, increasingly, the rational or mind soul with its less spatially immediate perceptions—a vaguer, less definite and more inward quality. Such a quality is harder to grasp. For this reason people gradually ceased to have any memory of their former lives. During the fifth post-Atlantean epoch, however, this awareness of past incarnations will reappear in a very specific way. And no one can understand human evolution without understanding the truths we are now describing. What emerges in humanity appears in diverse ways in the most varied regions of our globe. I have often pointed out[217] that we can expect a time to come in future, very specifically and significantly in the third millennium, when a certain capacity to look back to past lives, along with clear awareness of future lives, will become something possible for all. But this awareness will emerge in different ways in different regions, and it is extremely important to understand this.

Let us for a moment consider various wider regions where this will emerge: first in the East, in eastern Europe, and then extending into Asia, and thus the Orient; and then let us consider western Europe and America in particular. This future capacity to grasp the reality of reincarnation is being prepared in different ways in these two wider regions. In the West, in initiate circles, this is already very well known, and it is significant that the West reckons with esoteric capacities and also envisages employing these in external life. To overlook this is to fail to understand western developments and the whole influence of the West on humanity's history. The most important occurrences in the West, instigated by the Anglo-American race, are influenced by a more secret, intimate knowledge of evolving humanity. In describing what is involved in such matters we soon of course risk speaking in paradox since we are talking of things to which 'clever' people will respond by saying: Well, why aren't the initiates telling us about all this then? But you need only reflect on everything I have told you about Lucifer and Ahriman—what they do, feel and especially what they have accomplished—and then along come people who think they are cleverer than Lucifer and Ahriman, and would not have done things as they have, such as staying retrograde in their development and so on. But these things have to be properly understood. There are certain things one can do precisely because one is, in a sense, cleverer than a human being.

In the West, in particular, a tendency is emerging from certain secret underground sources to oppose reincarnation, to oppose recurring lives on earth. In certain groups of deeply initiated people of the Anglo-American race a battle is being waged against reincarnation itself. This is the paradox. Certain spiritual centres in the West are in a sense seeking to put an end to recurring lives on earth—to the regularity of alternating lives first between birth and death, and then between death and rebirth. The ultimate aim of this is to establish a quite different form of human life, and there are means by which this can be achieved. What they seek to do is the following: through a certain kind of schooling, the endowing of particular powers, to place the human soul in a state where it feels ever more closely related to earthly powers and conditions after death, thereby developing a strong attraction towards these earthly powers, though of course to spiritual-earthly powers. In consequence the human soul will depart as little as possible from earthly regions after death, staying very close to these earthly regions, thus retaining a certain influence on them and, by so doing, living on after death in connection with these regions. At the same time, in consequence, the soul after death will be relieved of the need really to enter a physical body again. This is a curious ideal to which the Anglo-American race aspires: no longer to return to earthly bodies but for souls after death to exert an ever greater influence on the earth, to acquire ever more earthly souls. This ideal therefore involves making life here on earth and life after death more closely resemble each other. This will be achieved—for now only among those who are schooled in this way, though such schooling will become ever more prevalent—by awakening a much greater, stronger sense of the earth in human beings than otherwise normal. Without a certain luciferic and ahrimanic influence at work on the human being in Lemurian and Atlantean times, the human soul would now feel less closely related to the physical body than it does. Without this influence, numerous people who regard their body as belonging to the earth—the majority—would now sense this relationship to their body and the way they live in it as similar to our feeling of connection with the ground we walk on, and no more than that. Thanks to the luciferic influence we feel very closely associated with our body nowadays, but less so with the earth itself. We think of the earth as being outside us, but our body as part and parcel of us. Yet from a certain higher spiritual perspective, we are as much outside our body, even when awake, as we are distinct and separate from the earth. In a sense our soul just steps upon our brain, which offers us the resistance we need to think. The luciferic and ahrimanic influence prevent us realizing this. Without this influence, as souls we would feel much further removed from our body than we do, regarding it rather like a hill upon the earth, albeit a mobile one like a sand dune, that supports us.

Certain Anglo-American circles are making this into a pragmatic wisdom, developing feeling capacities of the human body to a great degree in a way that strengthens this sense of connection to the human body. They seek to augment this sense of connection by additional powers that are not only bodily ones but bind the latter to the earth. By means of specific exercises, the people of this Anglo-American race are gradually meant to acquire the strong sense that their body belongs to the earth, is part of it. Besides feeling 'I am my arm or my leg' they should also feel that they are the force of gravity passing through their limbs, the weight pulling upon hands or arms. The aim therefore is to establish and develop a strong sense of physical affinity between the human body and earthly elements. The same kind of affinity exists strongly in certain species of ape today; they possess this affinity as their inner life if you like, and one can study it as a phenomenon of physiology and zoology. What already exists here can be introduced gradually into a system for educating human beings, a form of bodily education and schooling that increasingly accentuates the human being's coarser affinity with nature. I am not denigrating this or being critical but simply presenting facts to you: this results in a kind of pragmatic Darwinism which endows people with a closer relationship or affinity to the earth, binding them more closely to it. In a sense it is possible to make humankind more 'apelike'. This appears to be 'instinctive' but is being ably introduced and highly cultivated in particular forms of sport and similar domains. Thus the soul is coupled to the earth strongly through a feeling of physical affinity with it, bringing about the ideal I spoke of a moment ago, whereby the continual alternation between more spiritual life and more physical life is overcome. This ideal will lead eventually to souls living in future periods of earth's evolution as a kind of ghost, dwelling upon earth as a ghost of a sort. It is actually very interesting indeed to note that this ideal can primarily be cultivated only amongst the male population, and that this will therefore gradually lead—despite all external political measures, which often have the very opposite inward intent to their outward and apparent aim—to an increasing gulf between male and female. Anglo-American life of the mind, spirit and culture will advance through women, will be passed on to posterity, whereas what lives in male bodies will tend towards the kind of ideals I described, also shaping the future bodily configuration of the Anglo-American race.

If we now look eastwards we find a very different picture. Looking towards the East with keener perception is very appropriate for us today in central Europe. What will develop and evolve there in eastern Europe is at present entirely concealed, masked, suppressed really. What has established itself at present in eastern Europe is of course the very opposite of what must emerge there. In Greater Russia, as it is called, the battle waged against any cultural or spiritual life at the same time represents a battle against the very foundations of humanity's spiritual existence. The East is in fact where certain spiritual foundations of humanity must develop. And our era has little inclination to open its eyes and gain clear insight into what is happening. People sleepwalk through everything, despite the urgent need to form clear views about current events. Our contemporaries ought to form proper judgements about people such as Lenin and Trotsky, seeing them for what they are: the most aggressive enemies of humanity's true spiritual evolution—worse than the Roman Caesars, who are always described in damning terms, worse also than Machiavellian figures such as the Borgias of the Renaissance, who in terms of their opposition to the spirit were mere infants compared to the likes of Lenin and Trotsky. People today simply overlook these realities, and it is necessary to point them out.

There is one thing in particular to which people's attention should be drawn: the past four years ought to have shown everyone that the old legends of history should be radically revised. Compared to current events, we should realize that the Roman Caesars or the events of the Renaissance, with the colouring history has given them, are old wives' tales really. If you are happy with old wives' tales then you will be sleepwalking through the lessons we can learn from the recent past. If, on the other hand, we want to discern what is in preparation in the East, we will have to wake up a little to things hidden from view below the surface. There is really a great deal more hidden there than used to be the case, although we can already find the beginnings of this in key figures in the history of eastern Europe. A time will come, though it is still some way off, when people in eastern Europe develop insight into reincarnation, though in a different way from what I described in relation to the West. In the West we find a kind of battle waged against reincarnation. In the East there will be acceptance of it, assimilation of the truth of recurring lives on earth. Here human souls will long for an education that teaches them to perceive and experience not only what lives in them from birth to death but from one life on earth to the next. Education will point to certain things that these people of eastern Europe, in particular, will experience very powerfully. Children will be taught about something dwelling in the human being that they can feel and sense, that is more than their bodily life. Older people will teach younger ones to ask themselves what they feel within their soul. Through such questions, posed in many different ways, they will come to sense that something exists in them that has entered their body but existed previously on earth—has passed through death and will return again in future. At present this may be a dull, dim feeling; but then they will be prompted by their teachers to ask how this dim feeling or sense of things relates to the rest of their inner life. And as this education progresses, through all kinds of similar questions and formulations, young people will come to experience that this 'something' they dimly sense as living repeatedly on earth destroys their thinking, prevents them thinking, tries to kill off thoughts. And this will be a very important feeling, dawning in them and being developed in people of the East by their education, though in a very natural way, not inculcated. They will acquire a feeling that there is something in them that passes from one life to another but which also, as earthly human beings, deprives them of thinking, numbs this faculty and makes it void, kills it off. When I feel this deeper aspect within me, they will say, I cannot think properly, my thinking grows dull. This deeper aspect of my being undermines my thinking. I feel my eternal being within me, but I experience it almost as a murderer of my thoughts.

This sense or feeling will be one of many extremely interesting things emerging in eastern Europe and spreading into the world. Actually it strikes me that anyone with some knowledge of eastern European literature and art can discern the beginnings of this already. The works of Dostoyevsky[218] herald it in figures who strive to the best of their ability but as they do so come to feel like an inward murderer, a burier of their thoughts. This is because the consciousness soul must come to expression there in a very particular form, and is one of the elements of the human soul which, as I have said before, is most closely bound to the earth. As we advance towards the future, and the soul comes to sense its capacity to feel the reality of recurring lives on earth, this will be an experience different in kind from that of pre-Christian times, in ancient Greece say, when the sentient soul was experienced in its full vitality. No, gradually instead the rational or mind soul will also be experienced as something lying further back in us that kills off and deadens thoughts.

But education will not end there. These souls will feel themselves to be the inner grave of their own being, and yet a grave that makes space for a revelation of the world of spirit. This feeling will follow from the other, and I would like to characterize it now. Souls will say to themselves: 'I experience my eternal being, which passes on from one life to the next, as something that deadens my thinking exertions, eradicates my thinking; but in its place divine thinking streams in and fills the grave of my own thoughts.' The Spirit Self will arrive; the consciousness soul enters the grave and in this way the Spirit Self appears. I am no longer describing this merely schematically—here is the consciousness soul, and then the Spirit Self appears—but I want to give you a real sense of the nature of the human soul as the I gradually experiences this transition from the consciousness soul to the Spirit Self. I want to show how this dawns in the East, giving people there a sense that the eternal on earth—in decline since Graeco-Roman times—has developed in a way that destroys ordinary thinking, a thinking that emanates from the human being alone, leaving him empty but not empty in vain. Into this emptiness a new spiritual revelation gradually enters, initially in the form of the Spirit Self expanding in the human soul.

Such things do not emerge without significant inner dramas and tragedies. Countless people in the East, particularly, will experience profound inner tragedy and suffering through a sense that their intrinsic being annihilates their thinking. A certain weariness and dullness will come over people as they find that the ideal they hold dear, of seeking their true nature, does not bring them liberation initially, but instead an inner deadening and weariness.

The people of central Europe exist, in a sense, to bring objectivity to bear on these circumstances, to understand them and gain orientation in relation to them. They will only fulfil this task if they really attend to what is happening and developing. In doing so, though, they must recollect what I called a 'forgotten stream' of thought and culture in my book *The Riddle of Man*.[219] It really is extremely important for people to understand once more something that has largely been forgotten and once existed as a power to understand the whole world, to encompass the whole world in thought. Who nowadays still recognizes the grandeur of Friedrich Schlegel's view of all human culture, for instance? Great minds such as Schelling, Hegel and Fichte offered deep insights into the evolution of humanity, yet these are more or less forgotten now. There is much talk of Fichte today but those who speak most about such thinkers understand them the least. Think, too, how understanding could be enlivened if people really imbued themselves with the way in which Goethe saw the world. Much is necessary if this is to be achieved. We should return to a Goethean view of the world; but still more importantly we ourselves should state clearly how much we owe to Goethe. The relationship and affinity between our building in Dornach and the mind of Goethe is something, I believe, that many fail to grasp. It would be important to emphasize this.

This view of western and eastern culture is something that thinkers in the West and East also express. One just has to understand them properly, interpreting in the right way even what surfaces in political speeches in the West, and seeing how certain instincts that come to the fore are connected with the evolution of the human soul. The instinct for earthly dominion as this holds sway in Anglo-Americanism is closely connected with the ideal of becoming a kind of earthly ghost in the future. What announces itself in the East, on the other hand, can be found imbuing every sentence of the remarkable lecture which Rabindranath Tagore gave on 'The Spirit of Japan',[220] which can now be found in almost every bookshop. What I am speaking about is not found there in so many words, of course, but it pulses through all the sentiments which an eastern mind such as this—though from the Far East, from a more oriental point of view—says about developments in eastern Europe. It would be very important for people of both West and East, for people everywhere in the world, to recognize what the spirit substance of central Europe contains. Naturally people first attend to what is apparent outwardly and physically. If an oriental person wants to find out more about Goethe—and in Asia, very important books have been published recently, such as the volume I have mentioned before by Ku Hung Ming[221]—he is very likely to turn to the 'Goethe Society' whose headquarters are located in the city that was once the centre of Goethe's work.

And yet this same society cultivates Goethean culture in a very odd and hitherto unknown way. It would have been possible to make Goethe's work available and productive for a life of culture very far-reaching in its scope, and Baroness Sophie[222] has done things of immeasurable worth and maturity for Goetheanism. But then a Goethe Society was founded. Who represents it? Is it someone in whom the spirit of Goethe really lives? No. It is very characteristic of our time that this society is directed by a former finance minister.[223] But people sleepwalk through such things, although they shouldn't. People should open their eyes to what is happening in the world.

Recently I pointed out[224] that besides the one and a half billion people on earth there are another 540 million 'human hands' in the form of machines developed in recent centuries. This has introduced a major ahrimanic thrust into humanity's evolution. This ahrimanic impulse is based on something that has become very necessary: the scientific exploration of our surroundings. We talked about this last time. Over the past four centuries, scientific discoveries have necessitated a close study of nature, of laws at work in the natural world and its creatures. Human beings carry this scientific mode of enquiry into all sorts of other fields and disciplines too—for example into a study of history, where it does not belong. No scientist will be inclined to sing hymns or paeans of praise to nature as an all-embracing unity, which would be of little use to modern civilization. And yet 'pan-naturalism' outlooks of this kind do exist, and I will give you an example of this.

A historian called Layard[225] who was investigating the ancient city of Nineveh once asked the Cadi of Mosul to describe the character and function of his different servants, and the previous history of certain states in the region. This was far too detailed and scientific for the Cadi. He failed to understand why one could be interested in the different characters of his servants or the history of the region, which for him were just 'part of the landscape'. He said that such questions originated in 'European nonsense' about studying the natural world, and he replied to the researcher: 'Listen my son, the only true reality is believing in God. And this truth, believing in God, should restrain you from trying to investigate his deeds. Look up: you see there a star that circles around another. And you see a star with a long tail, which has taken many, many years to arrive here. It will take many, many years to depart from us again. Who would be so foolish as to try to investigate the orbits of this star? The hand that created it will also guide and direct it. Listen, my son, you say that this is not curiosity but that you have a greater thirst for knowledge than I do. If your knowledge has made you a better man than you once were, you are doubly welcome to me; but do not ask that I should concern myself with such things. I concern myself only with the knowledge that consists in faith in God. I despise all other knowledge. Or let me ask you this: has this knowledge, which stumbles all over the place, succeeded in giving you a second stomach? Or has it opened your eyes to paradise?' Thus spake the Cadi of Mosul in his diatribe against natural science.

You may smile at this, and its seemingly naive outlook. And yet spiritual science continually encounters something similar, although in a different realm. There are a great many 'Cadis of Mosul' in fact and they keep saying there is no need whatever to concern oneself with any spiritual matter beyond a faith in God. Just as the Cadi of Mosul rejected science, so a great many people today—in fact key figures in culture especially—reject the science of the spirit. A booklet has just been published, very well meaning in its way; and yet one finds there this sentence:

> What is wrong with spiritual science is its effort to know something about the world of spirit, whereas the real meaning of religious life consists in not knowing anything of this world, instead having the trust, the great trust, to believe in something one knows nothing of.

It is meant to be an excellent quality, therefore, to admit that one knows nothing but that one still accepts the divine. People have not yet realized as they should that this 'faithful' relationship to the world of spirit is really precisely the same as the Cadi of Mosul's view—which amused you—of the physical world of the senses, and knowledge of this world. It is really very important that humanity starts making the transition from knowledge of the natural world to a knowledge of the world of spirit. We need to be clear about this, for on it depends whether we can in future develop a world-view capable of laying the healthy foundations for human society. Our society can have no real basis in studies such as those nowadays termed 'economics'. Economics as it exists today consists either of old traditions that serve no further use, or dry straws in the wind. A national economy worthy of the name will only come about when a thinking drawn from the world of spirit is imbued with the power of ideas. The economic orthodoxies taught in schools find their ultimate consequences in the minds of enemies of humanity such as Lenin and Trotsky. Human powers of real future potential can only emerge in us through a knowledge of worlds of spirit. Today we may need to resort to paradoxes in speaking of the West and the East as I have done, and yet such paradox encompasses spiritual realities! Unless people can gain insight into these spiritual realities, earthly conditions will increasingly plummet into chaos. Concepts that still had some validity a few years back no longer mean anything. In all areas there is a need to relearn everything afresh. Religions will only continue to have meaning for people if they encompass real knowledge of the worlds of spirit. To do this—and this relates not only to their content but to the forms they have gradually assumed—they will need to learn that such forms and traditions no longer really speak to us inwardly, and can only do so by invoking real powers originating in the world of spirit. The 'Cadis of Mosul'—though not just from Mosul of course but everywhere—must fade from public discourse. I have put this very simply but I think you can feel that a very great deal more is contained in it.

But now we must consider the following specific question. How is it that transformations undergone by the human soul occurring from the twelfth century onwards and, in a broader sense, from the eighth and seventh centuries BC up to our own time have remained so hidden from human awareness? This is because there still resides in human nature, as one of the deepest mysteries in humanity, some quality of another world. We will only come to understand the human being if we succeed a little in fathoming this other world, which seeks to remain hidden. And next time we will speak further of this.

Lecture 18

BERLIN, 16 JULY 1918

I would like to continue the observations I began regarding the passage of the human soul through its diverse lives on earth in our current cycle of humanity, and to do so in a way which can shed some light on current events of immediate concern. With this in mind, I want to develop a theme today that is more concerned with outward occurrences, and then, in a week's time, take this theme in a more inward direction.

In its passage through successive lives on earth, we have described how the human soul, as self, learns and experiences something new in each incarnation. We will focus today on three periods in particular, the Egyptian-Chaldean, the Graeco-Roman period, and our own times. Let us also remember how things will be for souls today, in our time, who pass through their earthly incarnation and are then reborn after a comparatively normal period of time. While not true for all, this applies to a very great number.

I have repeatedly said,[226] and did so again last time, that souls now in earthly incarnation will largely return with some form of sure, inner knowledge—and I described this form more precisely last time—of successive incarnations. The future age will see this important new development in which souls pass from their current uncertainty about successive lives on earth to knowledge of this. As I said, we looked at this more precisely last time. However, there is something else I wish to emphasize.

I drew your attention to the importance of the period starting roughly with the eighth or seventh centuries BC. During the first few centuries of this time span a comparatively large number of souls were still able to look back to their former incarnations because of habits of ancient clairvoyance they retained. But having especially developed the sentient soul in these former lives, as they looked back they saw how they conducted themselves in the external world. They acquired something like a tangible picture of how a person walked around in the physical world, and what outwardly happened to him. But this is something that souls will not have in the forthcoming era, reckoned from today. As they look back their gaze will no longer be focused on sentient experience, on how a person walks about in physical space and what happens to him there; this recall will have less of a vividly real content in the sensory meaning, but instead a greater apprehension of soul nature.

I mention this again here so that you can see that in their successive lives souls undergo very diverse experiences. And one can really wonder why historians, and the public at large, think that human nature has changed so little over the ages. Ordinary historians—and most of them, though not all, are well meaning—invariably look back to a certain point when historical records began, and over this period the human soul is thought to have been configured in more or less the same way. A certain development is accepted, but scarcely radical in nature, and far less incisive than the account we draw from spiritual-scientific research. How can it be that people have so little sense of the transformations undergone by the human soul? This certainly seems problematic.

If we now consider historical events from the perspective of spiritual science, we find that for a long time now human beings have been held back from self-knowledge, from a knowledge of their own soul, rather than being led towards such knowledge. We can really only understand and perceive how the human soul changes from incarnation to incarnation if authentic self-knowledge comes into its own, and yet the events we will now reflect on have suppressed it to a very great degree. It is possible to cite significant instances of how self-knowledge has been suppressed in recent history. A certain fraternity you are all aware of, the Freemasons, no doubt believes, along with many of its well-meaning members, that it is helping those in its ranks towards self-knowledge.

This fraternity has diverse symbols which spiritual-scientific insights can tell us are profound and deeply meaningful and would all be well suited to lead people towards self-knowledge. But this does not happen. It is very curious: if you read the official histories of the Freemason movement, the more enlightened of them suggest it is necessary to go back only to the seventeenth or eighteenth centuries to acquaint oneself with modern Freemasonry. And yet the inner content of the Freemason symbols was in fact concealed from the seventeenth century onwards, transformed into something Freemasons regard, engage with and yet have ever less need to understand. If one were to investigate Freemason symbolism with a greater understanding of its meaning, this would certainly offer a path towards human self-knowledge since the symbols themselves have this potential. But actual developments took a different course, seeking to smother self-knowledge, render it impossible by a focus on merely outward symbols. A truthful view of what has happened here will discern that modern Freemasonry has developed, basically, with a view to rendering incomprehensible the symbols at the centre of this fraternity. It almost seems as if there were an unconscious plan, an intention, to render these symbols incomprehensible because human beings were seized with a fear of self-knowledge as modern Freemasonry was developing—amongst the enlightened Freemasons, not the mystical ones. There is a great deal of talk about self-knowledge, about the need for a human being to seek his higher, divine self and so forth. But it is all just talk, and in fact serves the purpose, largely, of obstructing rather than smoothing the path to self-knowledge. Where does this disinclination or fear of self-knowledge originate? Today I will explore this firstly from a more external point of view.

It is of course not just here, in Freemasonry, that this anxiety is apparent, but throughout our modern culture. It is a curious thing to realize that this modern culture of ours—especially wherever Christianity has spread—actually pursues efforts to conceal and suppress self-knowledge. This is extremely interesting and highly significant. Very few people make the effort nowadays to compare the beliefs they hold with better accounts from more distant times, nor to reflect on the nature of things that surface within them. If you study Herman Grimm's[227] book on the life of Michelangelo, you can do a rather interesting little inner experiment with it. Grimm has really written more about the age in which Michelangelo lived, from which he emerged. But try, with the aid of this book, to picture what the world around you would be like if you could walk around at that time of Michelangelo, then see if you can compare this world with the one in which you now live. There is a really huge difference! This does not necessarily mean very much in itself since it is not so very long, really, since Michelangelo's day. Something else emerges however if we now really focus our attention on the era, with its antecedents and after-effects, when the radical turning point of modern times occurred. If we look back to the three great periods which spiritual science describes for our current earth cycle, the third epoch closes around the eighth or seventh century BC, while the fourth epoch concludes at the beginning of the fifteenth century. Here, at the start of the fifteenth century, which is not so long ago, we can discern a radical change, a new departure in the soul experience of modern people. History rarely detects this or describes it. Why does it not? Precisely because of this fear of self-knowledge, of insight into the life of the human soul.

If you were to read accounts of an individual such as Bernhard of Clairvaux[228] you would find something very interesting. Bernhard, perhaps the most important figure of the twelfth century, of the era which concludes the fourth post-Atlantean cultural epoch, reveals a configuration of soul that simply became impossible in Europe after the fifteenth century. Today it is extremely difficult to re-imagine the soul life of such a person, since all the foundations for this are now lacking. But I recommend reading biographies of Bernhard so that you can see how others at the time were struck by his inner life. In reading these accounts of his life you can feel that they surpass the stories of miracles in the Gospels. The few sick people whom Christ Jesus himself heals in the Gospel accounts appear as nothing compared to the wonders accomplished by Bernhard almost twelve centuries later, news of which spread far and wide. He apparently heals far more people, giving eye-sight back to the blind and making the lame walk again. And accounts of the sermons given by Bernhard are so powerful that one gains the sense of a great spiritual aura emanating from his words. A reality, of which we can form very little idea now, lived in the words of this man. If one were to try to describe all that issued from him, it would meet with disbelief since nothing in our own time enables us to form a picture of the impression made by such a figure as Saint Bernhard. Even in these circles we lack the real basis for entering into the inner configuration of Bernhard's soul, but I would still like to emphasize one thing.

In this individual lived an utter devotion to the world of spirit, with which he merged completely. Nowadays it seems perfectly natural to us, if we undertake to do something but without success, to ask ourselves whether what we envisaged was right after all. Someone like Saint Bernhard never doubts, for whatever he undertakes or advises others to do he has invariably talked of beforehand with his God in the world of spirit. And even in misadventures such as those he experienced during the Crusades, when everything he advised had failed, he never for a moment doubted that his thoughts were completely right, and that the discrepancy between what happened in the outer reality of the sensory world and what he conceived by the guidance of the world of spirit is something that will in some way eventually be resolved.

Bernhard is a striking figure in this respect, but although he was of outstanding stature what I have said about him is not by any means confined to one individual but is a signature of that whole era. It is the signature of that particular era in Europe, starting around the third and fourth centuries AD and lasting until the thirteenth, fourteenth and fifteenth centuries. Naturally other things are in preparation during this period but they only come to the fore and really become determining characteristics of the times after the fourteenth or fifteenth centuries. Between the third and fifteenth century was a time when the power of faith grew ever stronger, was increasingly consolidated and became a determining influence on events. Please note here that I use words very carefully and with intent—something generally so in my lectures. If one were to substitute other words for the ones I have used, it would no longer be historically accurate. If instead of speaking of the consolidating power of faith one used the term 'consolidating piety' this would be quite wrong. That is not what I mean. It was the power of faith that lived in Bernhard. Certainly he was a pious man, but that is something one can also be as a person, in personal terms. Events in the centuries I am speaking of were informed, rather, by the power of faith living in, and at work in them.

The power of faith exists in every age but is not always historically decisive as it was then. Our own age will be followed by another when, albeit temporarily and sporadically, the power of faith will once again play a certain role. This is not yet true today. In future, for instance, the superstitions prevalent in modern, materialistic medicine will assume grotesque forms. The power of faith will play a great part then but things have not yet advanced so far. At present we can witness more of a twilight sleep amongst humanity, and this plays an incisive part in current historical events. But now we can ask this question: why or how was it that this power of faith became such a significant historical impulse in Europe, leading up to and introducing the fifth post-Atlantean epoch in which we now live?

Firstly, something very external provided the basis for this power of faith to develop: the same that largely brought about the fall of the Roman Empire. Historical impulses at work from the third and fourth centuries through to the fifteenth replaced the impulses driving the Roman Empire. Naturally the decline and fall of the Roman Empire was caused by several factors but one of these was the fact that money had gradually drained eastwards to the Orient during the course of Roman history. As the Roman Empire expanded, the legions were drawn ever further to its distant boundaries and soldiers' wages increasingly had to be paid in money rather than payments in kind as had been possible in a less extensive empire. Monetary wealth had actually passed to the Orient along with the extending empire, and Europe, in the early Christian centuries, from the third and fourth centuries, is characterized by its lack of money, its paucity of metal coinage. Various other things are connected with this, and it is important to keep one's feet on the ground when studying them, rather than indulging in mystical fantasies. We should keep a sober eye on reality. The art of alchemy, with its efforts to create gold, partly arose in Europe because all the money had drained away to the Orient. People thought they could make gold, create it instead, and regain wealth by this means. Underlying alchemy as this developed in the early Middle Ages is paucity of money caused by the Roman Empire's expansion. And to this is due in turn the influx of northern tribes into the impoverished Roman Empire, with their heathen culture, sentiments and outlooks, and little understanding of the strong social structures that had become ever more substantial under the influence of money. The Romans felt extremely uncomfortable about the loss of their monetary wealth towards the Orient, whereas invading Germanic tribes were perfectly happy with the situation.

The spread of Christianity came as this mood emerged in the Roman Empire. People are no longer aware of this, but in fact a profound spiritual outlook was borne upon the spreading waves of Christianity in these times of its early development. In theological circles, especially, there is still an irrational fear of what is called gnosis. If you ask people in theological circles why they dislike our spiritual science, or even fear it, they will often tell you that it could lead to a renewal or revival of gnosis, and this in itself is a reason to reject it. Although gnosis must surface in a different form, of course, from the one it had in the early Christian centuries, it is in reality nothing other than a positive knowledge of the world of spirit, a human capacity to gain insight into spiritual worlds just as one comes to understand physical worlds through the physical senses. You often meet people who mock all the disputes that once existed about, say, whether the Spirit issues from the Father or the Son, or is in some other way connected with these. People cannot make head or tail of such arguments nowadays, but in those times these ideas meant something. To write a true history of the early Christian centuries, you would need to know that there is meaning and spirit at the source of these dogmas, although people can no longer discover this. Borne on the waves of spreading Christianity was a profoundly significant spiritual apprehension which extends through into the ninth century. If you study the details of this expanding Christianity you can find that the later view that religious sensibility should be restricted to pervading oneself with the power of faith, without engaging with diverse aspects of the world of spirit, arose from a correct perception of the nature of the tribes from which the new Europe emerged. These heathen peoples had not got very far in their thinking, in the association and development of concepts that embrace the world of spirit. They were vigorous, powerful, primordially healthy people but they did not have the mental faculties to form very tangible ideas about anything spiritual.

Those who supported the spread of Christianity adapted to these tribes and their ways in order to do so. But because these people had a less developed thinking capacity, an appeal was made instead to their power of faith. And so we see how, in the tenth century, all spirit vision has more or less faded from Christianity and been compressed instead into the power of faith. The vision vouchsafed by this power of faith, the support felt to be offered by it, gradually became the inner content of people's souls. Souls lived differently then from now. You have to picture the experience a person of those days had in response to a legend. Let me tell you a simple legend that was widespread at the time. It runs as follows. Saint Bernhard was once riding upon a donkey and had a monk with him who, as one would say today, suffered from epilepsy. The monk kept falling over as he was leading the donkey. Bernhard turned to God to ask him that henceforth the monk should never suffer from epilepsy again without knowing this in advance. The legend goes on to say that the monk lived another 20 years and whenever he was to have an attack of epilepsy he knew of it beforehand and would lie down in bed so that no harm came to him as he fell.

A harmless, simple story—and yet one that had a deep effect and was widely recounted at the time. People felt their soul strengthened by the sustaining power of faith, and lived in the aura of this feeling.

It would not in fact have been possible for this power of faith to become so strong if Europe had not become increasingly isolated through the centuries. Money had drained away towards the Orient and trade had gradually ceased in consequence. For a certain period Europe was largely restricted to its agricultural produce; and it is a highly significant factor in Europe's development at this period that a third of the land passed to those who sustained this power of faith. A third of all land was held by the Church. It is as if all that lived in the fourth post-Atlantean epoch, and had simply been interrupted by the Roman element, was now compressed into this power of faith. But as the power of faith consolidated and rigidified, progress in real Christ consciousness was lost. We should not forget that a really elevated knowledge of Christ existed in the early Christian centuries in those who were able to place the Christ figure, the being of Christ, into the whole compass of the world of spirit and its powers. Those who were first seized by the grandeur of the figure of Christ were able to look up into worlds of spirit and as it were perceive this figure approaching the earth for aeons from spirit worlds, thus connecting the events of Golgotha with everything at work in the cosmos. Those who could interpret the events of Golgotha were powerfully moved by the fact that what was happening on earth was the influx of an event descending from worlds of great cosmic compass.

I am very aware that things are presented differently today. But when theologians say that we should return to simple, humble views of Christ Jesus from the early Christian centuries, they cling merely to their own predilections, and seek to conceal the majesty of the idea of Christ and the profound insight into the Mystery of Golgotha living in people then. Their preferred way of seeing things is to accentuate this supposed simplicity, in which Christ Jesus was nothing more, they like to think, than the 'simple man of Nazareth'. It is perhaps less surprising to find such views amongst younger people. The older generation ought to know, though, that a significant change has occurred with respect to such things in our time. I have often heard people saying that what spiritual science presents is almost incomprehensible. And yet only 30 years back simple country folk would have understood these things easily. Things have changed over the last few decades, but an older generation might still recall how farmers, people in rural communities, still read and absorbed books by people like Jakob Boehme[229] or Eckartshausen[230]—texts which make great efforts to enter into detailed aspects of the world of spirit. Our cultural life became much more superficial with the rise of the middle classes, who prefer to say that 'truth should be simple'—meaning only that everyone ought to be able to grasp it easily, without thinking too much. Nowadays there is little evidence left to show, even in humble hearts, that it was possible in the early Christian centuries to speak of lofty spiritual matters when one spoke of Christ Jesus, and that ordinary, 'simple' people could understand this. This means, therefore, that in subsequent centuries knowledge of Christ was in a sense covered over, concealed again from humanity, to prevent people getting too close to this knowledge.

In such matters, as opposed to our own imaginings, we need to look the truth squarely in the face. One of the deepest needs of our time is to learn to perceive truth and reality once more. I often recall the following instance because it is so vivid and tangible. On one occasion I was giving a lecture in Colmar[231] on Christianity and wisdom, and two Catholic priests were present. Naturally they had never heard such things as I was speaking of, and they came to me afterwards because of the novelty of the lecture for them—which played a part too—and the fact that they thought what I was saying was not at all bad. If one of their superiors had told them what to think about it beforehand, no doubt they would have considered it all nonsense. They only had one objection to what I had said: 'All you say is very fine,' they told me. 'It is a fine thing to speak about the spiritual world—but human beings don't understand this at all. We speak to people in a way they can understand.' I replied that it was not for them or for me to decide how to speak to humankind in line with our predilections. If our speech were governed by these predilections we would of course all think that our own way of putting things was the right one. But that was not the point, I said. Instead we should speak as our times oblige us to: not answering questions according to our preferred way of seeing the world but allowing reality itself to answer them. I continued my reply to them by asking if they were really speaking to all people. 'Not all people enter your church,' I said, 'and many stay away. And that in fact is reality's answer! I am speaking to those who stay away from the Church, who also have a right to find their way to Christ Jesus.' Thus one does not ask oneself what should be said, but tries to ask reality, ask the age we live in. The answers we give ourselves are things we already know and seem very self-evident; it is less easy to learn to understand the obligations imposed on us by the nature of our times. You will have to ponder a good deal to see what really underlies what I have now said.

What humanity needs today is to become objective, to learn to live more intimately with our surroundings. If we can understand what this means and take up the corresponding impulse, we will also come to recognize the truth of how, due to events during the centuries I have spoken of, higher knowledge gradually faded in Europe so that people no longer perceived the spiritual connection between the Mystery of

Golgotha and cosmic occurrences. Christ faded from European sensibilities and became confined to things people were able or wanted to grasp. But what matters is to grasp reality rather than to grasp what one wishes to. Nowadays one often hears people saying that we should seek God within us, and will find him there. Inwardly we should unite with our divine self in order to find God. People take offence especially at the emphasis of spiritual science on the existence of hierarchies we discover when we depart or emerge from this physical world we live in here, and at the idea that just as we find a wealth of physical phenomena here, so there we likewise find a richly complex world of spirit. People find it much more comfortable to turn directly to their own Christ within. But what do they actually find when they think they have an inner relationship to their God? What they call God is in fact often nothing other than the most immediate spirit being of the hierarchy of the angeloi, their own guardian angel whom they then worship as the highest divinity. Our belief that we have found God is not what matters, but instead we should truly understand the reality of this inner experience. In believing that they are inwardly imbued with the divine, people are in fact mostly only imbued with a being from the hierarchy of the angeloi or otherwise by their own I as it existed between their previous death and latest birth, living in the world of spirit before it united with their present physical body. There is an important word whose origin, very interestingly, is unknown. Etymological dictionaries can provide all sorts of fascinating derivations for most words but not for this one, the word God. Have a look in a German dictionary—this is the word whose origins philologists are most uncertain about. This is very significant, very characteristic. You see, what people are actually talking about when they speak of their God is either their own angel being or even their own self as it existed between death and their latest birth. What they experience—and I'm thinking here of those who are honest and authentic in their capacity to experience—is a reality. Reality is the important thing and not the illusions to which people succumb: that, say, they are worshipping one God. All they are referring to with this word is an experience of their angel or even in a sense just their own self either before or during its incarnation.

Spiritual science must investigate what underlies people's supposed experience of God, and many people oppose it precisely because they sense this. The whole of history from the third to the tenth centuries, and in fact really through to the fifteenth, aims to cover up the mysteries of Christ Jesus, to conceal them more than to reveal them. This is not critique but merely characterization. You see, if we are incapable of contemplating an objective account of things, we will never understand the powers governing developments at the beginning of the fifteenth century—the age of the consciousness soul. One can say that this age is heralded by blasts of thunder; and everything in the world of spirit tends towards the emergence of this consciousness soul with its two poles, both materialistic and spiritual. And it is from this perspective that we must view historical developments. We must invoke such pictures as these: from a strengthened and consolidated power of faith, appearing to us in its highest form in Saint Bernhard, issues the European tendency or inclination to replace Rome with Jerusalem, to found an anti-Roman Christianity centred in Jerusalem. This really underlies the Crusades. Gottfried von Bouillon[232] is not an emissary of the Roman popes but the figure who takes up the cause of the Crusades in order to erect a bulwark against Rome in Jerusalem and make Christianity independent of Rome. This idea was one that prevailed really for many centuries. Henry II,[233] the Holy Roman Emperor, then gave this the form of an *Ecclesia Catholica non Romana* (non-Roman Catholicism).

And thus we see that the European power of faith sends its emanation into the regions into which the Romans dispatched their gold! The Crusaders clash with gold and its consequences in the Orient: Roman gold on the one hand and oriental gnosis on the other. One has to consider the emanation, the aura surrounding the Crusades, which issues entirely from the European power of faith. That is one colouring of the picture. But let us add to this nuance—and we could paint it, if we wished, simply as colour tone—the other picture of the dawning age of the consciousness soul. How would we have to do this? By depicting the figure of Dandolo of Venice.[234] Born in 1108, the Doge of Venice went to Constantinople and was there blinded by the Byzantines; yet he was an incarnation of the spirit of Ahriman and, despite being unable to see, became Lord of Venice—the same Venice that infused the spirit of

Ahriman into the spirit I just described above. It is an important moment of world history when this Doge Dandolo conquers Constantinople and modifies the original spirit of the Crusades into its subsequent colouring. How did this happen?

You see, initially the Crusaders set out for the Orient to find what sacred relics still remained for the power of faith to light upon. This is what they sought, wishing to bring it back with them to Europe and pay homage to it. They wished to create a real bond between their power of faith and the actual events of the Mystery of Golgotha. And when Venice intervened, what became of the sacred relics? They were all collected up and formed the basis for capital gain, for the accumulation of wealth! Under the influence of Venice, these relics gradually became something like stocks and shares whose value kept on increasing. The era of capitalism began to spread through Dandolo, an incarnation of the ahrimanic spirit.

How did Venice succeed in reversing what had already occurred? It drew trade back from the Orient to Europe, rekindling the commercial life that could not have existed previously. And now we have to ask how Venice could grow so powerful commercially since Europe, basically, was so impoverished?

This resurgence in trade involved exchange. Basically, during the early part of the period I have been describing today, Europe was shut off from the Orient to which it had first given its metal coinage. Without coins, barter and exchange took place. We should repeatedly emphasize the historical fact of how Venice proceeded here. There is evidence of a large sale by Venice to Alexandria and Damietta, as the means of exchange to procure oriental goods in turn. What goods did Venice sell? Some aspects of this can easily be proven by documents, and much else could then be related to it as the basis for further research. In fact, a thousand people were sold by Venice. Human beings were used to initiate trade with the Orient again. People were sold to the Orient. If you follow this up you discover something remarkable to which ordinary history gives little attention: that the most important of the warriors used by Asia to undertake its great and successful European campaigns were the descendants of these people sold as a commodity. The core troops of Asian armies that later invaded Europe were descended from Venetians and people from other Italian cities who had been sold to the Orient.

We really ought to look behind the scenes of world history rather than adhering to the legends so often purported to be history, which are more in the nature of old wives' tales, even if historians of the status of Ranke proffer these legends. Our times are far too serious to avoid looking squarely at the truth. The most important thing to be learned from such truths is to avoid sleepwalking through current events but instead to follow them with alert attention. Something of huge proportions and ramifications is happening today but people fail to see it, do not wish to see it—wish instead to see everything in a confused and distorted way. If one hints merely at deeper aspects of human evolution and history, one is immediately dismissed with phrases found everywhere today in superficial newspaper articles, as far removed as possible from reality and productive truth.

Today I have endeavoured to draw your attention to some outward realities connected with the era in the fifteenth century, when a transition occurred from the mind soul to the consciousness soul. It would be very good indeed if people could integrate such things and reflect upon them, and this is something we need today in all areas. Nowadays people talk a great deal about how society, the structure of society, needs to develop in the future. Today I read something by someone who thinks himself very clever, or at least believes he has grasped a basic truth of economics. The profound truth he comes up with in the middle of his article is that we should regard society, social coexistence, as an organism. People consider it highly significant if they reject the idea of social mechanisms and replace this with the social organism. And yet this is the worst Wilsonism. I have often reiterated[235] that the essence of Wilsonism is to see society in terms of an organism only. But to understand social structure we need more than this concept; we need higher concepts, for social structure can never be regarded merely as an organism. It has to be understood as psychism, pneumatism, for spirit is also at work in all human coexistence. Our age has only impoverished concepts. We cannot establish a national economy without immersing ourselves in spirit knowledge, for it is only by this means that we can discover the meta-organism which surpasses merely organic life.

Nowadays, everywhere, we find that people lack good will to penetrate the spirit. Yet this is needed and without it there will be unforeseeable consequences. In the seventeenth century as I have mentioned before—for example in the last issue of the journal *Das Reich*[236]—Johann Valentin Andreae wrote *The Chymical Wedding of Christian Rosenkreutz*. This contains a great many of the impulses connected with the radical change that occurred in the fifteenth century. In fact the story is set in the fifteenth century too. It is very interesting to note that Johann Valentin Andreae wrote this story when he was 17—a 17-year-old boy, with an apparently immature intellect, and later on he rejected this story himself. The pietistic theologian Andreae, writing later, himself opposes everything he had earlier written in his *Chymical Wedding*. This is very interesting indeed; the life of Andreae shows us that he had not the least understanding of what he himself wrote in *The Chymical Wedding*. The worlds of spirit wished to reveal something to humanity that was connected with the whole sensibility of that era. Recently I found myself in a castle in central Europe[237] that has a chapel with symbols embodying this radical change at the start of the new era. There are some fairly primitive paintings on the walls of the staircase, but what do they depict? The 'chymical wedding of Christian Rosenkreutz'! One passes through this 'chymical wedding' to arrive at a Grail chapel. Then the Thirty Years War began, after the *Chymical Wedding* had been written down, and what had been intended by it was submerged in the tumult of this war.

This should teach us something, for it ought not to happen a second time. The spiritual development required of humanity since the fifteenth century must gradually come about; and next time we will speak of this from a more inward perspective.

Lecture 19

BERLIN, 23 JULY 1918

LET us explore this question: Why do people not realize that the content, the spiritual and cultural contents of the different epochs they pass through in different lives on earth are markedly different? Why do so many people believe that humankind has altered very little in millennia, since historical records began, whereas in fact spiritual science teaches us that souls have indeed changed essentially during the third, fourth and fifth post-Atlantean cultural epochs. We ourselves are now living in the fifth epoch. The knowledge we gain through the science of the spirit shows us that the human soul has definitely changed. But if we consider historical records as historians usually interpret them, they seem to give little indication of such changes.

To approach this question I recently tried to show[238] that in fact these changes do become apparent if we examine the soul aspect of humanity's history. I tried to explain how differently human souls experienced things in, say, the eleventh and twelfth centuries compared with today. As an illustration I tried to shed some light on the quality of soul of someone like Bernhard of Clairvaux in the twelfth century. One could do the same in relation to other souls. But before we pursue this further let us first return again to the core of this question and ask the following. What prevents a person from properly perceiving the changes he undergoes through succeeding earthly lives?

He is prevented first and foremost by the fact that, in our present stage of earthly evolution, he has very little perception of the true nature of his I, his real human essence. People would conceive of their own nature and being in very different ways if certain hindrances did not obstruct their view. Later we will speak further of these obstacles, but for now, as a kind of hypothesis, let us consider how a person would see himself in the world if he could perceive his true nature and being.

If people could do this they would observe a great change occurring in their personal life between birth and death. However old a person might be, whether 20, 30 or 50, he would be able to look back to his earlier life, back towards birth, and see himself in ongoing metamorphosis. He would grasp more clearly the changes he has undergone, and also form hopeful conceptions of the future with an eye to further such changes. In past lectures[239] I have spoken of these hopeful, forward-looking thoughts of the future.

The way we are today, we do not think very much about how we have changed over time because by and large we do not consider our soul nature sufficiently. However strange this may sound, people today always split themselves into two parts when they think of themselves. On the one hand they see their physical body, regarding it as something fairly constant and fixed during their whole life. They know that they have grown, of course, that they were once small and then grew taller, but that is more or less all they are aware of in relation to their outward physical nature. Take a simple fact: you cut your nails. Why? Because they grow. This is an example of how the outward corporeality of your organism is continually divested. You actually repulse your organism's physicality, pushing it outwards so that after a certain time, no more than six to seven years, what existed in you as matter and substance seven or eight years before is no longer present in you. You continually repulse or extrude your materiality, but are unaware of this—do not perceive that you are melting outwards and reconstituting yourself from within. Think how differently we would regard ourselves if we knew that we are in a sense repulsing our physical body continually, divesting ourselves of it and inwardly reconfiguring ourselves; if we observed this ongoing metamorphosis at work in us.

But this would connect with something else: if we really were fully aware that this body of ours is something we possess for no more than seven years, after which its former substance has been discarded, we would regard ourselves as far more spiritual than we usually do. We would no longer have the illusory idea that we were first small and then just grew bigger, but would know, rather, that the stuff we were made of as a young child has gone and what remains or persists in us is actually not material at all but something trans-material. If we took full cognizance of this we could look back on our life, back to childhood, and see what it is of us that has remained constant. Then we would recall ourselves in spiritual terms. We could absorb far more spiritual ideas about ourselves if we were aware of what actually occurs.

And something further would be associated with this: we would see ourselves in far less abstract terms. In a sense we transform ourselves into a spiritual point, speaking of this as our I. We think that our I was present in our childhood, and continued to be present in us, is still there now and so forth. But this I of ours is something we picture only as a kind of spiritual point. If we could entertain the idea that actually we are always melting away on the outside and reconstituting ourselves within, we would not be able to help comprehending this I of ours as the active, dynamic principle that instigates this divesting and reconstituting process. We would regard ourselves as something much more real and inwardly active. In brief, when considering our I we would not be contemplating our abstract I as we do now, but could survey how this I works upon our body in inner activity, leading it from one metamorphosis to another. Thus we would correct various really very mistaken ideas to which we are prone because of what I have described here. To say that we grow bigger during childhood is not correct, for the truth is more complex. In infancy our physical and corporeal activity is experienced more as being one with our soul-spiritual activity, and because of this our head organism is in closer proximity to our reproductive and sexual organism. Later these two experiences diverge and are differentiated, so that head experiences and bodily experiences become more detached from each other. The material organism that we were as children does not grow bigger since it is divested, melts away if you like. But we differentiate ourselves so that the two poles of our being grow more distant from each other. In consequence, substance is integrated into a configured body in which the two poles have drawn apart, and it seems to us as if we had just grown. But we do not simply grow; we become inwardly differentiated, and thereby connect at a later age with different outward things than in infancy. Later on our head organization inevitably stands at a further remove from direct earth forces than before. Our head elevates itself, and the fact that we grow is connected with this.

All these ideas change if we absorb and integrate the truth about such things. But we do not do so. We misconceive the continually metamorphosing and changing body and picture it growing out of itself, growing bigger; and therefore we fail to see what a rich, inward, mobile and living thing our I actually is, continually working upon us from birth to death. If we could picture ourselves in this way our ideas about this self would become unified. But modern human beings have not been able to conceive of themselves like this for a long time, and this is connected with human destiny and the whole evolution of our age. Rather than closely encountering his living, active I which in fact constitutes the organism from year to year, a person splits it: he regards his organism as something very consistent on the one hand, and on the other has an abstract and insubstantial view of his I. And then he sees himself as a sensory organism on the one hand, a corporeal organism, in consequence of which he cannot really come close to reality because things only make 'impressions' on him rather than revealing their true nature. He cannot get near to the 'thing in itself', instead only perceiving 'phenomena'. It is true that if we regard our flesh and blood as something fixed and consistent, this conclusion has a certain justification. Then, on the other hand, he considers his insubstantial I and discovers, say, a sense of duty living in it. He reflects upon all that can be summarized as categorical imperative in us, but in doing so splits into two what is encompassed in a whole. People thus become Kantians, splitting the unity of human nature into two separate parts, and this profoundly informs their way of thinking.

People today are not well fitted to comprehending the full scope of their nature in the world. They split themselves as I have described. But this in turn means that we never have the real nature of our soul before our eye of spirit, since the soul element is continually working upon and changing our body. Rather than a view of the soul we perceive our abstract body divided from our abstract I, without regard for our whole, unified human nature. This perception of our whole unified being would however lead us to see that this unified being changes greatly from incarnation to incarnation. The true, authentic human I, which conceals itself from our soul perception in the present moment, is what changes from one life to another. Of course, if you consider only the abstract 'I' rather than the tangible, active human I, you cannot discover that this I becomes so different from one life to the next. After all, in the abstract everything of some affinity is seen as identical. Naturally a soul retains similarities in successive lives, but on the other hand it changes a good deal, as we have always described, as we pass through human evolution from life to life. People do not perceive their true being because they fail to discern the whole mobility of their body and the very real living activity of their I. This is like a golden rule in relation to real knowledge of or insight into the human being. Why is this so?

The answer is provided by our knowledge of Ahriman and Lucifer. We split our being into two, on the one hand seeing our body as something that was once small and then grew larger, whereas in fact it continually renews itself. What do we actually perceive when we regard our body in this way? We perceive the ahrimanic, as this ahrimanic activity works upon us. Yet this ahrimanic quality is not our true human nature, but is, rather, the type or species that does remain the same through all ages. In looking upon our body as we do, therefore, we are perceiving the ahrimanic aspect of our nature, and in fact modern mainstream anthropology only describes this ahrimanic aspect. That is one half of what we see: our physical nature as we ourselves conceive and concentrate it. The other half is the abstract I, in a really very fluctuating state, living only a temporal existence as we envisage ourselves in life between birth and death. This encompasses our own education and upbringing, our morality or waywardness, our whole personal life. Yet we do not perceive the reality of our I as this works to transform our physical life. Instead we see it diluted, luciferically attenuated. Our physical corporeality is something we perceive as ahrimanically materialized, whereas we perceive our soul and spirit as luciferically attenuated.

If this were not so and we did not split ourselves in half to leave one pole of our being ahrimanic and the other luciferic, we would have a much closer relationship with the dead, who are continually amidst us, since we would also have a much closer connection with the world of spirit. We would comprehend the whole reality including the realm in which we live after passing through death and before we enter this world again through the portal of conception.

In fact we never really have a full perception of our being but on the one hand the illusory ahrimanic picture of our physical corporeality and on the other the illusory luciferic picture of our soul and spirit: two illusions about ourselves, between which, albeit imperceptibly, lives our true human reality. Yet it is of this human nature we must speak if we speak of the human being at all, since it is our true and intrinsic being that passes from one life to the next.

This insight into human nature is deeply significant, and shows us why people think that human beings remain the same through many succeeding ages. We must focus clearly on misguided ideas of the human being—the species or genus aspect that does remain constant through long ages, and on the other hand the false apprehension of soul and spirit that fails to see its living dynamic in our life. If people recognized how the spirit and soul change the body year by year, they would also grasp the huge transition that occurs when this spirit-soul enters physical corporeality at conception or departs from it again at death. We take no account, mostly, of how the spirit-soul works upon the body.

There is another way, too, to express what has just been said. Our ahrimanic view of the more or less fixed and finished human organism accounts for very little really of what we are. We merely live in this organism. The aspect of it we usually perceive as something ahrimanically condensed and concentrated originates much more from our last incarnation than from this one. From our various reflections this year,[240] and from previous ones too, you will realize that your physiognomy and other enduring aspects of your form really derive from your past incarnation, your last life. Everything associated with the physical body is much more connected with your last life than with this one. But people today, who do not believe they have had a previous life, cannot accept that such a life could have provided their current shape and form, their size and so forth. True understanding would require us to look back to our last life, and we would be helped in this if we could start to see the I as it works upon our organism, as I have described. We would become aware of all that we ourselves cannot shape and form in the present but what was formed in former lives. If one can really study the human being with insight, one knows how the soul and spirit work upon our organism. The human being emerges in a sense from this work, leaving behind, as apparently fixed form in ahrimanic perception, what remains from a former life as all that has previously been shaped.

If we can accustom ourselves to seeing the human being's nature as very dynamic and alive, when we meet another person it is always as if someone emerges from him as the present human being. Usually this is not perceived. The part that remains somewhat behind is the aspect of the person that was shaped in a former life. And very soon something steps into what emerges in this way. The emerging aspect is initially very transparent, one can say, and then grows more opaque. Because the spirit-soul manifests in activity, it condenses what has emerged; and then something emerges in turn from this which appears as a seed or germ for the next life on earth.

A person appears as a threefold being to someone who can comprehend the reality. Various mythological traditions have encapsulated this in symbolic form. You will no doubt recall numerous tales involving three generations, and this is because they refer to this emergence of the three aspects I have described. If you think of various portrayals of Isis, and some tales in Christian traditions, you will find an account of three successive figures who belong together. In reality this indicates what I have referred to. Of course such things can be interpreted materialistically if you have a mind to do so: grandmother, mother and child perhaps. But the three figures exist because they correspond to a perceived reality. Images from earlier times are best understood if you refrain from the academic fantasies of today which analyse such things arbitrarily. It is much more productive to recall what people actually perceived not so very long ago, and then portrayed what they saw in artistic form.

Reflections such as these become especially important if we realize that the Christ who passed through the Mystery of Golgotha has a connection—one we frequently speak of—with the authentic human I. If you think of the Pauline phrase[241] 'Not I but Christ in me', this 'in me' refers to the true I which for us today is hidden and concealed. To find the right relationship with Christ we must in a sense look upon this I in its spiritual reality. It is hard to see how certain words and phrases in the Gospels can be comprehended if no account is taken of this. Consider the phrase in the Gospel of St John[242] where the evangelist speaks of the Christ coming to humankind as to the place where he rightfully belongs. Translators of the Gospels usually render this as: 'He came unto his own and his own received him not.' But the passage then continues: 'But to all who did receive him, who believed in his name, he gave the right to become the children of God, who were born not of blood nor of the will of the flesh nor of the will of man, but of God.' And it becomes apparent therefore that he wished to come to all those who have such awareness. Yet outward people, or in other words all those usually in existence, are certainly 'born of blood and of the will of the flesh'. But the human being I have spoken of as the true and authentic one, who is not born of blood or the will of the flesh, comes from the world of spirit and only clothes himself in what comes from physical inheritance. The Gospel speaks of this authentic human being, and this is why it is so hard to comprehend and is so often wrongly interpreted—because it is pressed into the kinds of concepts that are current today. Without the ideas spiritual science can convey, such Gospel passages cannot be understood. Once we have these concepts, a light suddenly dawns on us in relation to the Gospels.

In regard to all these circumstances, we have to say that something of grandeur occurred in human evolution at the Mystery of Golgotha. As you know from my books and lectures,[243] this whole human I lived differently before this point from how it lived after it. The moment when the Mystery of Golgotha took place was at the same time one when the whole of human consciousness changed. Naturally this was because the Christ Being united with earthly evolution, as I have often described. Increasingly we should understand the nature of the Mystery of Golgotha and its relationship to humankind. Many exponents of the Gospels stumble over passages where, in one way or another, it is said that 'heaven descended to earth'. Among those who completely misunderstood this was Helena Petrovna Blavatsky,[244] who believed Christians were claiming that a kind of heavenly kingdom had descended to the earth but that otherwise nothing had altered—that ears of corn, say, or cherries, did not suddenly become twelve times bigger, and so forth. Her point is that things on earth remained unchanged; and this 'descent of the heavenly kingdom' becomes very problematic for many exegesists because they fail to understand it. The real meaning is this: until that point people experienced the spiritual realm within and through physical, earthly conditions by means of an atavistic clairvoyance; subsequently they had to raise themselves to the spirit, perceiving things in a realm of spirit that did indeed arrive. One has no need for the ingenious twists and turns proposed by many to explain this phrase but can simply accept the reality as it is described there.

When Christ passed through the Mystery of Golgotha human beings could no longer receive their spiritual existence by virtue of their merely physical existence but must now live in the spiritual world. Someone who lives only in the physical world no longer lives upon the earth but beneath it, since from the Mystery of Golgotha onwards it has become possible to live in the spirit. The spiritual realm has really come amongst us, and this expression can immediately be understood if we grasp it as I have suggested. Christ has a real relationship with the spirit, although initially this is to remain concealed. This ought only slowly to be imparted to human beings through their own endeavours. And only when we grasp this can we understand the real course of modern history since the Mystery of Golgotha. In the early centuries, Christianity as it arrived in the world through the Mystery of Golgotha implanted itself in the gnosis that was more or less still in existence. People had very spiritual ideas to comprehend the real nature of Christ Jesus. But then the Church acquired a definite form, as you can trace in history; but you have to understand what the task of this ecclesiastical form was from the third, fourth and fifth century onwards.

Please do not misunderstand me—spiritual science shows genuine and active tolerance towards all existing religious confessions and traditions, and has to be able to see the relative truth of their diverse traditions. Spiritual science does not favour one confession more than another. It seeks, rather, to bring to light the truth of different religious perspectives, carefully weighing them and refraining from one-sidedness. Spiritual science should not be seen to tend more towards a particular confession. It seeks to reveal knowledge of the spirit. For instance, spiritual science can well understand that it is a shame if many lose touch with what lies in Catholic rites and worship, and is aware of the benefits of such worship for culture. It is also fully aware that Catholic worship has been closely associated with fine works of art, and that Catholicism, far more than is realized, perpetuates various other religious confessions. There are deep mysteries at the heart of Catholic worship. But what I am speaking of here relates to something very different from the Catholic Mass, even though the latter has its own full justification and has been a huge stimulus to human creativity. Ecclesiastical forms received certain tasks and still possessed these—still possess them today in fact—when such fervent souls as Bernhard of Clairvaux emerged from the Church and lived in devotion to their God. We have to distinguish carefully here: the Church on the one hand, and figures such as Bernhard of Clairvaux and numerous others. What task did the Church have? Its task is to keep souls as distant as possible from knowledge of Christ, to prevent them coming too close to Christ.

Ecclesiastical history from the third and fourth centuries onwards largely reveals how human sensibility distances itself from real understanding of the Mystery of Golgotha. In the Church's development lies a certain opposition to understanding of Christ. This negative task of the Church is also justified, in that people continually had to strive anew to find Christ through the powers of their own soul. Basically, whenever people came to Christ throughout these centuries this involved opposition to, or rebellion against ecclesiastical thinking. Figures such as Bernhard of Clairvaux also really rebel against the Church. Even Thomas Aquinas[245] was regarded as a heretic in Church circles; he was frowned upon and his teachings were only adopted at a later stage. The path to Christ has really always involved pushing back against the Church, and people could only find their way towards Christ by effort, in a slow, gradual way. It is worth remembering that, for instance, the 'Waldensian sects' founded in the twelfth century by Petrus Waldus as yet had no knowledge of the Gospels, for ecclesiastical life had spread without them. A strange but curious fact! In the community that gathered around Petrus Waldus[246] people were sought out who could translate passages from the Gospels. In this way some knowledge of them arose, and thus a stream of heightened, Christian life began to flow from them. In consequence the Pope declared Petrus Waldus to be a heretic. Right up to these times in Europe too certain gnostic insights were prevalent, for instance amongst the Cathars, whose name can be translated as 'the pure ones'. But this gnostic wisdom sought to engender ideas, tangible ideas about Christ and the Mystery of Golgotha. The official Church did not want this, and thus the Cathars were also declared heretics.

It is very important to bring the clear light of awareness to bear on these things and distinguish the path of Christianity from that of the Church as institution. By drawing on spiritual-scientific foundations people today can forge a path to the true Christ, to a true idea of Christ. A great deal of modern history, too, becomes clear if we know that not everything invoking the name of Christ sought to convey understanding of the Mystery of Golgotha, but, on the contrary, often aimed to hinder it. These barriers to understanding are still in place in our own time, very much so! And here I would like to describe some things that are characteristic of this.

Efforts, including Protestantism, that arose in many places to oppose the Church, were due to this role of the Church in erecting barriers to an understanding of Christ, thus necessitating individual endeavour to attain such understanding. Petrus Waldus did this by seeking out the Gospels. Until then people only had the Church, not the Gospels. Even today there are many who have strange views about the relationship between the Church and the Gospels. I would like to read you an excerpt from a modern book[247] that is very characteristic of this. Here you can see that views which cast Petrus Waldus as a heretic, because he sought the path to Christ through the Gospels, still take root in our own time. Here is a passage from the book:

> The Gospels and the Epistles are of incomparable value to us as written documents testifying to revelation; yet they are neither the foundation upon which our faith first had to develop nor the sole source from which we may actively draw the contents of our faith. In our view, the Church is older than the holy scripts. We receive them from its hand and it offers the pledge of their credibility. In

> the face of the risks of handwritten accounts and the alteration of wording in the course of translation into all the languages of the earth, the Church must remain the only reliable interpreter of the meaning and scope of Gospel passages.

Thus rather than the words of the Gospels themselves, what the Church tells us should be sought in the Gospels is the decisive thing. I have to point this out since much naivety exists, even in our circles, in relation to this. Even in our circles you can often hear the view expressed that we would make more headway with the Catholic Church if we were seen to have a Christ-friendly stance. But this will not help us in the least with the Catholic Church. On the contrary, it puts us at loggerheads with it since nothing about Christ, and nothing that exceeds the scope of mere science, can be disseminated in the Catholic Church unless the Church itself first acknowledges this as an authorized doctrine. Anyone amongst us, therefore, who propounds ideas about Christ and thinks that this can be accepted by the Church, will be seen as heretical because the Church does not accord anyone the right to speak of Christ in any other than the strictly authorized way.

The author who wrote the above passage makes this very clear: 'A person of faith will of course hold views corresponding to those the scientist holds of the facts of his experience.' In other words, he is saying that the faithful must acknowledge Church tenets about the world of spirit in the same way that the eyes of a scientist give him information about the world. Then he continues:

> He must accept them as they are, not subtracting from or adding anything to them. And this acceptance and acknowledgement of the real state of affairs, as far as possible cleansed of all subjective tinge, is what is asked of him... The truths of revelation are likewise a given for those who grasp them in faith. They are also something concluded and complete. After the time of Christ they cannot be further enhanced, nor can they be diminished. All change or modification of their content is excluded.

This is written by someone fully rooted in what orthodox Catholicism has to propound. This orthodoxy will inevitably turn aside with some disdain from efforts initiated by figures such as Lessing to seek the soul and spirit once again. Lessing got as far as envisaging reincarnation, starting from a modern life of spirit. Everything founded on the Catholic Church, by contrast, is in inevitable and stark opposition to German culture and spiritual life as this flowed through Lessing, Herder, Goethe and Schiller. For this reason, the author whose work I quoted above, also writes:

> The edifice of ecclesiastical doctrine as nowadays acknowledged and presented by theologians was however not complete and concluded from the outset. What Christ told the Apostles, and these in turn proclaimed to the world, was not a methodically progressing and universal system but a wealth of truths that are all united, as in a single point, in the one fact of the story of our Lord, of God become man. But instruction of the faithful, and defence against attacks by heathens and misinterpretations by heretics made it necessary to connect these truths together systematically, to develop their full content and determine their precise meaning. This occurred in the form of doctrinal enactments by the organs appointed to do this; it was done, in the Catholic view, under the guidance of the Holy Spirit but at the same time with the collaboration of ecclesiastical studies initiated at an early stage in the Church's history.
>
> The revelation did not create a new language but drew on that already current, revising the meaning and enhancing the significance of individual words and phrases. Theology, too, which undertook to expound the contents of this revelation in an ordered and doctrinal way, and to penetrate it speculatively, required for this certain tools and aids, clearly defined terms to structure the material, special expressions to indicate comprehensibly relationships and connections that exceed the scope of daily experience. In this, Greek philosophy found its new, world-historic task: that of helping prepare the vessels into which was now poured an infinitely richer content from higher sources. Originally the source was Platonism, whose speculation, focused upon the supersensible, directly prompted this. Much later, after more than a millennium,

> when the most important constituents of revelation had long since found their doctrinal formulation, a close connection between theological disciplines and Aristotelian philosophy was forged, and continues to this day.

Thus it seems that since Aristotelian philosophy was reconciled with the Church back in medieval times it is still valid in the Church of today!

> With its aid, Saint Thomas Aquinas, a systematist par excellence, erected the great edifice of Church doctrine which in the following centuries, with only small modifications, determined the form, expression and mode of instruction of Catholic theology.

The gentleman who wrote this book realizes that what he calls Church doctrine emerged from a certain connection between the substance of Christian wisdom and the Aristotelianism of ancient Greece. He even envisages a future possibility—albeit still a long way off, for he expressly states 'in a future by no means yet approaching'—when people might view Christianity with quite different ideas and concepts. He asks what would have happened if Christianity had not spread via Greek philosophy but, as it might have done, through Indian philosophy. Everything would have assumed a different form. And yet he insists that we must stick with the form it has now received and cannot modify this with other outlooks emerging in the modern world. However, he does sense that this becomes problematic at some points: 'I only reject a frame of mind that, in areas where full freedom is accorded to scientific research, is deaf to all objections, however well justified, and clings instead to tradition.' Nevertheless, he does cling pretty securely to tradition! 'And finally we do have to concede some things in the same way that concessions were made to the Copernican system.' But the Church only conceded this in 1827! But he rejects justified attempts to comprehend Christianity anew, from the perspective of modern consciousness. He finds this most unappealing, and states:

> I can conceive that in a future by no means yet approaching, the connection between Aristotelian philosophy and theology will loosen, with concepts that are then no longer comprehensible and

> still less satisfying being replaced by others corresponding to a greatly enhanced state of knowledge.

He finds it 'conceivable' that something no one anyway any longer understands might be replaced by something else that, likewise, no one understands.

> This would not run counter to the Gospel's warning, for rather than pouring new wine into old wineskins, the reverse would be true: new vessels would be created in which to preserve the inexhaustible and intrinsically unaltered nature of the wine of the salvation doctrine and offer it to the faithful.

But this ought not to happen, since, as he goes on:

> These vessels must be suitable in nature. The attempts made in the seventeenth century with Cartesian ideas[248] and in the nineteenth century with the philosophy of Kant and Hegel admonish us to be cautious. A system of concepts that would replace the Aristotelian must, like the latter, emerge from a wealth of knowledge and contemporary awareness ... This conceptual framework would have to succeed in achieving widespread acceptance amongst thinking humanity. Even then its application to ecclesiastical theology would be hard to accomplish without all kinds of errors and confusion.

'Work' would be needed to engender the right understanding:

> After all, the same was true in the thirteenth century when, mediated by the Arabs, the whole of Aristotelian philosophy came to the awareness of the Christian Occident. There was a violent refusal to acknowledge it in many quarters. Even Thomas Aquinas was not spared hostility in this regard. Many at the time regarded him as an innovator against whom the defenders of the old, tried and tested school of thought must direct their attacks.

Human nature is remarkable in absolutely refusing, on principle, to allow something to surface that can very easily be conceived, where this involves suppression of an old understanding of Christianity by a newer one. Nor can we say that this account is naive. It is actually very scholarly, for the booklet concludes with a really very significant pointer to a religious order that has always set great store by cleverness and intellect, and took a quite different stance from that of Bernhard of Clairvaux or Francis of Assisi—who expressed more mystical and pious inclinations. The other religious order I am thinking of placed less emphasis on such things as mystical piety, instead accentuating a certain cleverness and intellectual comprehension of life. For this reason the booklet concludes as follows:

> I will end with a saying by Saint Ignatius Loyola,[249] adopted by the constitutions of the Jesuit order, and in recent times once again accorded significance in many quarters: 'A preoccupation and concern with science, if pursued with the pure striving of an act of worship, is, since it encompasses the whole human being, not less but more pleasing to God than practices of penance and expiation.'

In our times people have tried to awaken clear understanding in many diverse ways. Let me demonstrate this to you with an example. Today I have read some passages to you from a book which can show how some adopt a particular stance within the orthodoxy I described. A gentleman who has written an essay on the author of the booklet I quoted from can illustrate this further. It is important to note that this essay was written quite recently. Let me read you something from it:[250]

> In his talk given in 1893, entitled 'The Role of Science in Catholicism and the position of Catholic scholars in the present day', the author states: 'We Catholic scholars of the nineteenth century are convinced that there is no conflict between knowledge and faith, but that the nature of both can coexist in mutual harmony. We are certain that truth is not and cannot be twofold. God is the source of all truth, and has spoken to us through the Prophets and the Logos become man. He speaks to us in the doctrines of the Church but no less so in the laws of logic to which we must adhere, where we strive for knowledge of natural truths. And since God cannot contradict himself, so there can be no

> conflict between natural and supernatural laws, nor between the teachings of revelation and serious, honest laws of logic and a science which subscribes to methodological rules.' In stating this, however, he leaves philosophy in a cul-de-sac. Its 'freedom' appears to us to be no more than that of the fire enclosed in its grate or the prisoner shut in by walls. Simply having feet to walk around the exercise yard and hands to use for whatever activity is permitted does not make the prisoner free; and no more is a philosophy free whose principles are subject to the limiting dominion of faith. A Catholic philosophy inevitably contains a contradiction in that it is not freely self-determining.

If our science of the spirit were not freely self-determining it too would not be what it should be. The passage continues:

> Catholic philosophy has a predetermined path, whereas a philosophy that lays claim to academic rigour must adhere with relentless consistency only to what arises from independent research and thinking and is bound by the strict rules of enquiry and empirical proof. It must not be founded on a particular faith or any ecclesiastical dogma, for then it is no longer science but instead unscientific dogmatism. In the latter case it is determined not by scientific principles but by the articles of faith. Rather than pursuing its own unhindered way it acknowledges in advance a truth to which it subscribes rather than to the intrinsic, independent laws of enquiry.

And it is this, precisely, which is our contemporary task: to find the path upon which each individual soul can be founded on itself and its own experience. The Catholic text from which I quoted earlier therefore stands in crass opposition to the real tasks of our day and, as you see, there are people who realize this: that a scientific world-view is not possible if one starts from predetermined perspectives. And yet it seems to be very difficult nowadays to retain an unprejudiced point of view, despite the urgent need for this. The further advance of culture will depend on people discovering their inner connection with the world of spirit. Those who fail to see this are placing obstacles in the way of the most vital contemporary task. But seeing it is not enough—one also has to draw the right consequences from it. The curious thing today is that people can have insight but then draw quite different consequences. The author of the essay I just quoted from continues with a hymn of praise to the man whose views he has just taken issue with, which culminate in a Jesuit confession of faith. This man was Count Georg von Hertling; and the author of the essay that takes issue with his views concludes as follows:[251]

> Count Hertling is a decided individual. The word 'individual' means 'indivisibility', but this is at the same time the basis for inner nuance and fully structured organization. Here an individual soul, the soul of a tribe, and of a nation, merge and have a mutually enhancing effect. This unity of three in one is what renders him so strong, and stamps him with the quality of the one chosen to be the Chancellor of the German Empire.

Today we need to find ways to shape the vessel into which the fluidum of spiritual science must flow, and this can happen only if this vessel is a conduit whereby the human soul finds its own way to the life of spirit. It is vital to grasp this, connected as it is with the most necessary impulses of our age. You see, our age is asking us not only to gain greater understanding but, when we do, to draw the necessary consequences and act accordingly. Our science of the spirit will only be able to stand its ground in those who really have courage for the truth, otherwise contradictions as in the passage above will increasingly rear their heads. I also say this because, time and again, some naive minds amongst us are so delighted to discover apparent praise for some aspect of spiritual science. It is important to be very discerning here. Praise can actually be much more damaging to us than criticism, as long as the latter is honestly intended.

Recently, by chance, I read a review of a book by Hermann Heisler,[252] a Protestant theologian who collected some of his sermons in a book entitled *Life Questions, 17 Sermons by Hermann Heisler*. The review is very characteristic in its inconsistency, although some of our naive friends may count it among the offerings in which they take much pleasure. The reviewer writes:[253]

These sermons deserve special regard, if for no other reason because of the preacher himself. He was a Protestant priest in Steiermark and Bohemia for ten years, but then, alarmed by the risk of going stale in the routines of his work, left his calling and spent many years in profound study of science and philosophy. Eventually his inner vocation reasserted itself and he returned to it with fresh joy and love. Since he could not serve his fatherland with arms, he offered his spiritual services to the church in his native Baden, and was appointed to the diocese of Constance. It was there, in 1917, that he gave the 17 sermons which compose this book. Their content is outstanding in quality, displaying thorough engagement and acuity, and requiring some effort of audience and readers. The sermons do not seek to kindle beautiful feelings but, through serious cogitation, to shape conviction into knowledge. Thus they avoid any kind of sermonizing tone and almost read like well-considered yet popular academic treatises on religious problems. In particular I would mention a sermon on the much-debated concept of freedom, which arrives at the following true conclusion: 'Naturally compulsion always governs us. Even as free individuals we pursue goals that are most attractive to us. But the divine gift of freedom brought to us by Christ is that the lower temptations of the sensory world lose their compelling power over our soul, while the glory of the world of spirit gains inner ascendancy over us.' However, the quality of these sermons is not confined to their thoroughness of thinking but lies in the specific content of the thoughts expressed. Heisler is an enthusiastic theosophist or, as he himself would prefer to say, an adherent of spiritual science. This should not be confused, though, with a spiritualist belief in the materialization of spirits; but instead Heisler asserts that the spirit acts freely and independently of any material means. Our thoughts, he says, are powers which, though invisible, emanate from us with great potency and impress the stamp of our being upon all of nature with either beneficial or deleterious effects. This belief in the indestructible power of the spirit offers comfort in the sermon 'Our Dead Still Live', and assumes a surprising form in the sermon 'Destiny'. Based on the

> text of John, chapter 9 (the man born blind), Heisler here revives the ancient Indian and Orphic teaching of the migration of souls, or of reincarnation of the soul in an earthly body. In doing so, the preacher seeks to resolve the problem of what so often seems to be the injustice of destiny. Like Lessing in his *The Education of the Human Race* he wishes to awaken belief in destiny as divine education. To sum up Heisler's views one can say that he regards his whole spiritual science as a return to the New Testament, and that he presents it as a rigorous discipline and thus one which overcomes the Kantian division between knowledge and faith.

You might well say, Well what could be better than such a review? And yet the man who writes all this concludes as follows:

> Personally I reject this spiritual science and remain with Kant. And yet these sermons contain so many good things, and theosophy currently informs theology so significantly (e.g. in Rittelmeyer's essays), that I believe many, both theologians and lay people, will be well-served by reading them.

This is a very common phenomenon of our time—lack of inner strength and courage in people's thinking. The reviewer has only good things to say about the book, and one sees that he really does recognize something of value in it; and yet suddenly he states, 'Personally I reject this spiritual science'! There you have the fruits of what I described before, which are connected with many aspects of our modern culture.

In a week's time we will reflect further on this: the stream I described today, which then leads into social democracy and Bolshevism.

LECTURE 20

BERLIN, 30 JULY 1918

TODAY I will continue by outlining a few further things relating to our recent reflections. Understanding the present day with all its divergent currents of spiritual and materialistic views is extremely difficult, and one ought not to think that this confused picture of modern times can be understood without having the will to perceive how these times have long been in preparation as history slowly unfolded. Today, drawing on our spiritual-scientific insights, we will look back to what we call the fourth post-Atlantean epoch.

As you know, this epoch began around the year 747 BC, and ended as the fifteenth century began, in around 1413. The dates themselves must of course be regarded, like all such figures, as an approximation. In this period we find at work certain powers that have an inner consistency and mutual relationship, and differ essentially from all the powers prevailing both before and after this epoch. This time, during which the rational or mind soul developed in human nature, can be further subdivided into three smaller eras: the period starting around 747 BC—the date in fact when Rome was actually founded—and ending about 27 BC. The second period extends from this date, 27 BC, to roughly the end of the seventh century AD, that is to the year 693; and the last and shorter period lasts from 693 to around 1413. Since that time around 1413 we have been in a new phase of soul development with distinctive qualities with which we are already familiar. We can make a clear distinction in terms of human soul evolution between the fourth post-Atlantean epoch and the three preceding epochs of ancient India, ancient Persia and Egypt-Chaldea, and likewise between this fourth epoch and the fifth that follows it; and in the same way we can also clearly distinguish characteristic stages within this fourth epoch itself which are significant for the development of civilization. In each of these shorter phases we can observe how humanity progresses in particular ways.

Taking the first of these phases, 747 to 27 BC,* we will naturally think first and foremost of the peoples living around the Mediterranean, in whom we find developing a very particular state of soul. History tells us little about this since its ideas and concepts avoid engaging with really characteristic qualities. If we wish to properly characterize this period, and the inner factors of humanity's evolution at work then, we can say that during it human souls slowly detach themselves from a connection with the whole spiritual cosmos. If we look back to Egyptian and Chaldean times—the epoch of the sentient soul—human beings felt that their soul belonged to the cosmos. The sentient soul in human nature sensed that the human being is a part of the universe. We cannot properly describe Egyptian and Chaldean evolution without taking account of the fact that people in those times, in observing the cosmos around them, received through their senses and feelings something that came to expression in this awareness of harmony with the spiritual cosmos, of being part of it. Just as we can say that the fingers of our hands are and feel one with us, so people in ancient Egypt and Chaldea felt themselves one with the spiritual cosmos. This feeling for the cosmos underwent a crisis in the eighth century BC, was shaken to its roots. In the past human souls owed their sense of belonging with the cosmos to their ancient, atavistic and dreamy clairvoyance. In those days people did not perceive as we do today. In their sense perceptions they also perceived the spirit, the divine—a faculty which modern scholars, in their ignorance, call 'animism'. In this way people of those times felt intimately connected with the spirit of the cosmos.

This intimate connection faded, and on the one hand this led to many symptoms of decadence, while on the other it led to the wonders of

---

* Steiner actually says '27 years before the Mystery of Golgotha', and it is therefore not clear if he means 27 BC or 6 AD.

Greek culture. You see, the culture of ancient Greece is founded primarily on the human being's experience of standing in isolation in the universe, no longer as an intrinsic part of the cosmos but as a complete and self-encompassing human totality. In a sense the human being had emerged from the cosmos and embarked on an existence that was complete in itself. The beauties and wonders of Greek culture could never have emerged if a more ancient form of soul experience had continued to prevail—such as held sway in ancient India for instance—along with this sense of close belonging to the cosmos. The glories of Greek culture, which in other regions also surfaced as less delightful phenomena, all developed between the eighth and first centuries BC. Humanity withdrew into the realm of soul, into the purely human, approaching the Mystery of Golgotha as this period progressed. Let us not forget that the Mystery of Golgotha inevitably has a quality that cannot entirely be encompassed by human understanding, nor human supersensible understanding either. Some part of it inevitably evades our comprehension. What was accomplished as Christ entered earthly evolution cannot, as I have explained in various previous reflections, be summed up in human concepts or encompassed in human feelings. And connected with this is the fact that as this Mystery of Golgotha developed, in a sense civilized humanity was prepared for it in a way that did not allow full awareness or experience of this event to dawn. Instead it occurred alongside and at one remove from ordinary human experience. In terms of history, this is fairly clear: civilized humanity around the Mediterranean took little notice of Christ Jesus nor of what was happening in the far-flung Jewish province of Palestine. This scarcely figures even in Tacitus, writing a hundred years after the Mystery of Golgotha.

On the one hand therefore we have advancing civilization and on the other, at one remove from it, a current in which the Mystery of Golgotha occurred. These two streams flow alongside but separate from each other. This could only happen because, as the divine act was accomplished, civilization had shut itself off from the divine, and a life was unfolding which no longer had a direct connection with the spirit. A spiritual event took place upon the globe which human civilization itself ignored. In all former times it would have been inconceivable for such a division to exist between outward culture and a mystery event, since human culture in those days was fully informed by an awareness of divine, spiritual realities. It is very characteristic, highly significant, that the mundane culture running parallel to the Mystery of Golgotha had closed itself off and therefore was distanced from this event.

In the second period of this epoch, thus beginning around 27 BC and ending in AD 693, the whole of central European culture is basically founded on preventing any understanding of the Mystery of Golgotha from informing mundane civilization. It may seem very strange to you that I say this, since Christianity did indeed spread abroad through the central European culture of those times; and yet it spread in the way I recently described. The Mystery of Golgotha occurred in splendid isolation. Certainly, aspects of it reached mainstream culture in an external and dogmatic fashion. People knew that Christ had come, that he had disciples, brought this or that to humanity and made this or that remark about the human being's relationship to the divine. This entered mundane culture in the form of outward phrases and principles, and yet alongside these externalities it was also true that the whole of humanity, really, which absorbed Christianity during these centuries, remained distant from any inner understanding of the Mystery of Golgotha. It would have been possible to gain deeper insight into what actually happened at the Mystery of Golgotha with the aid of gnosis, and certain forms of preparation founded on traditional wisdom passed down from heathen peoples. But this did not happen. Such things were all declared heretical. Instead, trivial formulations were used as a narrow mould into which to pour Christianity—whose deeper aspects of course can never be limited and confined in this way. The Mystery of Golgotha can be comprehended only through the highest spiritual striving and the fruits of wisdom this can reveal.

The institutions established in the early Christian centuries really did not serve to connect people with the Mystery of Golgotha but instead inculcated something in people's souls that remained very distant from any sense of communion with it. Rather than fostering insight, the Church cultivated non-understanding of the Mystery of Golgotha. If you trace the history of the various Ecumenical Councils and all the ecclesiastical machinations during this period, you will find that all this aimed to inculcate dogmatic ideas in people of a kind that sought to ensure that everything connected with the Mystery of Golgotha would be conceived in terms far removed from the life of the human soul. We can sum all this up, albeit somewhat radically, by saying that people tried to equip themselves with certain ideas about the Mystery of Golgotha and its effects, and yet what they might find out about this was not the most important thing. Instead, they were intent on cultivating the sense that the Mystery of Golgotha did not directly concern them, and that Christ would ensure they were saved. There was a tendency increasingly to push the reality of these sacred, spiritual events into another realm altogether, rather than conceiving of them as being connected with what unfolds in the human breast. These two things were to be kept as far as possible sundered. An unconscious aim was at work here: a self-evident and yet not articulated intention, and this only surfaced clearly in the year 869 at the Eighth Ecumenical Council in Constantinople.[254] This goal was to prevent the human spirit from any direct, personal preoccupation with spiritual reality, which instead was to be confined to the Mystery of Golgotha. In other words, efforts were afoot to quash any personal, feeling engagement with the Mystery of Golgotha. It was to remain shrouded in incomprehension. By this means the Church sought gradually to subject people to its authority, allowing them only a mundane understanding of these mysteries, and increasingly cultivating the belief that one cannot reflect upon supersensible things since they are beyond the scope of an individual human soul. Human reflection was to limit itself to physical reality only, rather than developing powers suitable for seeking an understanding of the Mystery of Golgotha. In certain resolutions passed by the Eighth Ecumenical Council at Constantinople we find a clear articulation of efforts to prevent people in Europe from thinking for themselves, since human soul faculties were not to engage with the realm of living reality to which the Mystery of Golgotha belongs.

Precisely in this middle period of the fourth post-Atlantean epoch, therefore, from around 27 BC to AD 693, a belief was cultivated in humanity that all human knowledge and feeling was fit only for this sensory realm of existence. The non-sensory or supersensible realm, the other side of existence or whatever one wishes to call it was withdrawn from direct knowledge and perception, put beyond the scope of human feeling and faculties. Really we can only understand the history of this whole period if we consider this. Throughout these centuries all the actions of the Catholic Church aimed to inculcate in people the belief that their soul faculties were fit only for the physical realm, and the supersensible realm could approach them only without the involvement of their own powers of understanding and perception. Because of this, after the end of this middle period, thus around the eighth and ninth century, European humanity was plunged into a kind of darkness as far as the human soul's connection with the supersensible realm was concerned. Bernhard of Clairvaux is typical of a phenomenon that can be understood in this context, as someone standing beyond everything physical and sensory and devoting his soul entirely to all that exceeds the scope of natural human understanding. This fervour for what lies beyond human comprehension must be included in our view of someone like Bernhard, with his whole configuration of soul. In this figure particularly we can find traits of mighty grandeur since everything that is somewhat shifted or distorted can also have a beautiful, grand and glorious aspect. But in Bernhard, too, we will find characteristics of soul which show clearly that he emerged from the prevailing mood developing in western culture in these centuries. Besides Bernhard of Clairvaux one might name other figures; he is merely typical of them, for instance in the way he speaks to his followers of all that will be vouchsafed to them by the Crusade he intends to embark on. Then the Crusade fails, but how does this fervently devout man speak about the failure? Roughly as follows. If everything ends badly, the verdict on this failure may be meted out to me but not to God, for the divine can never be wrong. So even when a person knew himself to be closely connected with the divine, spiritual power underlying all reality, he makes a careful distinction between this reality and himself, saying that he will bear the blame but that truth and spiritual reality exist beyond such fault, beyond the current of existence on which the human soul is borne.

At the beginning of the third era of the fourth post-Atlantean epoch, therefore, a kind of darkness had come to shroud humanity. We can see this in the fact that human concepts no longer testify to a connection with real spiritual streams and impulses. If you study philosophy written in the centuries from the eighth to the fifteenth, you will find that it continually seeks to prove that spiritual reality cannot be grasped by human ideas and concepts. It was thought that this reality must be 'left to revelation', in the phrase of the time, and to ecclesiastical teachings.

Thus the power of the Church developed, emerging not only from theological impulses but from this doctrine that people must limit their own powers of cognition, their own faculties of soul, to physical and sensory life, and refrain from trying to fathom the supersensible realm with their thinking. The concept of faith arose from this at a later date, and was certainly not present in the early centuries as you can conclude from historical documents. This idea of faith states that faith, rather than knowledge, is the only possible human response to the divine. This division between the truth available to faith and that available to knowledge developed from these important historical contexts which underlie what I have been speaking of today.

Since the fifteenth century, roughly since the year 1413, we live—as the third millennium will show—in a period founded on everything that happened under influences such as those I have described. We carry this legacy with us; and yet at the same time an entirely new quality is also developing in this fifth post-Atlantean epoch. In that fourth epoch, if we survey its whole compass, we see the human soul being sundered from the divine, spiritual world, being directed to and becoming dependent upon merely external physical and sensory processes. This was a new development at that time, and did not exist, as I have said, in ancient Egyptian and Chaldean epochs. In our age something new is likewise entering, and humanity's task is increasingly to become more conscious so as to recognize all this, seeing on the one hand what has been passed down as legacy from a past epoch and what, on the other, is emerging as a new development in our own epoch. Let us first consider the legacy passed down to us.

As we saw, we have inherited a frame of mind in which we feel convinced that we must develop our soul life quite separately from the supersensible realm. The further legacy of this, as you will see the more carefully you study history, is a clear conviction—in which no room for doubt remains—that rooting human soul faculties in the sensory domain and shutting them off from the supersensible led to a situation in the fifth post-Atlantean epoch, thus since the fifteenth century, in which this whole supersensible realm was dismissed as an illusion. Firstly efforts were aimed at keeping human beings at a distance from the supersensible, as apparent in the Eighth Ecumenical Council in 869; and then, because the supersensible realm had been kept at arm's length as the Church saw fit, this realm came to be rejected altogether. A belief developed that human beings themselves had invented it, and that it had no reality. If we really wish to understand the origins of modern materialism we have to seek them in the Church itself. Naturally the Church is only the outward expression of deeper powers at work in human evolution, but we acquire insight into this evolution if we examine more carefully how one thing really emerges from another. In the fourth post-Atlantean epoch, right-thinking people believed that human powers of cognition were fit only for comprehending sensory things while the non-sensory had to be left to revelation unsullied by human thinking. Holding one's own individual views of the divine was deemed heretical, and would, they thought, lead only to error and illusion. The modern Marxist or Social Democrat, the true offspring of this view, has actually emerged from the Catholicism of former centuries, and holds that all science worthy of the name can only relate to processes in the physical world of the senses. No such thing as spiritual science can exist since the spirit is an illusion. The only acknowledged cultural domain that bears any relation to it is 'social science'—the science of social coexistence. This kind of outlook has of course assumed diverse forms in different cultural regions of the earth, but this is the general trend of it.

From the ninth century onwards, therefore, in central and western Europe, efforts were focused on cultivating belief in the supersensible without people knowing anything of it except through revelation—a kind of unknowing faith. The soul qualities of central European peoples had to be taken into account, could not simply be ignored. It would not have worked to tell people to focus only on food and drink and other pragmatic matters, and ignore things too lofty for them. In western Europe this would not have worked. This was done however in eastern Europe, and is the cause of the ecclesiastical division between eastern and western Europe. In eastern Europe people really were confined to a narrow focus on the sensory world: their powers were to be preoccupied with physical matters and develop in this realm. And what unfolded as the Orthodox Church belonged to the lofty heights of the mysteries, quite untinged by sensory things. Here there was a strict division between what people elaborated out of their human nature and the real world of spirit, which, in a rarefied atmosphere, floated far above people in the rites of worship.

What was the inevitable outcome of this? It was inevitable that, in various nuances of feeling, a view formed that only the sensory and physical realm has meaning. One can put it like this: powers of which no use is made, but which instead are locked away inside a person, do not develop; they wither. For centuries people were prevented from encompassing the supersensible in their mind or spirit, and thus their powers became ever less practised at doing so, and ultimately vanished altogether. This utter absence is something we now rediscover in modern socialist views. It is not their socialism itself that is so dire but the wholesale rejection of supersensible spirit, which leads people to confine their scope to the social structures of a mere human animal. The laming of the human being's supersensible powers led eventually to a focus on mere social structures for human animals. This arose because people were forced to cease connecting their soul with a living experience of the stream of life that brings the blessing of knowledge of the Mystery of Golgotha's meaning.

And what was this connected with? In this fourth post-Atlantean epoch, luciferic powers were working very strongly to detach the human being from the cosmos. These powers always seek to isolate the human being egotistically—to cut him off from the whole spiritual cosmos even in his knowledge of the physical cosmos. For this reason no science existed at the time when this sundering reached its peak. This is luciferic. And so we must say that the division between sense-based knowledge and supersensible dogmatism is luciferic in nature. The ahrimanic opposes the luciferic here—two adversaries of the human soul. This withering of supersensible human powers, leading to a purely brutish form of socialism—which is now set to have a devastating, destructive impact on humanity—must be ascribed to luciferic powers. The new element that is developing in our age is different in nature, is more ahrimanic. The luciferic seeks to isolate people, cut them off from the supersensible, spiritual realm, give them the illusion that they are a totality in themselves. By contrast the ahrimanic makes people afraid of the spirit, stops them approaching it, gives them the illusion that the spirit is not something that humankind can attain to. Whereas luciferic influence works through culture and education to keep human beings away from the supersensible, the ahrimanic does so through invoking fear of the spirit, a kind of intrinsic, bodily fear that has emerged particularly since the fifteenth century. While luciferic sundering from the spirit came to expression especially under the mantle of Orthodox Christianity in the East, ahrimanic sundering through fear was bred largely in the element of western culture, and quite particularly in American culture.

Such truths may feel uncomfortable to many, but they are true nevertheless; and we will make no headway today by talking in general terms—however mystically or theosophically—about our connection with the divine. We have to acknowledge reality: that is the only way to advance; and we can only create order again amidst our chaos by recognizing the distinctive nature of diverse streams that flow alongside each other. Each of these streams has a local origin, determined by particular conditions; but then it spreads and merges in a turbulent muddle with all the others to form what we call culture nowadays. I would call 'Americanism'—as a collective term not to be applied to individual Americans—everything that betrays fear of the spirit: the longing to live only with the physical plane, and at most also with what rises into this physical, sensory plane as coarse spirit, spiritualistic emanations and suchlike, which is not true spirit. Americanism is characterized by fear of the spirit. But this Americanism does not live merely in America itself—where it comes to very pronounced expression in the will character of the social realm—but above all in all science. Since the fifteenth century, this science has increasingly developed what we might call a 'fear of the spirit'. Science is regarded as objective only where it sheds all inwardly engendered living concepts. Observation of nature is meant to remain untinged by any idea or concept engendered in the human soul. Only dead and arid observation is accepted by science, not a living, spirit-imbued quality. To introduce an idea or concept into one's observations in the Hegelian fashion, which is a truly central European approach, or also in the way that Schelling or Goethe did, is regarded as a very suspect methodology. You see, people do not trust that they will grasp objective reality through their spiritual comprehension and experience. They think that they will open the doors to the arbitrary, to all that is not objective, by introducing the slightest subjective tinge into their observations and experience. But this is ahrimanic. Science is a kind of universal Americanism in so far as it abides by the principle of discarding anything subjective from the observation of phenomena; and this developed from a former luciferic spirit isolation in the fourth post-Atlantean epoch.

And so we have added a new element to that old legacy—something which, alongside what must develop productively and consciously in future, increasingly reveals its destructive powers. This new element is largely ahrimanic in nature, is fear of the spirit and has a destructive effect, a dissolving effect on all human culture which must after all be rooted in the spirit.

At the turning point from the fourth to the fifth post-Atlantean epoch, and especially during the fifth epoch, the impulses I have now described increasingly emerged. When America was discovered and European culture was transplanted there, this fear of the life of spirit developed. But a tension arose in human souls at the same time, for by their very nature the powers at work in European souls had a sense or intimation of their connection with the spirit in the cosmos. At the transition from the fourth to the fifth post-Atlantean epoch this tension emerged, during the centuries when modern history was developing. It was a tension due to a suppression of spirit in the human breast. You can say that this tension had to be stifled, partly through a clear understanding of the old legacy still present, and partly through a very realistic appraisal of the newly emerging ahrimanic element. Here there arose the spiritual stream whose influence is actually much greater than most people believe. I spoke about this from a different angle last time. This spiritual stream, Jesuitism, sought to perpetuate the human soul's isolation from the realm of spirit. The inner principle of Jesuitism involves directing human evolution along a path that can keep people at a remove from their connection with the supersensible, from their real connection with it. It is self-evident that this distancing or detachment can be achieved all the better if the supersensible realm is presented in strict, dogmatic terms as something that human cognition cannot reach. But on the other hand, the Jesuit approach forges strong connections with modern science and Americanism. The greatness of Jesuitism lies in its deep engagement with the physical sciences. The Jesuits excel in the realm of the physical, sensory sciences since they count on our primary fear of the spirit—a human attribute that must be counteracted by guiding our nature towards the world of spirit. They count on being able to make a social construct of this fear by telling people that they cannot and ought not to approach the spirit, and that they, the Jesuits, will mediate it to everyone else.

These two streams, of Americanism and Jesuitism, are in reciprocal interplay. But please do not take this too superficially. In all such things we have to try to discover the deeper impulses at work in humanity's evolution. If you look for the forces that have created our present catastrophe, you will discover a curious collaboration between Americanism, as I have defined it here, and Jesuitism. In surveying these things we find an old legacy working on in culture on the one hand, and on the other a new element. The luciferic legacy and this new ahrimanic element both stand in opposition to the true life of spirit as the redeeming element that humankind will need for its evolution. If we study a figure such as Bernhard of Clairvaux with the right inner sympathy we see that he tries to balance the physical, sensory focus of human cognition by opening his soul in pious fervour and elemental experience to the spiritual and the divine. The quality of enthusiasm enters his being. This one-sided inclination for the spirit in human souls has a correlate in our own time with an inclination towards the dark side of things. In the twelfth century we had Bernhard of Clairvaux, while our own century has figures like Lenin and Trotsky. Whereas we see an impulse towards the supersensible in the first instance, in these modern figures we find a hatred for the supersensible, albeit expressed in other words and content. That is the dark reverse of those earlier times: on the one hand the human soul pours itself into the divine, and on the other human nature pours itself into the animalistic and brutish, with the aim of sustaining nothing but social structure.

But we can only understand this if we are absolutely clear about one thing which is, however, very alien to modern comprehension. Our modern world sets great store by theories, believing in the content of programmatic ideas. I have often discussed this. Theoretical content is never the decisive thing, for what matters is the reality that takes effect, the efficacy of an idea. Before the world war, at the turn of the century, a modern Marxist would naturally have quoted the teachings of Marx, Engels and Lassalle as highly desirable doctrines for securing the well-being of humanity. People set great store by the content of programmes and schemas. But such things are never what count in reality; ideas never unfold in accordance with their content but through powers present in them quite distinct from their content. We only understand reality if we realize that ideas often have very little to do with reality but that their content has a separate existence alongside it. You can devise a beautiful plan, very well thought out, and can be inordinately pleased with it and enthusiastic about it—as we have seen in the case of Marxists. But none of this counts. For an era as unspiritual as ours this is just playing with fire. People think they are working to realize their ideas; yet anyone who knows how life develops will also know that quite different effects will come about from the intended ones. Ideas, we can say, give rise to monstrosities in cultural life if they are not received with spiritual understanding. But the ideas of Marxism cannot be received spiritually since they seek to eradicate the spirit. They will inevitably become monstrous, however lovely they appear. We should leave ideas to one side. Instead of thinking day has come on the earth by some power inherent in the earth itself, we should realize that day dawns because the sun rises. You can only explain the dawning day by looking beyond the immediate environment of the earth, and in the same way you can only understand current events by looking back to the distant past. You fail to understand Bolshevism if you overlook the fact that it is a consequence or after-effect of the Eighth Ecumenical Council in the year 869. You have to see Bolshevism as a result of the withering of spiritual powers that perceive the supersensible world. This is the inner connection needed for properly understanding what happens in the outer world, and for taking the right stance towards it. Those who can trace the threads of history find it appalling to see movements which think, arrogantly, that they can reform the world but which only count on the content of ideas without due regard to real effects. The content of an idea alone, however, fine or ugly, has nothing to do with it. Look at it like this: a child is born, a beautiful child. Its mother may be delighted. Mothers can of course be delighted even if the child is not so beautiful. The child grows up and becomes a good-for-nothing, perhaps a criminal. This does not mean, does it, that the child was not beautiful to start with? We are still entitled to perceive the child's beauty. It seems to us that there is a contradiction between such beauty and later events that were not envisaged. In the same way, ideas live amongst certain groups of people who admire them and wish to use them to reform the world. But these ideas turn into monsters! You see, in themselves ideas are something dead, and must first be enlivened by flowing into a living cultural context.

If you read modern socialist tracts and overlook certain differences between them, you will find that, despite dealing with different aspects of life and formulated in different ways, they actually very closely resemble tracts produced by Catholicism. Recently, for instance, I read you some passages from a pamphlet.[255] If you compare the thought forms in this pamphlet, the mode of thinking, with rampant socialist ideas tending towards Bolshevism, this whole anti-cultural trend, then you will find the same ideas, basically, as in a text by Lenin or Kautsky.[256] The one is a development of the other. Reading certain dogmatic socialist tracts, you quickly feel you are very much in a 'Catholic' world. The only real difference is that something forbidden in Catholicism, philosophizing about certain subjects, becomes a passion, a principle in Bolshevism: all knowledge and mental progress must be explained in terms of the class war. This principle arises from the principle of Catholicism. In its current form Bolshevism may only have a short existence but humanity will long be plagued by what underlies it.

We have to look clearly at all these things to realize how necessary it is for us to cultivate the right kind of spiritual life. Pie-in-the-sky thinking is of no use. What we need is to use spiritual perception to see reality clearly, and discover the connecting threads. Only if we grasp the full context can we intervene properly in world events, rather than living from old legacies or becoming fearful as new elements enter culture which can only lead us deep into chaos. In the brutish forms of socialism we have to see an elaboration of what developed in the fourth post-Atlantean epoch. This contains something luciferic: the luciferic Fall. What is happening now is like the punishment for this original sin: the powers that were not applied to supersensible perception have now really become incapable of it, and this is accompanied by hatred of and repugnance for the supersensible. This is indeed a kind of punishment for the fact that we turned away from the supersensible, and this can explain much that is currently happening in the world.

Impulses at work in human evolution come to expression in diverse ways, with different aspects and nuances. We can only understand what is happening in the world today by understanding these nuances.

As Christianity spread it took root in the people of Italy and Spain, and likewise in the population of what is now France and the British Isles. We know that the sentient soul was retained in Spain and Italy, while the rational or mind soul developed in French regions, the consciousness soul in the British Isles and the I here in central Europe. In eastern Europe, similarly, a culture of the Spirit Self will arise, though at present this exists only in hidden, germinal form and will unfold in the future.

If only people would consider western Europe in the light which spiritual science can shed on it! For instance, Italian traits—not the characteristics of individual Italians who of course can grow beyond mere regional stereotypes—develop differently from those of the French or British. In Britain national characteristics are connected with the consciousness soul. I have described these things in the past.[257] Through this mode of life in the consciousness soul, a person is driven out into the plane of physical reality, though this is less marked in the British Isles than in America. As a result of this, having been cut off from the supersensible by ecclesiastical developments, the human being is now led towards the cosmic realm again, but, as far as the consciousness soul is concerned, only towards external aspects of the cosmos. This means that the British only connect with the cosmos through economic principles. British thinking is largely informed by economics, by economic categories. If you grasp the inner connection between the consciousness soul and the physical world, you will see the inevitability of this; and likewise you will see how inevitable it is that the stereotype French character—not necessarily that of a French individual—develops political thinking in its close relationship with the rational or mind soul. Similarly, national characteristics in Italy and Spain develop a close connection with animality because of the direct involvement here of the sentient soul. I am only briefly outlining these things, but they do convey qualities that live in national characteristics.

If we consider German characteristics, which are currently involved in such tragic developments, we find that they draw upon the I. Light is shed on all of German history if we consider this fact, which becomes apparent through perception of the world of spirit. This human I, undergoing the least degree of outward development, remains our most spiritual aspect; and this is why German people, through the I, have the strongest spiritual connection with the world of spirit. They cannot forge an economic, political or animal connection with the cosmos. Instead they connect with it only as it manifests in cultural life through the soul of particular individuals—for the I always lives in individualities—and then flows out into the wider nation. German developments are apparent, most characteristically, in the substance of Goetheanism, and in the conceptions of Herder or Lessing, which lie one level higher than the physical, sensory plane of existence. For this reason one finds here a certain quality of alienation or distance from the physical realm, a feeling that these ideas and conceptions cannot fully belong to the physical, sensory realm. And this in turn is why, in recent decades, so much Americanism on the one hand and on the other so much that I do not wish to describe in further detail here has streamed through Germany and alienated it from its inherent national characteristics.

Eastern Europe will forge a connection with the spirit in a still higher way, developing a still more spiritual culture in opposition to what is now emerging for reasons I have described. But this is something for the future, and is not yet present—is still confined within brutish tendencies from which it will seek to emerge.

The countries of western Europe are still connected with the fourth post-Atlantean epoch as though by rightful inheritance and tradition. A newer element, although opposed to Americanism, lies in German nature: a certain relationship with the world of spirit, sought within the realm of spirit itself. A German, in following the inner dictates of his own inherent nature, does not fear the spirit but has a devoted inclination for it, as we find for example in typical, albeit higher form in Goetheanism.

In saying such things, of course, one has to express them rather radically—not out of chauvinism but through perception of realities. I definitely do not say this to curry favour with anyone. As you saw last time, I am capable of saying things, if necessary, that might equally cause offence. But this must be said: it has largely been forgotten in central Europe that German nature manifests a connection between the human spirit and the supersensible world, and that this connection, which needs to be further developed, stands in complete opposition to everything else coming to expression on earth today. If only we could recognize this, the past few decades would not, sadly, have brought us Americanism in this realm, and Bolshevism, and science and scholarship would have developed in a different way in central Europe. From my past reflections you know that Goetheanism could have given rise to a spiritual deepening of science and knowledge, but that Goetheanism remained in the margins, becoming only a one-sided pursuit also. Was it understood? Not so far. Yet it is the essence of German nature, and, as you can see from what I have said today, alien to other forms of scholarship and other national traits, which draw to a very large extent on old legacies and the new elements I described, as it were emerging from their shells.

We can see in various ways how Goetheanism has remained at one remove from materialistic science—of course people praise Goethe yet at the same time, as I said, they appoint a former finance minister as president of the Goethe Society.[258] The intrinsic element in German nature is something one has to feel as a continual reproach in other domains. People tend to defend themselves against something their own nature prevents them from acknowledging by scorning it. We must face this head-on. People cast scorn on anything they feel to be a reproach to them, taking refuge in this subjective defensiveness. This is an important psychological reality. Such scorn will become ever more widespread, and it will be rooted in a sense of discomfort at the distinctive relationship of the I to the spirit. We must not flinch from seeing this clearly. If we ourselves did not have so much philistinism and Americanism in us we would recognize the two opposite poles at work here—German Goetheanism and Americanism—and we would know that we can only adopt the right stance to currents flowing through the modern world if we can observe them with an entirely open mind. We ought to shed all chauvinism and see things objectively.

If we did so, however, we would no longer laud Americanism to the skies as we have been wont to do and, since the characteristic trait of this Americanism is fear of the spirit, would come to see that the American element will increasingly act as a radically evil driving force in current catastrophic events. Those who see it differently are short-sighted because they cannot survey the whole context. All that arises from the French political element, from the purely economic rigidity natural to the British, from the animal furore and 'sacred egotism' of the Italian people, is as nothing in the larger scheme of things compared to the truly evil element emerging from Americanism. You see, there are three currents whose inner affinity and confluence produces a destructive effect upon human evolution. In diverse ways each has assimilated old legacies and a new element, as I tried to outline briefly today. The destructiveness lies in these three currents: firstly in everything we can call Americanism, which increasingly tends to invoke fear of the spirit and make the world into a place where only physical life can unfold. This is actually quite different from the British tendency to try to make the world into a trading company. Americanism seeks to make it into a physical habitation, furnished as comfortably as possible, where one can live in comfort and prosperity. That is the political element of Americanism. If you cannot see this, you do not discern realities, are half asleep. The influence of this current will lead to the death of the human being's connection with the world of spirit. There lies in these American forces something that leads the earth to its end, a destructive element that ultimately spells annihilation for the earth since it blocks off the spirit. The second destructive current is not just Catholicism but all Jesuitism, which has a close affinity with Americanism. Whereas Americanism seeks to cultivate a fear of the spirit, Jesuitism tries to awaken a belief that we should not ourselves reach towards the spirit, which is beyond us, but allow spiritual wellsprings to be administered instead by those whom the Catholic Church appoints as its ministers. This current, too, wants the human powers which seek the spirit to wither. And the third current, emerging today in the East in such terrible symptoms, has its source in a socialism that addresses nothing but the human animal. Without seeing this dogmatically, Bolshevism has to be recognized as something it will be hard for humanity to overcome.

These are the three destructive elements at work in modern humanity. To recognize them so as to oppose them in the right way wherever they surface in current events is something only possible when we stand on spiritual-scientific foundations; and next week I will speak further of this.

LECTURE 21

BERLIN, 6 AUGUST 1918

IN our recent reflections[259] you will have seen that we are trying to shape ideas drawn from spiritual science in ways that can serve us when we seek to understand events occurring on a daily or hourly basis in our modern culture. Today, as a kind of last appendix to these reflections, I will offer what can be no more than aphoristic characterizations of our modern era, and connect these with various fundamental aspects introduced in the course of these lectures.

It is particularly noticeable today that of all the hindrances and obstacles apparent in modern culture, the mode of thinking, the nature of our ideas as these have evolved over recent centuries, gives people little capacity of foresight for approaching events. This becomes clear in the surprise experienced when events overtake us, seemingly without any capacity on our part to predict them or to believe that this might be possible. People think that what happens cannot be predicted, and that they must simply allow events to overtake them. Whenever one speaks of forthcoming occurrences, people are very surprised, or else they ironically discount this supposed longing for prophetic powers. If one draws attention to things now spreading across the globe from far eastern regions, emerging from causes I have recently commented on here, one meets with little understanding even though such developments are only too apparent. There is far too little desire to form real insights, and connected with this so little will to engage with truths that point, within natural limits, to what will happen in future. Of course I am not speaking, as you will realize, of any kind of soothsaying or misguided prophecy, but of a serious, scholarly outlook and mode of thought. This reluctance or inability to prefigure future developments has deep roots, but in general we can say that people are unaware of how far back the causes of things lie, and that on the whole they seek these causes in things that are far too close or superficial.

If I try to describe the causes of this relative blindness, I must seek it in a deeply rooted tendency in human souls today to embrace dead concepts and ideas rather than living ones. It is of course understandable that people cannot think about what is coming towards them in the same concept as they have formed of past events. But today people only give credence to what, as they say, can be 'proven'; and in seeking such proof they turn to that particular form of evidence of which they are nowadays so enamoured. A clear understanding of this particular mode of proof will show us that it serves only to confirm truths that relate to everything in decline in the universe, everything that is dying. This is why people today want a science, or just a mode of perception, that relates only to everything which dies. People who think themselves most enlightened have a predilection for knowledge and also for a form of will that relates to dying things. In the broadest sense there is a prevailing trend today, even if we are unaware of this, to engage only with decline. We fail to find the courage to conceive of living growth since this cannot be encompassed in such rigid and narrowly defined terms, nor proven in the same way as decline, or fading, dying tendencies. People defend themselves fiercely against more living forms of knowledge.

If one stands up and opposes such things, as one must, one runs the risk of being called a ridiculous fantasist and dilettante, or perhaps even worse. People today try to formulate concepts that can arm them against having to think of things with germinal potential for the future. Those who consider themselves most intelligent inoculate themselves against such fruitful thinking with concepts such as the 'conservation of matter and energy'[260] as this principle is nowadays formulated. Anyone who does not subscribe to this 'fundamental scientific principle' is regarded in certain circles of course as a 'blockhead'. And yet true perception of the cosmos will show us that matter and energy are transient and pass away; and that all knowledge we can gain of matter and energy is a knowledge of their transience. It is actually precisely because people wish to have a science of transient things, wish only to allow fading and dying things to figure in science, that they dogmatically decree that substance or energy are eternal, to have at least something they can hold fast to. This law of the conservation of matter and energy also plays an important role for lay people with no scientific training, and they project it vaguely into everything. The idea of the conservation of matter and substance thus finds its way into all popular textbooks and all contemporary thinking, becoming a supposed self-evident truth for people.

But we know from our reading of *Occult Science*[261] that evolution has passed through phases we refer to as those of Saturn, Sun, Moon and Earth. Nothing of what we refer to nowadays as substance and energy will endure beyond the stage of Venus evolution. By then even the most permanent of substances will have come to its end. We are now past the midpoint of planetary evolution, and are currently in the fifth period of the Earth phase of this evolution, somewhat beyond its midpoint. Having passed this midpoint we are already living in a declining phase of Earth evolution, or in other words in a phase of decline in which substance and energy are fading away again. And when we study physics and chemistry we would discern things properly if we recognize that insights gained in these fields relate only to transient things that will have disappeared no later than by the stage of Venus evolution. Nothing upon which modern science focuses today will ultimately endure; and the ideas and concepts invoked today to offer the kinds of proof of which people are so enamoured relate only to this kind of transience. The whole of science concerns itself with transient things.

We need to radically correct these ideas in this most fundamental of areas; and those who consider themselves to be the best-trained scientists will need to learn a great deal if they are to replace their current concepts with true ones. But why am I saying all this? It may well seem to you that in general such a thing is of no great importance.

Actually it is. You see, these ideas which people acquire and which then live in all their thinking inform other ideas and concepts according to which people live, and inform also their will and actions. Social concepts, political ideas, are informed by the mode of thinking thus developed. They are formed in accordance with the distinctive use one makes of such forces, whereby thoughts and concepts are considered to be only transient; and this has a knock-on effect on people's daily thinking. We can see this in particularly striking form if we study the social programmes of those who consider themselves the most progressive—the programmes of many socialists for instance, which are all the rage in many circles, and are all based in one way or another on the theory formulated by Karl Marx. Marxism is currently the bane of Russia because—for reasons I explained last time—it informs current historical developments there. This Marxist outlook is at the same time the most extreme expression of the will to engage only with, and control, dying things. If you study Marxist ideas you find that the most fanatical Marxists believe they possess ideas of great future potential; and yet in fact these ideas can only relate to everything that fades and withers. This appears in a naive way especially in this 'socialist' outlook, since it invariably refuses to establish any fruitful ideas of the future. Instead it preaches the eradication of ideas, propounding the abolition of all that currently exists, as a way of allowing something new to emerge by itself miraculously out of the resulting turmoil and confusion. I'm putting this radically; but then there are many too who, as we saw in the last lecture, abide by the teachings of the Church through many centuries and interpret the events of recent centuries in dogmatic ecclesiastical terms, and so we must say that this outlook basically entirely refuses to cultivate ideas of future potential. It seeks only to produce ideas that can destroy all that has been established in the past. Those who propound these doctrines think there is future potential in their ideas; but what counts is how ideas become reality. In truth these ideas have no potential to establish anything new but are concerned only to introduce destruction into existing institutions. This socialism appears to me like a lady—though of course I'm harking back to the past here—who cannot bear to wear crinoline, and detests hooped petticoats. This must change, says she. And what does she do? She lines it inside so that it looks just the same as it did before, outwardly, but is now lined with padding. This is what the socialists are doing: instead of using new ideas to make fruitful the institutions that have emerged in the course of history, they leave them as they are, basically, simply taking the place of those who once administered these institutions. They preserve the petticoats and pad them out with lining. Here too we find an extreme outlook embodied in nothing but a longing to administer and manage all that is fading and dying. What is the cause of this?

It is because the concepts in today's merely sense-based science, founded on a reasoning faculty that recognizes sensory perception alone, can only engage with all that withers and dies. It can only meet with elements of nature that lead towards death, not its living aspects. Science cannot comprehend life and living things. In culture, too, life is not comprehended—not germinal growth but only what dies. You see, this germinal growth can only be encompassed in imaginations, by attaining at least the first level of higher knowledge as I have described in *Knowledge of the Higher Worlds*.[262] To reach certain higher forms of knowledge relating to perception of growing, living things, we also need to be able to employ Intuition and Inspiration. In approaching phenomena with past concepts, people can go on talking till the cows come home but they will never get beyond an engagement with decline and death unless they enter into what supersensible faculties alone can perceive of growth and life. Today things really are on a knife-edge. Without certain forms of knowledge, without perception of the spirit, humanity will plunge into cultural chaos, which we are already familiar enough with.

We need a renewal of the mysteries, and this is also something that the science of the spirit seeks to attain. For this, of course, the meaning of the ancient mysteries first has to be grasped; and then also the meaning of the period of history which was in a sense an intermediate phase between these ancient mysteries and the new ones that are still to come. All this must be understood. Pupils of the ancient mysteries were astonished to find, as they were taught in vivid ways, that ancient, atavistic, clairvoyant faculties and occult knowledge were inevitably declining. This was something they could not grasp themselves through their knowledge and vision for it could be comprehended only through initiation into the mysteries. They were taught that something else, another condition, would dawn in humanity, replacing ancient, clairvoyant vision of the world of spirit. Mystery pupils were shown that this old form of soul condition, this appearance of world breadths in

Imagination, was on its way out. This was explained to them roughly as follows. What can be seen on earth with the physical senses does not as such contain the intrinsic secrets of earth existence. These secrets can only be revealed if the human soul is granted clairvoyant vision of the mysteries of the cosmos and all extra-telluric reality, so that what happens in the extra-telluric cosmos dawns in this soul. This was what ancient clairvoyant vision showed—the non-physical realities of the spiritual cosmos, rather than what was happening on earth. And these mystery pupils were taught that such knowledge and perception, this ascent into the cosmos, would no longer be possible in future. And those who were to penetrate the Christ Mystery were granted insight into something else as well.

This, roughly, was the conception that arose: although ancient seers did not speak of Christ, their inspirations came from the world in which Christ had always dwelt, since he is a cosmic being. Christ lives in the whole cosmos and everything streaming from it as this is revealed to atavistic clairvoyance. But from the time when the Mystery of Golgotha was to occur, people no longer had access to this as they once had. What happened? Well, the Christ descended from this world, from the cosmos down to earth. Christ had to descend to humankind because the spiritual cosmos was no longer accessible to people as it had once been in ancient times and they could no longer have found Christ there by the old means. It died away, this mode of knowledge and sensibility of soul in which the world where Christ lived was formerly perceived, and therefore Christ had to descend to humankind. And so he did. And thus everything which illumined minds had ever perceived of the world of spirit in ancient heathen mystery rites and in heathen mystery knowledge had now to be comprised in the Christ. Vision of it had to be found in Christ. We have to realize what kind of cosmic being had descended to the earth from the cosmos as Christ. That is one aspect.

The other was as follows. Reason and the senses, as I said, can only perceive transient things, a knowledge of transience when they consider all of nature, and social and cultural life too. Everything now existing will come to an end by the Venus phase of evolution. Despite believing that cultural ideas, ideas about society, have growth potential, people very often stand in the stream of decline as they entertain them. What the senses perceive and all that can be grasped by reason has no germ of future potential but is wedded to death. If this were all that existed there would only be death knowledge, for the reality that surrounds us is itself wedded to death. Where can we look to find anything enduring therefore? Where can we find a realm of eternal reality that will survive beyond this outward existence of ours which is wedded to death? Where do we find something truly conserved? Atoms and forces which are thought to endure forever according to belief systems and superstitions rooted in the physical will in fact go under.

We find this only in the human being himself. Of all creatures, animals, plants, minerals, all the air, water and everything else that will go under, there is one thing only that will be preserved beyond earthly evolution and other phases of evolution that follow it, and this is what lives within ourselves. Only we human beings bear within us on earth something that endures. It is misguided to speak of the conservation of atoms and matter; we can speak only of the conservation of something within ourselves. Yet this can be perceived only by means of Imagination, Inspiration and Intuition. Nothing that is not perceived by supersensible perception endures. Everything in the sensory world is transient; and the supersensible, which endures, can therefore also only be encompassed by supersensible perception. We walk upon the earth and within us lies everything that will survive of earth existence. If we wonder where to look for the germ of what will survive the Earth, Jupiter and Venus phases of evolution and what of modern culture will endure into a culture of the future, we have to recognize that nothing of the physical earth and cosmos will survive, but only what lies within us. In the part of our being which is accessible only to supersensible perception we find something that bears the germ of the future. We cannot really speak of the future at all unless we have the will to comprehend the supersensible. Otherwise our ideas of the future are false. And this is why the Christ had to descend from worlds that were becoming ever more unavailable to human perception: he had to unite with the human being, establishing his dwelling place in Jesus and thus becoming Jesus Christ, because only in a human body could be found the future potential of earthly evolution. In Christ we thus have the cosmic element which was directly comprehended only through ancient perception; and in Jesus, to whom the Christ came, we have the only possible bearer of the germ of the future in the human will. We fail to understand Christ if we see him only as Christ, or only as Jesus. The Christ of whom the ancient teachings of docetism[263] spoke—a kind of Gnostic doctrine—can no longer be comprehended and was available only to ancient clairvoyance. We do not understand Jesus if we fail to grasp that Christ entered him. If we do not acknowledge Christ within Jesus we do not comprehend that only through the germ of humanity on earth will cosmic reality be rescued for the future.

To understand that Christ Jesus is a dual being is a great and important task. Yet at the same time many have sought to hinder such understanding. In modern times diverse efforts have been made to assign to oblivion the knowledge that Christ lived in Jesus. On the one hand we have the extreme theological doctrine that speaks only of the 'simple man of Nazareth'[264] and thus really only of a person endowed with our ordinary sensory nature rather than of the one who bears the germ of our future potential. Then there is a society, too, that was founded to oppose the idea of Christ, and to this end to establish a false idea of Jesus: the Society of the Jesuits, which largely exists to drive out the Christ from the Jesus-Christ picture, leaving only Jesus as a kind of tyrant looming over evolving humanity. All this must be seen in context. The diverse impulses to which I am referring act more powerfully in modern life than people realize. They act very powerfully and intensely. If we do not open our eyes fully to these things and seek to grasp the real effects of what is happening, we will continually be surprised by all that comes. In many respects our modern culture is far too sluggish to recognize such things. Spiritual-scientific concepts are far too difficult for many, and people therefore denigrate them as unscientific fantasy and dilettantism. For reasons I have explained they condemn themselves at the same time to dispensing with anything of real future potential.

Around us we see a wasteland today, and chaos into which old religious confessions and cultural traditions have led us. In the midst of this chaos which people very naively regard as war although it has gone far beyond warfare to become something quite different, we find a wasteland of ideas and outlooks. Only by grasping the supersensible, the spiritual realm, would ideas arise that are not barren. Today we must decide either to engage with decline and death and become a pupil of Lenin or to reckon with the supersensible, which encompasses what must emerge in future. I am not talking about the lone individual Lenin whose ideas are currently causing such mischief in eastern Europe; I take him more as the symbol of a chronic condition, for there are many Lenins spread far and wide, in one field or another. The realm of dying and death is the only one people are seeking out and engaging with at present.

Let us recall something I once said here: that a plant lives, and can be described as a living entity. But when modern science tackles plant life today it does not find a living quality, which is supersensible, but describes substances that are the vehicle for life, the dead, mineral aspects. In modern science you will find an account only of the mineral, and in fact death-bearing, constituents of living things; and therefore people cannot raise themselves to really fruitful ideas about nature. The concepts prevalent in modern botany do not accord with life; instead they describe the minerals that make up living entities, and circulate within them. As soon as one goes beyond this circulating mineral element in plant, animal or the human being each of these is found to be quite different in nature from the way it is usually described.

Consider the zoologist von Uexkuell,[265] who wrote an essay entitled *The Battle for the Soul of the Animal*. This gentleman displays a masochistic cruelty in relation to all psychology or anything the least related to it. I say 'masochistic cruelty' because of the following sentiments in his essay: 'There is no need to determine whether there is such a thing as the soul or not, but only that science cannot make anything of it.' A properly cruel or ferocious person actually kills something, whereas someone who is 'masochistically cruel', like this Mr Uexkuell, just dabbles a little in killing, tries it out. This is typical of modern science though people fail to notice because they turn aside from it. People do not like rupturing the partition that sunders them from their surroundings and so they cannot break through to find the concepts that are really needed for understanding these surroundings.

From the science of the spirit we know that the core, integral nature of the human being descends from worlds of spirit and connects with our flesh and blood, the material covering in which we are enclosed between birth and death, or rather between conception and death. Nowadays scientists study issues surrounding conception and birth, embryonic development—but these fields cannot be studied since this research addresses only the dead elements embedded in life. This will never enable people to understand the only thing that can make the human being comprehensible: the fact that when we descend from worlds of spirit we are received by father and mother and then pass through the whole of foetal development. Science today holds to the arrogant view that a father and mother give a child its existence, and that since they are the core of the family and the family is the foundation for social community, so social communities, as enlarged families, think that they own the human being. But this mean little idea is very far from the truth.

What does a human being receive in the act of conception, and what does he gain from it? We receive here—as spiritual science can show us—the capacity to become a mortal creature. The act of conception endows us with the possibility of dying. This is the inevitable consequence of other things I have described in various books. At the moment of conception already, we integrate into us what makes it possible for us to die here on earth. The whole of life from birth to death is a development towards death, and death is inoculated into us at conception. Our nature as living entity and human being is not somehow created at conception but instead this moment inoculates our otherwise immortal being with the opportunity to die. Parents, in fact, can only give their offspring the gift of death—although this is putting it radically of course: the opportunity to bear a mortal body here on earth. The life within this body has to descend from the spiritual world. What descends from the world of spirit enables this whole organism of ours, the whole mechanism with which we are clothed on earth, which we receive at conception with the germ of death, to be alive. We need to learn to connect the human being again, in his most tangible appearance, with the evolution of the spiritual cosmos. And to do this we have to move beyond cowardly fears and timid apprehensions to really tackle the loftiest problems facing science. If we shy away from them we will not even understand the things that live in our closest proximity.

We can say that the most diverse peoples live also in our immediate proximity. Just think of the misguided thoughts which Woodrow Wilson has summoned from the idea of nations and peoples. We have often spoken of this. We have to realize that the idea of different races will never be properly understood if we do not engage with the whole of earthly evolution. Why is it that the population of the globe has been divided into these different races and nations?

Spiritual science teaches us that world evolution began with the Saturn embodiment of the earth, followed by the Sun embodiment, the Moon stage and now our current Earth stage. This will be followed by a Jupiter embodiment and so forth. But we should not see this too schematically, with an ancient Saturn planet transforming smoothly into the Sun, then Moon and Earth stages. Rather, this evolution is a continuous alternation in which the sun first separates from the earth and then the moon does: bodies separate then reunite and separate again. What I have just referred to as cosmic evolution, involving this separation, played a part in ancient clairvoyance. What can be summed up as the human germ of the future remained unconsciously present in this clairvoyance, remained 'chthonic', as it is called in ancient seership, in the ongoing advance of earthly evolution. You see, what comes from the universe was destined to die and was preserved only by virtue of luciferic power. And thus diverse differentiations entered from the cosmos and developed into nations and races; but these cosmic forces were impregnated with luciferic powers. In contrast to these diverse, differentiated peoples there stands—as was understood by a better era than our own—the universal human, and this has a quite different origin. We can speak of this in the abstract but we will only speak of its reality by truly grasping the germ of the future within us, which contains nothing national or nationalistic. This is a quality that did not descend from the cosmos but which Christ approached and united himself with. The Christ did not unite himself with any national trait as, say, Jehovah did, but instead with the universal human. He was in the community of gods from whom nations developed but he departed from this realm when it was ripe for decline, came to earth and took up dwelling in the universal human. It is the greatest blasphemy to invoke the name of Jesus Christ for anything partisan, for anything other than the universal human, and it is in this sense only that we can say: 'Not I but Christ in me.'[266]

This is one of the most vital insights for the future: to understand Christ Jesus' relationship to humanity, and also to grasp that everything of a national or nationalistic nature is outside the realm of Christ Jesus and is an old residue of something that was already ripe for decline at the time of the Mystery of Golgotha. All things cling on beyond their time like withered fruit. What was ripe for decline has clung on only as a science that turns its focus upon decline and death, and which, like modern science or the social sciences, concerns itself only with ideas that can engage with decline—either all that withers and dies in nature or cultural decline.

In cultural history we can sometimes see a real clash occurring between this decline, which seeks to live in dead, abstract ideas, considering them significant, and the impulse to grasp hold of the human seed which alone has future potential. I have frequently referred to an important conversation between Goethe and Schiller,[267] when these two were once at a meeting of the Research Association in Jena. The botanist Batsch[268] had given a lecture, and as Schiller was leaving he said to Goethe: this botanical approach fragments everything, dispels all unifying impetus. At this, Goethe, in a few characteristic strokes, described to Schiller his approach to plant metamorphosis. And then the latter said: but that is not your experience, it is just an idea. Schiller was unable to raise himself to vision of the human being who bears the future within him, nor of the resulting ability to find, in turn, a future-sustaining power in the world, which is the supersensible. And therefore he replied to Goethe that the latter's perception was not experience or observation but merely an idea. And Goethe responded by saying: well, then I see my ideas with my eyes. He felt what he was describing to be something he also saw, and was as real to him as anything he might have observed with his physical senses. Here then we have two figures face to face: Schiller who could not raise his perception to the supersensible but entertained only the dead, abstract idea, and Goethe who sought to draw from what he perceived in nature something that bears futurity within it, the eternal in the human being, for whom 'everything transient is but a metaphor'. He sought to unite what he perceived outside him with something eternal; and he was not understood because he had vision of something supersensible and enduring and looked upon this as if observing sensory phenomena. What our time needs, therefore, is to develop this Goethean approach. Insight will only come when we realize that something like the diverse religious confessions, including those founded on the Old Testament, and especially Catholicism, are only a perpetuation of something old that has clung on past its time, a withered branch of evolution that has to assert itself through outward power structures. This redundant impetus is accompanied by something that seeks to bear nothing but transience, impermanence into the future, and this is Americanism; and this explains the affinity between Americanism and Jesuitism, as I described it last time.

Goetheanism stands in opposition to all such phenomena. In saying this I don't wish to fix dogmatically on a name. One has to use names to point to something that goes far beyond a name's narrower scope. By 'Goetheanism' I do not mean what Goethe thought up to 1832, but rather what may take another millennium or so to be thought along Goethean lines; all that can develop from Goethe's vision and ideas. It is due to this that everything clinging to withering powers regards Goetheanism in any form as its enemy. Here we can witness the greatest cultural paradoxes. It is highly paradoxical that one of the most inventive books on Goethe was, however unlikely this seems, written by a Jesuit, Father Baumgartner.[269] This is a book that delves deeply into Goethe. It is characteristic of course that anything associated with Jesuitism will oppose Goethe; and yet this is a spirited, deep book, not flitting superficially over its subject. It really does summon the man and describe him vividly—unlike another book by the English aristocrat Lewes[270] who calls Goethe a mere eighteenth-century philistine to whom no regard is due. The Jesuit book on Goethe on the other hand reveals a real cultural paradox, and here one can see the opposing forces that clash within one author's mind.

On a smaller scale we find the same thing in our own circles. As long as we were regarded as a 'small sect', few people bothered attacking anthroposophy. But now that it has greater prominence, the fiercest attacks are launched on us, particularly by Jesuit circles. It no longer suffices for the periodical *Stimmen der Zeit*[271] to publish an article opposing us but it devotes whole issues to the subject. This is why I keep emphasizing that we should not think that we will appeal to the better nature of these circles by explaining to them that we are invoking Christ, that we are cultivating an understanding of Christ. These people are fiercely opposed to such a thing! This is precisely what they want to prevent. Anything that is not a part of ecclesiastical doctrine should not be asserted about Christ, in their view. Let us therefore cease to be so naive as to believe that we can appease Catholicism by explaining that we are good Christians. It is this very thing—that we do all in our power to nurture Christianity—that makes Catholicism our greatest enemy. Such naivety in regard to these things must increasingly be banished from our circles. Instead we should become ever more discerning, clear-sighted about the powers, both declining and dawning, that live around us. We must reach further than the small longing so prevalent amongst us to seek just a little bit more of an imaginative faculty. I have often said this. Instead of securing ourselves just a little bit of an imaginative world, we must be able to relate our spiritual science to contemporary cultural ideas, becoming keen observers of what actually lives in the modern world. Only spiritual science gives a perspective that can enable us to really observe this world. Many come to me and tell me that they have seen one thing or another. Well, they certainly have. Imaginations are not so far removed from human evolution, and will increasingly approach us. Many ask me, for instance, whether it was the Guardian of the Threshold they saw. But it is not so easy just to reply 'yes' or 'no' to such a question, since the answer encompasses the whole of human evolution. Yet the answers have been given. At present I am revising my book *Occult Science*,[272] a new edition of which is about to be published; and I find that it actually includes everything needed to answer such questions. All necessary caution with regard to them, all checks and balances one needs, are carefully described there. The feelings one needs to develop are described there too. And these things are clearly indicated, although you will have to read the book with sufficient care to see this. I would have had to write 30 volumes to explain every detail of what is contained in *Occult Science*. In reading this book you have to think for yourself too, and draw your own conclusions; and this is perfectly possible. I don't like writing huge tomes, but if you read this book carefully you will discover that, certainly, seeking the supersensible world will bring you an encounter with the Guardian of the Threshold. Yet this encounter is not as simple or straightforward as having a dreamy imagination, which is the most comfortable way of entering the world of spirit. The encounter with the Guardian of the Threshold is a tragedy, a battle for survival involving all concepts and laws of cognition, and all human connections with the spiritual world, with Ahriman and Lucifer too. By encountering the Guardian of the Threshold you enter catastrophic circumstances. If, by contrast, you see just a dreamlike imagination before you, this means that you are trying to slip easily past this encounter, to have a dream of the Guardian of the Threshold as substitute for the real encounter.

It is necessary to approach these things with healthy thinking, which, as will then become apparent, contains the basis for curing all superstition and everything that opponents of spiritual science accuse it of. Besides this, a healthy mode of thinking that can raise itself to experience of the spiritual realm contains all germinal power we need in order to emerge from the current catastrophe in which the world is plunged. We will be led out of it by something that is not comprehended on earth, or not alone in the sensory realm, not in ruinous institutions that exploit and misuse resources, but in something that is not yet in existence! We must find burning enthusiasm for grasping something not yet present; yet this can only be grasped by comprehending and pursuing a mode of supersensible knowledge rather than by looking back to the past. People such as Kautsky prefer to look back to the past and base their view of humanity's future on anthropology. To understand present social conditions they study past states when we were as yet scarcely human. Those such as Kautsky are the true sons of a misunderstood Catholicism. Yet looking back to the past like this will not help, since back then the foundations of our modern era were created only by atavistic, instinctive powers. In the future nothing will any longer be based on instinct; and if people try to draw on what is still present in them from ancient, instinctive times, they will never reach the future potential in them that can lead us out of catastrophe. We need a true stance towards the world of spirit in order to develop a real, engaged and serious understanding of the present.

I would have to speak for many hours if I were to address such themes more fully and examine issues that are currently of much concern. But over the summer weeks, when we will not be meeting, you will come far in an understanding of the cosmic Christ and the earthly Jesus if you really meditate on all we have been discussing here, culminating in the need to perceive a dual Christ-Jesus figure. You will see that the cosmic Christ descended from worlds of spirit since these worlds were henceforth to be closed to human vision, and because the human being was destined to grasp the seed of future potential that lies within himself. In this cosmic Christ and in the earthly, the humanistic Jesus, and the union of both, lies much that can help solve the riddle of the cosmos, at least the part of it that concerns humanity. Within the human being lies the seed of the future. But this seed must be fertilized by Christ Jesus. If this does not happen, the seed will become ahrimanically configured, and the earth will end in error and confusion. Thus we find solutions to a great many contemporary questions by fathoming the Christ-Jesus secret. But you should not seek these solutions in a superficial way through what is often regarded as theosophy, mysticism or suchlike, through some 'union with the spirit' or a 'merging with the universe'. Instead, try to really discern what is happening around us today, and to comprehend it through what you draw from the science of the spirit. As all kinds of issues start to be resolved you will increasingly discover that humanity today truly seeks practical not theoretical answers. If it does not try to cultivate the spirit it will find itself in a cul-de-sac and be forced to acknowledge that it cannot get any further. Wherever we fail to pursue the spirit, to journey spiritually, we will find that our efforts wither on the bough.

Whether or not people will strive spiritually is of great importance for humanity's future. Today I want to plant in your hearts a sense of the feelings that can emerge and develop from our recent reflections. It is also very likely that this is the last time we will meet in this hall,[273] which we have become fond of over many years, and where many of these lectures have been held. These were the first premises we furnished in accordance with our own ideas, although of course only within a given scope. We furnished it as we did because our spiritual-scientific endeavours ought not to be something merely theoretical but should come to expression in everything that surrounds our human encounters. This hall is now being taken from us and we must seek another, but naturally, in present circumstances, we will not be able to furnish it in the same way that we furnished this one. We will have to make do with whatever premises we find. We have become attached to this hall since it cannot be assumed that we can speak of our connection with the spirit elsewhere in the same way as here, where we attempted to configure some aspects of the space as we did, on a larger scale, in Dornach. In earlier times we often had to make do. Some among you may still recall us holding lectures in a pub. I stood there with an audience in front of me, and behind me the publican was drawing pints. On another occasion we gathered in a kind of barn. We had been promised a different space but we were only given that one in the end. In other cities I sometimes lectured in pubs too, some of which had no proper floor, and we had to cope with such things. But in fact at core we cannot wish this, and to say we can speak of the spirit in the same loving way anywhere, in any space at all, would be to misunderstand the nature of our movement. Spirit exists to penetrate, imbue and configure matter. And this applies too to social and economic life as I suggested today.

Because of all this we will find it very difficult indeed to say farewell to this hall in a few weeks time, and to leave these premises that anthroposophists so kindly helped to furnish and decorate. But a departure and farewell such as this is also something we must regard in the proper way, as a kind of symbol. Over forthcoming decades people will have to take their leave from much that they hold dear. People do not realize this as yet, and will be surprised when it comes. But those who have really grasped the inmost impulse of spiritual science will recognize that, whatever uncertainties approach, one thing will not founder or waver: what we have encompassed in the spirit and what we have spiritually resolved to realize. All that we do when we act out of the spirit, irrespective of how it appears amidst the tumult of the present, will turn out to be for the best.

Our departure from this place can therefore stand as a symbol. We must find other premises, but we will carry with us a core and foundation which we know not only to be that of our own deepest inner being but also the deepest inner being of the world, upon which humanity must build if it wishes to build well. Spiritual science gives us a sure and firm conviction that what we draw from it and pursue by its means cannot be taken from us by anyone, and that it cannot be taken from humanity either, but that it must lead human conditions to a state of greater health. We may well not yet know how we will accomplish many things, but we will accomplish what is needed if we hold fast to the science of the spirit. Let us grasp fully the significance of Goetheanism for spiritual science, and at the same time recognize, as I recently explained,[274] that the world today scorns and disparages everything associated with central European culture of the eighteenth and early nineteenth century. Nevertheless, if we become fully aware of these things we can still stand our ground and recognize that whatever may come this central European culture will bear fruit in humanity's future progress. Humanity's future depends on it. The adversaries of this central European culture scorn and disparage it precisely because they do not wish to embrace humanity's true future, preferring to evade it. We can however acknowledge this central European culture to the full, recognizing its spiritual nature and knowing that we can build upon these foundations. And then we can also be sure that even if every devil in Christendom conspires to bring about this culture's downfall, it will not founder. But equally, that only what is connected with the true spirit will not go under.

NOTES

Textual sources. The lectures of 22 and 29 January 1918 were taken down in shorthand by Hedda Hummel, and the other 19 lectures by Walter Vegelahn. The original shorthand transcripts have not survived, and this volume is based on typescripts of the lectures prepared by the stenographs from their shorthand versions.

R. Friedenthal and S. Loetscher were responsible for reviewing/revising the 3rd edition of 1991, and they made alterations and amendments listed in detail in the current German edition. Quotations cited by Rudolf Steiner were compared with their respective sources and, where necessary, corrected. An index of names and a detailed contents page were added, and notes were checked and enlarged, in particular in relation to Rudolf Steiner's many references to other lectures.

Titles of cycles and lectures. The original lectures bore no titles or summary of contents. Vegel's initial typescripts of lectures 8 to 21 (2nd and 3rd cycle) were however given titles. According to one report Vegelahn often went to see Rudolf Steiner after a lecture to ask him for a title for it (see Karl Boegner in *Mitteilungen aus der anthroposophischen Arbeit in Deutschland*, Michaelmas 1959). It can therefore be assumed that these titles are attributable to Steiner himself.

The origin of the title of the first series is not known. However, since it was given already in the first edition of 1922, we can assume that it was either provided by Steiner or fully approved by him. We can assume this likewise for the overall title of the first two cycles, and the original title of the 3rd.

The titles of the first five lectures were altered in the 1967 edition. Originally they were as follows: 22 January, 'The Place of Spiritual Science Today'; 29 January, 'Enhancing Insight into the Nature of the Human Being'; 5 February, 'The Living and the Dead'; 5 March, 'Our Dead and World Thoughts'; and 12 March, 'The Human Being's Connection with the World of Spirit'.

In the 1967 edition, the lecture titles were only given in the list of contents, and this has been retained in the present edition.

Drawings. The original board drawings by Rudolf Steiner to accompany the lectures of 26 March and 9 April have not survived. Since the shorthand transcript is not extant either, the outline sketches in the typescript had to be used as the basis for the drawings done by Hedwig Frey.

Earlier editions. These lecture series were published in 1922 by Marie Steiner's Philosophisch-Anthroposophischer Verlag in Berlin (3 vols.) in so-called 'cycle format', and were enumerated throughout as follows:

Lectures 1–7: cycle 48
Lectures 8–14: cycle 49
Lectures 15–21: cycle 50

The first edition published in the GA or Collected Works appeared in 1967, both in a single volume and in three separate volumes. Some of these separate editions were later bound together in one volume and sold. The numerical order of the lectures was retained, and the 3rd cycle was given in its present title. Notes were added to this edition.

The lecture of 30 March 1918 also appeared in *Gäa Sophia. Jahrbuch der Naturwissenschaftlichen Sektion am Goetheanum,* vol. II, Dornach 1927, and that of 5 February in the paperback series *Rudolf Steiner—Themen aus dem Gesamtwerk*, vol. 15: *Das Leben nach dem Tode*, Verlag Freies Geistesleben, Stuttgart 1987.

1. During the war, Rudolf Steiner spoke these or similar words in countries affected by the war before every lecture he gave to members of the Anthroposophical Society.
2. GA 153, six lectures in Vienna, 1914.
3. Lectures of 5, 7, 12 and 14 November 1917, GA 73.
4. Lecture of 7 November 1917.
5. Herman Grimm, 1828–1901, art and literature scholar. In: *Fragmente*, vol. 1, Berlin and Stuttgart 1900, in the chapter 'Einleitende Bemerkungen zu den Fragmenten', p. v.
6. Edward Gibbon, 1737–94, English historian. *History of the Decline and Fall of the Roman Empire*, 6 vols., London 1782–8.
7. Leopold von Ranke 1795–1886, historian, founder of modern academic history.
8. Karl Lamprecht, 1856–1915, historian.
9. Reference to Woodrow Wilson, 1856–1924, President of the United States from 1912 to 1920 and his 'Fourteen Points'.
10. See the lecture cycle of GA 177, 14 lectures, Dornach 1917, especially the lecture of 8 October 1917. Steiner is also referring here to two further lectures, one in Bern on 30 November 1917 and the other in Basel on 24 November 1917, both published GA 72.
11. Karl Marx, 1818–83, founder of socialist theories.
12. Rudolf Steiner spoke of this in detail in his lecture of 16 November 1917 in St Gallen on the 'mystery of the double', published in GA 178.
13. Carl Gustav Jung, 1875–1961, physician. See *Die Psychologie der unbewussten Prozesse. Ein Überblick über die modern Theorie und Methode der analytischen Psychologie*, Zurich 1917.
14. Ibid, pp. 18 ff. See also pp. 62 ff in this volume.
15. Ibid, pp. 85 ff.
16. Ibid. The passages in Jung read: 'Only during the Enlightenment did people discover that the gods did not really exist but were only projections. As such they were over and done with. Yet the psychological function that corresponds to them was by no means over and done with but lapsed into the unconscious, thus poisoning people through an excess of libido that had previously been invested in worship of divine images. The devaluing and

suppressing of such a powerful function as the religious sensibility naturally has weighty consequences for the psychology of the individual.' (See pp. 115 f in the German edition.) And: 'The concept of God is an essentially necessary psychological function that is irrational in nature, and it has absolutely nothing to do with the question about God's existence. This latter question is in fact one of the stupidest anyone can ask. After all, we are fully aware that we cannot think up a god for ourselves let alone imagine that he really exists, as little as we can conceive of a process that is not inevitably causally determined.' (See p. 91 in the German edition.)

17. See the lecture on 1 June 1913 in the cycle on the *Bhagavadgita* in GA 146 (9 lectures, Helsingfors, 1913). Cf. also the address to a Russian audience in Helsingfors on 5 June 1913, in GA 158.
18. Pedro II, 1825–91, Emperor of Brazil from 1831 to 1889 (prince regent until his crowning in 1841).
19. *The New Freedom*, 1913 and *Mere Literature and Other Essays*, 1893.
20. See, for example, the lectures of 23 November 1908 in GA 108, 17 September 1910 in GA 125 and 24 August 1911 in GA 129.
21. GA 21.
22. GA 15.
23. For, example, on 12 January 1918 in GA 180.
24. See the cycle on cosmic and human metamorphosis in GA 175. Cf. also the lectures of 21 October 1916 in GA 171 and 21 January in GA 174.
25. See, for example, the lectures of 31 July and 7 August 1916 in GA 170.
26. See 'Das Schädelgerüst aus sechs Wirbelknochen auferbaut' in Goethe's scientific writings published in *Kuerschner's Deutsche National-Litteratur* and reprinted as GA 1a.
27. See, for example, the lecture of 7 December 1915 in GA 157a and the lecture of 5 September 1915 in GA 163.
28. This probably refers to the lecture of 24 January 1918 in GA 67. Cf. also the lecture of 11 November 1917 in GA 178.
29. See, for instance, the lecture of 24 January 1918 in GA 67 and 11 May 1917 in GA 174b.
30. An alchemist, thought to have been a fifteenth-century Benedictine monk. A series of texts were published under his name around 1600. His 'collected works' were published in three volumes in Hamburg in 1717 and 1740.
31. Theodor Svedberg, 1884–1971, chemist, Nobel Prize winner. See *Die Materie. Ein Forschungsproblem in Vergangenheit und Gegenwart* 1912 (German edition 1914).
32. Dr Friedrich Rittelmeyer, 1872–1938, a Protestant theologian and later co-founder and chief coordinator of the Christian Community. See his essay 'Von der Theosophie Rudolf Steiners' in *Die Christliche Welt*, 1917, nos 33–5.
33. Johannes Mueller, 1864–1949, Protestant theologian and writer, in *Die Christliche Welt*, 1918, nos 2–4.
34. GA 21. In a lecture on 26 June 1917 (GA 176) Rudolf Steiner tackled Dessoir's chapter on anthroposophy in detail. Cf. also Friedrich Rittelmeyer's essay 'Max Dessoir und Rudolf Steiner' in *Süddeutschen Monatsheften*, 1917, issue 1.

35. Max Dessoir, 1867–1947, in his book *Vom Jenseits der Seele. Die Geheimwissenschaften in kritischer Beleuchtung*, Stuttgart 1917, the chapter 'Anthroposophie'.
36. See pp. 16 f., and note 21, in relation to Dessoir's replies to Rudolf Steiner's essay in *Riddles of the Soul*.
37. See note 33 above to Johannes Mueller, op. cit., no. 2, column 21: 'Today theosophy is running a propaganda campaign of a type and intensity that are hard to match.'
38. Mueller writes in his article: 'It is this that I hold against Steiner above all, not least in the interests of theosophy itself: that he had made of the occult world a sensation to titillate the curiosity and prurience of human superstition. Anyone who has read about the themes of his lectures, for years now, in posters advertising them, will think only with distaste of the way they evoke a base desire for sensation or play to the longings of grieving relatives in hearing about the other side.'
39. In relation to the essay by Johannes Mueller cited above, cf. the book by Friedrich Rittelmeyer *Johannes Müeller und Rudolf Steiner*, Nuremberg 1918.
40. GA 8.
41. GA 4.
42. Johannes Mueller, *Die Bergpredigt, verdeutscht und vergegenwärtigt*, Munich 1906.
43. See, for example, the lecture of 9 March 1915 in GA 157.
44. GA 21.
45. Friedrich Theodor Vischer, 1807–87, poet and writer on aesthetics.
46. See note 2.
47. Rudolf Steiner spoke about this, for example, on 24 October 1915 in Dornach, in GA 254.
48. Richard Wagner, *Parsifal*, Act 1.
49. See, for example, the lectures of 26 February 1916 in GA 65 and 19 October 1917 in GA 72.
50. See, for example, the lectures of 27 March and 3 April 1917 in GA 175.
51. Wilhelm Wundt, 1832–1920, philosopher, psychologist and physician. He founded the first institute for experimental psychology in Leipzig. See also p. 143 in this volume.
52. See the lecture of 5 February 1918 in this volume.
53. Ibid. See also the lecture of 13 February 1917 in GA 175.
54. *The Tempest*, Act 4, Scene 1.
55. Lectures of 9 and 10 December 1917, in GA 179.
56. Gotthilf Heinrich Schubert, 1780–1860, physician and scientist. See *Über Ahnen und Wissen*, Munich 1848, chapter 4: 'Das menschliche Ahnungsvermögen'. The example of going for a walk does not figure there, but similar instances do.
57. See the lecture of 5 February 1918 in this volume; and also the lecture of 23 February 1918 in GA 174b.
58. See the lecture of 5 February 1918 in this volume; and also the lectures of 14 February 1918, GA 174a, and 23 February 1918, GA 174b.
59. GA 121.

60. Rabindranath Tagore, 1861–1941, Indian philosopher and poet and freedom campaigner. Tagore came from a Bengali family descended from a Sanskrit playwright of the eighth century called Bhatta-Naranja. See Tagore's lecture 'The Spirit of Japan'. Rudolf Steiner's personal library contained all three German editions of this lecture.
61. Tagore: 'No doubt we wish to appropriate their machines, though not with the heart but only with the brain. We will try them out and build sheds for them, but we will not admit them to our homes and temples.'
62. Tagore: 'The creative spirit of Europe has endowed its peoples with the strength for organization, as this appears particularly in politics, trade and in scientific disciplines. The creative spirit of Japan has shown to you the beauty of nature and given you the power to realize it in life.' And: 'My brothers, when the red flames of this mighty fire send forth their prattling laughter to the stars, you will place your trust in the stars and not in the destroying fire. For once this fire has consumed itself and gone out, leaving a pile of ashes as memorial, the light of eternity will shine out once more in the East—in the Orient where the morning light of human history was born. And who knows: perhaps this day is already dawning and the sun has already risen upon the eastern horizon. Then, like the singers my ancestors, I will greet this eastern sun which is destined to illumine the whole world once more.' See also the whole lecture.
63. Tagore: 'You must always have felt a strong undertone of fear whenever the West spoke of the possibility that an eastern people could rise to ascendency again. The reason for this is that the power through which the West rules is an evil one. So long as it has this power on its side alone, the West feels safe while the rest of the world trembles. The modern civilization of Europe must, if it is to live, seek to have Satan and his potencies in its exclusive service. Its whole war-readiness and diplomacy are focused on this single goal. Yet all these costly rites for invoking the evil spirit will lead, upon a path of outward flourishing, to the very edge of the abyss.'
64. Sophie von Sachsen-Weimar, 1824–97; cf. Rudolf Steiner's comments about her in GA 31.
65. Georg Kreuzwendedich Count of Rheinbaben, 1855–1921, was the Prussian finance minister in Weimar. Cf. also p. 253 in this volume.
66. Plato, 427–347 BC, Greek philosopher, pupil of Socrates. The school he founded in the Grove of Akademos became the model for all future 'academies'.
67. Socrates, *c.* 469–399 BC, Greek philosopher.
68. Alexander Moszkowski, 1851–1934, Berlin journalist, chiefly known as a humorist.
69. For example, E. Rasmussen: *Jesus. Eine vergleichende psychopathologische Studie*, Leipzig 1905.
70. See the lecture of 5 March 1918 in this volume.
71. For instance, in the following lectures: 1 January 1912, GA 134; 14 April 1914, GA 153; 6 November 1917, GA 178.
72. For instance, in the lectures of 10 and 11 November 1917, GA 178; also the lecture of 22 January 1918 in this volume and the related note.

73. The lecture of 7 March 1918, GA 67.
74. See the chapter 'Some Effects of Initiation' in *Knowledge of the Higher Worlds*, GA 10.
75. GA 153.
76. The lecture of 12 March 1918 in this volume.
77. For example, in the lecture of 28 August 1915, GA 163.
78. The lecture of 14 March 1918, GA 67.
79. Cf. the lecture of 5 February 1918 in this volume.
80. See the lecture of 12 March 1918 in this volume.
81. See the lecture of 29 January 1918 in this volume. There Rudolf Steiner says: 'The kind of knowledge, by contrast, that can be entirely assimilated by the rest of the organism would be one which later, in recalling it, would invoke in us qualities such as love, joy and warmth of heart. How we structure lessons so that, for the rest of his life, a person can look back on his education with warmth of heart, joy and a certain feeling of bliss is connected with the deepest mysteries of humanity.'
82. Cf. pp. 167 f. in this volume.
83. Steiner refers to this in many lectures in his collected works; see also the lecture of 29 January 1918 in this volume.
84. Immanuel Kant, 1724–1804, philosopher, mathematician, scientist.
85. The lectures did not appear until 1927. GA 128.
86. 14 March 1918, in GA 67. See also the lecture of 21 March 1918, ibid.
87. For example in the following lectures: 6 March 1911, GA 127; 8 June 1913, GA 150; 28 January 1917, GA 174; and 16 November 1917, GA 178.
88. GA 121.
89. See for instance p. 49 of this volume.
90. For example, the lectures of 13 February 1917, GA 175 and 11 December 1917, GA 179.
91. For instance, the lectures of 29 January and 26 March, GA 178.
92. The lecture of 14 March 1918, GA 67. See also the lecture of 16 November 1917, GA 178.
93. See notes 9 and 19.
94. See note 5.
95. It is not clear which passages in Grimm and Wilson Steiner is referring to here. However, cf. the lecture on 14 March 1918, GA 67, where it is apparent that Steiner is speaking of the verdicts of Grimm and Wilson on Macaulay and Gibbon. See also the detailed accounts in the lecture of 16 October 1918 in GA 182, and in the 'answers to questions' on 17 October 1918, GA 277.
96. Cf. the lecture of 29 November 1917, GA 182.
97. For example, see the lectures of 8 October 1906, GA 96; 10 and 23 October 1915, GA 154; and 7 August 1916, GA 170.
98. GA 20.
99. Nicolaus Copernicus, 1473–1543, Polish astronomer, canon, mathematician, physician, jurist, humanist and originator of the heliocentric worldview.
100. Steiner is referring to the lecture series he gave in various cities to members of

the society. In his *Autobiography* (GA 28, chapter XXXV) he says this: 'These lectures were attended only by members with some basic knowledge of anthroposophy. One could speak to them in the same way as to more advanced students. The stance I adopted in these internal lectures was different from what was necessary in published books.' Transcripts of these lectures were privately printed, but Steiner did not have the time to check or revise them, and they were intended only for the members of the society. By 1918 around 30 lecture cycles were available in print.

101. See note 84.
102. Arthur Schopenhauer, 1788–1860, philosopher.
103. The essay was entitled 'Frederick the Great and Macaulay' and published in *Fünfzehn Essays, Erste Folge*, Berlin and Guetersloh, 1884. The passage runs as follows: 'It is conceivable that the spirit of a human being, released from corporeal bands, might float above the earth somewhat like a mere reflection of events. This is not some article of faith but just a fantasy. Let us assume that for some people immortality consists in them floating over the earth unconstrained by what formerly blinded them, so that all destinies of the earth and human beings, from the birth of our planet onwards, were revealed to them. They would perceive the past as a weft of harmonious beauty ... Now suddenly, let us continue dreaming, the spirit who surveys everything thus freely is compelled to unite again with the body of a mortal human being. Even if this person possessed the greatest talents of any or every kind, would he still be able to recall this former condition? He would be born at a particular date, with father and mother, a nation, a social class, a heart that loves and hates, vanity, pain, joy, doubt, despair, delight. And when therefore, even for a moment, would he be capable of the free clarity that was formerly his element? Previously he saw human hearts like a glass beehive, with their thoughts flying in and out and labouring in the world; and now he is compelled to guess their hidden secrets.'
104. The passage reads: 'However, I assert that only so much *actual* science will be discovered in any natural treatise as there is mathematics to be found therein.' In the preface to *Metaphysische Anfangsgründe der Naturwissenschaft*, 1786.
105. See the lectures of 29 January and 26 and 30 March 1918 in this volume. Also the lectures of 31 July, and 5 and 7 August 1917 in *The Riddle of Man*, GA 20.
106. For instance, see the lecture of 26 March 1918 in this volume.
107. Plato: see note 66.
108. Aristotle, 384–322 BC, a pupil of Plato and teacher of Alexander the Great.
109. See Timaeus, chapter 16, paragraphs 79–82, verses 45b–47c.
110. City of the Mandubian Celts on Mount Auxois, near the modern village of Alise-Sainte-Reine in the department of Côte-d'Or. It was destroyed by Caesar in 52 BC. Cf. also lectures in Dornach on 11 and 16 July 1920, GA 198.
111. Napoleon III, 1808–73, French Emperor from 1852 to 1870.
112. Vercingetorix was a Gaul of the Arverni tribe and leader of the great rebellion against Caesar in 52 BC. This was successful initially but he was

eventually surrounded by Caesar's forces and forced to surrender. He was executed in Rome by Caesar in 46 BC, after six years imprisonment.

113. Gaius Julius Caesar, 100–44 BC, Roman military leader and statesman.
114. For example, see the lectures of 11 April 1914, GA 153; 17 April 1914, GA 154; and 27 June 1916, GA 168.
115. First appearing in *Lucifer-Gnosis*, many editions of this lecture were published. GA 34 and Tb 658.
116. GA 9, in the chapter 'The Soul in the Soul World After Death'.
117. GA 153.
118. See the lectures in this volume dated 19 and 26 March and 1 April 1918.
119. See *Faust*, Part 2, Act 2, Laboratory (Homunculus); line 6924.
120. Origen, *c.* AD 185–253/4, founder of Christian Gnosis.
121. See pp. 43 f. in this volume.
122. Cf. p. 44 in this volume, and the related note.
123. Jakob Frohschammer, 1821–93. *Über den Ursprung der menschlichen Seelen. Rechtfertigung des Generatianismus*, Munich 1854, in the chapter entitled 'Der Präexistentialismus. I. Generatianismus und Einfachheit des Geistes'. Cf. also his book *Die Philosophie des Thomas von Aquino*, Leipzig 1889, Vorrede, p. VIII, where he states this: '... my theory, that the souls of children originate from their parents since the latter engender living human beings and not just bodies or even animals which God must each time directly infuse with a newly created soul ...'
124. GA 21.
125. Lecture of 7 March 1918, GA 67.
126. Cf. pp. 28–30 in this volume, and the related note.
127. Max Wentscher: *Einführung in die Philosophie* (Sammlung Göschen 281), Berlin and Leipzig 1912, p. 59: 'And similarly "supranaturalism" is really what lends *tradition* such huge power. With good will, everyone can discover what is natural within himself; and this enables us to check our own judgements. But what is supernatural, which we do not all experience within us, must simply be accepted by others in good faith; the individual cannot check it, and it therefore inevitably gives rise to an unfree, dependent sensibility. This is compounded by the fact that the priests and the Church have always known how to nurture and strengthen traditional faith in the supernatural, which the masses anyway have a liking for, by making it seem that the soul's destiny in the *other realm* is dependent on such "true faith". Anyone therefore who does not wish to put his soul's redemption at risk is required to be obedient in his faith, and is thus irredeemably exposed to excessive moral judgements relating to the incomprehensible world of the supersensible, as traditional faith has taught it to be.'
128. Cf. the lecture of 1 April 1918 in this volume and note 97.
129. See the lecture of 12 March 1918 in this volume. Cf. also that of 1 April 1918.
130. See the lecture of 24 January 1918, GA 67.
131. See the lecture of 1 April 1918 in this volume and note 97.
132. As well as many related accounts in later lectures, see the lecture of 9 July 1918 in this volume.

133. August Strindberg, 1849–1912, Swedish dramatist.
134. Fritz Mauthner, 1849–1923, writer and philosopher. *Beiträge zu einer Kritik der Sprache*, 3 vols, Berlin 1901/02.
135. John Stuart Mill, 1806–73, English philosopher, politician and economist.
136. Herbert Spencer, 1820–1903, English philosopher.
137. GA 4. This was the second, substantially enlarged and expanded edition, Berlin 1918.
138. 'Die Geisteswissenschaft als Anthroposophie und die zeitgenössische Erkenntnismethode. Persönlich-Unpersönliches' in *Das Reich*, Munich 1917/18, Book 2 (July 1917); reprinted in GA 35, pp. 307 ff. in the German edition.
139. Eduard von Hartmann, 1842–1906, philosopher. *Philosophie des Unbewussten*, 1969. In relation to E. von Hartmann, see for example Rudolf Steiner's essay on him in GA 30 and his comments in his *Autobiography*, GA 28.
140. Cf. the letters to and from E. von Hartmann in GA 38 and GA 39, especially letters nos 364, 400 and 517 in vol. 2.
141. See Beiträge zur Rudolf Steiner Gesamtausgabe, nos 85/86, Dornach 1984, 'Zur Philosophie der Freiheit. Kommentare und Randbemerkungen von Eduard von Hartmann'.
142. The sentence is formulated differently here than it is in *The Philosophy of Freedom*; to compare this with the German edition see p. 107, lines 1–11 of the latter, and p. 133 with the related note.
143. The lecture of 15 April 1918, GA 67.
144. See his work *Die Welt als Wille und Vorstellung* ('The world as will and idea'), 6 vols, Rudolstadt 1819, in the edition *Sämtliche Werke in 12 Bänden*, with an introduction by Dr Rudolf Steiner, Stuttgart and Berlin (undated, 1894), vols 2–6.
145. See note 143.
146. See for example the lecture on 15 November 1917, GA 178 and 15 April 1918, see note 143.
147. Oscar Hertwig, 1849–1922, anatomist, pupil of Ernst Haeckel. *Das Werden der Organismen. Eine Widerlegung von Darwins Zufallstheorie*, Jena 1916; and *Zur Abwehr des ethischen, des sozialen, des politischen Darwinismus*, Jena 1918.
148. The passage reads: 'We ought to enquire into the laws of the configuration of lifeless nature in physics and chemistry, and the laws of configuration of living beings in biology, along with their modes of action, by using methods that resemble those which, in astronomy, have made it possible to cloak processes occurring in the heavens in fixed forms which we call natural laws.' Oscar Hertwig in *Zur Abwehr* ...
149. Emil Dubois-Reymond, 1818–96, German physiologist. 'Über die Grenzen des Naturerkennens', lecture given to the 45th assembly of German scientists and physicians in Leipzig on 14 August 1872; published Leipzig 1872.
150. 'Goethes Horoskop' in *Berliner Tageblatt*, no. 161, 28 March 1918, evening edition.
151. Franz Boll, philologist. Sternglaube und Sterndeutung. *Die Geschichte und das Wesen der Astrologie*, Leipzig and Berlin 1918.

152. Franz Boll: 'Noch einmal Goethes Horoskop', *Berliner Tageblatt*, no. 192, 16 April, morning edition.
153. Flavius Claudius Julianus, 332–63, Caesar from 361 to 363. The Christians called him the 'Apostate' because he sought to renew the heathen mysteries as an initiate of the Mysteries of Eleusis. In relation to Julian see also GA 175, especially the lecture of 19 April 1917.
154. Julius Robert Mayer, 1814–78, physician and scientist. The treatise referred to here was entitled 'Bemerkungen über die Kräfte in der unbelebten Natur', and appeared in *Liebigs Annalen*, 1942, vol. 42. (It is also included in: R. *Mayer über die Erhaltung der Kraft*, vier Abhandlungen, Voigtländers Quellenbücher, Leipzig, vol. 12.)
155. Friedrich Ueberweg, 1826–71, philosopher. *Grundriss der Geschichte der Philosophie*, 1863–66. He refers to Mayer there in Part 3 ('Die Neuzeit'), vol. 2 (*Nachkantische Systeme und Philosophie der Gegenwart*), 8th edition 1897, p. 293: 'In his books (of 1842, 1845 and 1850), Julius Robert Mayer discussed and demonstrated that only the quality of energy alters but is indestructible in amount, and that heat too is only a kind of movement, or that heat and movement transform into one another; and that a law of immutable relationships between movement and heat can also be expressed in numerical terms. He speaks of this numerical quantity as the mechanical equivalent of heat.'
156. James Prescott Joule, 1818–89, English physicist, brewer; was the first to empirically determine the mechanical heat equivalent.
157. Hermann L.F. von Helmholtz, 1821–94, physiologist and physicist. Particularly relevant here is his treatise 'Über die Erhaltung der Kraft' (1847).
158. Charles Robert Darwin, 1809–82, English scientist, physician, geologist and botanist. *On the Origin of Species by Means of Natural Selection* was published in 1859.
159. Robert Chambers, 1802–71, bookseller and writer. *Vestiges of the Natural History of Creation*, Edinburgh 1844 (appeared anonymously).
160. Jean Baptiste Lamarck, 1744–1829, French scientist.
161. Published in London, 1831. See also the chapter 'Historical Sketch' in Charles Darwin *On the Origin of Species* (see note 158).
162. Robert Hamerling, 1830–89, Austrian poet.
163. See the previous lecture on 9 April 1918 in this volume.
164. Lecture of 15 April 1918, GA 67.
165. See also Rudolf Steiner's lecture of 23 April 1918, GA 174b, and 30 June 1918, GA 182. See also Ernst Neumann, *Vorlesungen zur Einführung in die experimentelle Pädagogik und ihre psychologischen Grundlagen*, 3 vols, 1907. See also the next note.
166. The following excerpts in the text originate in the article 'Die Entwicklung der Psycho-Technik in Deutschland während des Krieges' by Dr Curt Piorkowski, published in the journal *Deutsche Politik. Wochenschrift für Welt- u. Kulturepolitik*, Weimar and Berlin, issue 16 of 19 April 1918.
167. Words spoken by Pylades in Goethe's *Iphigenia*, Act 2, Scene 1, verse 665 f.
168. See Leo Königsberger, *Hermann von Helmholtz*, 3 vols, Braunschweig 1902–3.
169. See the lecture of 6 May 1918 in GA 271.

170. See page 30 in this volume and note 34.
171. Ibid.
172. In the first edition of *Jenseits der Seele* (see note 34), p. 254, footnote.
173. The following passage illustrates how Dessoir tackles Steiner's statements: '... I would ask the reader, furthermore, to urgently take note of the fact that he does not live in the sixth but in the fifth "post-Atlantean epoch". However, you may believe me when I say that I am not all that concerned about the numerical mistake I made here, since I regard these post-Atlantean periods as ... an empty miasma (p. XI of the Preface). See also page 30 in this volume and note 34.
174. Review of Dessoir's book *Vom Jenseits der Seele* by E. Utitz in the journal *Kantstudien*, vol. XXII (1981), issue 4, pp. 464 ff.
175. Vladimir Ilyitch Lenin (Uljanov), 1870–1924, leader of the Bolsheviks and founder of the USSR. Leon Trotsky (real name Leib Bronstein), 1879–1940, close collaborator with Lenin.
176. Lecture of 14 April 1914, GA 153 p. 174.
177. On 11 April 1913 in a lecture on *Faust*, GA 272.
178. Dornach performances of *Faust* do portray this.
179. *Faust* Part 1, Martha's Garden, lines 3438 ff.
180. Ibid., Night, Gothic Room, lines 512 f.
181. Ibid., words of the Earth Spirit, lines 512 f.
182. Ibid., lines 514 f.
183. Words of Faust, ibid., lines 602–5.
184. Jakob Minor, 1855–1912, literary historian. *Goethes Faust. Entstehungsgeschichte und Erklärung*, 2 vols, Stuttgart 1901. In vol. 2, p. 28, he writes: 'If we find him (Goethe) at this period in such tortured struggle with his poetic works and, most unusually for him, continually stopping and starting in his creative productivity, we can seek the reason for this, I believe, in this change in his outlook on life, as this comes most faithfully to expression in his poetic output. At the time Goethe was nearly 50; and as far as I know the first lament about approaching age originates at the time of his Swiss travels in the beautiful poem "Swiss Alps". In the *puer eterna*, hitherto used only to creative vision, thought now appears in a more central role as the prefiguring of the wisdom of old age.'
185. Ibid., Prologue in Heaven, lines 338 f.
186. Ibid., lines 320 f.
187. This was first published in Berlin in 1902 by the Theosophischer Bibliothek. In 1918 it was republished as volume one of a study of Goethe, GA 22.
188. This third part had originally been published in 1899 in the *Magazin für Literatur*, Berlin no. 34, 26 August 1899, and as a separate pamphlet (Berlin). This first version has been reprinted in GA 30.
189. GA 8.
190. Friedrich Paulsen, 1846–1908, philosopher and pedagogue, from 1878 professor at Berlin University.
191. Gideon Spicker, 1840–1912, former Capuchin monk, later professor of philosophy.
192. See for example the lectures of 5 February and 14 May 1918 in this volume.

193. See for example the lecture of 5 February 1918 in this volume. See also the lecture in Bern on 29 November 1917, GA 182.
194. In *Das Reich* (Munich), issues of April 1916 and January 1917. Reprinted in GA 35.
195. GA 10.
196. GA 13.
197. For example, Rudolf Steiner spoke about Otto Weininger on 18 March 1908, GA 56, and on 29 July 1916, GA 170. See also the lecture of 21 September 1924, GA 238, in relation to the karma of the anthroposophical movement.
198. Otto Weininger, 1880–1903, philosopher. *Geschlecht und Charakter*, Vienna and Leipzig 1903. See also the note above.
199. Steiner is referring to the book *Über die letzten Dinge*, with a biographical foreword by Dr Moriz Rappaport. Weininger wrote this book in the last year of his life in Italy (see Foreword, pp. XVIII f.) and it was published posthumously in 1907.
200. See note 120.
201. See for example the lectures of 1 and 9 April in this volume.
202. 'Die Chymische Hochzeit des Christian Rosenkreutz', Part III, was published in *Das Reich* (Munich) in April 1918. The article was reprinted in GA 35. Baron von Bernus, the editor of *Das Reich*, had written to Steiner on 11 January 1916 to ask him to write an introduction to the *Chymical Wedding*, which was due to be republished for the first time in the journal that year. Von Bernus wrote as follows: 'If it were possible for you to write an introduction to this republished version, even a short one, this would of course be highly significant.' Rudolf Steiner replied to Bernus in a letter of 20 March 1918, and we see from his words how he regarded this task: 'In my article I have gone as far as is possible at present in interpreting the *Chymical Wedding*. I would only be able to delve deeper if anyone should dispute the spirit of my interpretation. In the present context it is, I am sure, not necessary to take any further account of exoteric literature on Rosenkreutz than I have done at the end of my piece. What I say at the very end about Andreae's relationship to Rosicrucianism originates from my spiritual-scientific research. This however will elicit objections from anyone who has previously written on this theme. But my spiritual-scientific research is well-founded. If I should be called upon to describe this underlying context—for instance because objections are raised—this would exceed the scope of an essay on the *Chymical Wedding* itself. For the time being I think that I have written enough.' The whole text of *The Chymical Wedding of Christian Rosenkreutz, Anno 1459*, by Johann Valentin Andreae, is available in English from Wynstones Press.
203. Christian Rosenkreutz: a figure of the fourteenth/fifteenth century whom mainstream history does not regard as historical, but is known from Rosicrucian literature. See also the note on Johann Valentin Andreae. Christian Rosenkreutz was supposedly a German of aristocratic birth who lived from 1378 to 1484. According to Rudolf Steiner he was a real historical individual. See also GA 130.

204. Johann Valentin Andreae, 1586–1654, a Lutheran pastor in Wuerttemberg and writer. Few still contest that Andreae did indeed write the *Chymical Wedding*; but there is no consensus about whether or not he is the author of the so-called Rosicrucian manifestoes in the *Fama Fraternitatis*, Cassel 1614, and of the *Confessio Fraternitatis*, Cassel 1615. His works are: *Vita ipso conscripta*, edited by F.H. Rheinwald, Berlin 1849; *Turris Babel sive Judiciorum de Fraternitate Rosaceae Crucis Chaos*, Strasbourg 1619; *Die Chymische Hochzeit des Christian Rosenkreutz Anno 1459*, Strasbourg 1616. Frances A. Yates explored Andreae's life and work in detail in her book *The Rosicrucian Enlightenment*, 1972. See also p. 270 in this volume.
205. See the lecture of 29 June 1921 in Bern, Dornach 1986.
206. Franz Reuleaux, 1829–1905. 'Cultur und Technik', a lecture given at the Lower Austrian Trade Association on 14 November 1884, published in Vienna, 1884. On p. 12 he says of manganism and naturalism: 'I wish to use an old word, generalized for our present purposes, and call "manganism" the use and application of natural forces, whose laws have been recognized and understood. By contrast, I will refer to the other stance which does little in relation to natural forces other than stand before them defensively, at the most drawing a few formulae from them by mysterious and surreptitious means, as "naturalism".'
207. Ibid., p. 16. The passage runs: 'Art and scientific technology are not mutually exclusive. But greater exertions are needed to do justice to both—greater stability and spiritual immersion in subtle aesthetic laws in order to ward off the disruptive attacks of the machine. In Austria and Germany we can see from today's living dynamic in these two realms that they can both be developed alongside each other.'
208. Two plays by Edouard Schuré, *The Sacred Drama of Eleusis* and *The Children of Lucifer*, were performed for the first time in 1907 and 1909 respectively. In 1910 Rudolf Steiner wrote his first Mystery Play, *The Portal of Initiation*, performed in the same year. It was followed by three further plays by Steiner. See GA 14.
209. To accompany Schuré's play *The Children of Lucifer*, Rudolf Steiner gave the lecture cycle 'The Orient in the Light of the Occident. The Children of Lucifer and the Brothers of Christ', GA 113. He likewise accompanied his own four Mystery Plays with a lecture cycle each, now to be found, respectively, in GA 122 (for *The Portal of Initiation*), GA 129 (for *The Probation of the Soul*), GA 138 (for *The Guardian of the Threshold*) and GA 147 (for *The Soul's Awakening*).
210. Today this group stands in a special room at the Goetheanum in Dornach.
211. Mieta Waller-Pyle, 1883–1954, from around 1907 a friend and close artistic collaborator with Marie Steiner-von Sivers and Rudolf Steiner.
212. Louise Edith Maryon, 1872–1924, sculptor and artistic colleague of Rudolf Steiner.
213. Georg Korf: *Die andere Seite der Welt*, 1914.
214. In 1911 Annie Besant, president of the Theosophical Society, founded the Star of the East order with C.W. Leadbeater. The order was intended to publicize the young Jiddu Krishnamurti (1895–1986), under the name of

Alcyone, as the second coming of Christ. Krishnamurti later distanced himself from this role and dissolved the order.

215. See the lecture of 25 June 1918 in this volume.
216. Ibid.
217. Ibid. See also the lecture of 2 April 1918 in this volume.
218. Fyodor Mikhailovich Dostoyevsky, 1821–81, Russian author.
219. GA 20.
220. See note 60.
221. Author of a book cited by Steiner on various occasions, *The Spirit of the Chinese People* (1922).
222. Sophie von Sachsen-Weimar, see note 64.
223. See note 65.
224. See the lecture of 3 July 1918 in this volume.
225. Sir Austen Henry Layard, 1817–94, English statesman, archaeologist and writer. *See Discoveries in the Ruins of Nineveh and Babylon*, 1853.
226. See lecture of 25 June 1918 in this volume.
227. Herman Grimm, 1828–1901, *Das Leben Michelangelos*, 1860–63, 2 vols.
228. Bernhard of Clairvaux, 1091–1153, Doctor of the Church and one of the most important of medieval mystics. In 1147 he called on people to join the Second Crusade, and was its most active supporter. Pope Alexander III conferred sainthood on him in 1174.
229. Jakob Boehme, 1575–1624, a shoemaker in Goerlitz by profession. He was a mystic and philosopher, and the first to write his works in German.
230. Karl von Eckartshausen, 1752–1803, a mystic who wrote alchemical works.
231. On 21 November 1905, unpublished.
232. Baron of Niederlothringen, leader of the First Crusade. After conquering Jerusalem in 1099 he bore the name 'The Protector of the Sacred Grave'. He died in 1100.
233. Henry II, the Holy, 973–1024, last of the Saxon kings, made a saint in 1146. In his published works, Steiner refers to the Saxon king Henry II in similar ways in various lectures. The formulation 'Ecclesia Catholica non Romana' has not been sourced.
234. Enrico Dandolo, 1108–1205, Doge of Venice in 1192.
235. See for example the lectures of 1 June 1913 and 22 March 1917, GA 66.
236. See the lecture of 25 June 1918 in this volume and note 202.
237. On 17 June 1918, Rudolf Steiner, with Marie Steiner and the Polzer and Klima families, visited Karlstein Castle near Prague. The pictures referred to, depicting the life of Saint Wenzel (tenth century), are ascribed to the Strasbourg painter Nikolas Wurmser, and are said to have been painted between 1356 and 1365. However, one can also discern in them a representation of the *Chymical Wedding of Christian Rosenkreutz*. See Ludwig Polzer-Hoditz: *Erinnerungen an Rudolf Steiner*, Dornach 1985, p. 98 and the appendix in that volume by Julie Klima, pp. 291 ff. For a description of the individual pictures, see Hanna Kraemer-Steiner: *Geistimpulse in der Geschichte des tschechischen Volkes von den Ursagen bis Karl* IV, Stuttgart 1971, pp. 132 ff. See also J. Neuwirth, *Mittelalterliche Wandgemälde und Tafelbilder der Burg Karlstein in Böhmen*, Prague 1896.

238. In the lecture of 16 July 1918 in this volume.
239. See for instance the lectures of 10 and 17 July in GA 176.
240. See for example the lecture of 29 January 1918 in this volume.
241. Galatians 2:20.
242. John 1:11–13.
243. Apart from Steiner's books, see also the lectures of 2 and 8 February 1910 in GA 116; also the lecture of 16 November 1908, GA 107.
244. Helena Petrovna Blavatsky, 1831–91 founded the Theosophical Society in 1875. See *Secret Doctrine. The Synthesis of Science, Religion and Philosophy*.
245. Thomas Aquinas, 1225–74, known as Doctor Angelicus, an outstanding philosopher and scholastic. Sainthood was conferred on him in 1323.
246. Petrus Waldus founded the Waldensian movement in 1177.
247. Georg Freiherr von Hertling, 1843–1919, professor of philosophy, German Chancellor from 1917. *Das Princip des Katholicismus und die Wissenschaft*, Freiburg 1899. The passages either quoted or freely rendered on the following pages can be found on the following pages of that book: 15, 41, 42, 83, 44, 45 and 102.
248. Renatus Cartesius, 1596–1650, a French mathematician, physicist and philosopher who wrote under the name of René Descartes.
249. Quoted in Gothein, *Ignatius von Loyola*, Halle 1895, p. 420.
250. Bernhard Muenz, 'Der deutsche Reichskanzler als Philosoph', printed in *Österreichische Rundschau*, Vienna and Leipzig, vol. 55, issue 2, 15 April 1918.
251. Ibid.
252. Hermann Heisler, *Lebensfragen*. 17 Predigten, Konstanz and Leipzig 1918.
253. D. Schuster in the *Hannoverscher Kurier*, 18 July 1918, evening issue.
254. See also the lecture of 5 February 1918 in this volume, and GA 175.
255. By Hertling, see p. 288 and the corresponding note.
256. Karl Kautsky, 1854–1928, a socialist politician and writer.
257. See GA 157 and GA 121, in the latter especially the lecture of 16 June 1910. See also the lecture of 30 March 1918 in this volume.
258. See pp. 281 f. in this volume and the corresponding note.
259. This may refer to the comments on pp. 249 f. in this volume.
260. See the lecture of 16 April 1918 in this volume.
261. GA 13.
262. GA 10.
263. Docetism (from the Greek, meaning 'shine'): Christian heretics who held various forms of the view that, since matter was evil, Christ's corporeal nature was only appearance and his death an optical illusion. Those who subscribed to some form of docetism included the Manichaeans, the Bogomils and the Cathars.
264. See for instance Heinrich Weinel, *Jesus im neunzehnten Jahrhundert*, Tuebingen and Leipzig 1903, Introduction pp. 6 f. The passage runs: ... 'Naturally it is not the Christ of the past, the divine being of the old dogma, but Jesus of Nazareth to whom the men of our day turn again with questions regarding his answers to their cares and woes. For long, long ages, this simple, courageous man was concealed in the radiant glory of the king of heaven ...'
265. Jakob von Uexkuell, 1864–1944, zoologist. *Im Kampf um die Tierseele*,

Wiesbaden 1902, p. 19: 'To our opponents I would expressly say that we do not claim animals possess no psyche but only that it is not possible to gain any direct experience that would answer this question.'

266. See note 241.
267. See 'Verfolg: Glückliches Ereignis' in: *Goethes Naturwissenschaftliche Schriften*, edited and annotated by Dr Rudolf Steiner in *Kuerschner's Deutsche National-Litteratur*, 5 vols (1884–97), reprinted in Dornach 1975, GA 1a–e, vol. 1, GA 1a, pp. 111 ff.
268. August Karl Batsch, 1761–1802, professor of natural history in Jena.
269. Alexander Baumgartner S.J., 1841–1910, literary historian. *Goethe. Sein Leben und seine Werke*, 2 vols, Freiburg i. Br. 1885/86.
270. George Henry Lewes, 1817–78, English writer. *The Life and Works of Goethe*, London 1855.
271. *Stimmen der Zeit. Katholische Monatschrift für das Geistesleben der Gegenwart*, Freiburg i. Br. The articles in question were: Josef Kreitmaier, 'Vom Expressionismus', issue 10, July 1918; Otto Zimmermann, 'Anthroposophische Irrlehren, ibid., and 'Der anthroposophische Mystizismus', issue 12, September 1918.
272. At the time Steiner was working on the new, greatly revised and enlarged edition. It was published in Leipzig in 1920.
273. At Geisbergstrasse 2 in Berlin. Later the Berlin branch of the Anthroposophical Society occupied premises in Potsdamer Strasse.
274. See the lecture of 22 January 1918 in this volume.

RUDOLF STEINER'S COLLECTED WORKS

The German Edition of Rudolf Steiner's Collected Works (the *Gesamtausgabe* [GA] published by Rudolf Steiner Verlag, Dornach, Switzerland) presently runs to 354 titles, organized either by type of work (written or spoken), chronology, audience (public or other), or subject (education, art, etc.). For ease of comparison, the Collected Works in English [CW] follows the German organization exactly. A complete listing of the CWs follows with literal translations of the German titles. Other than in the case of the books published in his lifetime, titles were rarely given by Rudolf Steiner himself, and were often provided by the editors of the German editions. The titles in English are not necessarily the same as the German; and, indeed, over the past seventy-five years have frequently been different, with the same book sometimes appearing under different titles.

For ease of identification and to avoid confusion, we suggest that readers looking for a title should do so by CW number. Because the work of creating the Collected Works of Rudolf Steiner is an ongoing process, with new titles being published every year, we have not indicated in this listing which books are presently available. To find out what titles in the Collected Works are currently in print, please check our website at www.rudolfsteinerpress.com (or www.steinerbooks.org for US readers).

Written Work

CW 1 Goethe: Natural-Scientific Writings, Introduction, with Footnotes and Explanations in the text by Rudolf Steiner

CW 2 Outlines of an Epistemology of the Goethean World View, with Special Consideration of Schiller

CW 3 Truth and Science

CW 4 The Philosophy of Freedom

CW 4a Documents to 'The Philosophy of Freedom'

CW 5 Friedrich Nietzsche, A Fighter against His Time

CW 6 Goethe's Worldview

CW 6a Now in CW 30

CW 7 Mysticism at the Dawn of Modern Spiritual Life and Its Relationship with Modern Worldviews

CW 8 Christianity as Mystical Fact and the Mysteries of Antiquity

CW 9 Theosophy: An Introduction into Supersensible World Knowledge and Human Purpose

CW 10 How Does One Attain Knowledge of Higher Worlds?

CW 11 From the Akasha-Chronicle

CW 12	Levels of Higher Knowledge
CW 13	Occult Science in Outline
CW 14	Four Mystery Dramas
CW 15	The Spiritual Guidance of the Individual and Humanity
CW 16	A Way to Human Self-Knowledge: Eight Meditations
CW 17	The Threshold of the Spiritual World. Aphoristic Comments
CW 18	The Riddles of Philosophy in Their History, Presented as an Outline
CW 19	Contained in CW 24
CW 20	The Riddles of the Human Being: Articulated and Unarticulated in the Thinking, Views and Opinions of a Series of German and Austrian Personalities
CW 21	The Riddles of the Soul
CW 22	Goethe's Spiritual Nature And Its Revelation In 'Faust' and through the 'Fairy Tale of the Snake and the Lily'
CW 23	The Central Points of the Social Question in the Necessities of Life in the Present and the Future
CW 24	Essays Concerning the Threefold Division of the Social Organism and the Period 1915–1921
CW 25	Cosmology, Religion and Philosophy
CW 26	Anthroposophical Leading Thoughts
CW 27	Fundamentals for Expansion of the Art of Healing according to Spiritual-Scientific Insights
CW 28	The Course of My Life
CW 29	Collected Essays on Dramaturgy, 1889–1900
CW 30	Methodical Foundations of Anthroposophy: Collected Essays on Philosophy, Natural Science, Aesthetics and Psychology, 1884–1901
CW 31	Collected Essays on Culture and Current Events, 1887–1901
CW 32	Collected Essays on Literature, 1884–1902
CW 33	Biographies and Biographical Sketches, 1894–1905
CW 34	Lucifer-Gnosis: Foundational Essays on Anthroposophy and Reports from the Periodicals 'Lucifer' and 'Lucifer-Gnosis,' 1903–1908
CW 35	Philosophy and Anthroposophy: Collected Essays, 1904–1923
CW 36	The Goetheanum-Idea in the Middle of the Cultural Crisis of the Present: Collected Essays from the Periodical 'Das Goetheanum,' 1921–1925
CW 37	Now in CWs 260a and 251
CW 38	Letters, Vol. 1: 1881–1890
CW 39	Letters, Vol. 2: 1890–1925
CW 40	Truth-Wrought Words
CW 40a	Sayings, Poems and Mantras; Supplementary Volume
CW 42	Now in CWs 264–266
CW 43	Stage Adaptations
CW 44	On the Four Mystery Dramas. Sketches, Fragments and Paralipomena on the Four Mystery Dramas
CW 45	Anthroposophy: A Fragment from the Year 1910

Public Lectures

CW 51	On Philosophy, History and Literature
CW 52	Spiritual Teachings Concerning the Soul and Observation of the World
CW 53	The Origin and Goal of the Human Being
CW 54	The Riddles of the World and Anthroposophy
CW 55	Knowledge of the Supersensible in Our Times and Its Meaning for Life Today
CW 56	Knowledge of the Soul and of the Spirit
CW 57	Where and How Does One Find the Spirit?
CW 58	The Metamorphoses of the Soul Life. Paths of Soul Experiences: Part One
CW 59	The Metamorphoses of the Soul Life. Paths of Soul Experiences: Part Two
CW 60	The Answers of Spiritual Science to the Biggest Questions of Existence
CW 61	Human History in the Light of Spiritual Research
CW 62	Results of Spiritual Research
CW 63	Spiritual Science as a Treasure for Life
CW 64	Out of Destiny-Burdened Times
CW 65	Out of Central European Spiritual Life
CW 66	Spirit and Matter, Life and Death
CW 67	The Eternal in the Human Soul. Immortality and Freedom
CW 68	Public lectures in various cities, 1906–1918
CW 69	Public lectures in various cities, 1906–1918
CW 70	Public lectures in various cities, 1906–1918
CW 71	Public lectures in various cities, 1906–1918
CW 72	Freedom—Immortality—Social Life
CW 73	The Supplementing of the Modern Sciences through Anthroposophy
CW 73a	Specialized Fields of Knowledge and Anthroposophy
CW 74	The Philosophy of Thomas Aquinas
CW 75	Public lectures in various cities, 1906–1918
CW 76	The Fructifying Effect of Anthroposophy on Specialized Fields
CW 77a	The Task of Anthroposophy in Relation to Science and Life: The Darmstadt College Course
CW 77b	Art and Anthroposophy. The Goetheanum-Impulse
CW 78	Anthroposophy, Its Roots of Knowledge and Fruits for Life
CW 79	The Reality of the Higher Worlds
CW 80	Public lectures in various cities, 1922
CW 81	Renewal-Impulses for Culture and Science—Berlin College Course
CW 82	So that the Human Being Can Become a Complete Human Being
CW 83	Western and Eastern World-Contrast. Paths to Understanding It through Anthroposophy
CW 84	What Did the Goetheanum Intend and What Should Anthroposophy Do?

Lectures to the Members of the Anthroposophical Society

CW 88	Concerning the Astral World and Devachan
CW 89	Consciousness—Life—Form. Fundamental Principles of a Spiritual-Scientific Cosmology
CW 90	Participant Notes from the Lectures during the Years 1903–1905
CW 91	Participant Notes from the Lectures during the Years 1903–1905
CW 92	The Occult Truths of Ancient Myths and Sagas
CW 93	The Temple Legend and the Golden Legend
CW 93a	Fundamentals of Esotericism
CW 94	Cosmogony. Popular Occultism. The Gospel of John. The Theosophy in the Gospel of John
CW 95	At the Gates of Theosophy
CW 96	Origin-Impulses of Spiritual Science. Christian Esotericism in the Light of New Spirit-Knowledge
CW 97	The Christian Mystery
CW 98	Nature Beings and Spirit Beings—Their Effects in Our Visible World
CW 99	The Theosophy of the Rosicrucians
CW 100	Human Development and Christ-Knowledge
CW 101	Myths and Legends. Occult Signs and Symbols
CW 102	The Working into Human Beings by Spiritual Beings
CW 103	The Gospel of John
CW 104	The Apocalypse of John
CW 104a	From the Picture-Script of the Apocalypse of John
CW 105	Universe, Earth, the Human Being: Their Being and Development, as well as Their Reflection in the Connection between Egyptian Mythology and Modern Culture
CW 106	Egyptian Myths and Mysteries in Relation to the Active Spiritual Forces of the Present
CW 107	Spiritual-Scientific Knowledge of the Human Being
CW 108	Answering the Questions of Life and the World through Anthroposophy
CW 109	The Principle of Spiritual Economy in Connection with the Question of Reincarnation. An Aspect of the Spiritual Guidance of Humanity
CW 110	The Spiritual Hierarchies and Their Reflection in the Physical World. Zodiac, Planets and Cosmos
CW 111	Contained in CW 109
CW 112	The Gospel of John in Relation to the Three Other Gospels, Especially the Gospel of Luke
CW 113	The Orient in the Light of the Occident. The Children of Lucifer and the Brothers of Christ
CW 114	The Gospel of Luke
CW 115	Anthroposophy—Psychosophy—Pneumatosophy
CW 116	The Christ-Impulse and the Development of 'I'-Consciousness
CW 117	The Deeper Secrets of the Development of Humanity in Light of the Gospels

CW 118	The Event of the Christ-Appearance in the Etheric World
CW 119	Macrocosm and Microcosm. The Large World and the Small World. Soul-Questions, Life-Questions, Spirit-Questions
CW 120	The Revelation of Karma
CW 121	The Mission of Individual Folk-Souls in Connection with Germanic-Nordic Mythology
CW 122	The Secrets of the Biblical Creation-Story. The Six-Day Work in the First Book of Moses
CW 123	The Gospel of Matthew
CW 124	Excursus in the Area of the Gospel of Mark
CW 125	Paths and Goals of the Spiritual Human Being. Life Questions in the Light of Spiritual Science
CW 126	Occult History. Esoteric Observations of the Karmic Relationships of Personalities and Events of World History
CW 127	The Mission of the New Spiritual Revelation. The Christ-Event as the Middle-Point of Earth Evolution
CW 128	An Occult Physiology
CW 129	Wonders of the World, Trials of the Soul, and Revelations of the Spirit
CW 130	Esoteric Christianity and the Spiritual Guidance of Humanity
CW 131	From Jesus to Christ
CW 132	Evolution from the View Point of the Truth
CW 133	The Earthly and the Cosmic Human Being
CW 134	The World of the Senses and the World of the Spirit
CW 135	Reincarnation and Karma and their Meaning for the Culture of the Present
CW 136	The Spiritual Beings in Celestial Bodies and the Realms of Nature
CW 137	The Human Being in the Light of Occultism, Theosophy and Philosophy
CW 138	On Initiation. On Eternity and the Passing Moment. On the Light of the Spirit and the Darkness of Life
CW 139	The Gospel of Mark
CW 140	Occult Investigation into the Life between Death and New Birth. The Living Interaction between Life and Death
CW 141	Life between Death and New Birth in Relationship to Cosmic Facts
CW 142	The Bhagavad Gita and the Letters of Paul
CW 143	Experiences of the Supersensible. Three Paths of the Soul to Christ
CW 144	The Mysteries of the East and of Christianity
CW 145	What Significance Does Occult Development of the Human Being Have for the Sheaths—Physical Body, Etheric Body, Astral Body, and Self?
CW 146	The Occult Foundations of the Bhagavad Gita
CW 147	The Secrets of the Threshold
CW 148	Out of Research in the Akasha: The Fifth Gospel
CW 149	Christ and the Spiritual World. Concerning the Search for the Holy Grail

CW 150 The World of the Spirit and Its Extension into Physical Existence; The Influence of the Dead in the World of the Living
CW 151 Human Thought and Cosmic Thought
CW 152 Preliminary Stages to the Mystery of Golgotha
CW 153 The Inner Being of the Human Being and Life Between Death and New Birth
CW 154 How does One Gain an Understanding of the Spiritual World? The Flowing in of Spiritual Impulses from out of the World of the Deceased
CW 155 Christ and the Human Soul. Concerning the Meaning of Life. Theosophical Morality. Anthroposophy and Christianity
CW 156 Occult Reading and Occult Hearing
CW 157 Human Destinies and the Destiny of Peoples
CW 157a The Formation of Destiny and the Life after Death
CW 158 The Connection Between the Human Being and the Elemental World. Kalevala—Olaf Åsteson—The Russian People—The World as the Result of the Influences of Equilibrium
CW 159 The Mystery of Death. The Nature and Significance of Middle Europe and the European Folk Spirits
CW 160 In CW 159
CW 161 Paths of Spiritual Knowledge and the Renewal of the Artistic Worldview
CW 162 Questions of Art and Life in Light of Spiritual Science
CW 163 Coincidence, Necessity and Providence. Imaginative Knowledge and the Processes after Death
CW 164 The Value of Thinking for a Knowledge That Satisfies the Human Being. The Relationship of Spiritual Science to Natural Science
CW 165 The Spiritual Unification of Humanity through the Christ-Impulse
CW 166 Necessity and Freedom in the Events of the World and in Human Action
CW 167 The Present and the Past in the Human Spirit
CW 168 The Connection between the Living and the Dead
CW 169 World-being and Selfhood
CW 170 The Riddle of the Human Being. The Spiritual Background of Human History. Cosmic and Human History, Vol. 1
CW 171 Inner Development-Impulses of Humanity. Goethe and the Crisis of the 19th Century. Cosmic and Human History, Vol. 2
CW 172 The Karma of the Vocation of the Human Being in Connection with Goethe's Life. Cosmic and Human History, Vol. 3
CW 173 Contemporary-Historical Considerations: The Karma of Untruthfulness, Part One. Cosmic and Human History, Vol. 4
CW 174 Contemporary-Historical Considerations: The Karma of Untruthfulness, Part Two. Cosmic and Human History, Vol. 5
CW 174a Middle Europe between East and West. Cosmic and Human History, Vol. 6
CW 174b The Spiritual Background of the First World War. Cosmic and Human History, Vol. 7

CW 175	Building Stones for an Understanding of the Mystery of Golgotha. Cosmic and Human Metamorphoses
CW 176	Truths of Evolution of the Individual and Humanity. The Karma of Materialism
CW 177	The Spiritual Background of the Outer World. The Fall of the Spirits of Darkness. Spiritual Beings and Their Effects, Vol. 1
CW 178	Individual Spiritual Beings and their Influence in the Soul of the Human Being. Spiritual Beings and their Effects, Vol. 2
CW 179	Spiritual Beings and Their Effects. Historical Necessity and Freedom. The Influences on Destiny from out of the World of the Dead. Spiritual Beings and Their Effects, Vol. 3
CW 180	Mystery Truths and Christmas Impulses. Ancient Myths and their Meaning. Spiritual Beings and Their Effects, Vol. 4
CW 181	Earthly Death and Cosmic Life. Anthroposophical Gifts for Life. Necessities of Consciousness for the Present and the Future.
CW 182	Death as Transformation of Life
CW 183	The Science of the Development of the Human Being
CW 184	The Polarity of Duration and Development in Human Life. The Cosmic Pre-History of Humanity
CW 185	Historical Symptomology
CW 185a	Historical-Developmental Foundations for Forming a Social Judgement
CW 186	The Fundamental Social Demands of Our Time—In Changed Situations
CW 187	How Can Humanity Find the Christ Again? The Threefold Shadow-Existence of our Time and the New Christ-Light
CW 188	Goetheanism, a Transformation-Impulse and Resurrection-Thought. Science of the Human Being and Science of Sociology
CW 189	The Social Question as a Question of Consciousness. The Spiritual Background of the Social Question, Vol. 1
CW 190	Impulses of the Past and the Future in Social Occurrences. The Spiritual Background of the Social Question, Vol. 2
CW 191	Social Understanding from Spiritual-Scientific Cognition. The Spiritual Background of the Social Question, Vol. 3
CW 192	Spiritual-Scientific Treatment of Social and Pedagogical Questions
CW 193	The Inner Aspect of the Social Riddle. Luciferic Past and Ahrimanic Future
CW 194	The Mission of Michael. The Revelation of the Actual Mysteries of the Human Being
CW 195	Cosmic New Year and the New Year Idea
CW 196	Spiritual and Social Transformations in the Development of Humanity
CW 197	Polarities in the Development of Humanity: West and East Materialism and Mysticism Knowledge and Belief
CW 198	Healing Factors for the Social Organism
CW 199	Spiritual Science as Knowledge of the Foundational Impulses of Social Formation

CW 200 The New Spirituality and the Christ-Experience of the 20th Century

CW 201 The Correspondences Between Microcosm and Macrocosm. The Human Being—A Hieroglyph of the Universe. The Human Being in Relationship with the Cosmos: 1

CW 202 The Bridge between the World-Spirituality and the Physical Aspect of the Human Being. The Search for the New Isis, the Divine Sophia. The Human Being in Relationship with the Cosmos: 2

CW 203 The Responsibility of Human Beings for the Development of the World through their Spiritual Connection with the Planet Earth and the World of the Stars. The Human Being in Relationship with the Cosmos: 3

CW 204 Perspectives of the Development of Humanity. The Materialistic Knowledge-Impulse and the Task of Anthroposophy. The Human Being in Relationship with the Cosmos: 4

CW 205 Human Development, World-Soul, and World-Spirit. Part One: The Human Being as a Being of Body and Soul in Relationship to the World. The Human Being in Relationship with the Cosmos: 5

CW 206 Human Development, World-Soul, and World-Spirit. Part Two: The Human Being as a Spiritual Being in the Process of Historical Development. The Human Being in Relationship with the Cosmos: 6

CW 207 Anthroposophy as Cosmosophy. Part One: Characteristic Features of the Human Being in the Earthly and the Cosmic Realms. The Human Being in Relationship with the Cosmos: 7

CW 208 Anthroposophy as Cosmosophy. Part Two: The Forming of the Human Being as the Result of Cosmic Influence. The Human Being in Relationship with the Cosmos: 8

CW 209 Nordic and Central European Spiritual Impulses. The Festival of the Appearance of Christ. The Human Being in Relationship with the Cosmos: 9

CW 210 Old and New Methods of Initiation. Drama and Poetry in the Change of Consciousness in the Modern Age

CW 211 The Sun Mystery and the Mystery of Death and Resurrection. Exoteric and Esoteric Christianity

CW 212 Human Soul Life and Spiritual Striving in Connection with World and Earth Development

CW 213 Human Questions and World Answers

CW 214 The Mystery of the Trinity: The Human Being in Relationship with the Spiritual World in the Course of Time

CW 215 Philosophy, Cosmology, and Religion in Anthroposophy

CW 216 The Fundamental Impulses of the World-Historical Development of Humanity

CW 217 Spiritually Active Forces in the Coexistence of the Older and Younger Generations. Pedagogical Course for Youth

CW 217a	Youth's Cognitive Task
CW 218	Spiritual Connections in the Forming of the Human Organism
CW 219	The Relationship of the World of the Stars to the Human Being, and of the Human Being to the World of the Stars. The Spiritual Communion of Humanity
CW 220	Living Knowledge of Nature. Intellectual Fall and Spiritual Redemption
CW 221	Earth-Knowing and Heaven-Insight
CW 222	The Imparting of Impulses to World-Historical Events through Spiritual Powers
CW 223	The Cycle of the Year as Breathing Process of the Earth and the Four Great Festival-Seasons. Anthroposophy and the Human Heart (Gemüt)
CW 224	The Human Soul and its Connection with Divine-Spiritual Individualities. The Internalization of the Festivals of the Year
CW 225	Three Perspectives of Anthroposophy. Cultural Phenomena observed from a Spiritual-Scientific Perspective
CW 226	Human Being, Human Destiny, and World Development
CW 227	Initiation-Knowledge
CW 228	Science of Initiation and Knowledge of the Stars. The Human Being in the Past, the Present, and the Future from the Viewpoint of the Development of Consciousness
CW 229	The Experiencing of the Course of the Year in Four Cosmic Imaginations
CW 230	The Human Being as Harmony of the Creative, Building, and Formative World-Word
CW 231	The Supersensible Human Being, Understood Anthroposophically
CW 232	The Forming of the Mysteries
CW 233	World History Illuminated by Anthroposophy and as the Foundation for Knowledge of the Human Spirit
CW 233a	Mystery Sites of the Middle Ages: Rosicrucianism and the Modern Initiation-Principle. The Festival of Easter as Part of the History of the Mysteries of Humanity
CW 234	Anthroposophy. A Summary after 21 Years
CW 235	Esoteric Observations of Karmic Relationships in 6 Volumes, Vol. 1
CW 236	Esoteric Observations of Karmic Relationships in 6 Volumes, Vol. 2
CW 237	Esoteric Observations of Karmic Relationships in 6 Volumes, Vol. 3: The Karmic Relationships of the Anthroposophical Movement
CW 238	Esoteric Observations of Karmic Relationships in 6 Volumes, Vol. 4: The Spiritual Life of the Present in Relationship to the Anthroposophical Movement
CW 239	Esoteric Observations of Karmic Relationships in 6 Volumes, Vol. 5

CW 240	Esoteric Observations of Karmic Relationships in 6 Volumes, Vol. 6
CW 243	The Consciousness of the Initiate
CW 245	Instructions for an Esoteric Schooling
CW 250	The Building-Up of the Anthroposophical Society. From the Beginning to the Outbreak of the First World War
CW 251	The History of the Goetheanum Building-Association
CW 252	Life in the Anthroposophical Society from the First World War to the Burning of the First Goetheanum
CW 253	The Problems of Living Together in the Anthroposophical Society. On the Dornach Crisis of 1915. With Highlights on Swedenborg's Clairvoyance, the Views of Freudian Psychoanalysts, and the Concept of Love in Relation to Mysticism
CW 254	The Occult Movement in the 19th Century and Its Relationship to World Culture. Significant Points from the Exoteric Cultural Life around the Middle of the 19th Century
CW 255	Rudolf Steiner during the First World War
CW 255a	Anthroposophy and the Reformation of Society. On the History of the Threefold Movement
CW 255b	Anthroposophy and Its Opponents, 1919–1921
CW 256	How Can the Anthroposophical Movement Be Financed?
CW 256a	Futurum, Inc. / International Laboratories, Inc.
CW 256b	The Coming Day, Inc.
CW 257	Anthroposophical Community-Building
CW 258	The History of and Conditions for the Anthroposophical Movement in Relationship to the Anthroposophical Society. A Stimulus to Self-Contemplation
CW 259	The Year of Destiny 1923 in the History of the Anthroposophical Society. From the Burning of the Goetheanum to the Christmas Conference
CW 260	The Christmas Conference for the Founding of the General Anthroposophical Society
CW 260a	The Constitution of the General Anthroposophical Society and the School for Spiritual Science. The Rebuilding of the Goetheanum
CW 261	Our Dead. Addresses, Words of Remembrance, and Meditative Verses, 1906–1924
CW 262	Rudolf Steiner and Marie Steiner-von Sivers: Correspondence and Documents, 1901–1925
CW 263/1	Rudolf Steiner and Edith Maryon: Correspondence: Letters, Verses, Sketches, 1912–1924
CW 264	On the History and the Contents of the First Section of the Esoteric School from 1904 to 1914. Letters, Newsletters, Documents, Lectures
CW 265	On the History and from the Contents of the Ritual-Knowledge Section of the Esoteric School from 1904 to 1914. Documents, and Lectures from the Years 1906 to 1914, as well as on New Approaches to Ritual-Knowledge Work in the Years 1921–1924

CW 266/1	From the Contents of the Esoteric Lessons. Volume 1: 1904–1909. Notes from Memory of Participants. Meditation texts from the notes of Rudolf Steiner
CW 266/2	From the Contents of the Esoteric Lessons. Volume 2: 1910–1912. Notes from Memory of Participants
CW 266/3	From the Contents of the Esoteric Lessons. Volume 3: 1913, 1914 and 1920–1923. Notes from Memory of Participants. Meditation texts from the notes of Rudolf Steiner
CW 267	Soul-Exercises: Vol. 1: Exercises with Word and Image Meditations for the Methodological Development of Higher Powers of Knowledge, 1904–1924
CW 268	Soul-Exercises: Vol. 2: Mantric Verses, 1903–1925
CW 269	Ritual Texts for the Celebration of the Free Christian Religious Instruction. The Collected Verses for Teachers and Students of the Waldorf School
CW 270	Esoteric Instructions for the First Class of the School for Spiritual Science at the Goetheanum 1924, 4 Volumes
CW 271	Art and Knowledge of Art. Foundations of a New Aesthetic
CW 272	Spiritual-Scientific Commentary on Goethe's 'Faust' in Two Volumes. Vol. 1: Faust, the Striving Human Being
CW 273	Spiritual-Scientific Commentary on Goethe's 'Faust' in Two Volumes. Vol. 2: The Faust-Problem
CW 274	Addresses for the Christmas Plays from the Old Folk Traditions
CW 275	Art in the Light of Mystery-Wisdom
CW 276	The Artistic in Its Mission in the World. The Genius of Language. The World of Self-Revealing Radiant Appearances—Anthroposophy and Art. Anthroposophy and Poetry
CW 277	Eurythmy. The Revelation of the Speaking Soul
CW 277a	The Origin and Development of Eurythmy
CW 278	Eurythmy as Visible Song
CW 279	Eurythmy as Visible Speech
CW 280	The Method and Nature of Speech Formation
CW 281	The Art of Recitation and Declamation
CW 282	Speech Formation and Dramatic Art
CW 283	The Nature of Things Musical and the Experience of Tone in the Human Being
CW 284/285	Images of Occult Seals and Pillars. The Munich Congress of Whitsun 1907 and Its Consequences
CW 286	Paths to a New Style of Architecture. 'And the Building Becomes Human'
CW 287	The Building at Dornach as a Symbol of Historical Becoming and an Artistic Transformation Impulse
CW 288	Style-Forms in the Living Organic
CW 289	The Building-Idea of the Goetheanum: Lectures with Slides from the Years 1920–1921
CW 290	The Building-Idea of the Goetheanum: Lectures with Slides from the Years 1920–1921

CW 291	The Nature of Colours
CW 291a	Knowledge of Colours. Supplementary Volume to 'The Nature of Colours'
CW 292	Art History as Image of Inner Spiritual Impulses
CW 293	General Knowledge of the Human Being as the Foundation of Pedagogy
CW 294	The Art of Education, Methodology and Didactics
CW 295	The Art of Education: Seminar Discussions and Lectures on Lesson Planning
CW 296	The Question of Education as a Social Question
CW 297	The Idea and Practice of the Waldorf School
CW 297a	Education for Life: Self-Education and the Practice of Pedagogy
CW 298	Rudolf Steiner in the Waldorf School
CW 299	Spiritual-Scientific Observations on Speech
CW 300a	Conferences with the Teachers of the Free Waldorf School in Stuttgart, 1919 to 1924, in 3 Volumes, Vol. 1
CW 300b	Conferences with the Teachers of the Free Waldorf School in Stuttgart, 1919 to 1924, in 3 Volumes, Vol. 2
CW 300c	Conferences with the Teachers of the Free Waldorf School in Stuttgart, 1919 to 1924, in 3 Volumes, Vol. 3
CW 301	The Renewal of Pedagogical-Didactical Art through Spiritual Science
CW 302	Knowledge of the Human Being and the Forming of Class Lessons
CW 302a	Education and Teaching from a Knowledge of the Human Being
CW 303	The Healthy Development of the Human Being
CW 304	Methods of Education and Teaching Based on Anthroposophy
CW 304a	Anthroposophical Knowledge of the Human Being and Pedagogy
CW 305	The Soul-Spiritual Foundational Forces of the Art of Education. Spiritual Values in Education and Social Life
CW 306	Pedagogical Praxis from the Viewpoint of a Spiritual-Scientific Knowledge of the Human Being. The Education of the Child and Young Human Beings
CW 307	The Spiritual Life of the Present and Education
CW 308	The Method of Teaching and the Life-Requirements for Teaching
CW 309	Anthroposophical Pedagogy and Its Prerequisites
CW 310	The Pedagogical Value of a Knowledge of the Human Being and the Cultural Value of Pedagogy
CW 311	The Art of Education from an Understanding of the Being of Humanity
CW 312	Spiritual Science and Medicine
CW 313	Spiritual-Scientific Viewpoints on Therapy
CW 314	Physiology and Therapy Based on Spiritual Science
CW 315	Curative Eurythmy
CW 316	Meditative Observations and Instructions for a Deepening of the Art of Healing
CW 317	The Curative Education Course

CW 318	The Working Together of Doctors and Pastors
CW 319	Anthroposophical Knowledge of the Human Being and Medicine
CW 320	Spiritual-Scientific Impulses for the Development of Physics 1: The First Natural-Scientific Course: Light, Colour, Tone, Mass, Electricity, Magnetism
CW 321	Spiritual-Scientific Impulses for the Development of Physics 2: The Second Natural-Scientific Course: Warmth at the Border of Positive and Negative Materiality
CW 322	The Borders of the Knowledge of Nature
CW 323	The Relationship of the various Natural-Scientific Fields to Astronomy
CW 324	Nature Observation, Mathematics, and Scientific Experimentation and Results from the Viewpoint of Anthroposophy
CW 324a	The Fourth Dimension in Mathematics and Reality
CW 325	Natural Science and the World-Historical Development of Humanity since Ancient Times
CW 326	The Moment of the Coming Into Being of Natural Science in World History and Its Development Since Then
CW 327	Spiritual-Scientific Foundations for Success in Farming. The Agricultural Course
CW 328	The Social Question
CW 329	The Liberation of the Human Being as the Foundation for a New Social Form
CW 330	The Renewal of the Social Organism
CW 331	Work-Council and Socialization
CW 332	The Alliance for Threefolding and the Total Reform of Society. The Council on Culture and the Liberation of the Spiritual Life
CW 332a	The Social Future
CW 333	Freedom of Thought and Social Forces
CW 334	From the Unified State to the Threefold Social Organism
CW 335	The Crisis of the Present and the Path to Healthy Thinking
CW 336	The Great Questions of the Times and Anthroposophical Spiritual Knowledge
CW 337a	Social Ideas, Social Reality, Social Practice, Vol. 1: Question-and-Answer Evenings and Study Evenings of the Alliance for the Threefold Social Organism in Stuttgart, 1919–1920
CW 337b	Social Ideas, Social Realities, Social Practice, Vol. 2: Discussion Evenings of the Swiss Alliance for the Threefold Social Organism
CW 338	How Does One Work on Behalf of the Impulse for the Threefold Social Organism?
CW 339	Anthroposophy, Threefold Social Organism, and the Art of Public Speaking
CW 340	The National-Economics Course. The Tasks of a New Science of Economics, Volume 1
CW 341	The National-Economics Seminar. The Tasks of a New Science of Economics, Volume 2

CW 342	Lectures and Courses on Christian Religious Work, Vol. 1: Anthroposophical Foundations for a Renewed Christian Religious Working
CW 343	Lectures and Courses on Christian Religious Work, Vol. 2: Spiritual Knowledge—Religious Feeling—Cultic Doing
CW 344	Lectures and Courses on Christian Religious Work, Vol. 3: Lectures at the Founding of the Christian Community
CW 345	Lectures and Courses on Christian Religious Work, Vol. 4: Concerning the Nature of the Working Word
CW 346	Lectures and Courses on Christian Religious Work, Vol. 5: The Apocalypse and the Work of the Priest
CW 347	The Knowledge of the Nature of the Human Being According to Body, Soul and Spirit. On Earlier Conditions of the Earth
CW 348	On Health and Illness. Foundations of a Spiritual-Scientific Doctrine of the Senses
CW 349	On the Life of the Human Being and of the Earth. On the Nature of Christianity
CW 350	Rhythms in the Cosmos and in the Human Being. How Does One Come To See the Spiritual World?
CW 351	The Human Being and the World. The Influence of the Spirit in Nature. On the Nature of Bees
CW 352	Nature and the Human Being Observed Spiritual-Scientifically
CW 353	The History of Humanity and the World-Views of the Folk Cultures
CW 354	The Creation of the World and the Human Being. Life on Earth and the Influence of the Stars

SIGNIFICANT EVENTS IN THE LIFE OF RUDOLF STEINER

1829: June 23: birth of Johann Steiner (1829–1910)—Rudolf Steiner's father—in Geras, Lower Austria.

1834: May 8: birth of Franciska Blie (1834–1918)—Rudolf Steiner's mother—in Horn, Lower Austria. 'My father and mother were both children of the glorious Lower Austrian forest district north of the Danube.'

1860: May 16: marriage of Johann Steiner and Franciska Blie.

1861: February 25: birth of *Rudolf Joseph Lorenz Steiner* in Kraljevec, Croatia, near the border with Hungary, where Johann Steiner works as a telegrapher for the South Austria Railroad. Rudolf Steiner is baptized two days later, February 27, the date usually given as his birthday.

1862: Summer: the family moves to Mödling, Lower Austria.

1863: The family moves to Pottschach, Lower Austria, near the Styrian border, where Johann Steiner becomes stationmaster. 'The view stretched to the mountains ... majestic peaks in the distance and the sweet charm of nature in the immediate surroundings.'

1864: November 15: birth of Rudolf Steiner's sister, Leopoldine (d. November 1, 1927). She will become a seamstress and live with her parents for the rest of her life.

1866: July 28: birth of Rudolf Steiner's deaf-mute brother, Gustav (d. May 1, 1941).

1867: Rudolf Steiner enters the village school. Following a disagreement between his father and the schoolmaster, whose wife falsely accused the boy of causing a commotion, Rudolf Steiner is taken out of school and taught at home.

1868: A critical experience. Unknown to the family, an aunt dies in a distant town. Sitting in the station waiting room, Rudolf Steiner sees her 'form,' which speaks to him, asking for help. 'Beginning with this experience, a new soul life began in the boy, one in which not only the outer trees and mountains spoke to him, but also the worlds that lay behind them. From this moment on, the boy began to live with the spirits of nature...'

1869: The family moves to the peaceful, rural village of Neudörfl, near Wiener-Neustadt in present-day Austria. Rudolf Steiner attends the village school. Because of the 'unorthodoxy' of his writing and spelling, he has to do 'extra lessons.'

1870: Through a book lent to him by his tutor, he discovers geometry: 'To grasp something purely in the spirit brought me inner happiness. I know that I first learned happiness through geometry.' The same tutor allows him to draw, while other students still struggle with their reading and writing. 'An artistic element' thus enters his education.

1871: Though his parents are not religious, Rudolf Steiner becomes a 'church child,' a favourite of the priest, who was 'an exceptional character.' 'Up to the age of ten or eleven, among those I came to know, he was far and away the most significant.' Among other things, he introduces Steiner to Copernican, heliocentric cosmology. As an altar boy, Rudolf Steiner serves at Masses, funerals, and Corpus Christi processions. At year's end, after an incident in which he escapes a thrashing, his father forbids him to go to church.

1872: Rudolf Steiner transfers to grammar school in Wiener-Neustadt, a five-mile walk from home, which must be done in all weathers.

1873–75: Through his teachers and on his own, Rudolf Steiner has many wonderful experiences with science and mathematics. Outside school, he teaches himself analytic geometry, trigonometry, differential equations, and calculus.

1876: Rudolf Steiner begins tutoring other students. He learns bookbinding from his father. He also teaches himself stenography.

1877: Rudolf Steiner discovers Kant's *Critique of Pure Reason*, which he reads and rereads. He also discovers and reads von Rotteck's *World History*.

1878: He studies extensively in contemporary psychology and philosophy.

1879: Rudolf Steiner graduates from high school with honours. His father is transferred to Inzersdorf, near Vienna. He uses his first visit to Vienna 'to purchase a great number of philosophy books'—Kant, Fichte, Schelling, and Hegel, as well as numerous histories of philosophy. His aim: to find a path from the 'I' to nature.

October 1879–1883: Rudolf Steiner attends the Technical College in Vienna—to study mathematics, chemistry, physics, mineralogy, botany, zoology, biology, geology, and mechanics—with a scholarship. He also attends lectures in history and literature, while avidly reading philosophy on his own. His two favourite professors are Karl Julius Schröer (German language and literature) and Edmund Reitlinger (physics). He also audits lectures by Robert Zimmermann on aesthetics and Franz Brentano on philosophy. During this year he begins his friendship with Moritz Zitter (1861–1921), who will help support him financially when he is in Berlin.

1880: Rudolf Steiner attends lectures on Schiller and Goethe by Karl Julius Schröer, who becomes his mentor. Also 'through a remarkable combination of circumstances,' he meets Felix Koguzki, a 'herb gatherer' and healer, who could 'see deeply into the secrets of nature.' Rudolf Steiner will meet and study with this 'emissary of the Master' throughout his time in Vienna.

1881: January: '... I didn't sleep a wink. I was busy with philosophical problems until about 12:30 a.m. Then, finally, I threw myself down on my couch. All my striving during the previous year had been to research whether the following statement by Schelling was true or not: *Within everyone dwells a secret, marvelous capacity to draw back from the stream of time—out of the self clothed in all that comes to us from outside—into our innermost being and there, in the immutable form of the Eternal, to look into ourselves*. I believe, and I am still quite certain of it, that I discovered this capacity in myself; I had long had an inkling of it. Now the whole of idealist philosophy stood before me in modified form. What's a sleepless night compared to that!'

Rudolf Steiner begins communicating with leading thinkers of the day, who send him books in return, which he reads eagerly.

July: 'I am not one of those who dives into the day like an animal in human form. I pursue a quite specific goal, an idealistic aim—knowledge of the truth! This cannot be done offhandedly. It requires the greatest striving in the world, free of all egotism, and equally of all resignation.'

August: Steiner puts down on paper for the first time thoughts for a 'Philosophy of Freedom.' 'The striving for the absolute: this human yearning is freedom.' He also seeks to outline a 'peasant philosophy,' describing what the worldview of a 'peasant'—one who lives close to the earth and the old ways—really is.

1881–1882: Felix Koguzki, the herb gatherer, reveals himself to be the envoy of another, higher initiatory personality, who instructs Rudolf Steiner to penetrate Fichte's philosophy and to master modern scientific thinking as a preparation for right entry into the spirit. This 'Master' also teaches him the double (evolutionary and involutionary) nature of time.

1882: Through the offices of Karl Julius Schröer, Rudolf Steiner is asked by Joseph Kürschner to edit Goethe's scientific works for the *Deutschen National-Literatur* edition. He writes 'A Possible Critique of Atomistic Concepts' and sends it to Friedrich Theodor Vischer.

1883: Rudolf Steiner completes his college studies and begins work on the Goethe project.

1884: First volume of Goethe's *Scientific Writings* (CW 1) appears (March). He lectures on Goethe and Lessing, and Goethe's approach to science. In July, he enters the household of Ladislaus and Pauline Specht as tutor to the four Specht boys. He will live there until 1890. At this time, he meets Josef Breuer (1842–1925), the co-author with Sigmund Freud of *Studies in Hysteria*, who is the Specht family doctor.

1885: While continuing to edit Goethe's writings, Rudolf Steiner reads deeply in contemporary philosophy (Eduard von Hartmann, Johannes Volkelt, and Richard Wahle, among others).

1886: May: Rudolf Steiner sends Kürschner the manuscript of *Outlines of Goethe's Theory of Knowledge* (CW 2), which appears in October, and which he sends out widely. He also meets the poet Marie Eugenie Delle Grazie and writes 'Nature and Our Ideals' for her. He attends her salon, where he meets many priests, theologians, and philosophers, who will become his friends. Meanwhile, the director of the Goethe Archive in Weimar requests his collaboration with the *Sophien* edition of Goethe's works, particularly the writings on colour.

1887: At the beginning of the year, Rudolf Steiner is very sick. As the year progresses and his health improves, he becomes increasingly 'a man of letters,' lecturing, writing essays, and taking part in Austrian cultural life. In August–September, the second volume of Goethe's *Scientific Writings* appears.

1888: January–July: Rudolf Steiner assumes editorship of the 'German Weekly' (*Deutsche Wochenschrift*). He begins lecturing more intensively, giving, for example, a lecture titled 'Goethe as Father of a New Aesthetics.' He meets and becomes soul friends with Friedrich Eckstein (1861–1939), a vegetarian, philosopher of symbolism, alchemist, and musician, who will introduce him to various spiritual currents (including Theosophy) and with whom he will meditate and interpret esoteric and alchemical texts.

1889: Rudolf Steiner first reads Nietzsche (*Beyond Good and Evil*). He encounters Theosophy again and learns of Madame Blavatsky in the Theosophical circle around Marie Lang (1858–1934). Here he also meets well-known figures of Austrian life, as well as esoteric figures like the occultist Franz Hartmann and Karl Leinigen-Billigen (translator of C.G. Harrison's *The Transcendental Universe*). During this period, Steiner first reads A.P. Sinnett's *Esoteric Buddhism* and Mabel Collins's *Light on the Path*. He also begins travelling, visiting Budapest, Weimar, and Berlin (where he meets philosopher Eduard von Hartmann).

1890: Rudolf Steiner finishes volume 3 of Goethe's scientific writings. He begins his doctoral dissertation, which will become *Truth and Science* (CW 3). He also meets the poet and feminist Rosa Mayreder (1858–1938), with whom he can exchange his most intimate thoughts. In September, Rudolf Steiner moves to Weimar to work in the Goethe-Schiller Archive.

1891: Volume 3 of the Kürschner edition of Goethe appears. Meanwhile, Rudolf Steiner edits Goethe's studies in mineralogy and scientific writings for the *Sophien* edition. He meets Ludwig Laistner of the Cotta Publishing Company, who asks for a book on the basic question of metaphysics. From this will result, ultimately, *The Philosophy of Freedom* (CW 4), which will be published not by Cotta but by Emil Felber. In October, Rudolf Steiner takes the oral exam for a doctorate in philosophy, mathematics, and mechanics at Rostock University, receiving his doctorate on the twenty-sixth. In November, he gives his first lecture on Goethe's 'Fairy Tale' in Vienna.

1892: Rudolf Steiner continues work at the Goethe-Schiller Archive and on his *Philosophy of Freedom*. *Truth and Science*, his doctoral dissertation, is published. Steiner undertakes to write introductions to books on Schopenhauer and Jean Paul for Cotta. At year's end, he finds lodging with Anna Eunike, née Schulz (1853–1911), a widow with four daughters and a son. He also develops a friendship with Otto Erich Hartleben (1864–1905) with whom he shares literary interests.

1893: Rudolf Steiner begins his habit of producing many reviews and articles. In March, he gives a lecture titled 'Hypnotism, with Reference to Spiritism.' In September, volume 4 of the Kürschner edition is completed. In November, *The Philosophy of Freedom* appears. This year, too, he meets John Henry Mackay (1864–1933), the anarchist, and Max Stirner, a scholar and biographer.

1894: Rudolf Steiner meets Elisabeth Förster Nietzsche, the philosopher's sister, and begins to read Nietzsche in earnest, beginning with the as yet unpublished *Antichrist*. He also meets Ernst Haeckel (1834–1919). In the fall, he begins to write *Nietzsche, A Fighter against His Time* (CW 5).

1895: May, *Nietzsche, A Fighter against His Time* appears.

1896: January 22: Rudolf Steiner sees Friedrich Nietzsche for the first and only time. Moves between the Nietzsche and the Goethe-Schiller Archives, where he completes his work before year's end. He falls out with Elisabeth Förster Nietzsche, thus ending his association with the Nietzsche Archive.

1897: Rudolf Steiner finishes the manuscript of *Goethe's Worldview* (CW 6). He moves to Berlin with Anna Eunike and begins editorship of the *Magazin für Literatur*. From now on, Steiner will write countless reviews, literary and philosophical articles, and so on. He begins lecturing at the 'Free Literary Society.' In September, he attends the Zionist Congress in Basel. He sides with Dreyfus in the Dreyfus affair.

1898: Rudolf Steiner is very active as an editor in the political, artistic, and theatrical life of Berlin. He becomes friendly with John Henry Mackay and poet Ludwig Jacobowski (1868–1900). He joins Jacobowski's circle of writers, artists, and scientists—'The Coming Ones' (*Die Kommenden*)—and contributes lectures to the group until 1903. He also lectures at the 'League for College Pedagogy.' He writes an article for Goethe's sesquicentennial, 'Goethe's Secret Revelation,' on the 'Fairy Tale of the Green Snake and the Beautiful Lily.'

1898–99: 'This was a trying time for my soul as I looked at Christianity. . . . I was able to progress only by contemplating, by means of spiritual perception, the evolution of Christianity. . . . Conscious knowledge of real Christianity began to dawn in me around the turn of the century. This seed continued to develop. My soul trial occurred shortly before the beginning of the twentieth century. It was decisive for my soul's development that I stood spiritually before the Mystery of Golgotha in a deep and solemn celebration of knowledge.'

1899: Rudolf Steiner begins teaching and giving lectures and lecture cycles at the Workers' College, founded by Wilhelm Liebknecht (1826–1900). He will continue to do so until 1904. Writes: *Literature and Spiritual Life in the Nineteenth Century; Individualism in Philosophy*; *Haeckel and His Opponents; Poetry in the Present;* and begins what will become (fifteen years later) *The Riddles of Philosophy* (CW 18). He also meets many artists and writers, including Käthe Kollwitz, Stefan Zweig, and Rainer Maria Rilke. On October 31, he marries Anna Eunike.

1900: 'I thought that the turn of the century must bring humanity a new light. It seemed to me that the separation of human thinking and willing from the spirit had peaked. A turn or reversal of direction in human evolution seemed to me a necessity.' Rudolf Steiner finishes *World and Life Views in the Nineteenth Century* (the second part of what will become *The Riddles of Philosophy*) and dedicates it to Ernst Haeckel. It is published in March. He continues lecturing at *Die Kommenden*, whose leadership he assumes after the death of Jacobowski. Also, he gives the Gutenberg Jubilee lecture before 7,000 typesetters and printers. In September, Rudolf Steiner is invited by Count and Countess Brockdorff to lecture in the Theosophical Library. His first lecture is on Nietzsche. His second lecture is titled 'Goethe's Secret Revelation.' October 6, he begins a lecture cycle on the mystics that will become *Mystics after Modernism* (CW 7). November-December: 'Marie von Sivers appears in the audience....' Also in November, Steiner gives his first lecture at the Giordano Bruno Bund (where he will continue to lecture until May, 1905). He speaks on Bruno and modern Rome, focusing on the importance of the philosophy of Thomas Aquinas as monism.

1901: In continual financial straits, Rudolf Steiner's early friends Moritz Zitter and Rosa Mayreder help support him. In October, he begins the lecture cycle *Christianity as Mystical Fact* (CW 8) at the Theosophical Library. In November, he gives his first 'Theosophical lecture' on Goethe's 'Fairy Tale' in Hamburg at the invitation of Wilhelm Hubbe-Schleiden. He also attends a gathering to celebrate the founding of the Theosophical Society at Count and Countess Brockdorff's. He gives a lecture cycle, 'From Buddha to Christ,' for the circle of the *Kommenden*. November 17, Marie von Sivers asks Rudolf Steiner if Theosophy needs a Western-Christian spiritual movement (to complement Theosophy's Eastern emphasis). 'The question was posed. Now, following spiritual laws, I could begin to give an answer....' In December, Rudolf Steiner writes his first article for a Theosophical publication. At year's end, the Brockdorffs and possibly Wilhelm Hubbe-Schleiden ask Rudolf Steiner to join the Theosophical Society and undertake the leadership of the German section. Rudolf Steiner agrees, on the condition that Marie von Sivers (then in Italy) work with him.

1902: Beginning in January, Rudolf Steiner attends the opening of the Workers' School in Spandau with Rosa Luxemberg (1870–1919). January 17, Rudolf Steiner joins the Theosophical Society. In April, he is asked to become general secretary of the German Section of the Theosophical Society, and works on preparations for its founding. In July, he visits London for a Theosophical congress. He meets Bertram Keightly, G.R.S. Mead, A.P. Sinnett, and Annie Besant, among others. In September, *Christianity as Mystical Fact* appears. In October, Rudolf Steiner gives his first public lecture on Theosophy ('Monism and Theosophy') to about three hundred people at the Giordano Bruno Bund. On October 19–21, the German Section of the Theosophical Society has its first meeting; Rudolf Steiner is the general secretary, and Annie Besant attends. Steiner lectures on practical karma studies. On October 23, Annie Besant inducts Rudolf Steiner into the Esoteric School of the Theosophical Society. On October 25, Steiner begins a weekly series of lectures: 'The Field of Theosophy.' During this year, Rudolf Steiner also first meets Ita Wegman (1876–1943), who will become his close collaborator in his final years.

1903: Rudolf Steiner holds about 300 lectures and seminars. In May, the first issue of the periodical *Luzifer* appears. In June, Rudolf Steiner visits

London for the first meeting of the Federation of the European Sections of the Theosophical Society, where he meets Colonel Olcott. He begins to write *Theosophy* (CW 9).

1904: Rudolf Steiner continues lecturing at the Workers' College and elsewhere (about 90 lectures), while lecturing intensively all over Germany among Theosophists (about 140 lectures). In February, he meets Carl Unger (1878–1929), who will become a member of the board of the Anthroposophical Society (1913). In March, he meets Michael Bauer (1871–1929), a Christian mystic, who will also be on the board. In May, *Theosophy* appears, with the dedication: 'To the spirit of Giordano Bruno.' Rudolf Steiner and Marie von Sivers visit London for meetings with Annie Besant. June: Rudolf Steiner and Marie von Sivers attend the meeting of the Federation of European Sections of the Theosophical Society in Amsterdam. In July, Steiner begins the articles in *Luzifer-Gnosis* that will become *How to Know Higher Worlds* (CW 10) and *Cosmic Memory* (CW 11). In September, Annie Besant visits Germany. In December, Steiner lectures on Freemasonry. He mentions the High Grade Masonry derived from John Yarker and represented by Theodore Reuss and Karl Kellner as a blank slate 'into which a good image could be placed.'

1905: This year, Steiner ends his non-Theosophical lecturing activity. Supported by Marie von Sivers, his Theosophical lecturing—both in public and in the Theosophical Society—increases significantly: 'The German Theosophical Movement is of exceptional importance.' Steiner recommends reading, among others, Fichte, Jacob Boehme, and Angelus Silesius. He begins to introduce Christian themes into Theosophy. He also begins to work with doctors (Felix Peipers and Ludwig Noll). In July, he is in London for the Federation of European Sections, where he attends a lecture by Annie Besant: 'I have seldom seen Mrs. Besant speak in so inward and heartfelt a manner....' 'Through Mrs. Besant I have found the way to H.P. Blavatsky.' September to October, he gives a course of thirty-one lectures for a small group of esoteric students. In October, the annual meeting of the German Section of the Theosophical Society, which still remains very small, takes place. Rudolf Steiner reports membership has risen from 121 to 377 members. In November, seeking to establish esoteric 'continuity,' Rudolf Steiner and Marie von Sivers participate in a 'Memphis-Misraim' Masonic ceremony. They pay forty-five marks for membership. 'Yesterday, you saw how little remains of former esoteric institutions.' 'We are dealing only with a "framework"... for the present, nothing lies behind it. The occult powers have completely withdrawn.'

1906: Expansion of Theosophical work. Rudolf Steiner gives about 245 lectures, only 44 of which take place in Berlin. Cycles are given in Paris, Leipzig, Stuttgart, and Munich. Esoteric work also intensifies. Rudolf Steiner begins writing *An Outline of Esoteric Science* (CW 13). In January, Rudolf Steiner receives permission (a patent) from the Great Orient of the Scottish A & A Thirty-Three Degree Rite of the Order of the Ancient

Freemasons of the Memphis-Misraim Rite to direct a chapter under the name 'Mystica Aeterna.' This will become the 'Cognitive-Ritual Section' (also called 'Misraim Service') of the Esoteric School. (See: *Freemasonry and Ritual Work: The Misraim Service*, CW 265). During this time, Steiner also meets Albert Schweitzer. In May, he is in Paris, where he visits Edouard Schuré. Many Russians attend his lectures (including Konstantin Balmont, Dimitri Mereszkovski, Zinaida Hippius, and Maximilian Woloshin). He attends the General Meeting of the European Federation of the Theosophical Society, at which Col. Olcott is present for the last time. He spends the year's end in Venice and Rome, where he writes and works on his translation of H.P. Blavatsky's *Key to Theosophy*.

1907: Further expansion of the German Theosophical Movement according to the Rosicrucian directive to 'introduce spirit into the world'—in education, in social questions, in art, and in science. In February, Col. Olcott dies in Adyar. Before he dies, Olcott indicates that 'the Masters' wish Annie Besant to succeed him: much politicking ensues. Rudolf Steiner supports Besant's candidacy. April-May: preparations for the Congress of the Federation of European Sections of the Theosophical Society—the great, watershed Whitsun 'Munich Congress,' attended by Annie Besant and others. Steiner decides to separate Eastern and Western (Christian-Rosicrucian) esoteric schools. He takes his esoteric school out of the Theosophical Society (Besant and Rudolf Steiner are 'in harmony' on this). Steiner makes his first lecture tours to Austria and Hungary. That summer, he is in Italy. In September, he visits Edouard Schuré, who will write the introduction to the French edition of *Christianity as Mystical Fact* in Barr, Alsace. Rudolf Steiner writes the autobiographical statement known as the 'Barr Document.' In *Luzifer-Gnosis*, 'The Education of the Child' appears.

1908: The movement grows (membership: 1,150). Lecturing expands. Steiner makes his first extended lecture tour to Holland and Scandinavia, as well as visits to Naples and Sicily. Themes: St. John's Gospel, the Apocalypse, Egypt, science, philosophy, and logic. *Luzifer-Gnosis* ceases publication. In Berlin, Marie von Sivers (with Johanna Mücke (1864–1949) forms the *Philosophisch-Theosophisch* (after 1915 *Philosophisch-Anthroposophisch*) *Verlag* to publish Steiner's work. Steiner gives lecture cycles titled *The Gospel of St. John* (CW 103) and *The Apocalypse* (104).

1909: *An Outline of Esoteric Science* appears. Lecturing and travel continues. Rudolf Steiner's spiritual research expands to include the polarity of Lucifer and Ahriman; the work of great individualities in history; the Maitreya Buddha and the Bodhisattvas; spiritual economy (CW 109); the work of the spiritual hierarchies in heaven and on earth (CW 110). He also deepens and intensifies his research into the Gospels, giving lectures on the Gospel of St. Luke (CW 114) with the first mention of two Jesus children. Meets and becomes friends with Christian Morgenstern (1871–1914). In April, he lays the foundation stone for the Malsch model—the building that will lead to the first Goetheanum. In May, the International Congress of the Federation of European Sections of the

Theosophical Society takes place in Budapest. Rudolf Steiner receives the Subba Row medal for *How to Know Higher Worlds*. During this time, Charles W. Leadbeater discovers Jiddu Krishnamurti (1895–1986) and proclaims him the future 'world teacher,' the bearer of the Maitreya Buddha and the 'reappearing Christ.' In October, Steiner delivers seminal lectures on 'anthroposophy,' which he will try, unsuccessfully, to rework over the next years into the unfinished work, *Anthroposophy (A Fragment)* (CW 45).

1910: New themes: *The Reappearance of Christ in the Etheric* (CW 118); *The Fifth Gospel; The Mission of Folk Souls* (CW 121); *Occult History* (CW 126); the evolving development of etheric cognitive capacities. Rudolf Steiner continues his Gospel research with *The Gospel of St. Matthew* (CW 123). In January, his father dies. In April, he takes a month-long trip to Italy, including Rome, Monte Cassino, and Sicily. He also visits Scandinavia again. July–August, he writes the first mystery drama, *The Portal of Initiation* (CW 14). In November, he gives 'psychosophy' lectures. In December, he submits 'On the Psychological Foundations and Epistemological Framework of Theosophy' to the International Philosophical Congress in Bologna.

1911: The crisis in the Theosophical Society deepens. In January, 'The Order of the Rising Sun,' which will soon become 'The Order of the Star in the East,' is founded for the coming world teacher, Krishnamurti. At the same time, Marie von Sivers, Rudolf Steiner's co-worker, falls ill. Fewer lectures are given, but important new ground is broken. In Prague, in March, Steiner meets Franz Kafka (1883–1924) and Hugo Bergmann (1883-1975). In April, he delivers his paper to the Philosophical Congress. He writes the second mystery drama, *The Soul's Probation* (CW 14). Also, while Marie von Sivers is convalescing, Rudolf Steiner begins work on *Calendar 1912/1913*, which will contain the 'Calendar of the Soul' meditations. On March 19, Anna (Eunike) Steiner dies. In September, Rudolf Steiner visits Einsiedeln, birthplace of Paracelsus. In December, Friedrich Rittelmeyer, future founder of the Christian Community, meets Rudolf Steiner. The *Johannes-Bauverein*, the 'building committee,' which would lead to the first Goetheanum (first planned for Munich), is also founded, and a preliminary committee for the founding of an independent association is created that, in the following year, will become the Anthroposophical Society. Important lecture cycles include *Occult Physiology* (CW 128); *Wonders of the World* (CW 129); *From Jesus to Christ* (CW 131). Other themes: esoteric Christianity; Christian Rosenkreutz; the spiritual guidance of humanity; the sense world and the world of the spirit.

1912: Despite the ongoing, now increasing crisis in the Theosophical Society, much is accomplished: *Calendar 1912/1913* is published; eurythmy is created; both the third mystery drama, *The Guardian of the Threshold* (CW 14) and *A Way of Self-Knowledge* (CW 16) are written. New (or renewed) themes included life between death and rebirth and karma and reincarnation. Other lecture cycles: *Spiritual Beings in the Heavenly Bodies and in the Kingdoms of Nature* (CW 136); *The Human Being in the Light of Occultism, Theosophy, and Philosophy* (CW 137); *The Gospel of St. Mark* (CW 139); and *The Bhagavad Gita and the Epistles of Paul* (CW 142). On May 8, Rudolf Steiner celebrates White Lotus Day, H.P. Blavatsky's death day, which he had faithfully observed for the past decade, for the last time. In August, Rudolf Steiner suggests the 'independent association' be called the 'Anthroposophical Society.' In September, the first eurythmy course takes place. In October, Rudolf Steiner declines recognition of a Theosophical Society lodge dedicated to the Star of the East and decides to expel all Theosophical Society members belonging to the order. Also, with Marie von Sivers, he first visits Dornach, near Basel, Switzerland, and they stand on the hill where the Goetheanum will be built. In November, a Theosophical Society lodge is opened by direct mandate from Adyar (Annie Besant). In December, a meeting of the German section occurs at which it is decided that belonging to the Order of the Star of the East is incompatible with membership in the Theosophical Society. December 28: informal founding of the Anthroposophical Society in Berlin.

1913: Expulsion of the German section from the Theosophical Society. February 2–3: Foundation meeting of the Anthroposophical Society. Board members include: Marie von Sivers, Michael Bauer, and Carl Unger. September 20: Laying of the foundation stone for the *Johannes Bau* (Goetheanum) in Dornach. Building begins immediately. The third mystery drama, *The Soul's Awakening* (CW 14), is completed. Also: *The Threshold of the Spiritual World* (CW 147). Lecture cycles include: *The Bhagavad Gita and the Epistles of Paul* and *The Esoteric Meaning of the Bhagavad Gita* (CW 146), which the Russian philosopher Nikolai Berdyaev attends; *The Mysteries of the East and of Christianity* (CW 144); *The Effects of Esoteric Development* (CW 145); and *The Fifth Gospel* (CW 148). In May, Rudolf Steiner is in London and Paris, where anthroposophical work continues.

1914: Building continues on the *Johannes Bau* (Goetheanum) in Dornach, with artists and co-workers from seventeen nations. The general assembly of the Anthroposophical Society takes place. In May, Rudolf Steiner visits Paris, as well as Chartres Cathedral. June 28: assassination in Sarajevo ('Now the catastrophe has happened!'). August 1: War is declared. Rudolf Steiner returns to Germany from Dornach—he will travel back and forth. He writes the last chapter of *The Riddles of Philosophy*. Lecture cycles include: *Human and Cosmic Thought* (CW 151); *Inner Being of Humanity between Death and a New Birth* (CW 153); *Occult Reading and Occult Hearing* (CW 156). December 24: marriage of Rudolf Steiner and Marie von Sivers.

1915: Building continues. Life after death becomes a major theme, also art. Writes: *Thoughts during a Time of War* (CW 24). Lectures include: *The Secret of Death* (CW 159); *The Uniting of Humanity through the Christ Impulse* (CW 165).

1916: Rudolf Steiner begins work with Edith Maryon (1872–1924) on the sculpture 'The Representative of Humanity' ('The Group'—Christ, Lucifer, and Ahriman). He also works with the alchemist Alexander von Bernus on the quarterly *Das Reich*. He writes *The Riddle of Humanity* (CW 20). Lectures include: *Necessity and Freedom in World History and Human Action* (CW 166); *Past and Present in the Human Spirit* (CW 167); *The Karma of Vocation* (CW 172); *The Karma of Untruthfulness* (CW 173).

1917: Russian Revolution. The U.S. enters the war. Building continues. Rudolf Steiner delineates the idea of the 'threefold nature of the human being' (in a public lecture March 15) and the 'threefold nature of the social organism' (hammered out in May-June with the help of Otto von Lerchenfeld and Ludwig Polzer-Hoditz in the form of two documents titled *Memoranda*, which were distributed in high places). August–September: Rudolf Steiner writes *The Riddles of the Soul* (CW 20). Also: commentary on 'The Chymical Wedding of Christian Rosenkreutz' for Alexander Bernus (*Das Reich*). Lectures include: *The Karma of Materialism* (CW 176); *The Spiritual Background of the Outer World: The Fall of the Spirits of Darkness* (CW 177).

1918: March 18: peace treaty of Brest-Litovsk—'Now everything will truly enter chaos! What is needed is cultural renewal.' June: Rudolf Steiner visits Karlstein (Grail) Castle outside Prague. Lecture cycle: *From Symptom to Reality in Modern History* (CW 185). In mid-November, Emil Molt, of the Waldorf-Astoria Cigarette Company, has the idea of founding a school for his workers' children.

1919: Focus on the threefold social organism: tireless travel, countless lectures, meetings, and publications. At the same time, a new public stage of Anthroposophy emerges as cultural renewal begins. The coming years will see initiatives in pedagogy, medicine, pharmacology, and agriculture. January 27: threefold meeting: ' We must first of all, with the money we have, found free schools that can bring people what they need.' February: first public eurythmy performance in Zurich. Also: 'Appeal to the German People' (CW 24), circulated March 6 as a newspaper insert. In April, *Towards Social Renewal* (CW 23) appears—'perhaps the most widely read of all books on politics appearing since the war.' Rudolf Steiner is asked to undertake the 'direction and leadership' of the school founded by the Waldorf-Astoria Company. Rudolf Steiner begins to talk about the 'renewal' of education. May 30: a building is selected and purchased for the future Waldorf School. August–September, Rudolf Steiner gives a lecture course for Waldorf teachers, *The Foundations of Human Experience (Study of Man)* (CW 293). September 7: Opening of the first Waldorf School. December (into January): first science course, the *Light Course* (CW 320).

1920: The Waldorf School flourishes. New threefold initiatives. Founding of limited companies *Der Kommende Tag* and *Futurum A.G.* to infuse spiritual values into the economic realm. Rudolf Steiner also focuses on the sciences. Lectures: *Introducing Anthroposophical Medicine* (CW 312); *The Warmth Course* (CW 321); *The Boundaries of Natural Science* (CW 322); *The Redemption of Thinking* (CW 74). February: Johannes Werner

Klein—later a co-founder of the Christian Community—asks Rudolf Steiner about the possibility of a 'religious renewal,' a 'Johannine church.' In March, Rudolf Steiner gives the first course for doctors and medical students. In April, a divinity student asks Rudolf Steiner a second time about the possibility of religious renewal. September 27–October 16: anthroposophical 'university course.' December: lectures titled *The Search for the New Isis* (CW 202).

1921: Rudolf Steiner continues his intensive work on cultural renewal, including the uphill battle for the threefold social order. 'University' arts, scientific, theological, and medical courses include: *The Astronomy Course* (CW 323); *Observation, Mathematics, and Scientific Experiment* (CW 324); the *Second Medical Course* (CW 313); *Colour*. In June and September-October, Rudolf Steiner also gives the first two 'priests' courses' (CW 342 and 343). The 'youth movement' gains momentum. Magazines are founded: *Die Drei* (January), and—under the editorship of Albert Steffen (1884–1963)—the weekly, *Das Goetheanum* (August). In February–March, Rudolf Steiner takes his first trip outside Germany since the war (Holland). On April 7, Steiner receives a letter regarding 'religious renewal,' and May 22–23, he agrees to address the question in a practical way. In June, the Klinical-Therapeutic Institute opens in Arlesheim under the direction of Dr. Ita Wegman. In August, the Chemical-Pharmaceutical Laboratory opens in Arlesheim (Oskar Schmiedel and Ita Wegman are directors). The Clinical Therapeutic Institute is inaugurated in Stuttgart (Dr. Ludwig Noll is director); also the Research Laboratory in Dornach (Ehrenfried Pfeiffer and Günther Wachsmuth are directors). In November–December, Rudolf Steiner visits Norway.

1922: The first half of the year involves very active public lecturing (thousands attend); in the second half, Rudolf Steiner begins to withdraw and turn toward the Society—'The Society is asleep.' It is 'too weak' to do what is asked of it. The businesses—*Der Kommende Tag* and *Futurum A.G.*—fail. In January, with the help of an agent, Steiner undertakes a twelve-city German lecture tour, accompanied by eurythmy performances. In two weeks he speaks to more than 2,000 people. In April, he gives a 'university course' in The Hague. He also visits England. In June, he is in Vienna for the East–West Congress. In August–September, he is back in England for the Oxford Conference on Education. Returning to Dornach, he gives the lectures *Philosophy, Cosmology, and Religion* (CW 215), and gives the third priests' course (CW 344). On September 16, The Christian Community is founded. In October–November, Steiner is in Holland and England. He also speaks to the youth: *The Youth Course* (CW 217). In December, Steiner gives lectures titled *The Origins of Natural Science* (CW 326), and *Humanity and the World of Stars: The Spiritual Communion of Humanity* (CW 219). December 31: Fire at the Goetheanum, which is destroyed.

1923: Despite the fire, Rudolf Steiner continues his work unabated. A very hard year. Internal dispersion, dissension, and apathy abound. There is conflict—between old and new visions—within the Society. A wake-up call is needed, and Rudolf Steiner responds with renewed lecturing vitality. His focus: the spiritual context of human life; initiation science; the course of the year; and community building. As a foundation for an artistic school, he creates a series of pastel sketches. Lecture cycles: *The Anthroposophical Movement; Initiation Science* (CW 227) (in England at the Penmaenmawr Summer School); *The Four Seasons and the Archangels* (CW 229); *Harmony of the Creative Word* (CW 230); *The Supersensible Human* (CW 231), given in Holland for the founding of the Dutch society. On November 10, in response to the failed Hitler-Ludendorff putsch in Munich, Steiner closes his Berlin residence and moves the *Philosophisch-Anthroposophisch Verlag* (Press) to Dornach. On December 9, Steiner begins the serialization of his *Autobiography: The Course of My Life* (CW 28) in *Das Goetheanum*. It will continue to appear weekly, without a break, until his death. Late December–early January: Rudolf Steiner re-founds the Anthroposophical Society (about 12,000 members internationally) and takes over its leadership. The new board members are: Marie Steiner, Ita Wegman, Albert Steffen, Elisabeth Vreede, and Günther Wachsmuth. (See *The Christmas Meeting for the Founding of the General Anthroposophical Society*, CW 260). Accompanying lectures: *Mystery Knowledge and Mystery Centres* (CW 232); *World History in the Light of Anthroposophy* (CW 233). December 25: the Foundation Stone is laid (in the hearts of members) in the form of the 'Foundation Stone Meditation.'

1924: January 1: having founded the Anthroposophical Society and taken over its leadership, Rudolf Steiner has the task of 'reforming' it. The process begins with a weekly newssheet ('What's Happening in the Anthroposophical Society') in which Rudolf Steiner's 'Letters to Members' and 'Anthroposophical Leading Thoughts' appear (CW 26). The next step is the creation of a new esoteric class, the 'first class' of the 'University of Spiritual Science' (which was to have been followed, had Rudolf Steiner lived longer, by two more advanced classes). Then comes a new language for Anthroposophy—practical, phenomenological, and direct; and Rudolf Steiner creates the model for the second Goetheanum. He begins the series of extensive 'karma' lectures (CW 235–40); and finally, responding to needs, he creates two new initiatives: biodynamic agriculture and curative education. After the middle of the year, rumours begin to circulate regarding Steiner's health. Lectures: January–February, *Anthroposophy* (CW 234); February: *Tone Eurythmy* (CW 278); June: *The Agriculture Course* (CW 327); June–July: *Speech Eurythmy* (CW 279); *Curative Education* (CW 317); August: (England, 'Second International Summer School'), *Initiation Consciousness: True and False Paths in Spiritual Investigation* (CW 243); September: *Pastoral Medicine* (CW 318). On September 26, for the first time, Rudolf Steiner cancels a lecture. On September 28, he gives his last lecture. On September 29, he withdraws to his studio in the carpenter's shop; now he is definitively ill. Cared for by Ita Wegman, he continues working, however, and writing the weekly installments of his *Autobiography* and *Letters to the Members/Leading Thoughts* (CW 26).

1925: Rudolf Steiner, while continuing to work, continues to weaken. He finishes *Extending Practical Medicine* (CW 27) with Ita Wegman.
On March 30, around ten in the morning, Rudolf Steiner dies.

INDEX